Paul Cézanne

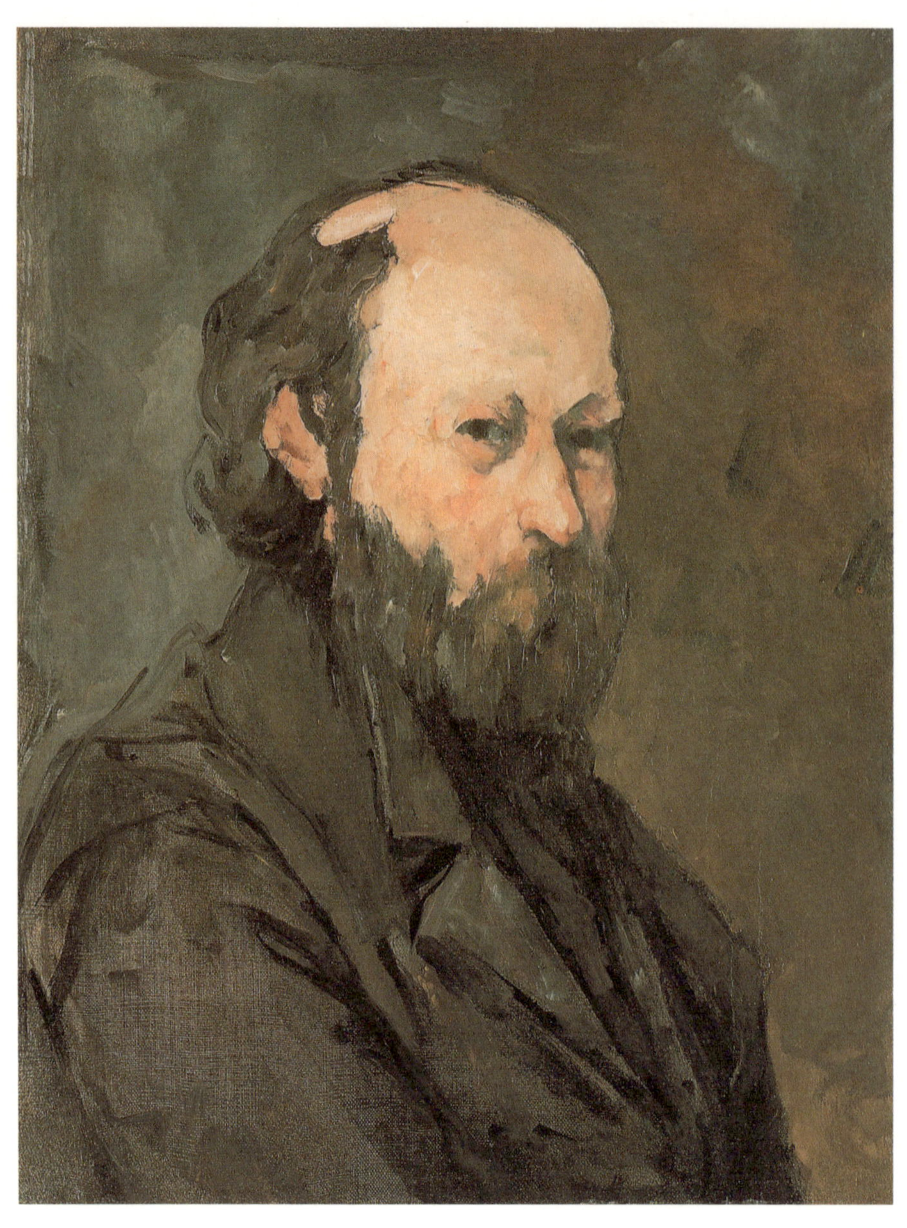

Self-Portrait, c. 1878–80.
Oil on canvas, 61 × 47 cm (23¾ × 18½ in.).
The Phillips Collection, Washington, DC

Paul Cézanne

Drawings and Watercolours

Christopher Lloyd

For Ellen Josefowitz
and in memory of Paul
8 JUNE 1952–18 MARCH 2013

Publisher's Note: All works are by Paul Cézanne
unless otherwise stated.
Measurements are height before width.

First published in the United Kingdom in 2015 by
Thames & Hudson Ltd, 181A High Holborn,
London WC1V 7QX

First paperback edition 2019

Reprinted 2023

Paul Cézanne: Drawings and Watercolours © 2015 and 2019
Thames & Hudson Ltd, London
Text © 2015 and 2019 Christopher Lloyd

British Library Cataloguing-in-Publication Data
A catalogue record for this book is available from
the British Library

ISBN 978-0-500-29521-2

Printed and bound in China by Toppan Leefung Printing Limited

Be the first to know about our new releases,
exclusive content and author events by visiting
thamesandhudson.com
thamesandhudsonusa.com
thamesandhudson.com.au

Contents

Nothing is stranger in his life than the contrast between the idea the public formed of Cézanne and the reality. He was one of those men destined to give rise to a legend which completely obscured the reality. He was spoken of as the most violent of revolutionaries … and all the time he was a timid little country gentleman of immaculate respectability who subscribed wholeheartedly to any reactionary opinion which might establish his 'soundness'. He was a timid man who really believed in only one thing, 'his little sensation'; who laboured incessantly to express this peculiar quality and who had not the faintest notion of doing anything that could shock the feelings of any mortal man or woman. No wonder then that when he looked up from his work and surveyed the world with his troubled and imperfect intellectual vision he was amazed and perturbed at the violent antagonism which he had all unconsciously provoked. No wonder that he became a shy, distrustful misanthrope, almost incapable of any association with his kind.

ROGER FRY

Preface

Books on Paul Cézanne are legion and come in many forms: catalogues raisonnés, editions of the letters, monographs, biographies, and selections of various kinds. The present book surveys the artist's development through his numerous drawings and watercolours. Cézanne was an ardent exponent of the art of drawing, which makes the study of his works on paper both worthwhile and revealing. The purpose of this publication is to encourage people to look more closely at Cézanne's works on paper and to acknowledge their significance in his *oeuvre*. Apart from the Introduction, the six chapters are arranged thematically, encompassing the main aspects of the artist's working life. Although the dating of his works is one of the central issues in studies on Cézanne, detailed discussion on the chronology of specific drawings or watercolours is not the purpose of this book. Close analysis of Cézanne's theories on art and speculative interpretations on hidden meanings of certain of his works – the Scylla and Charybdis of the literature on Cézanne – are also avoided: the first leads to philosophical disquisition or aesthetics and the second to psychology. Readers should bear in mind that the popularity of Cézanne's drawings and watercolours has over the years been such that in some cases overexposure to light might have resulted in some fading or change in the colour of the paper. Also, some of those drawings once, or remaining, in sketchbooks may have suffered from rubbing or have evidence of offsetting.

Detailed references for the epigraph on p. 6 and those at the head of each of the six chapters are given at the end of the Bibliography. It should be noted that the epigraphs to chapters 4 and 5 are taken from a questionnaire entitled *Mes Confidences*, first published by Adrien Chappuis in *The Drawings of Paul Cézanne* (1973), where it is given a suggested date of 1866–69, which is generally considered to be too early.

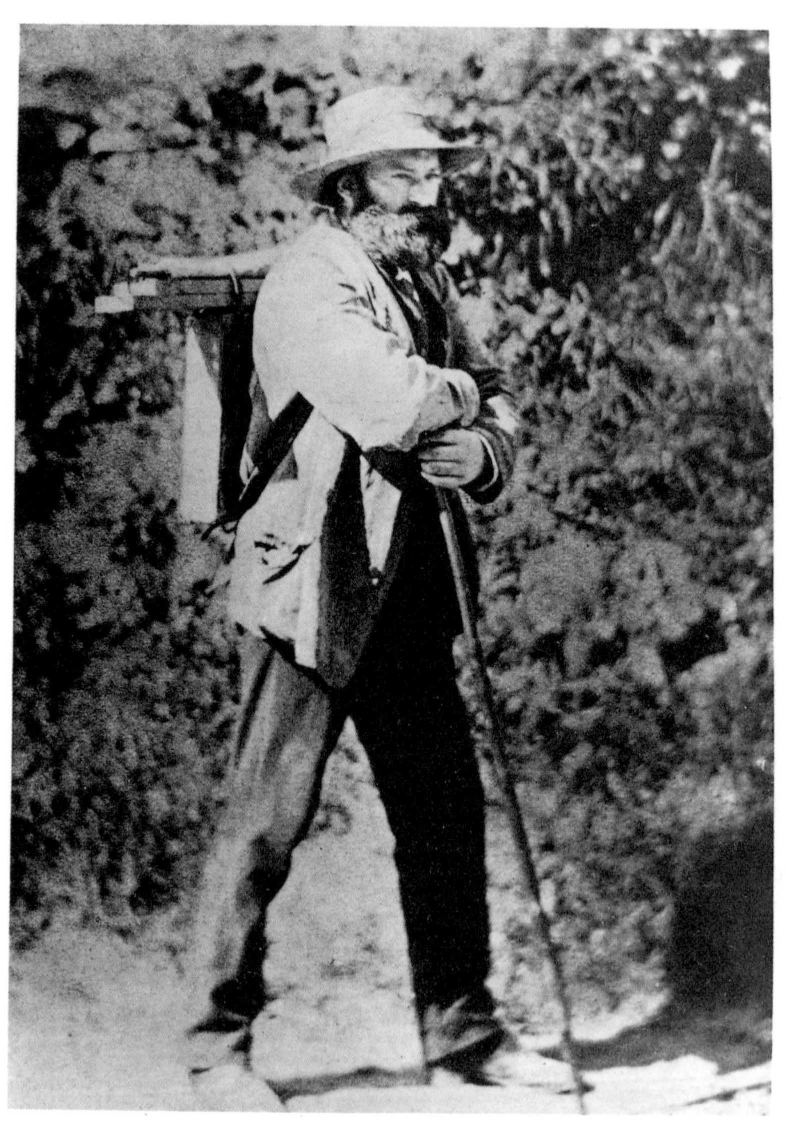

1. Paul Cézanne at Auvers-sur-Oise, *c.* 1874

Introduction

Paul Cézanne [1] changed the course of art in Europe. His independence, sense of purpose and technical accomplishments stemmed from a powerful personality totally dedicated to his vocation. The numerous drawings and watercolours, in addition to his paintings, that he produced during the closing decades of the nineteenth century transcended everything in art that had gone before.

That Cézanne proved so influential was due to his determination to retain his artistic freedom and his belief in the autonomy of individual works of art. Allied to this was his indefatigable search for solutions to those problems posed by the depiction of reality. This approach resulted in a totally new vision for painting based on a distinctive manner of looking and a novel system of application. The core belief for Cézanne was that an artist experienced certain sensory perceptions (what he called *sensations*) when confronting a motif and that it is his function to record those perceptions as truthfully and as accurately as possible. For this he devised a new pictorial language based on a range of carefully considered and precisely measured brushstrokes (what he termed *réalisation*).

Cézanne was admired and respected by his immediate contemporaries, especially Camille Pissarro, Claude Monet and Auguste Renoir, even if they were at first puzzled by his working methods and exasperated by his eccentricities. But, significantly, he was held in even greater awe by major artists of the emerging twentieth century, such as Pablo Picasso, Georges Braque, Henri Matisse, Fernand Léger, Wassily Kandinsky, Alberto Giacometti and Robert Delaunay. Similarly, the long list of artists who have owned paintings or drawings by Cézanne, which includes Pissarro, Monet, Edgar Degas, Renoir, Gustave Caillebotte, Paul Gauguin, Picasso, Matisse, Henry Moore, Graham Sutherland and Jasper Johns, is in turn testament to the fascination that his work has held for his confrères. In his book *Art* (1914), the writer and critic Clive

Bell hinted at the full extent of Cézanne's influence when he described
the artist as the 'Christopher Columbus of a new continent of form'. Bell
argued that 'Cézanne discovered methods and forms which have revealed
a vista of possibilities to the end of which no man can see.'

At first, in the late 1860s, Cézanne's work was met with ridicule and
suspicion, but gradually during the following two decades he gained
admirers – mostly fellow artists and a few discerning collectors – so
that by the second half of the 1890s, when he began to be promoted
by dealers, some sense of his importance was becoming more widely
acknowledged. This was particularly so among the young. Cézanne had
no fully developed theory about his art, and he was reluctant to write or
speak about it, so that what we do know about his thinking and working
practices is for the most part based on written accounts of visits made
by members of the younger generation to see him during his final years.
These included artists such as Emile Bernard, Charles Camoin and
Maurice Denis; writers such as Joachim Gasquet, Louis Aurenche and
Roger Marx; the poet Léo Larguier; and the archaeologist Jules Borély.
To a certain extent these accounts overlap and are repetitious, but they
are immensely instructive.

The proof of Cézanne's achievement lies, however, in the works
themselves, which exist in considerable numbers: nearly one thousand
paintings, over six hundred watercolours and roughly one and a half
thousand drawings. In the final analysis no hierarchical distinction
should be made between the paintings and the watercolours or drawings
in the case of Cézanne. Regardless of the difference in media, he
considered both to be exploratory in his search for a definitive means
of visual representation. This is why the faintest line or the most
transparent wash made by Cézanne on paper cannot be ignored.

Most of the drawings were done in sketchbooks of varying sizes
and importance. Only seven of these have survived more or less intact
with their linen covers, but there is evidence to show that eighteen or
so were once in use. Others may have been completely destroyed or are
simply missing. The drawings are mainly made in pencil of varying
hardness, sometimes with watercolour additions. Several pages are
predominantly in watercolour, which was a medium he favoured from the
start and showed an increasing preference for from the 1880s. Pen and
ink is occasionally used early on and the softer media – black chalk and
charcoal – only intermittently. Pastel occurs once.

The subject matter of the drawings is diverse but limited in scope,
even to the point of repetition: topographical views, copies of old master
paintings and sculpture (often from casts) of various dates, domestic
surroundings, preliminary ideas for imaginary compositions with

subsequent developments, and studies of his immediate family, namely his wife, Hortense Fiquet, and their son, Paul. Unlike the *Notebooks* of Degas, there are few notations, lists, addresses or aide-memoires. The pages of the sketchbooks are often crowded and visually confusing, but they are also sometimes scarcely touched. Sketches include false starts, partially realized ideas, fully resolved compositions and, on occasions, doodles by his small son.

Cézanne used his sketchbooks randomly and even within each one there is a disregard for the sequence of the pages. It is as though he constantly picked up the nearest one to hand, regardless of previous usage. The chronology of each of the main sketchbooks therefore varies widely as a result of this habit of starting one and returning to it at subsequent intervals. Several of the watercolours and the more interesting of the finished drawings in pencil were extracted for sale by Cézanne's wife and son towards the end of his life as a prelude to the gradual dispersal of the studio contents by both of them after his death. Although Cézanne did make many drawings on single sheets of larger dimensions, especially watercolours dating from the 1890s, the pages in the sketchbooks reveal the essence of Cézanne's draughtsmanship. They show him to have been an intensely private man, but at the same time someone deeply committed to perfecting the process of making art in order to record the world as he saw it with the greatest verisimilitude and probity.

Never at any stage was Cézanne a precise or accurate draughtsman in the context of academic teaching, and sometimes his drawings can appear to be extraordinarily inept. On the other hand, however slight, his drawings are always made with deliberation and with a sense of purpose, and the watercolours from the 1880s onwards are exceptional. Many of the Impressionists – Edouard Manet, Berthe Morisot, Renoir, Pissarro – showed an aptitude for watercolour and among the Post-Impressionists Gauguin, Vincent van Gogh and particularly Paul Signac also favoured the medium. But, on the whole, the watercolours made by those artists are not innovative, whereas those by Cézanne reveal unusual powers of visual analysis and sensitivity in execution, as well as an overall mastery of technique, that have never been surpassed.

Throughout his life Cézanne was tormented by self-doubt and feelings of inadequacy and these were only exacerbated by his own conviction that he would never actually succeed in his search for the means of making the most faithful rendition of nature. A letter written to Bernard on 12 May 1904 is characteristic of this mood: 'I am proceeding very slowly. Nature appears to me very complex, and the improvements to be made are never-ending. One must see one's model clearly and feel it exactly right, and then express oneself with distinction and force.'

It is our good fortune that the efforts he made in this search
amounted to some of the most absorbing art ever produced, which
Gasquet summarized as being derived from 'the most acute sensibility
at grips with the most searching rationality – that is the whole drama,
the story, the sum of Paul Cézanne's life'.

The artist was born on 19 January 1839 in the south of France, at
Aix-en-Provence, which is situated some twenty miles to the north of the
Mediterranean port of Marseille. His parents, Louis-Auguste Cézanne
(1798–1886) and Anne-Elisabeth-Honorine Aubert (1814–97) did not
actually marry until 1844. Louis-Auguste [2] was a successful hatmaker,
who in 1848 became a banker. Elisabeth had been a former employee in
her husband's first business. Cézanne had a difficult relationship with
his father, who often exerted his authority as the paterfamilias. Having
wanted his son to become a lawyer or even a banker, he was put out
when met with disobedience. During his first years as an artist, therefore,
Cézanne was dependent on a meagre allowance from his father, who, it
should be said, never positively discouraged his son from following his
chosen career. Cézanne's financial position improved somewhat when
Louis-Auguste made an initial division of his assets in 1881 prior to the
artist coming into his full inheritance five years later. Cézanne had a
closer and more open relationship with his mother, who had a personal
interest in art and encouraged her son's artistic ambition.

The couple had two other children besides Paul: Marie (1841–1921)
and Rose (1854–1909). Of these, Marie was resolutely pious, never
married and slightly disapproved of her brother. Cézanne commented,
'I who am not practical in life, I lean on my sister, who leans on her
adviser, a Jesuit (those people are very strong), who leans on Rome.'
Rose was more worldly and in 1881 married a lawyer, Maxime Conil
(1853–1940). They owned a farmhouse called Bellevue in the countryside
to the southwest of Aix-en-Provence where Cézanne sometimes worked,
particularly during the late 1880s, until it was sold in 1895.

The status of the family was considerably enhanced when in 1859
Louis-Auguste purchased a *bastide* called the Jas de Bouffan ('House of
the Winds') on the outskirts of Aix-en-Provence to the west. Formerly
owned by one of Louis XIV's most celebrated generals, Claude Louis
Hector, Duc de Villars, the property comprised the main building, a
retainer's house and a farmhouse. The principal features of the large
garden were an allée lined with chestnut trees, an ornamental pool with
a fountain, and an orangery. The whole site amounted to some fifteen
hectares and included tenant farmers and vineyards. On acquisition
the buildings were fairly dilapidated and had a faded grandeur, but it
quickly became a place of great significance for Cézanne as a retreat with

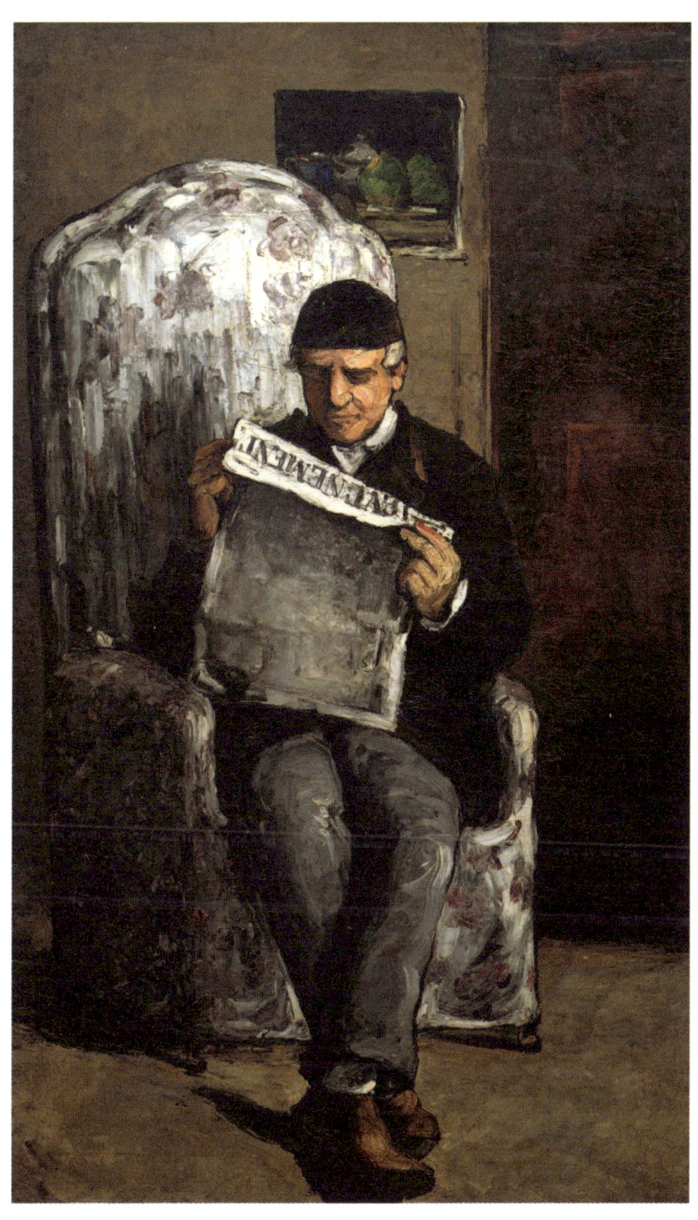

2. *The Artist's Father, Reading 'L'Evénement'*, 1866.
Oil on canvas, 198.5 × 119.3 cm (78⅛ × 47 in.).
National Gallery of Art, Washington, DC

family associations where he could paint undisturbed. He inherited the property jointly with his sisters in 1886 on their father's death, but two years after their mother died in 1897 the decision was made, largely at the insistence of Rose's husband, Maxime, to sell the Jas de Bouffan, a move that caused the artist considerable anguish.

Throughout his life Cézanne remained fervently proud of his Provençal origins. On the other hand, the importance of Paris for training to be an artist and for making those contacts essential for establishing a reputation was undeniable. Towards this end for most of his life Cézanne regularly rented apartments and studios in the city and often painted motifs in the immediate environs and beyond, but he remained at heart a man of the Midi and openly demonstrated this affiliation to the point of exaggeration in dress, speech and manners. He developed a profound distaste for metropolitan life, which he equated with the pursuit of materialism and a craving for bourgeois ideals.

Historically Provence was recognized as being at the heart of Mediterranean culture. The growth of regionalism in France during the second half of the nineteenth century in opposition to the tentacular influence of Paris led to a revival of interest in Provençal institutions, literature, language, folkloric customs and festivals, and architecture. This renaissance was promoted by the Félibrige Society founded in 1854 by the local poet Frédéric Mistral. Cézanne was never formally a member, but he knew its leading lights, among whom were Antoine-Fortuné Marion, Professor of Zoology and Palaeontology at Marseille University, the writers and amateur artists Numa Coste and Antony Valabrègue, and the younger poet Gasquet. In addition, Cézanne was aware of work by leading Provençal artists such as François-Marius Granet, Emile Loubon, Paul Guigou and Adolphe Monticelli – the last a close friend also admired by Vincent van Gogh.

Cézanne's preoccupation with Provence can be seen as part of this cultural renaissance. He was at first attracted by the fishing village of L'Estaque on the Bay of Marseille, which, owing to the arrival of the train, was being developed as a tourist resort, as well as becoming more industrialized. After 1886 when he began to spend more time in the south following his father's death, motifs closer to Aix-en-Provence held sway, particularly Mont Sainte-Victoire, which was the dominant landmark in the region and the site of a famous victory won in 102 BC by the Roman general Gaius Marius over the Teutonic and Cimbrian tribes. Ultimately, Mont Sainte-Victoire became a personal symbol with an almost spiritual significance for the artist. Similarly, he saw the surrounding landscape of pine trees, quarries, caves and rocks as arcadia.

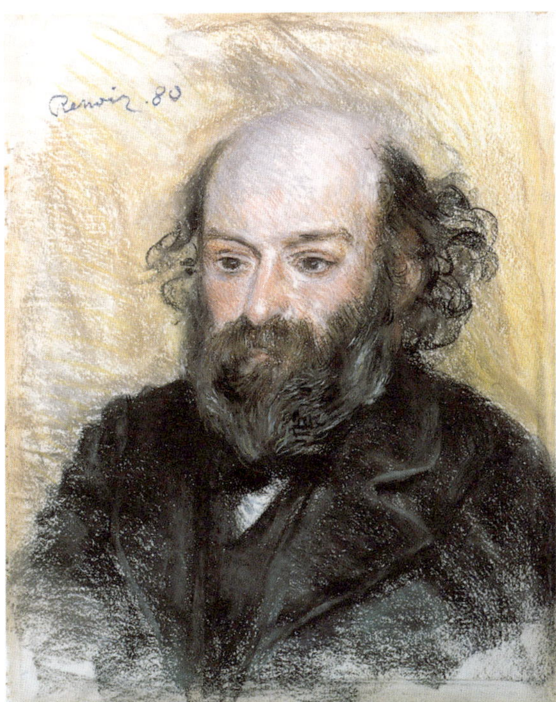

3. Auguste Renoir,
Paul Cézanne, 1880.
Pastel, 53.5 × 44.4 cm
(21 × 17 ½ in.).
Private collection

The scenes of bathers – a long-running theme – were couched in bucolic terms, evoking comparison with the pastoral poetry of Virgil, just as the subjects of the final portraits seem like images of a vanished race.

Cézanne often tried to entice other artists to the south. In a letter of 2 July 1876 he wrote rhapsodically to Pissarro from L'Estaque: 'It's like a playing card. Red roofs against the blue sea … There are the olive trees and the pines that always keep their leaves. The sun is so fierce that objects seem to be silhouetted, not only in black or white, but in blue, red, brown, violet.'

Renoir [3] visited in 1882 and again in 1883–84 with Monet, and then more briefly in 1888 and 1891, but Pissarro never came. Gauguin and Vincent van Gogh shared a studio in neighbouring Arles for nine weeks in 1888, after which Van Gogh stayed on alone until 1890 at the asylum at nearby Saint-Rémy. But of these contemporaries it was only Renoir who finally settled in the south after 1900 in appreciation of its advantages. For Cézanne, Provence was truly a place combining myth with reality and his interpretation of the landscape was a fusion of elements from the past and the present. As he wrote to the collector

Victor Chocquet on 11 May 1886: 'I must tell you that I am still occupied with painting and that there are treasures to be carried away from this region, which has not yet found an interpreter to match the nobility of the riches displayed.'

Cézanne, of course, was well on his way to becoming that interpreter. His initiation into art, however, had been slow and hesitant, even painful at times. This was not due solely to any opposition from his father, but the result of his own uncertainties. He attended two schools in Aix-en-Provence: the Ecole Saint-Joseph (1849–52) and the Collège Bourbon (1852–58). Here his bent seemed to be more towards literature than art, although in 1857 he registered for classes held at the Ecole Spéciale et Gratuite de Dessin. He clearly had little aptitude for passing examinations, but on the other hand, he did gain a thorough knowledge of classical literature. He knew the writings of Virgil, Horace, Tacitus and Lucretius, among others, extremely well and continued to quote from them in later life. At the same time, his love for a wide range of French literature grew with Alfred de Musset, Honoré de Balzac, Hippolyte Taine, Stendhal, Gustave Flaubert, Victor Hugo and Charles Baudelaire among his favourite authors.

Another advantage of Cézanne's school years was the number of friendships he formed and some with people who had distinguished careers in other fields: the novelist Emile Zola, the scientist Baptistin Baille (later professor of Optics and Acoustics at the Ecole de Physique et de Chimie Industrielles of the City of Paris), the sculptor Philippe Solari, and the writer Marius Roux. Three of these friends – Cézanne, Zola, Baille – called themselves the 'Inseparables'; their correspondence, which is full of versifying and verbal games and in Cézanne's case with some illustrations, attests to the carefree pleasures pursued during their school days on the banks of the river Arc. Zola describes this frolicking in the second chapter of his novel *L'Oeuvre* (1886), in which the main character is a painter named Claude Lantier who is largely based on Cézanne.

Aix-en-Provence gradually lost its savour for these younger citizens. They found it too conservative and old-fashioned. Zola, in particular, was keen to leave for Paris and began the exodus, encouraging Cézanne to follow. Having struggled with law studies at the university in Aix-en-Provence in order to fulfil his father's wishes, the artist finally set out for the capital in the spring of 1861, but this proved to be a false start, since after only five months he returned home and began to work in his father's bank. Just over a year later Cézanne went back to Paris and stayed until the summer of 1864. This constant travelling between Paris and Provence became a routine that Cézanne kept up for most of his working life, even after he settled into the family home at the Jas de

Bouffan in 1886. After the sale of this house in 1899 he rented a small apartment in Aix-en-Provence itself at 23 Rue Boulegon, where he had a makeshift studio. His main studio during the final years was at Les Lauves, situated on a hillside just to the north of the city with a view eastwards towards Mont Sainte-Victoire. The building with its terrace and garden was acquired in 1901 and duly converted to suit Cézanne's purposes. The studio was threatened with demolition during the 1950s, but was saved and is now open to the public.

Paris offered everything that an aspiring painter needed, but from the outset it was a place where Cézanne felt himself to be an outsider. He failed to gain a place at the prestigious Ecole des Beaux-Arts (Cézanne dubbed the students 'Bozards'), but enrolled instead at the Académie Suisse, an open studio on the Ile de la Cité, which for a nominal fee offered an alternative to the more traditional teaching of the Ecole. Significantly, it was at the Académie Suisse that he met like-minded artists such as Pissarro, Monet, Armand Guillaumin, Antoine Guillemet and the Puerto Rican Francisco Oller. He also registered as a copyist in the Musée du Louvre in 1863 and 1868. Cézanne did, however, try very hard to have his work accepted for exhibition at the annual Salon in Paris, which he dubbed the 'Salon de Bouguereau' after the popular academic painter William Bouguereau (1825–1905). Inclusion at the Salon was the traditional way of gaining recognition from the critics and the public. Although he submitted regularly to the Salon until 1884, Cézanne succeeded in being accepted only once, in 1882 with a portrait. The persistence with which he persevered with the Salon is extraordinary and in a perverse way it is as though he was seeking validation through having his work refused by the authorities.

From the start Cézanne was an uncompromising artist. His early works, even those with traditional subject matter such as portraits and still lifes, are overwhelmingly powerful. The compositions are direct and unfussy, the colour strong, and the style rhythmical, rugged and aggressive, with much use of the palette knife: it is a manner of painting that the artist himself described as his 'manière couillarde' ('ballsy'). Even more surprising are the subject pictures in which Cézanne's fertile imagination is made vividly apparent by the inclusion of scenes of eroticism, violence and fantasy. These are painted in an animated, burlesque style comparable in some respects with popular art. Their treatment shows how even at the outset of his career the artist was capable of making extraordinary innovations, as though reinventing established religious and secular iconography. Guillemet informed Oller in a letter of 12 September 1866 that Cézanne's early style 'makes Manet look like Ingres in comparison'. The unconventionality of these works

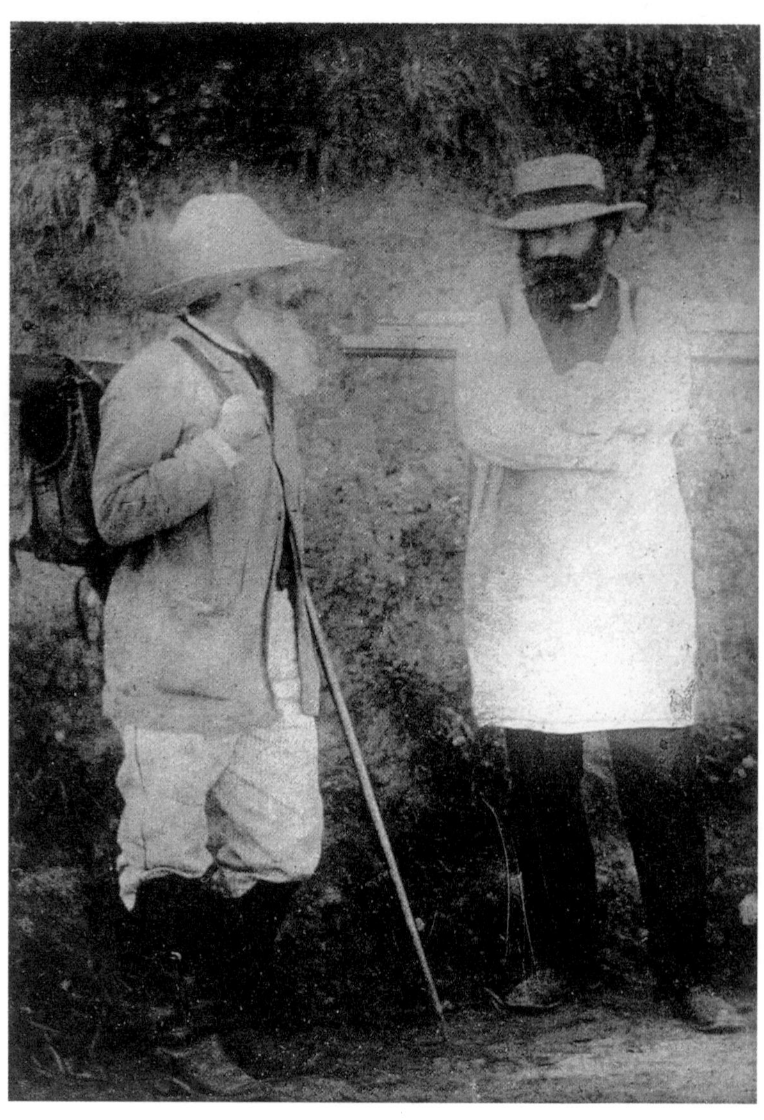

4. Camille Pissarro and Paul Cézanne, *c.* 1872–74

challenged the authorities, perplexed the public, outwitted the critics and intrigued fellow artists. An affinity with strong painters such as Gustave Courbet, Honoré Daumier and Edouard Manet meant that Cézanne's stance was instinctively close to avant-garde art.

The passion that is so characteristic of Cézanne's early work is sometimes referred to as his 'romantic' phase, implying that it was dominant for a short period, but, in fact, it never really abated, continuing in the extensive treatment of male and female bathers that emerged in the early 1870s and became such a major part of Cézanne's *oeuvre* later. Nonetheless, that early passion needed at some stage to be brought under control so that the artist could develop a calmer, more deliberate style. The schooling of Cézanne, or the sublimation of his anarchic pictorial energies, was due to Pissarro, with whom he established a working relationship during the 1870s, particularly during the years 1872–74, 1875 and 1877, continuing until 1882. Sometimes during these years the artists worked side-by-side depicting motifs previously explored by Pissarro alone at Pontoise and Auvers-sur-Oise to the northwest of Paris [4]. Here Cézanne learnt how to look at the landscape objectively and to analyse its constituent elements as part of creating a structured composition that was then laid on the canvas in clearly defined areas of pure colour.

By the early 1880s both painters had begun to grow apart. Cézanne adopted a style of brushwork now known as his 'constructive stroke', comprising areas of colour applied to the canvas in parallel strokes of varying thickness spread like a mesh across the surface; Pissarro started to explore the pointilliste technique favoured by the Neo-Impressionists. However, Cézanne never forgot his debt to Pissarro, and, as the American writer and collector Gertrude Stein later expressed it, 'Pissar[r]o indeed was the man from whom all the early Cézanne lovers heard about Cézanne'.

It is no surprise, therefore, that Cézanne exhibited with the Impressionists on two out of eight possible occasions, namely at the first exhibition in 1874 (April–May) and the third in 1877 (April). His contribution in 1874 was three paintings, which, owing to their style, were received by the critics and public alike with incomprehension. In 1877, Cézanne's contribution was far greater and more varied, numbering sixteen items in all, but the reception was just as negative. Nonetheless, growing interest in Cézanne's work outside Paris was demonstrated in 1890 when Octave Maus, the secretary of the avant-garde society Les XX, in Brussels, invited him to participate in one of their exhibitions, and further invitations were extended from that city by Les XX's successor, Libre Esthétique, in 1901 and 1904.

Essentially, the 1880s and 1890s were the decades when Cézanne emerged as a mature artist with an independent outlook pursuing those subjects that most absorbed him – landscape, bathers, still life – and painting them in great numbers. Even so, he retained an abiding uncertainty of the type expressed in a letter written to Zola on 24 September 1879, 'I'm still trying to find my way, pictorially. Nature presents me with the greatest problems.'

Fuelling this uncertainty was the fact that during the 1870s and 1880s Cézanne had failed to impress the public. Only a few dealers, collectors and critics were sympathetic and helped to sustain him. Of the critics, Zola, who had been such a support at the start, began to waver in the 1870s and then after the publication of *L'Oeuvre* became estranged, but younger writers such as Joris-Karl Huysmans, Gustave Geffroy, Georges Lecomte and Octave Mirbeau were more impressed. The earliest dealer to stock paintings by Cézanne, but not in great numbers, was Julien Tanguy (known as Père Tanguy), who also supplied the artist with his materials for painting and drawing. Tanguy often displayed pictures in the window of his small gallery and it was from him that Victor Chocquet, a customs official, acquired his first Cézanne before befriending the artist and becoming the earliest serious collector of his work.

It was at Tanguy's gallery that another dealer interested in contemporary art, Ambroise Vollard, discovered Cézanne and became the chief outlet for his work, handling over two-thirds of the artist's *oeuvre*. The exhibition Vollard organized in 1895 (November–December) of one hundred and fifty paintings and watercolours was Cézanne's first one-man show: he was aged fifty-six. It was a revelation. Pissarro, Degas, Monet and Renoir all acquired works on that occasion, which was followed in quick succession by other one-man exhibitions at Vollard's gallery in 1898, 1899, 1901 and 1902. Cézanne's work was for the first time suddenly available in significant quantities. It also gained him public attention, thereby enabling a far wider spectrum of collectors to obtain paintings or watercolours, as opposed to just fellow artists and friends, and allowing critics to become better acquainted with his style.

Vollard's success at promoting Cézanne gave the painter greater confidence and the prices charged by the dealer became indicative of the increase in the artist's standing. As such, the art market emerged as a more significant indicator of artistic success than the award of any medal at the official Salon. Cézanne was also being accorded space at public venues in Paris such as the Salon d'Automne, held in the Grand Palais (or sometimes the Petit Palais). Cézanne's association with this Salon began in 1904 when an entire room was devoted to thirty-one paintings and two drawings by him, and continued with smaller displays of paintings in 1905 and 1906. Following the artist's death on 23 October 1906, a memorial exhibition (1–22 October 1907), which included fifty-six works, was also organized by the Salon d'Automne.

The growth in Cézanne's reputation took some time, but when it happened it was sudden, spreading first in Europe and then very extensively in America. As the artist aged, Vollard increasingly conducted business with the artist's wife, Hortense Fiquet [5], or, more usually, his son, Paul [6]. After Cézanne's death, leaving Paul *fils* as the sole beneficiary, many paintings and watercolours were sold to Vollard with Hortense's blessing. Vollard shared several items with the Galerie Bernheim-Jeune, which was run by the two brothers Josse and Gaston Bernheim-Jeune, who had visited the artist in 1902. The dealer Paul Durand-Ruel, who had done most to support the Impressionists during the 1870s, was slower to appreciate the merits of Cézanne.

The artist was not someone who helped his own cause. His forbidding appearance could be distinctly off-putting. The domed forehead, which became more pronounced with baldness, slightly curved nose, prominent eyebrows and bulging eyes signalled a daunting presence. Furthermore, the whole face was framed by an abundance of hair, including a beard. The numerous self-portraits – painted and drawn – made during every decade of his life suggest that Cézanne was keen to cultivate a persona, but at every stage he undoubtedly remained a formidable figure, even later in life when he could be calmer and more dignified. Dress, too, suggests an indifference to fashion. Jackets of various types, hats of many descriptions, dungarees and boots – all spattered in paint – made it quite clear that Cézanne saw himself as an artisan with a job of work to do. He regarded painting as a form of hard labour carried out in the open countryside in all weathers rather than in the comfort of a heated, well-lit studio. Just as he was not afraid to be seen in public dressed in this way, thereby declaring his strong commitment to art, so he was not afraid to behave with the manners of a Provençal peasant. He retained a strong regional accent, which he took pleasure in exaggerating when in Paris. With characteristic nonchalance he greeted Manet at the Café Guerbois in 1866, 'I won't offer you my hand, Monsieur Manet, I haven't washed for eight days.'

An American painter, Matilda Lewis, left a vivid account of meeting Cézanne at Monet's house at Giverny in 1894:

> When I first saw him I thought he looked like a cut-throat with large red eyeballs standing out from his head in a most ferocious manner, a rather fierce-looking pointed beard, quite grey, and an excited way of talking that positively made the dishes rattle. I found later on

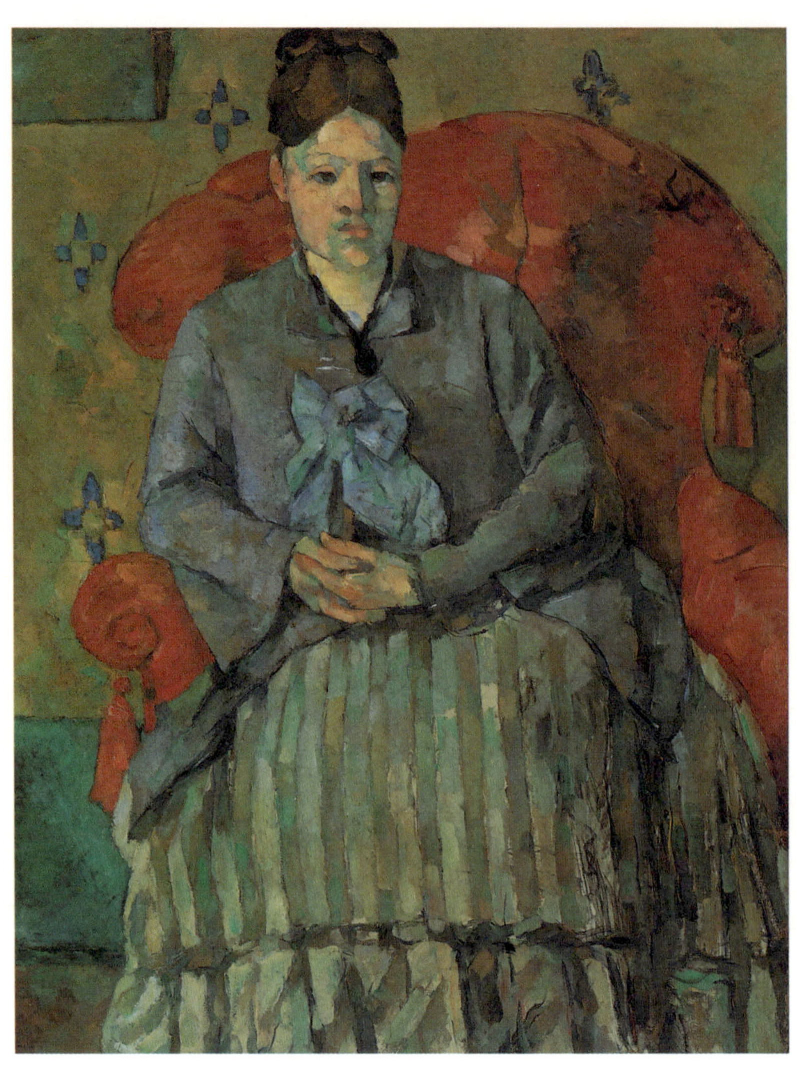

5. *Madame Cézanne in a Red Armchair, c.* 1877.
Oil on canvas, 72.4 × 55.9 cm (28½ × 22 in.).
Museum of Fine Arts, Boston

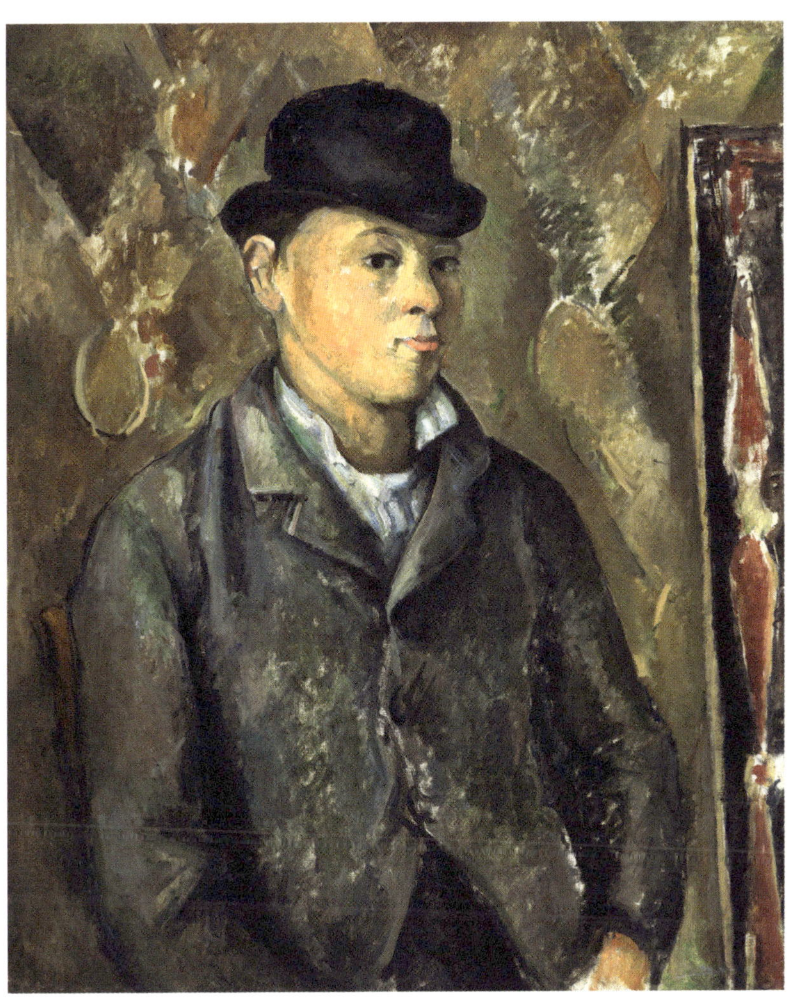

6. *The Artist's Son, Paul*, 1885–90.
Oil on canvas, 65.3 × 54 cm (25¾ × 21¼ in.).
National Gallery of Art, Washington, DC

that I had misjudged his appearance, for far from being fierce or a
cut-throat, he has the gentlest nature possible, *comme un enfant* as
he would say. His manners at first rather startled me – he scrapes his
soup plate, then lifts it and pours the remaining drops in the spoon;
he even takes his chop in his fingers and pulls the meat from the
bone. He eats with his knife and accompanies every gesture, every
movement of his hand, with that implement, which he grasps firmly
when he commences his meal and never puts down until he leaves
the table. Yet in spite of the total disregard of the dictionary of
manners, he shows a politeness towards us that no other man here
would have shown.

The forceful nature of Cézanne's personality is such that he served
as the model for painters described in two novels in addition to Zola's
L'Oeuvre: *La Proie et L'Ombre* (1878) by Marius Roux and *Madame
Meuriot* (1890) by Paul Alexis – both these authors were well known
to Cézanne and Zola.

Cézanne was of course capable of putting on an act and it would
be wrong to dismiss him as a simpleton. Well educated and widely read,
he could easily be overcome by shyness when young and throughout
life he disliked physical contact. Zola, in fact, regarded the artist's
rudeness as a mask for his shyness. As he grew older he also became
more reserved and preferred to stay in the south, so causing people to
visit him while working, which he did constantly. Cézanne's wit was
ironic and is best demonstrated by the way he signed certain letters:
'*Pictor semper virens*' ('painter still vigorous') in a draft to Marius Roux
of 1878–79; 'painter by inclination' to Geffroy on 4 April 1895; and
'*Bête noire de Roujon*' (the Director of the Beaux-Arts) to Gasquet on
5 September 1903. Painting was an obsession and in its pursuit he could
be reticent, standoffish, prickly, stubborn, dismissive, offensive – all
aspects of his anti-conformist character that were exacerbated after the
onset of diabetes, which was diagnosed around 1890 and which may have
affected his eyesight. When not feeling offended he was well mannered
to the point of fastidiousness and after his emotional outbursts and
sudden departures he always apologized, usually in writing, for the
offence caused.

With age Cézanne became more conservative in outlook, writing
to one his nieces, Paule Conil, on 1 September 1902: 'I well remember
Establon and the once so picturesque shores of L'Estaque. Unfortunately,
what we call progress is nothing but the invasion of bipeds, who won't
stop until they have transformed everything into hideous streets with
gas lamps and – even worse – electric light.' And to Paule's elder sister,
Marthe, on receiving an invitation to her first communion in 1899 he

replied on 16 May: 'Remember me in your prayers, for once we have begun to grow old, we can find no greater support and consolation than in religion.'

Cézanne, in fact, drew great strength from his immediate family, although painting was always a priority. Early in 1869 in Paris he met Hortense Fiquet (1850–1922), who had been born into a farming family in the village of Saligney in the French Jura on the eastern side of France close to Switzerland. The family had moved to Paris sometime in the late 1850s. Her father returned to the Jura in 1867 after his wife's death, but Hortense decided to stay on in Paris working as a seamstress while also modelling for artists. Her liaison with Cézanne was kept secret from the artist's father, but not from his mother, who also knew about the birth of their only child, Paul, on 4 January 1872 in the capital. The small allowance that Cézanne received from Louis-Auguste was scarcely sufficient to maintain a family and so the artist was forced to borrow money from the increasingly successful and productive Zola. Eventually, in 1878, misdirected letters led to the artist's father discovering the identity of Hortense and the existence of the younger Paul. Cézanne officially married Hortense on 28 April 1886 in Aix-en-Provence in a ceremony attended by both his parents.

Hortense Fiquet was a vital presence in Cézanne's life, but her role has been misunderstood partly owing to the artist's family and friends briefing against her. She was nicknamed La Boule ('the Dumpling'), referring no doubt to her shape; Paul *fils*, more affectionately, was called Le Boulet ('the Little Dumpling'). Cézanne painted his wife at least twenty-six times over twenty years and taken as a group these can be seen to complement the artist's own series of twenty-six self-portraits executed over forty years. Although Hortense and the younger Paul did live for long periods at a time in Aix-en-Provence, she was never allowed to treat the Jas de Bouffan as her home and on the whole she much preferred Paris. For much of the time husband and wife seemed to act independently of one another, even on some occasions living in separate apartments when in the same city.

Unlike Cézanne, Hortense liked to travel and in 1890 she even succeeded in enticing him to Switzerland for five months which was his only trip abroad. 'My wife likes only Switzerland and lemonade', Cézanne once quipped – a dismissive remark not unlike Harry Lime's observation made in the film *The Third Man* (1949) that five hundred years of democracy and peace in Switzerland resulted in the invention of the cuckoo clock. Another, less protracted, trip was made in the summer of 1896 to Haute Savoie where the destination was Talloires on the shores of Lake Annecy close to the Swiss border. Here Cézanne painted only a single picture – a view of the Château de Duingt seen across the lake (Courtauld Gallery, London). On these trips he missed Provence, pretended to his family to be bored and remained unenthusiastic about the landscape. Indeed, he regarded the views as rather tame and more suitable for 'the travel albums of young ladies'.

Cézanne's family regarded Hortense as vulgar and materialistic. In their opinion she was always greedy for money and much too keen to go shopping, play cards or gamble. She was, therefore, kept at a distance. At the time of Cézanne's death both Hortense and Paul were in Paris and did not attend the bedside. However, the evidence suggests that they were deterred by the rest of the family from travelling to Aix-en-Provence. And when they went to the south for the funeral they only just arrived in time.

Whatever shortcomings Hortense may have had, the real point is that she was a constant in Cézanne's life and fulfilled his expectations of what a wife should be. Her role was to be both present and absent and in this she succeeded. She may not have been impressed by his painting or understood what he was trying to achieve, but her features were one of his principal subjects and one that he treated with the utmost respect in both his paintings and drawings. That he cared for her is evident from his punctiliousness over enquiring in letters about the state of her health, as physically she was never very strong. In addition, her two surviving letters show that she was not unintelligent or unresourceful: one is to Chocquet's wife, Marie, written on 1 August 1890 on private matters and the other to the painter Bernard dating from 10 September 1905 on business affairs. Following Cézanne's death and the settlement of his estate, Hortense lived the rest of her life in some comfort until her own death in 1922. Paul *fils* married Renée Rivière, the daughter of the influential critic Georges Rivière, in 1913. His father-in-law wrote one of the earliest and most interesting scholarly monographs on Cézanne: *Le Maître Paul Cézanne* (1923). Both mother and son, therefore, died in the knowledge that Paul Cézanne's reputation was becoming well established and that his place in the history of art was assured [7].

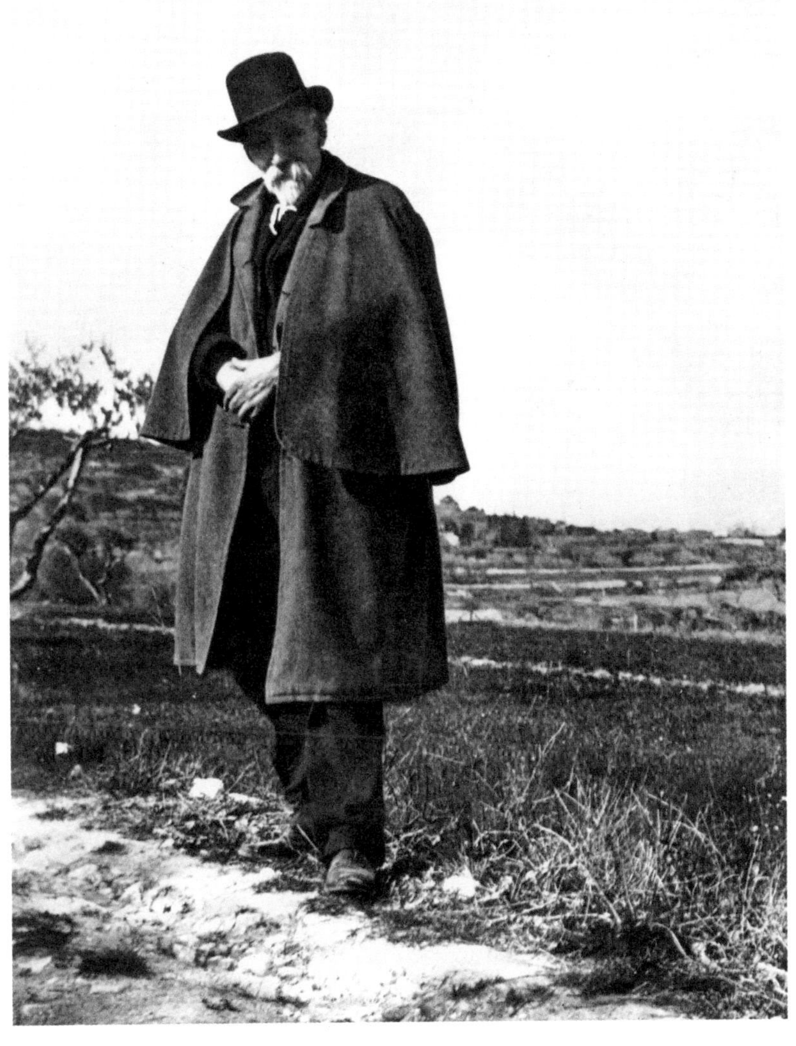

7. Paul Cézanne at Les Lauves, Aix-en-Provence, 1904.
Photograph by Emile Bernard

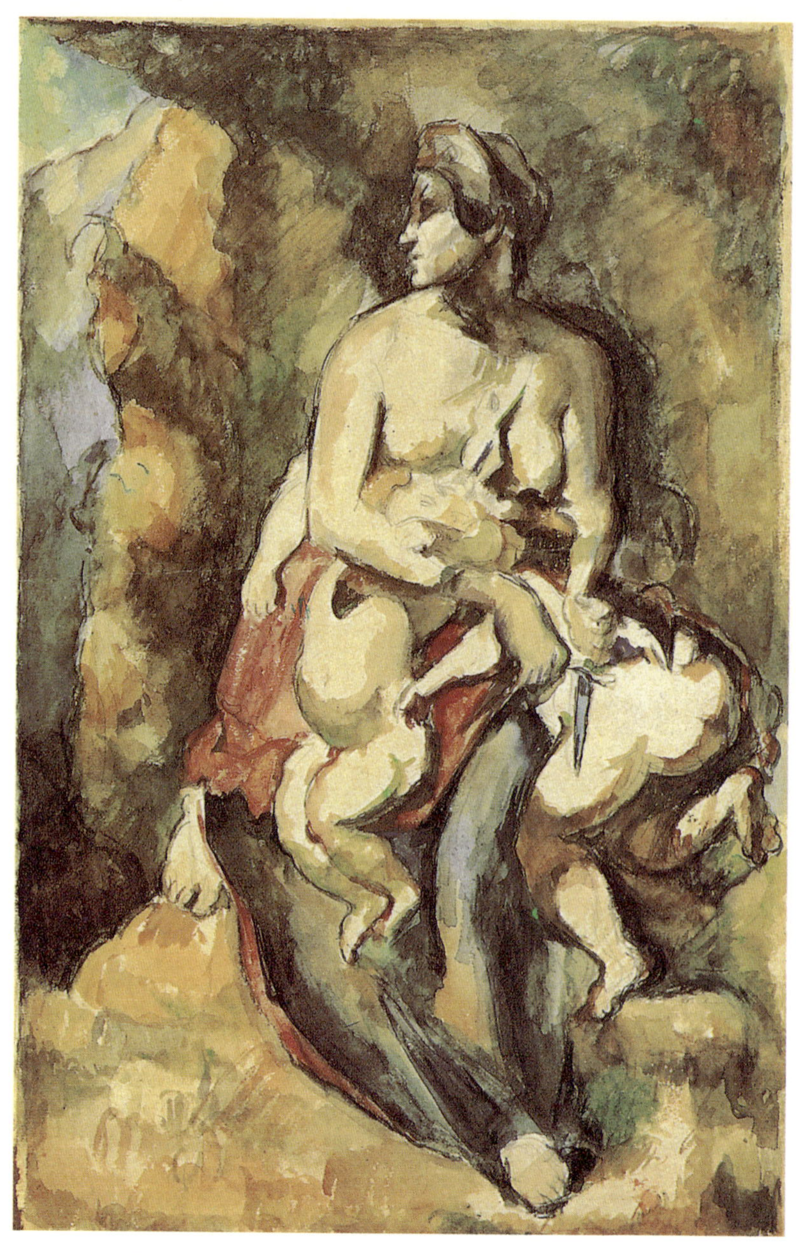

8. *Medea (after Delacroix)*, 1880–85.
Pencil with watercolour and gouache, 39.5 × 26.1 cm (15½ × 10¼ in.).
Kunsthaus Zurich

CHAPTER ONE

Past Masters

*'One has to go to the Louvre by way of nature and
come back to nature by way of the Louvre.'* Paul Cézanne

The basis of Cézanne's art was a fine balancing act between tradition
and innovation. He approached the art of the past in a spirit of enquiry
endeavouring to learn from his forerunners and to build upon their
achievements. What is surprising is how widely he searched and how
long he devoted to finding answers to the problems he encountered in
his creative struggles. Cézanne certainly looked at work by the greatest
old masters – both painters and sculptors – but without spurning
his immediate predecessors or even the Salon artists of his own day.
Similarly, it seems that his visual curiosity was never-ending, beginning
in Aix-en-Provence when he was setting out and continuing right up to
those final years when he was himself being asked for guidance by the
younger generation.

Cézanne certainly advocated the close examination of works by
earlier masters, but at the same time he was careful to warn against the
danger of becoming a *pasticheur*, wherein lay the danger of surrendering
artistic individuality. As he wrote to Emile Bernard in 1905: 'The Louvre
is the book from which we learn to read. However, we should not be
content with holding onto the beautiful formulas of our illustrious
predecessors. Let us go out to study beautiful nature, let us try to capture
its spirit, let us seek to express ourselves according to our individual
temperaments.' In short, Cézanne's purpose in examining his visual
heritage was emulation and not imitation.

The evidence for Cézanne's interest in the art of the past lies pre-
eminently in the drawn copies he made after specific works. These are
surprisingly numerous: roughly four hundred in all and dating not, as
might be expected, just from the earlier part of his career, but also from
the 1880s and notably from even after 1890 when he was at the height
of his powers. In effect, the habit and the need for copying never left
him and indeed it seems to have increased towards the end of his life.

Nearly a third of the total number of copies was produced after 1890, reflecting not only Cézanne's longing for constant reassurance but also how extensively his artistic dilemmas intensified during his final years. Copying, for Cézanne, therefore, was a coordinated exercise dedicated to stimulating his visual imagination, developing his pictorial skills and improving his technical abilities.

Since the Renaissance the practice of making copies had been a much-valued part of the process of training artists. The establishment of academies of art in major European cities during the seventeenth and eighteenth centuries affirmed the practice and made it an important element in the method of teaching. Cézanne's own first experience of this system was in Aix-en-Provence after he registered at the Ecole Spéciale et Gratuite de Dessin in 1857. The Ecole was housed in the same building as the Musée des Beaux-Arts (now the Musée Granet) and his teacher there from 1857 to 1862 was Joseph Gibert. It was at this stage that Cézanne began to make copies from prints and plaster casts, in addition to life drawings from posed models.

On first settling in Paris he expected to continue his training at the prestigious Ecole des Beaux-Arts, but he failed the entrance examination and so was forced to act independently. He duly attended the Académie Suisse, worked in the studio of Joseph Villevieille (also originally from Provence), and registered as a copyist in the Musée du Louvre. A pattern immediately emerges from these early affiliations whereby Cézanne embraces both the traditional (Villevieille's studio) and the radical (the Académie Suisse) while also choosing to go his own way as a copyist in the Louvre. From the outset, therefore, Cézanne refused to be doctrinaire in his approach to art and it is apparent that no formal system could accommodate his creative personality or his range of interests.

There is a list of the contents of Cézanne's final studio at Les Lauves on the outskirts of Aix-en-Provence. Made after his death, and supplemented by accounts given by visitors, the list testifies to Cézanne's profligacy in the examination of sources. By no means definitive, the forty items include reproductions of works by, among others, Luca Signorelli, Peter Paul Rubens, Nicolas Poussin, François Boucher, Claude-Joseph Vernet, Jacques-Louis David, Eugène Delacroix, Thomas Couture, Jean-François Millet, Daumier and Jean-Louis Forain. There were two plaster casts: an ungainly *Ecorché* associated with Michelangelo and a pretty *Cupid* then attributed to Pierre Puget. Finally, there was also an assortment of reference books such as parts of Charles Blanc's *Histoire des Peintres de toutes les Ecoles* (issued in fourteen volumes between 1848 and 1876), illustrated journals such as *Le Magasin Pittoresque*, *L'Artiste*, *L'Illustration,* and fashion magazines such as *La Mode Illustré*. This list, in effect, provides some insight into Cézanne's voracious appetite for visual sources and his almost reckless methods of satiating them, perhaps only comparable with the habits of Picasso and Francis Bacon.

The two principal locations where Cézanne made his copies were the Musée du Louvre, which after the French Revolution and the empire of Napoleon I comprised one of the greatest collections of art in the world, and the Musée de Sculpture Comparée (opened in 1882) in the Palais du Trocadéro, comprising mainly casts of famous sculptures. A variety of illustrations found in books, periodicals or journals supplemented and extended the range of possibilities. Whereas in the eighteenth century making copies from the masterpieces hanging in the Grand Galerie of the Louvre had been the prerequisite of the favoured student, as can be seen in paintings by Hubert Robert, now, in contrast, innumerable reproductions of works of art by recognized masters could be found in the pages of the popular press available to all. A cultural laissez-faire was thus created enabling someone like Cézanne to forage at will, giving him the freedom to pillage and plunder tradition as much as he liked.

The teaching at the Ecole des Beaux-Arts laid emphasis on the accuracy with which a copy should be made after prolonged examination and intricate execution, but too often this resulted in a deadening effect and reduced the skill of drawing to a formula. The type of copying that Cézanne pursued was more instantaneous and based on a more spontaneous response to a work of art, which in turn demanded a more notational style. The purpose of this kind of copying was to release an artist's imagination rather than to imprison it. Copying in this way, therefore, honoured tradition, but also, more importantly, offered an escape from it, which is why it appealed to Cézanne.

The advantages can be seen in his earliest copies, such as *The Dead Christ* after the reproduction of a drawing in black chalk in the Louvre by Fra Bartolommeo, made *c.* 1511 for the painting of *The Pietá* (Pitti Palace, Florence). In Cézanne's copy the broken accented outlines and sudden outbursts of hatching in different media from the original are the direct result of his own creative impulse rather than the Florentine artist's. Cézanne had a similar reaction to another reproduction of a drawing in the Louvre, in this case by Luca Signorelli, which he hung over his bed in his last apartment at 23 Rue Boulegon in Aix-en-Provence. *Study of a Man Seen from the Back Carrying a Body* was made by Signorelli in pen and brown ink with white highlights in connection with one of his frescoes (*Torments of the Damned*) in the Capella di San Brizio (Capella Nova) in the Duomo at Orvieto dating from 1499–1504. But, again using different media from the original, Cézanne [10]

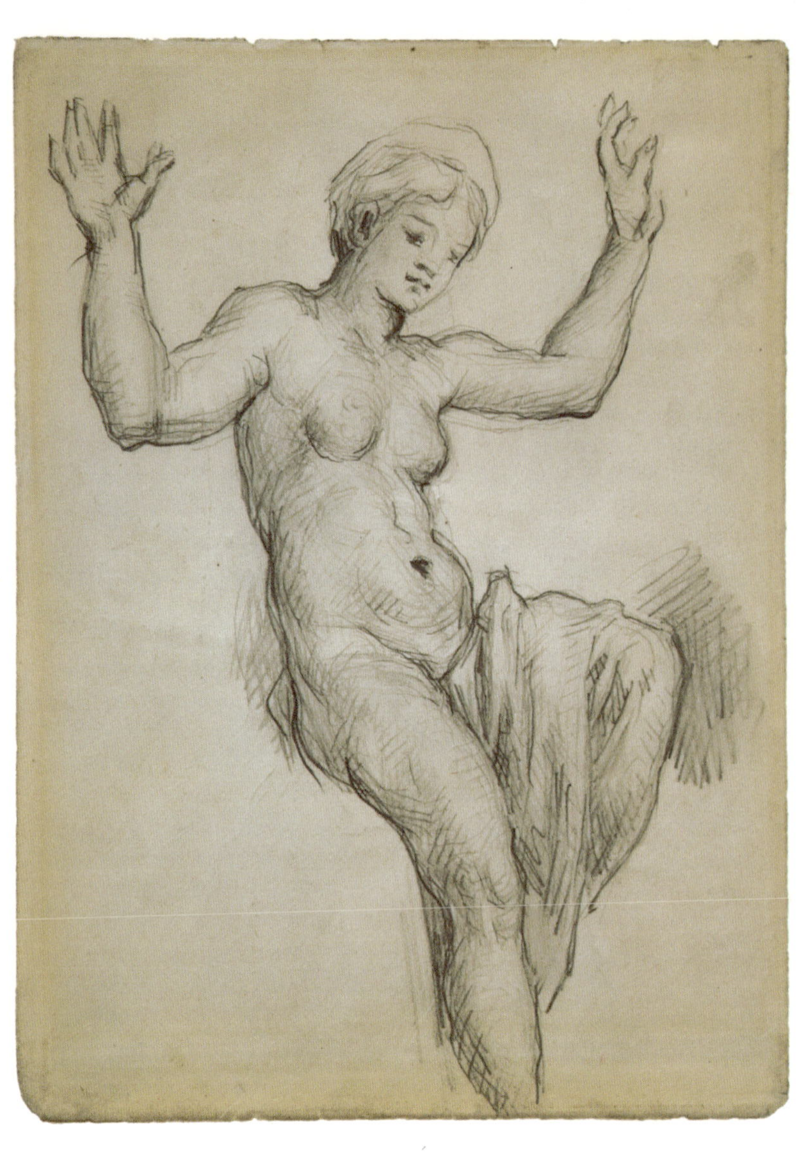

9. *Venus (after Raphael)*, *c.* 1866–69.
Pencil, 24 × 17 cm (9½ × 6¾ in.).
Private collection

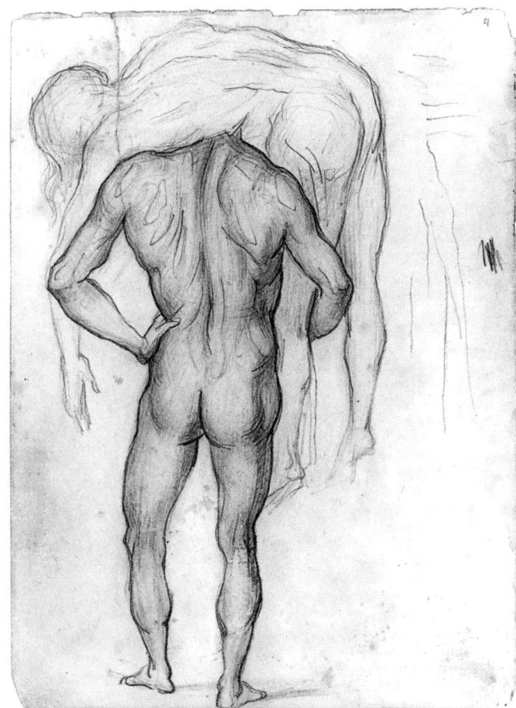

10. *Study of a Man Seen from the Back Carrying a Body (after Signorelli)*, *c*. 1867–70.
Pencil and red crayon, 24 × 18 cm (9½ × 7 in.).
Private collection

translates the delicate hatching, smooth modelling and careful highlighting of Signorelli's study into a series of accented or redrawn lines for the contours and broken lines for the pronounced musculature of the body.

In a similar way, Cézanne animates one of Raphael's finest late drawings (*c*. 1518) of *Venus and Psyche*, which was made in red chalk for the fresco cycle in the Villa Farnesina in Rome. The short reinforced outlines, small pockets of deep shadow and sporadic outbursts of cross-hatching that characterize Cézanne's copy [9] in pencil bring the pose of Venus to life, whereas Raphael's perfect technique virtually embalms the figure. Interestingly, Cézanne observed that Raphael was an artist 'always controlled by his model', which explains why he stated a preference for Michelangelo whom he classified as a 'constructor'.

A more elaborate technique was employed by Cézanne for a copy he made towards the end of the 1870s of Titian's painting *Concert Champêtre* (*c*. 1510), which was one of the most famous pictures in the Louvre. Attributed to Giorgione during the nineteenth century, Stendhal – one of Cézanne's favourite writers – observed that he 'never grew tired of looking at it'. Cézanne's copy [11] in pencil and watercolour is almost certainly done from memory, since there are some fundamental differences from the painting: the head and body of the figure standing on the left are turned inwards rather than outwards and the setting is far less bucolic, perhaps hinting at an interior as opposed to a landscape. There is almost a caricatural feel to Cézanne's copy and he may in fact have been in the process of devising a variation on Titian's theme, as Delacroix did in his painting *Women of Algiers in their Apartment* (Musée du Louvre, Paris) of 1834. A comparable copy, but one much later in date, of the painting by Caravaggio, *The Entombment of Christ* (1604) in the Pinacoteca Vaticana in Rome, must have been based on a black-and-white engraving. Cézanne has relied on the print for the outlines of the composition, but he has added the watercolour freely and without due regard to the colours used by Caravaggio in the original.

The wide range of Cézanne's visual sources during the 1860s and 1870s indicates an underlying uncertainty in his allegiances. Of his immediate predecessors, however, the dominant inspiration was Delacroix, in whose work he recognized not only compositional brilliance and technical sophistication, but also an underlying sympathy for humanity. An early two-sided drawing shows Cézanne examining on the recto the mural of *The Entombment* (1843–44) painted by Delacroix for the church of Saint-Denys-du-Saint Sacrement in Paris and on the other, by contrast, engaging with the huge ceiling painting of *Apollo Vanquishing the Serpent Python* (1850–51) in the Galerie d'Apollon in the Louvre. Although Cézanne knew many of Delacroix's paintings at first hand, he made both the copies on this single sheet from illustrations in two different journals and not from the original works. The copy of *The Entombment* [13] reveals the degree to which Cézanne relished the compacted energy and concentrated emotion of Delacroix's compositions. The intensity is captured by the repeatedly overdrawn lines, sudden outbursts of hatching, and emphatic accents at the centre of the composition reinforcing its diagonal thrusts. As it happens, there is a similarity between the slumped head and arm of Christ and the female figure in Cézanne's painting of *The Abduction* (Provost and Fellows of King's College, Cambridge, on loan to the Fitzwilliam Museum) of 1867, which demonstrates how he could put his copies to use.

Delacroix was one of Cézanne's major formative influences, but he was a controversial figure whose treatment of subject matter even in his own lifetime was often misinterpreted. His death in 1863 prompted a vigorous debate on his place within French art. A notable voice in the discussion was Baudelaire's, who wrote that 'Delacroix was passionately in love with passion, and coldly determined to seek the means of expressing it in the most visible way.' As a devoted admirer of Baudelaire, Cézanne would undoubtedly have read these words, but on a more fundamental level he must have felt a kinship with Delacroix, whose life had been totally dedicated to an art that seemed, according to the tenets of Romanticism, to be so all-embracing. Baudelaire also referred to Delacroix as 'a volcano artistically concealed beneath a bouquet of flowers'. Outwardly polite, courteous and intelligent, he was at the same time aloof, disdainful and enigmatic. He rarely dropped his mask and it is only occasionally in his *Journal* or his wonderful letters that his real character can be glimpsed. His paintings and drawings reveal a supremely gifted artist full of sensibility, extremely well read and with a profound love of nature.

Knowledge and admiration for Delacroix deepened as Cézanne's own career evolved. He made copies of portraits of him from photographs, as well as after the famous *Self-Portrait* (*c.* 1837) in the Louvre; he collected paintings and prints by Delacroix in addition to numerous reproductions; and he devised a composition entitled *The Apotheosis of Delacroix* [14], which he began in the early 1870s and worked on into the 1890s, but developed only as far as a small painting, tantamount to no more than an oil sketch. In addition to the portraits of Pissarro, Monet and the artist himself, Cézanne also includes in *The Apotheosis* one of his first supporters, Victor Chocquet (on the left, standing next to the tree), who owned over eighty works by Delacroix alongside which were soon to be hung paintings by Renoir and Cézanne.

The supreme example of Cézanne's admiration for Delacroix is the watercolour of *Medea* [8], which is based on a print after the painting of 1838 now hanging in the Musée des Beaux-Arts in Lille. This depicts the moment when Medea, having been spurned by her husband, Jason, takes her revenge by killing their two children. The combination of literary allusion and sense of drama heightened by the degree of personal suffering and the cruel outcome epitomize Romantic art. The iconography of a woman with children usually denoted an allegorical representation of Charity, but Medea is a scene of infanticide. The horror is increased by the solidity of the composition, which is based on a pyramid, but any suggestion of composure is shattered by the urgency with which Medea turns her head and grasps hold of her writhing children. The figure is seen slightly from below, which gives it an impression of monumentality. The impact of Cézanne's representation of this terrible scene is made even more dramatic by the highlighting of the flesh tones against which the dagger is seen and which contrast so vividly with the draperies and the background. What has clearly fascinated Cézanne in looking at this particular work is the controlled fury that the treatment of such a subject demands. No greater homage to Delacroix could have been made by Cézanne than this superlative copy of one of the earlier master's finest works.

The numerous copies made by Cézanne reveal many of his proclivities, but they were not intended to be a comprehensive account of the history of art in the manner of an encyclopedia. There are, in fact, a number of anomalies. Cézanne particularly appreciated Venetian Renaissance art as represented by Titian, Veronese and Tintoretto. Veronese's enormous canvas of *The Marriage of Cana* (1562–63) in the Louvre overwhelmed him and it became a talisman, but he only made two partial copies from it. There was a similar restraint over Titian and Tintoretto, which was all the more puzzling in the case of the former since he was well represented in the Louvre. Spanish art also interested Cézanne, as it did Manet, but his knowledge of El Greco, Alonso Cano, Velázquez, Murillo and Goya seems to have been gleaned principally from the relevant volumes of Blanc's *Histoire des Peintres*.

Even more puzzling is the fact that there is only a limited number of copies of the two French painters who were of the greatest significance for Cézanne's development. The balance and harmony of Nicolas Poussin's landscapes and the emotional range of his narrative compositions were an inspiration and a challenge to him, but Cézanne scarcely made any copies from his works in the Louvre. Similarly, Jean-Siméon Chardin's still lifes must have appealed to him for their simplicity of design and straightforward rendering of the subject. But, again, there are only two copies. For Cézanne Chardin was a starting point as regards the selection and disposition of objects within a still-life composition – perhaps more than any Spanish or Dutch artist – but there is no thorough exploration of this antecedence on paper.

A complete survey of Cézanne's copies reveals that his approach changed during the second part of his life. From the 1880s copying was undertaken more in accordance with the specific problems he was encountering as an artist at any one moment. There was, therefore, a greater emphasis on the figure at this point. This is apparent, for example, when Cézanne returns in *c.* 1885–90 to Signorelli and looks at the reproduction of another of his drawings in the Louvre – *Standing Male Nude* made *c.* 1508–10 in black chalk in connection with *The Flagellation* (Ca' d'Oro, Venice). The figure is seen in three-quarters profile from behind standing on tiptoe and reaching upwards with the arms raised above the head. Apart from the pose, Cézanne has also commandeered everything else that characterizes the drawing, concentrating on the twisting, gymnastic stance, and the curves of the body made by the shoulders, buttocks, thighs and calves. Pliant, redrawn outlines and areas of loose hatching, as in the small of the back, combine to show not just how the various parts of the body are fitted together, but also its elegance in movement. Such a figure pertains to Cézanne's continuing interest in compositions of bathers during the 1880s and 1890s.

Like Delacroix before him, Cézanne revered Rubens for his narrative inventiveness and his skills as a colourist. He returned again and again to the extensive series of twenty-four vast canvases depicting the life of Marie de' Medici originally painted for the Palais du Luxembourg in Paris and dating from 1622–25 but hanging in the Louvre from 1816. One of the masterpieces of the Baroque era, the cycle is an unsurpassed demonstration of Rubens's ability to treat history as allegory with vigour, imagination and conviction, but without loss of clarity. Cézanne carefully chose certain passages from two of the canvases: the naiads from *The Disembarkation of Marie de' Medici at Marseilles* [15] and the pivotal figure of Bellona from *The Death of Henry IV and the Proclamation of the Regency* [16]. More to the point is that he returned on several occasions to these particular figures, which helped him to clarify the ideas he was evolving in connection with the scenes of bathers.

Cézanne relishes the dramatic poses, voluptuous bodies, varied expressions and powerful sense of drawing found in these works by Rubens, which combine emotional intensity with clear exposition – boundless energy with notable articulacy. Ultimately, the appeal of Rubens for Cézanne lay in the ability of the Baroque master to work on such a large scale and yet still manage to weave so many figures together in a unified composition dependent on interlocking poses and interweaving gestures. Each canvas could be broken down into its different constituent elements, but in the end it was how these elements interconnected that was the key. And Cézanne diligently searched for those pivotal areas where Rubens makes such vital links.

The fact that Cézanne was intrigued by sculpture of all types in all materials might be considered surprising since he was himself solely a painter. Yet one of the Renaissance artists he most admired, Tintoretto, frequently made innumerable drawings after sculpture that he kept in his studio – pieces after the antique and Michelangelo. Cézanne, too, treasured the casts he kept and which on occasion he included in paintings: the *Écorché* associated in the nineteenth century with Michelangelo and the *Cupid* traditionally attributed to Puget [17, 18]. But it was in the Louvre or the Musée du Sculpture Comparée where Cézanne repeatedly copied sculpture extending in date from antiquity through the Renaissance and up to his own day, with items by François Rude, Antonin Mercié and Antoine-Louis Barye.

The painter did, however, have a special penchant for French sculpture of the seventeenth and eighteenth centuries. This is demonstrated by the thirty or so copies he made after the work of Puget, who had the additional advantage in Cézanne's opinion of having been born in Marseille. Cézanne, according to Gasquet, said, 'Puget has the mistral in him, that's what makes his marble move', and he made more copies after this artist than any other, including Rubens. Also admired by Delacroix, Puget was trained in Italy and developed a Baroque manner of working that was highly individual and emotionally intense. His headstrong and difficult temperament particularly appealed to Romantic artists and gave his sculpture immense dynamism and complexity.

Sculpture offered several advantages to a copyist such as Cézanne. Seen in the round and stationary each piece could be drawn from several different viewpoints of varying difficulty. The artist, in effect, stalks his prey marvelling at the number of changing profiles while he tries to unlock its inner energy. This is how Cézanne approached Puget's *Milo of Crotona* of 1671–82 [19, 20], *Hercules Resting* of 1661 [21] and Michelangelo's *Dying Slave* of 1513–15 [22], or Jean-Baptiste Pigalle's *Mercury* of 1744 [23]. The sequences of drawings after these particular sculptures reveal how each time Cézanne approached them he observed, or chose to examine, a new aspect. Any stylistic differences in the copies are more than just of chronological significance; rather, they imply a difference of interpretation expressed through such cumulative features as the flow, repetition or strength of the lines. Many of the sculptures selected by Cézanne had originally been displayed out of doors and had weathered, thereby reducing the sharpness, or depth, of the cutting and blurring the expressions. Essentially though, it was the spiralling rhythms set up by turning heads, flailing arms and twisting limbs that he sought out in order to discover how within a fixed pose such a variety of expressions and extremes of movement could be reduced to manageable forms in his own paintings. Cézanne noticed, for example, how Puget's strong carving created pools of shadow in the marble that reminded him of chiaroscuro in paintings. He in fact said that 'Puget worked like a painter'.

Antique sculpture continued to set the standards against which all later work was to be measured and Cézanne duly paid homage to the classical tradition that had also been so important for Rubens. The clear outlines and direct carving of Hellenistic sculpture gave it a poise and dignity that was instantly pleasing to the eye. The curves of the *Crouching Venus* (2nd century AD) [24], the reserve of the *Venus de' Milo* (180–100 BC) [25], and the military bearing of the *Borghese Mars* (1st or 2nd century AD) [26] excited Cézanne as much as they did Rubens.

Portraiture was an equally important part of antique sculpture, which
in turn inspired Renaissance artists. Busts of Roman emperors [29] and
Renaissance rulers [30] are both found in Cézanne's sketchbooks. But,
in addition, by looking at seventeenth- and eighteenth-century sculpture
he could explore a whole cross-section of humanity: rulers, aristocrats,
mistresses, divines, philosophers, soldiers, artists. Such portraits were a
challenge to draw because of the variety of the carving needed to render
hair, skin, clothes, accessories and wigs [31, 32].

Rarely, however, were Cézanne's copies of sculpture exact, detailed
or complete. Often they were deliberately unfinished, like a series of
visual *aperçus*, ending in a flurry of loose, repeated lines that give his
copies a timeless or even a modern appearance. Rather, what was of
intrinsic value for him was the gauging and representation of the distance
that he put between himself and the sculpture – an elusive space that
was defined by the endlessly shifting light, or particles of dust in the air,
and sometimes by the presence of neighbouring sculptures. Effectively,
Cézanne was looking for ways to represent the existence of a three-
dimensional object by suggesting something as abstract as the agitation
of air surrounding it, on the basis that objects are defined as much by the
space they displace as by that which they occupy. This engagement with
something that was virtually invisible is particularly acute in the copies
after Renaissance sculpture [30].

The variety and number of copies made by Cézanne throughout
his life amount to a vital piece of evidence for a proper appreciation
of his own art. They highlight the two complementary characteristics
found in his paintings: the search for order and balance associated with
the mind and the articulation of passion and emotion governed by the
heart. The copies provide clues as to how Cézanne set about resolving
this personal dichotomy, which he himself acknowledged as being central
to his being. The emphasis on sculpture in particular had repercussions
in wholly unrelated and surprisingly divergent areas such as portraiture,
scenes of bathers, and the rocky landscape of Provence. As such,
Cézanne's copies must be seen as uniting the various disparate elements
in his art, thereby defining its character and providing it with its own
identity. In making such copies with so much diligence and discipline
Cézanne was not enslaving himself to the past, which he so greatly
respected. He was, in fact, looking to the future. As he wrote to Roger
Marx on 23 January 1905, 'In my opinion, one does not replace the past,
one only adds a new link.'

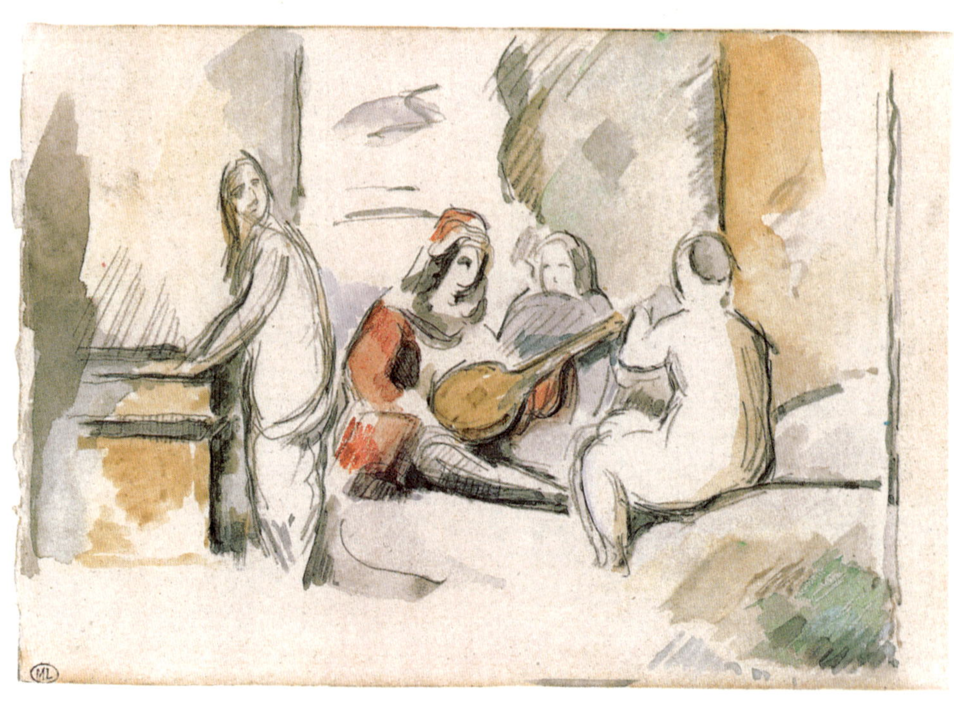

11. *Concert Champêtre (after Titian), c.* 1878.
Pencil, watercolour and gouache, 12 × 18 cm (4¾ × 7 in.).
Musée du Louvre, Paris

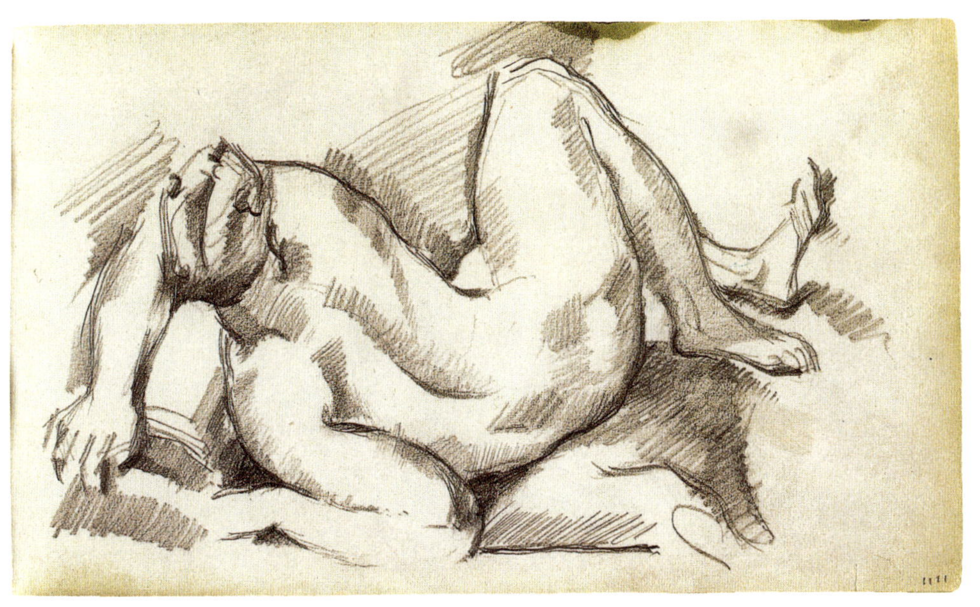

12. *Allegorical Figure of a River God (after Delacroix), c.* 1878–81.
Pencil, 12 × 21 cm (4¾ × 8¼ in.).
The Art Institute of Chicago

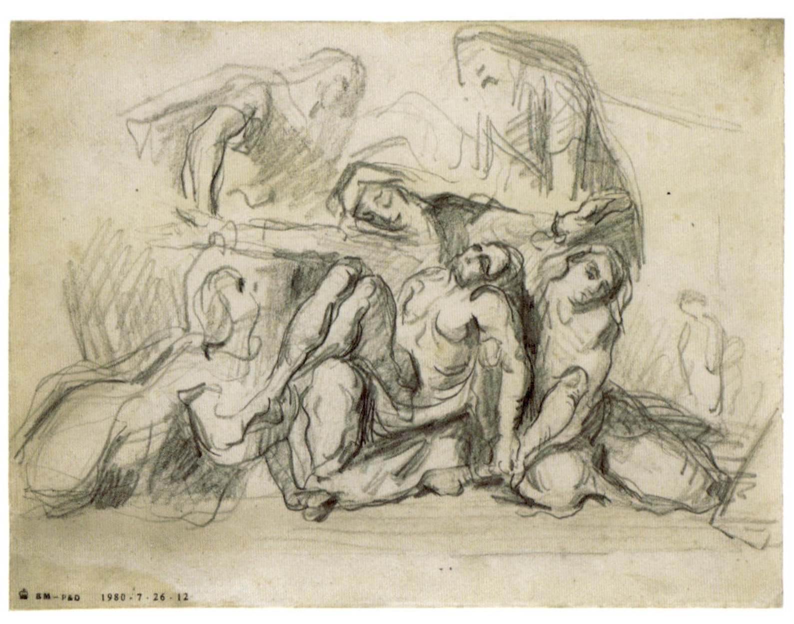

13. *The Entombment (after Delacroix), c. 1866–67.*
Pencil, 18 × 24 cm (7⅛ × 9½ in.).
British Museum, London

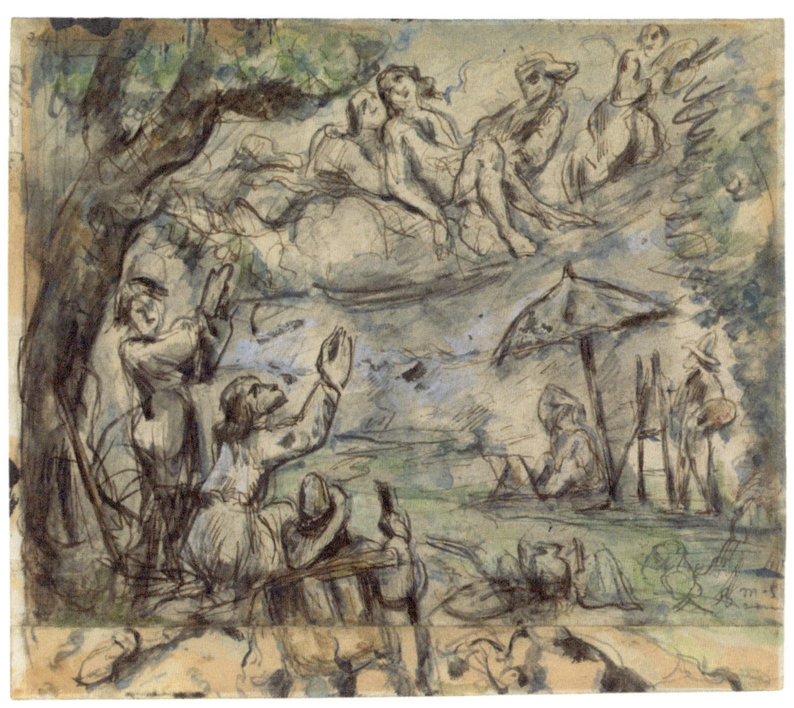

14. *The Apotheosis of Delacroix, c.* 1878–80.
Pen and brown ink, watercolour heightened with
gouache, over pencil, 20 × 23.3 cm (7⅞ × 9⅛ in.).
British Museum, London

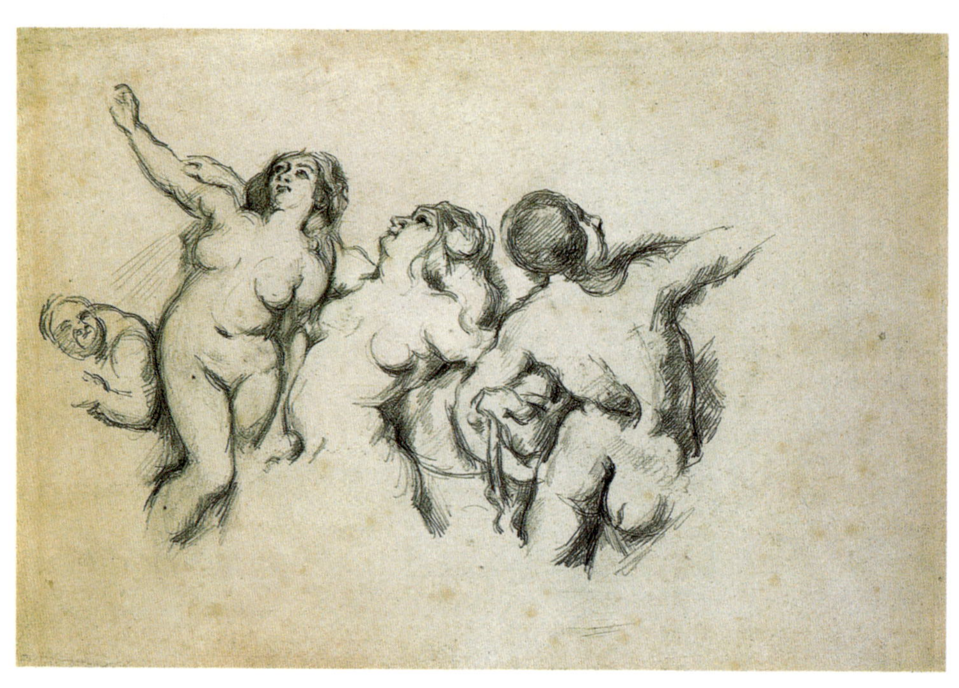

15. *Three Naiads (after Rubens)*, 1876–79.
Pencil, 31 × 45 cm (12¼ × 17¾ in.).
Private collection

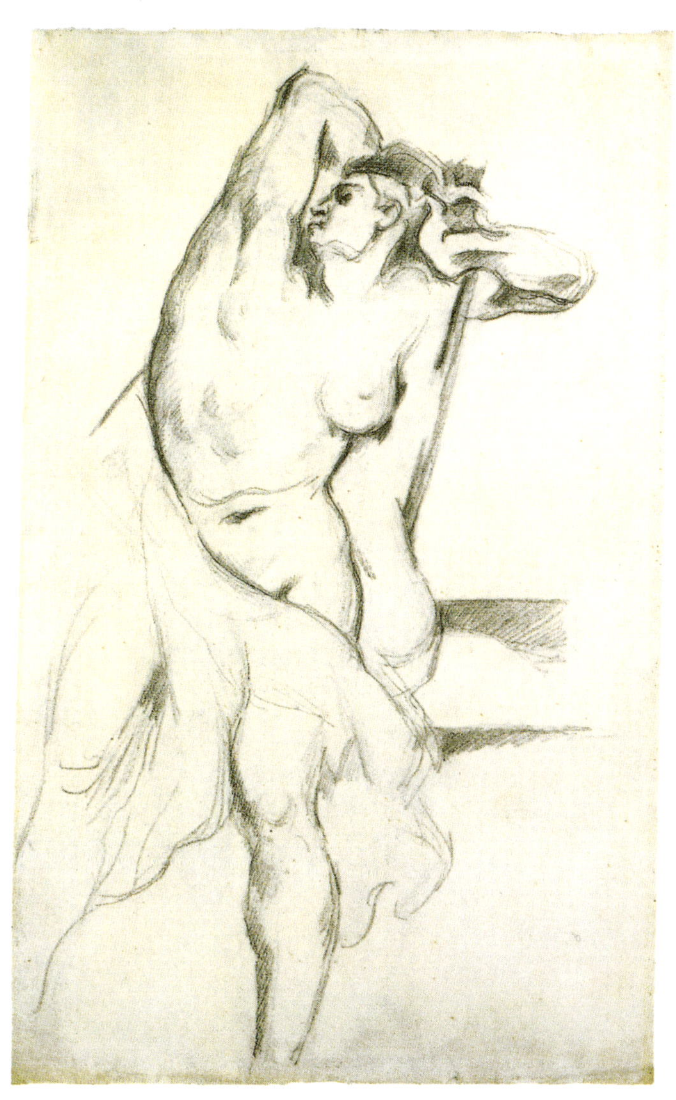

16. *Bellona (after Rubens)*, 1879–82.
Pencil, 48 × 30 cm (18⅞ × 11¼ in.).
Private collection

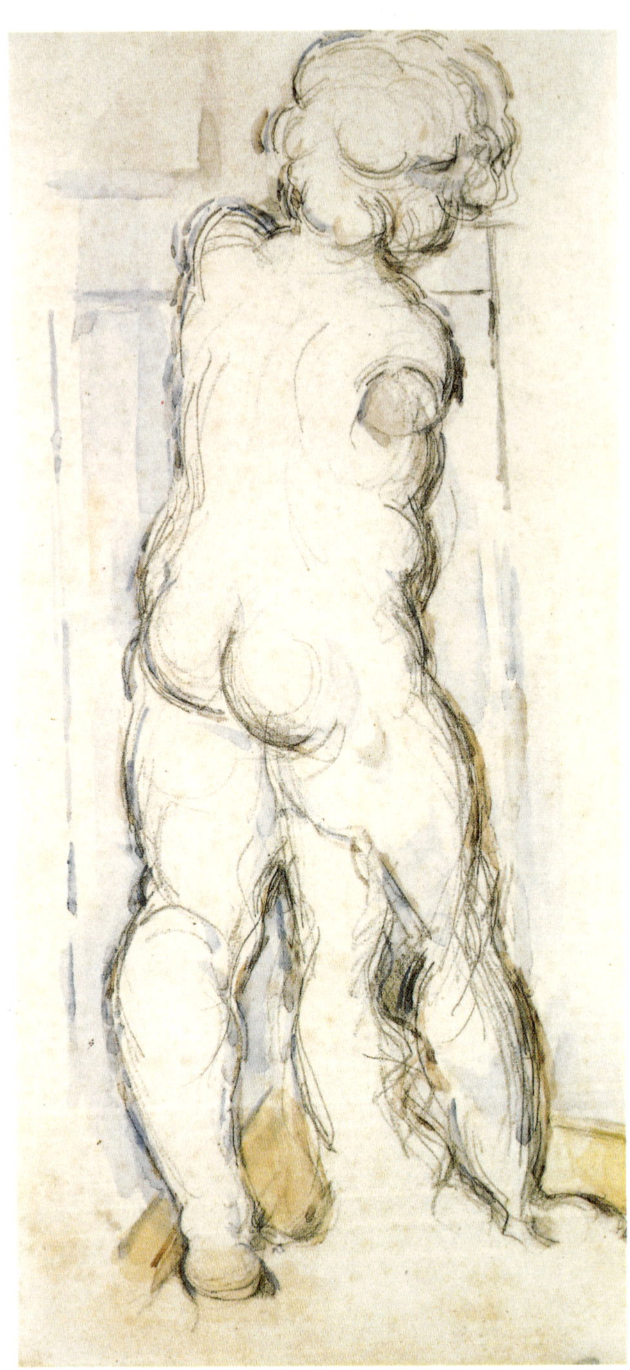

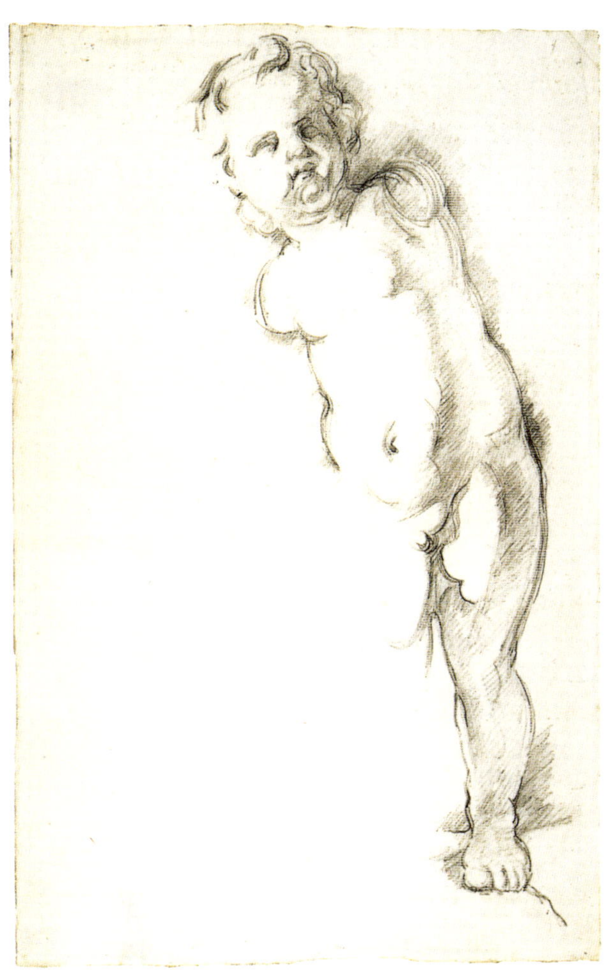

OPPOSITE

17. *Plaster Cupid* [traditionally stated to be after Puget], 1900–04.
Pencil and watercolour, 48 × 22.5 cm (18⅞ × 8⅞ in.).
Private collection

ABOVE

18. *Plaster Cupid* [traditionally stated to be after Puget], *c.* 1890.
Pencil, 49.7 × 32.2 cm (19½ × 12¾ in.).
British Museum, London

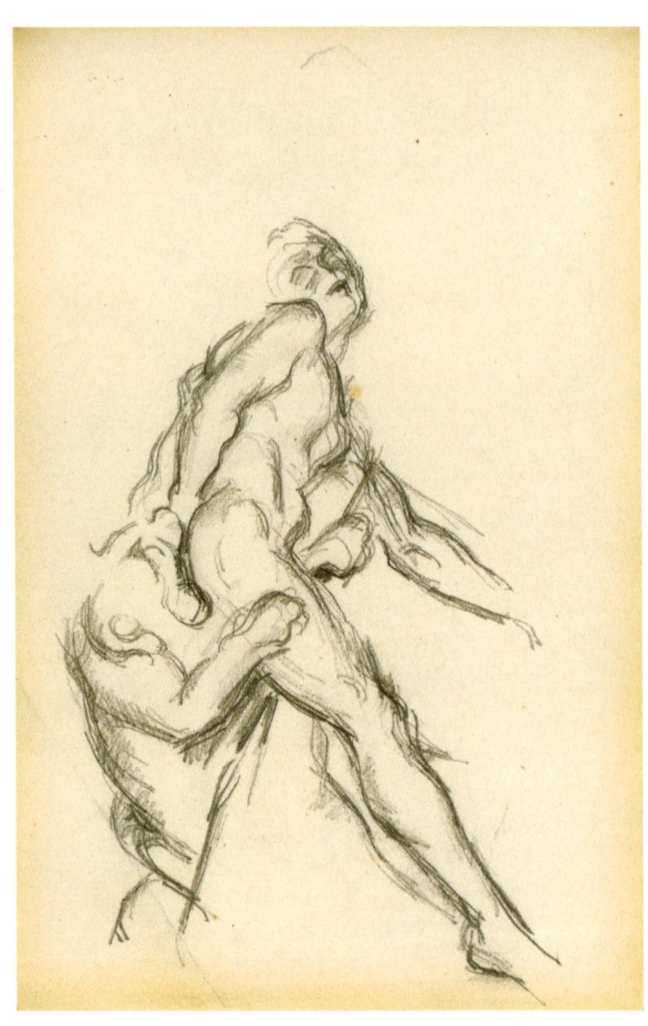

ABOVE
19. *Milo of Crotona (after Puget)*, 1880–83.
Pencil, 23.7 × 15.2 cm (9⅜ × 6 in.).
National Gallery of Art, Washington, DC

OPPOSITE
20. *Milo of Crotona (after Puget)*, 1897–1900.
Pencil, 21.2 × 13.1 cm (8⅜ × 5⅛ in.).
Kunstmuseum Basel

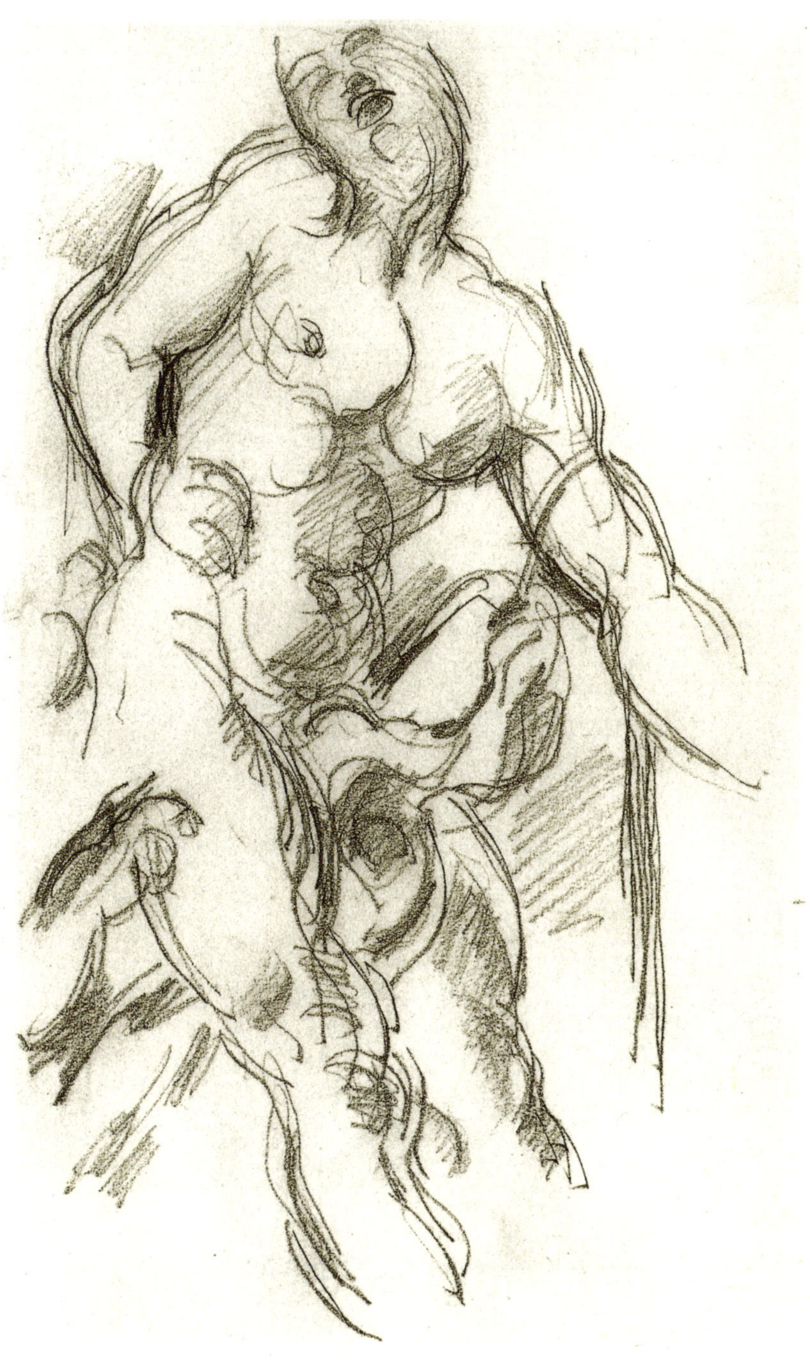

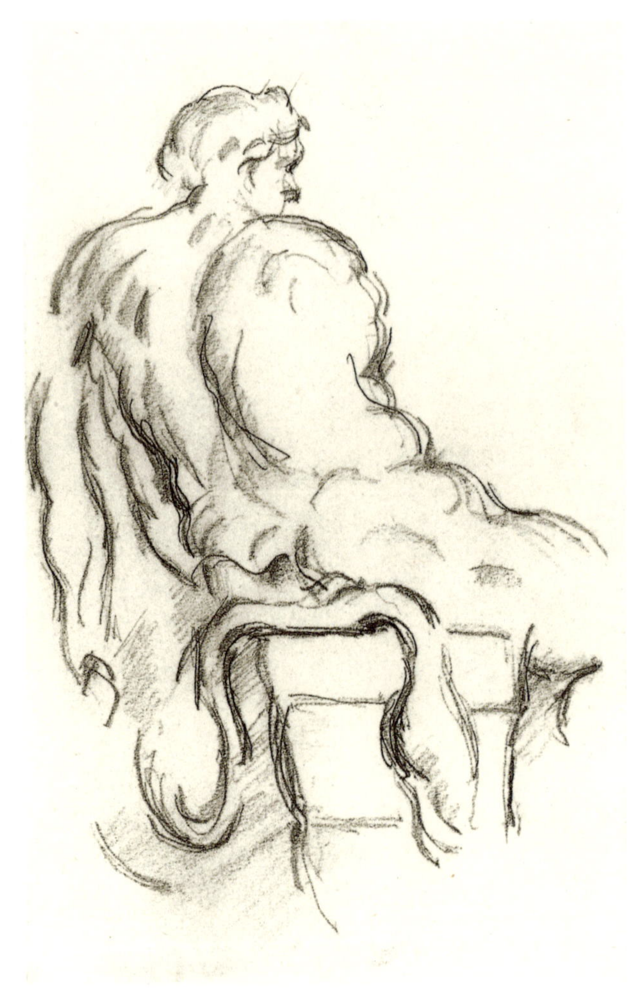

21. *Hercules Resting (after Puget)*, 1894–97.
Pencil, 19.8 × 12.5 cm (7¾ × 4⅞ in.).
Kunstmuseum Basel

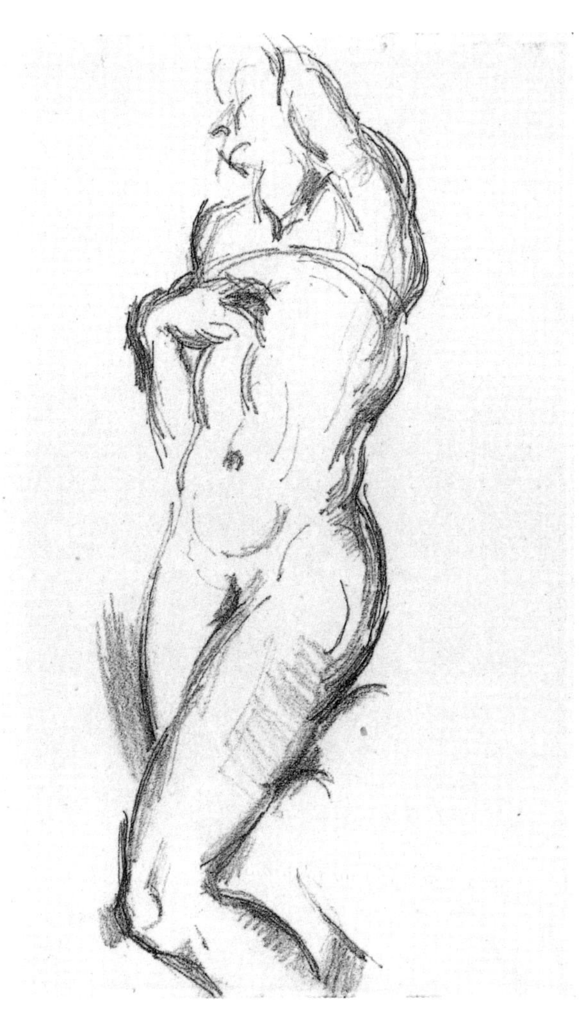

22. *The Dying Slave (after Michelangelo)*, 1885–90.
Pencil, 21.6 × 12.7 cm (8½ × 5 in.).
Kunstmuseum Basel

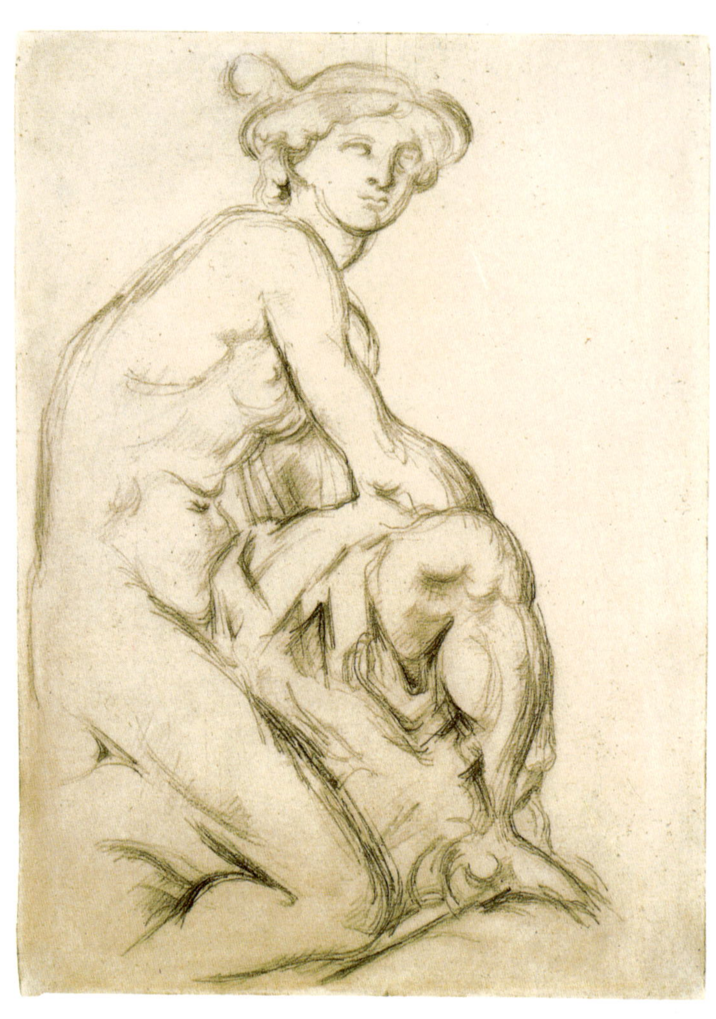

ABOVE
23. *Mercury (after Pigalle)*, c. 1890.
Pencil, 38 × 25 cm (15 × 9⅞ in.).
Museum of Modern Art, New York

OPPOSITE
24. *Crouching Venus (after the Antique)*, c. 1894–97.
Pencil, 23 × 15 cm (9 × 5⅞ in.).
Musée du Louvre, Paris

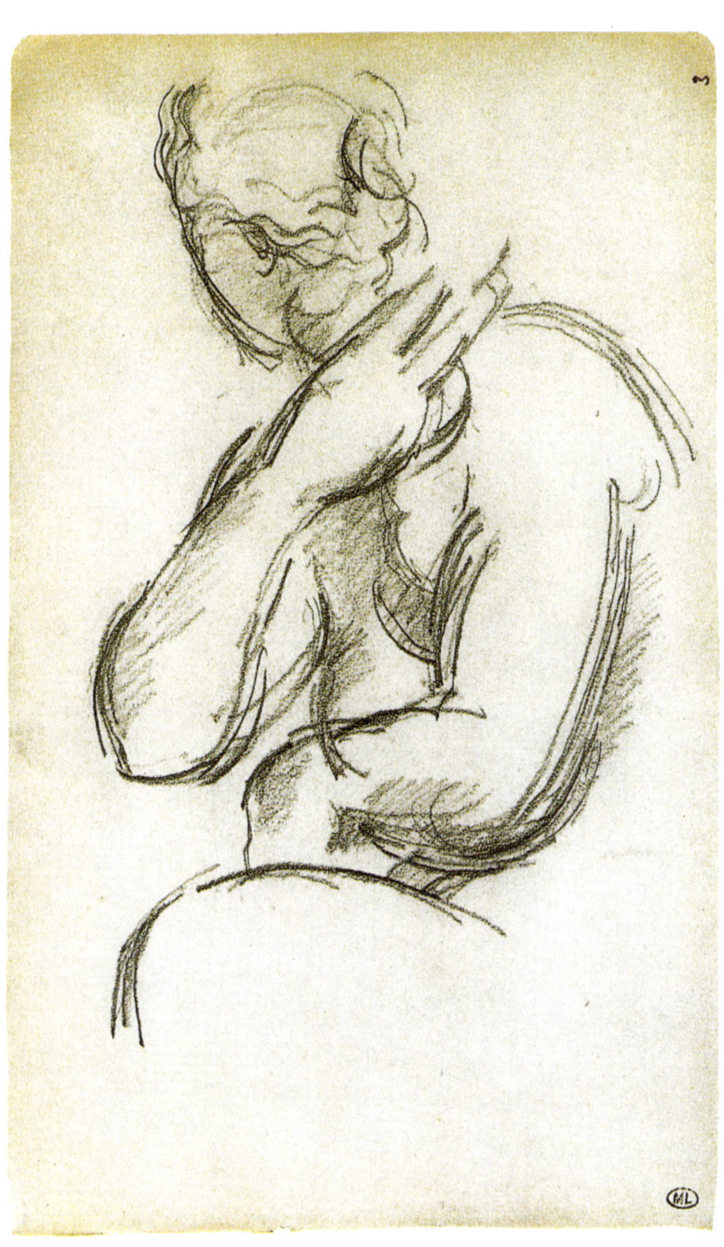

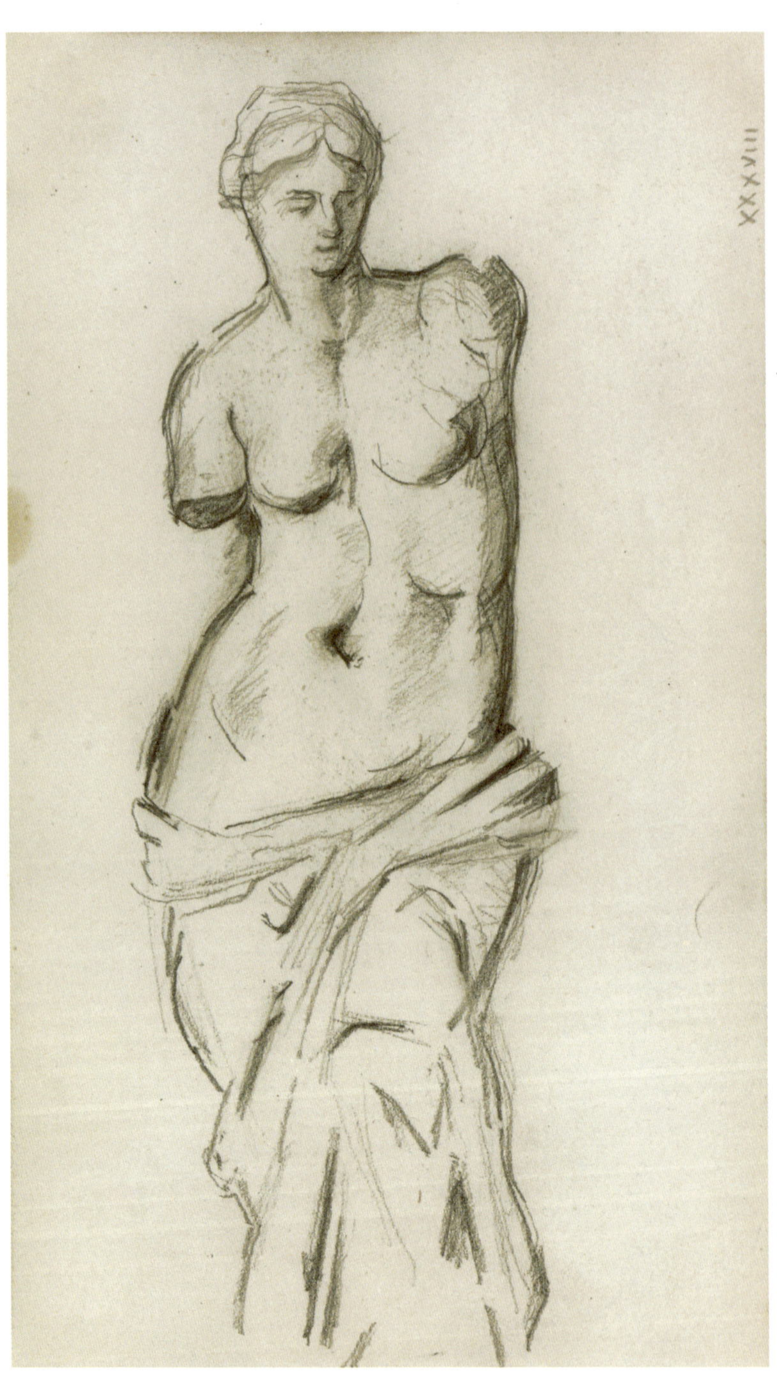

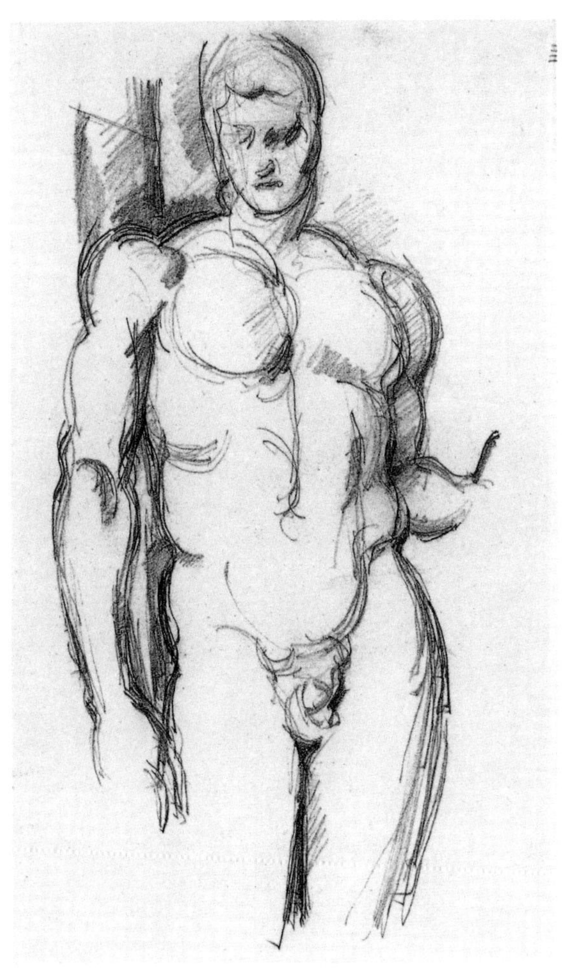

OPPOSITE
25. *Venus de Milo (after the Antique)*, *c.* 1872–73.
Pencil, 21.5 × 12.2 cm (8½ × 4¾ in.).
Formerly collection of Adrien Chappuis

ABOVE
26. *The Borghese Mars (after the Antique)*, *c.* 1895.
Pencil, 20.5 × 12.2 cm (8 × 4¾ in.).
Kunstmuseum Basel

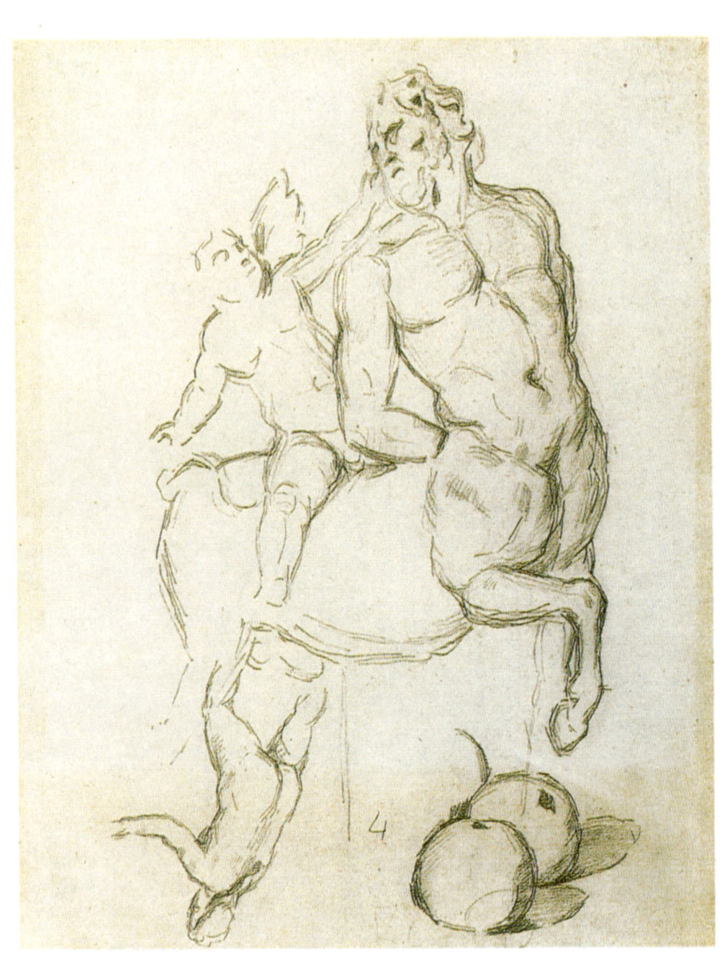

ABOVE
27. *Sheet of Studies with Centaur and Cupid (after the Antique)*, 1879–82.
Pencil, 37.9 × 31.3 cm (15 × 12⅜ in.).
Albertina, Vienna

OPPOSITE
28. *The Dancing Satyr (after the Antique)*, c. 1894–98.
Pencil, 22 × 14 cm (8⅝ × 5½ in.).
Musée du Louvre, Paris

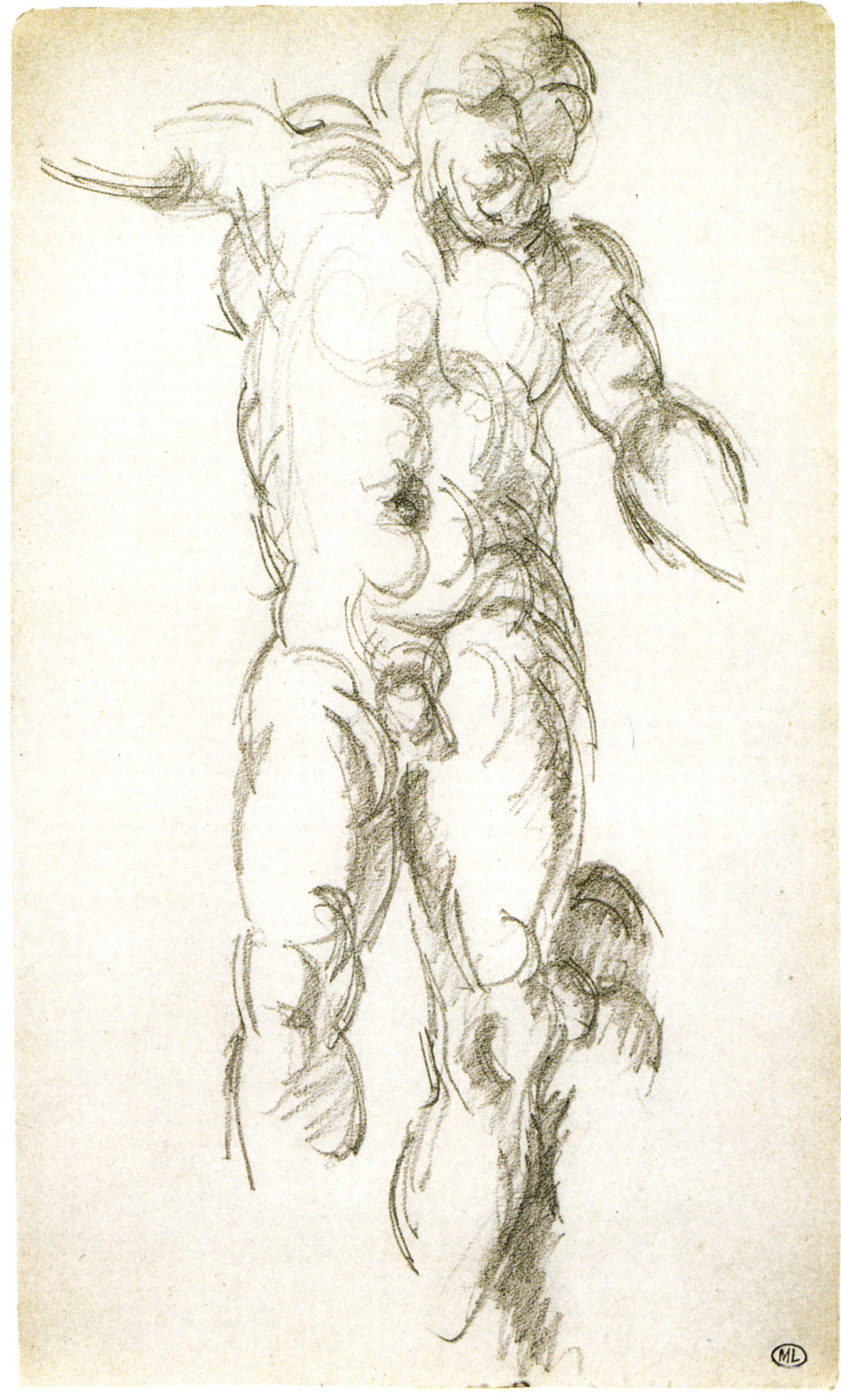

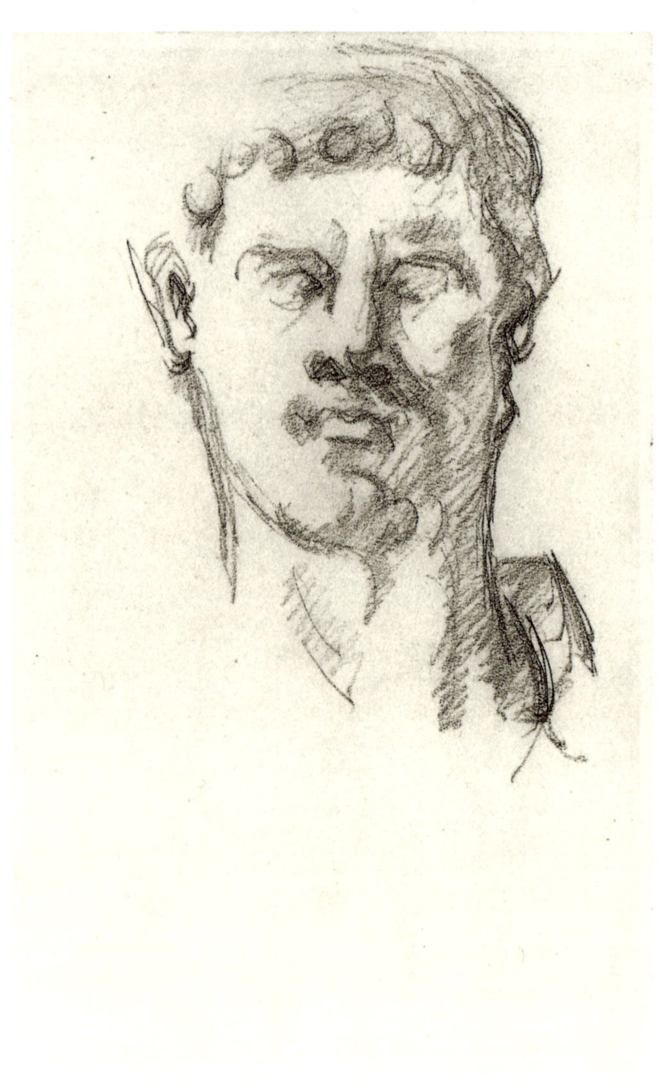

29. *Head of the Emperor Titus (after the Antique), c.* 1900.
Pencil, 21 × 13.1 cm (8¼ × 5⅛ in.).
Kunstmuseum Basel

30. *Filippo Strozzi (after Benedetto da Maiano),* 1881–84.
Pencil, 21.4 × 13.1 cm (8⅜ × 5⅛ in.).
Kunstmuseum Basel

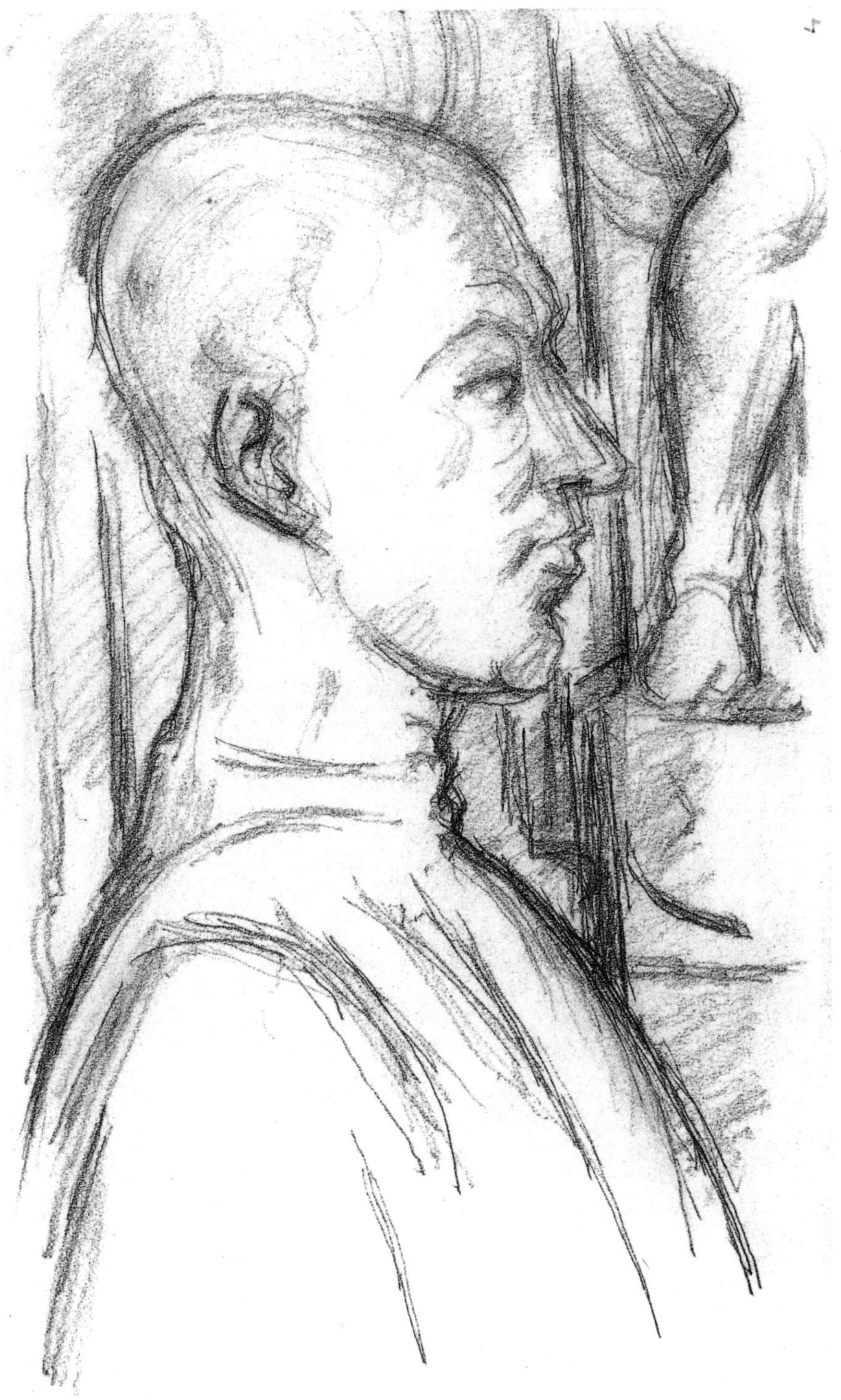

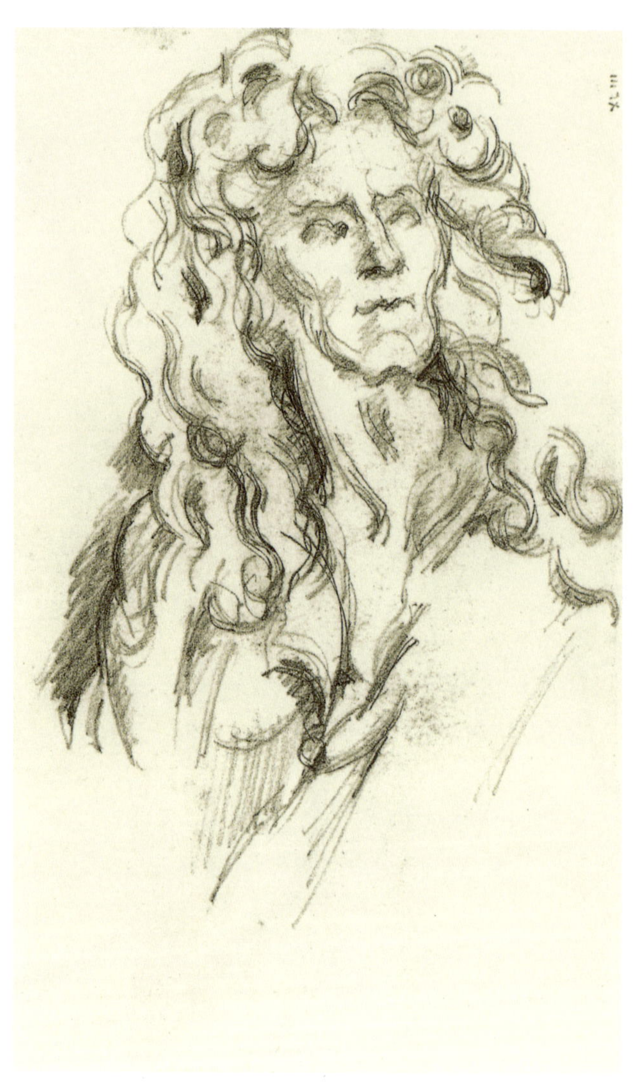

ABOVE

31. *Pierre Mignard (after Desjardins)*, 1892–95.
Pencil, 20.5 × 12.4 cm (8⅛ × 4⅞ in.).
Kunstmuseum Basel

OPPOSITE

32. *Pierre Mignard (after Desjardins)*, c. 1892–9.
Pencil, 22 × 14 cm (8⅝ × 5½ in.).
Musée du Louvre, Paris

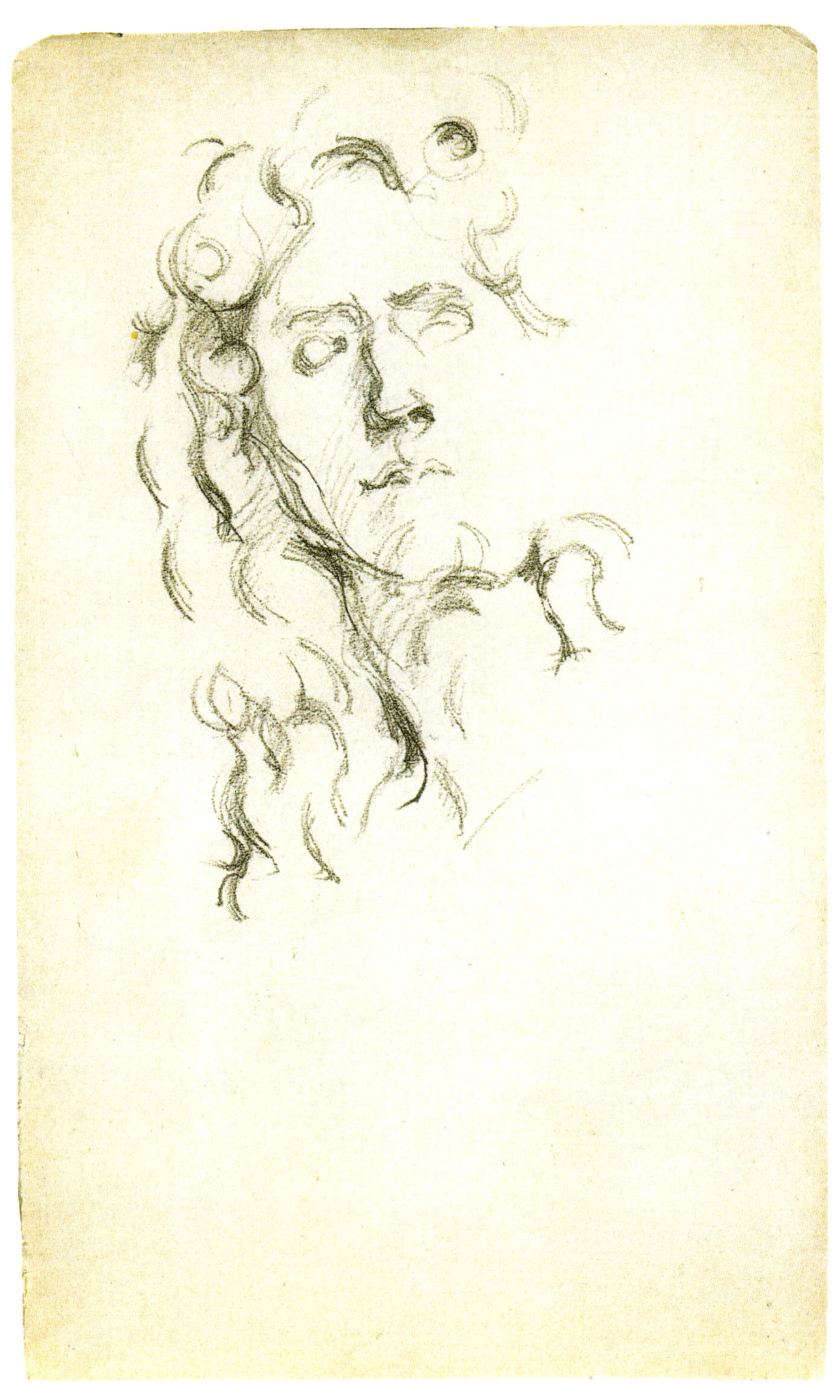

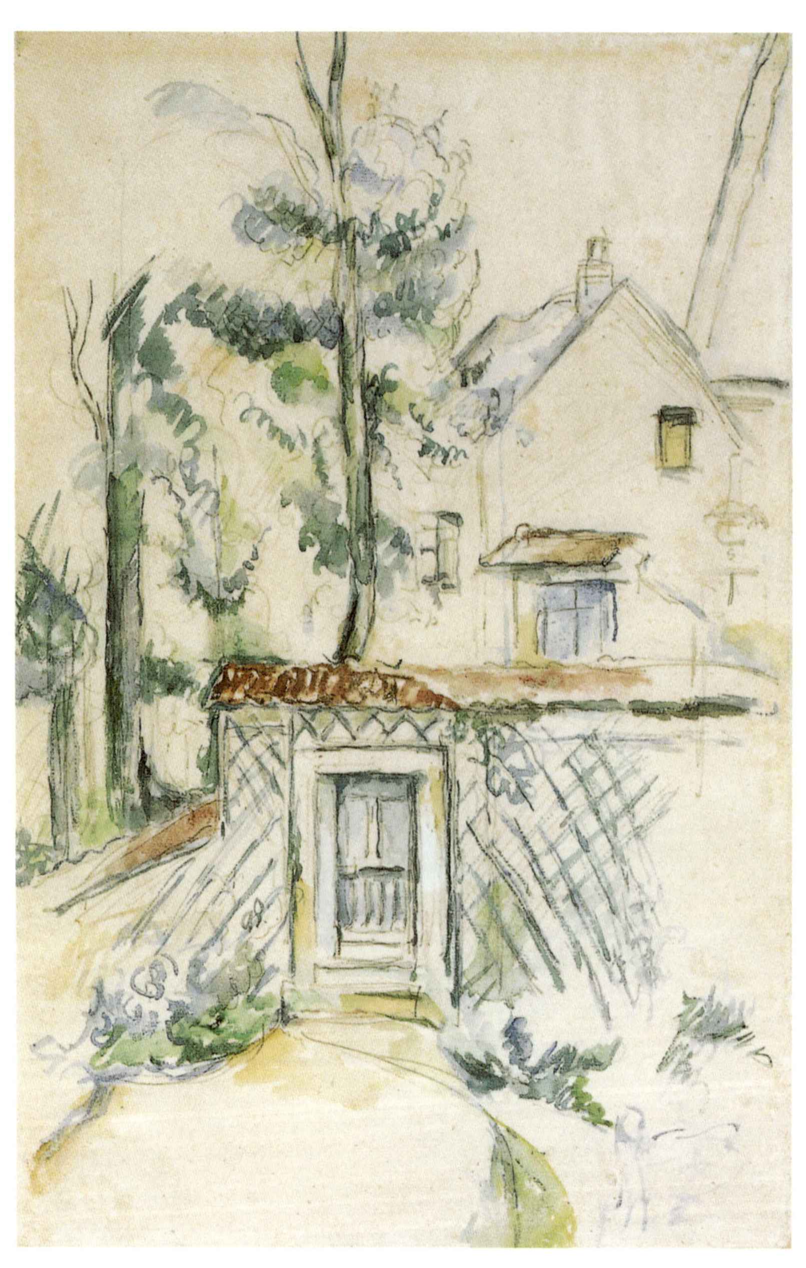

33. *Garden Entrance*, 1872–77.
Pencil and watercolour, 47.8 × 31.2 cm (18⅞ × 12¼ in.).
Metropolitan Museum of Art, New York

CHAPTER TWO

The Impact of Impressionism

'Matisse, "What is an impressionist?" Pissarro, "An impressionist is a painter who never paints the same picture, who always paints a new picture."'

When Cézanne left Aix-en-Provence for Paris in 1862 he did so full of aspirations, but plagued by uncertainties. Having spent a few months in the capital during the previous year he had no difficulty in establishing a routine. He returned to the Académie Suisse, registered as a copyist in the Musée du Louvre and persevered with trying to have his work exhibited at the annual Salon. The support of his school friend Emile Zola, who at this early stage of his career was beginning to gain a reputation as a journalist and critic, continued. And, in addition, Cézanne began to form his own friendships with artists he met at the Académie Suisse: Pissarro, Monet, Guillaumin, Guillemet and Oller.

Cézanne's uncertainties stemmed from the fact that he did not know exactly what sort of artist he wanted to be or what kind of art he wanted to produce. The Salon was the accepted route to success and he made numerous attempts to have his work exhibited there, but he was regularly frustrated by having these early submissions rejected by the jury. The disappointment was such that in 1866 he wrote a letter of complaint to Comte de Nieuwerkerke, Minister of Fine Arts, suggesting that a Salon des Refusés should be reconstituted along the lines of the one in 1863 when Manet exhibited his painting *Déjeuner sur l'Herbe*. Not surprisingly, as an unknown and somewhat eccentric painter, Cézanne's petition was unsuccessful.

The range of works produced by Cézanne during the 1860s in his attempt to impress the Salon jury was remarkable and it has perhaps not been sufficiently realized to what extent in this first decade of concentrated activity he was in so many ways already a complete artist. Portraits, still lifes, landscapes and imaginary narrative subjects abound, but the strength and directness of these pictures, as well as their daring treatment, were antithetical to the academic style favoured

by the Salon authorities. Thick layers of paint often trowelled on with
a palette knife, strong throbbing colours, ungainly figures, inaccurate
drawing, confrontational poses and lack of finish appeared shocking
and alarming.

The same wide range of subject matter and challenging technique
are also found in Cézanne's watercolours of the 1860s. Some of these
were made in connection with projected paintings, but nearly all stand
as works of art in their own right. They are usually of small dimensions
with clearly defined compositions. The surfaces are densely worked with
pencil (or occasionally with pen and ink) applied in conjunction with
watercolour and often heightened with gouache. As with Cézanne's early
paintings, the viewer is aware in these early watercolours of a traditional
medium being stretched to its limits or its potential being reassessed.

Straightaway it seems that Cézanne was keen to attach a greater
significance to his watercolours than was customary in mid-nineteenth-
century France where the medium was generally regarded as subsidiary
to painting and principally a vehicle for illustrations of various kinds.
It was certainly acknowledged that the liquidity of the medium allowed
artists a more spontaneous response to their observations, leading to
greater speed of execution and considerable freedom in handling, which
could not be achieved with oil paint. Romantic artists such as Théodore
Géricault and Delacroix made watercolours as a way of recording
their impressions more immediately, which in turn encouraged them to
examine subjects that they might otherwise have overlooked. And, as
Baudelaire maintained when he championed the work of Constantin
Guys, watercolour was the perfect medium for capturing the ephemeral
nature of modern life where everything appears to be in a state of flux.
By contrast, Cézanne seems to have favoured watercolour for almost the
opposite reasons, namely as a viable alternative to painting, allowing for
a more thorough and prolonged analysis of motifs.

In fact, by the early 1880s Cézanne only very rarely used watercolour
as part of the preparatory process and had instead begun to regard it as a
medium in which he could capture the effects of nature more definitively
than perhaps in his paintings. The exploration of that possibility led to
his late watercolours of the 1890s, which are very different in style from
those of the 1860s and are now regarded as being some of the greatest
ever made. The early watercolours, however, already reveal a surprising
interdependency between pencil, wash and gouache, to the extent that
their crowded, tight-knit compositions and opaque surfaces seem to
be almost overworked. There is a sense in which such works as *Still
Life: Flowers and Fruit* [34], *The Wine Grog* [43], *The Diver* [44], *The
Abduction* [45], *Landscape with Rock* [46], or *House in Provence* [47],

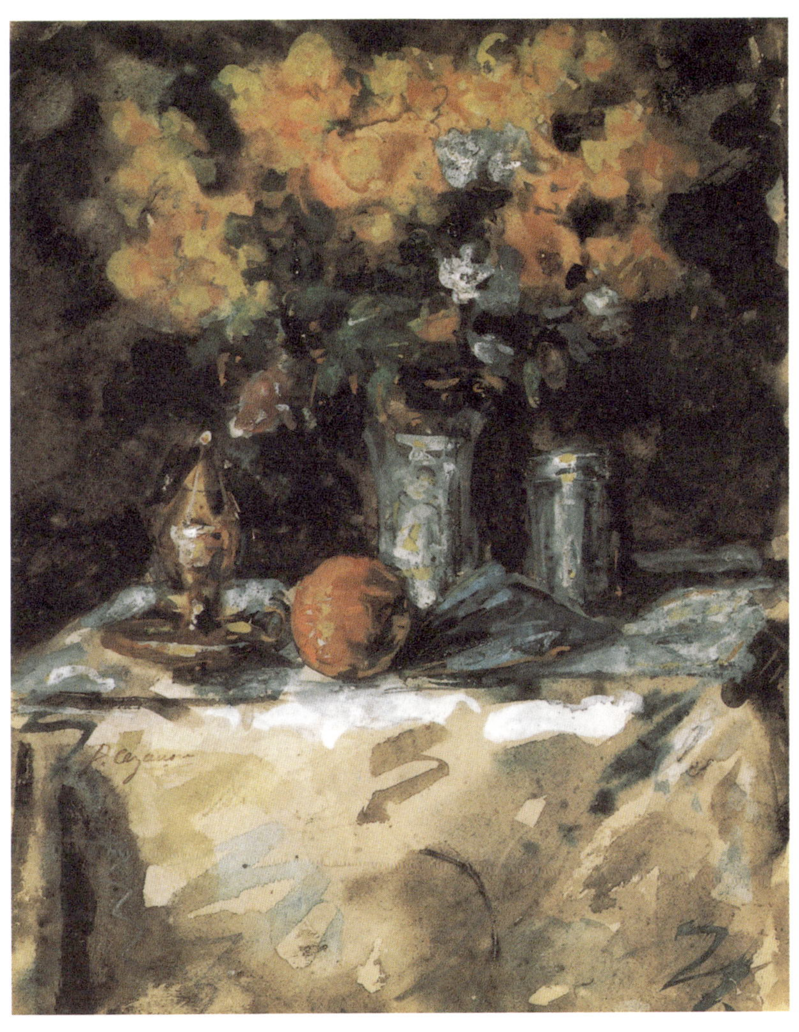

34. *Still Life: Flowers and Fruit*, 1865–67.
Pencil, watercolour and gouache, 18 × 14 cm (7⅛ × 5½ in.).
Private collection

show Cézanne learning about the technique of watercolour while at the same time also thinking about how to extend it into new areas. This is perhaps why they exude such a feeling of impatience and frustration.

Cézanne's work had the appearance of being untutored and, indeed, to a certain degree he was self-taught. The 'primitive' aspects of his early style that mainstream critics remarked upon and condemned was justified in so far as Cézanne was an artist who possessed a natural talent that needed to be tamed. He certainly demonstrated what avant-garde critics of the day referred to as 'temperament', but, as Zola warned as early as 1861, 'Paul may have the genius of a great painter; he will never have the genius to become one.' Fortunately, the independence of spirit and innovative practices that so unsettled Salon juries were recognized as positive virtues by fellow artists at the Académie Suisse. After seeing the exhibition of Cézanne's work organized by Vollard in 1895, Pissarro wrote to his eldest son, Lucien, on 4 December: 'Didn't I judge rightly in 1861 when Oller and I went to see the curious *provençal* at the Académie Suisse where Cézanne's figure drawings were ridiculed by all the important artists.' The talk at the Académie Suisse was the need to challenge the stranglehold of the Académie des Beaux-Arts and how to undermine its orthodoxies. Pissarro was particularly outspoken in these respects and, in his letter of 12 September 1866 to Oller, Guillemet emphasizes the anarchist leanings of their discussions:

> The Louvre will be burned; museums and antiquities will disappear, and as [Pierre-Joseph] Prudhon said, from the ashes of the old civilization a new art will rise. Fever is burning in us. The gap between today and tomorrow is a whole century long. Today's gods are not tomorrow's: let's seize our weapons, and, with a feverish hand, get hold of the insurrection *knife*. Let us destroy and build again (*et monumentum exegi aere perennius*) [I have built a monument more lasting than bronze – Horace, *Odes*, Book 30, line 1]. Courage, brother. Let's keep tight ranks between us: there are too few of us not to share our common cause. They are throwing us out: we will shut the fucking door in their face. The classics are falling apart. Nieu[wer]kerke is slipping off his pedestal. Let us launch an assault and overtake that treacherous creature … Let us only trust ourselves: Let's all build up paint with full impasto and dance on the bellies of those horrified bourgeois … Work, old woman, keep up the courage: impasto, and just the right patches of colour – and we will prevail in the end. Pissarro is sending his warmest greetings, and we all, including Cézanne, are hoping to see you soon.

Even Cézanne, though, balked in retrospect at Pissarro's radicalism when on 26 September 1906 he wrote to his son describing Bernard as 'an intellectual blocked by the memories of museums, who doesn't look at nature enough, and this is the main point, to get away from any and every school. So Pissarro was not mistaken; he went a bit far, however, when he said that all the artistic necropolises should be burned down.'

A further passage in Guillemet's letter of 12 September 1866 to Oller hints at how quickly reputations in the art world of mid-nineteenth-century Paris could change. Guillemet declares that just as Courbet's position as the *enfant terrible* in art had been usurped by Manet, so, too, would Manet in turn be usurped by Cézanne. This was an amazingly bold prediction to have been making in the mid-1860s and few others would have countenanced it.

Artists like Cézanne and his associates at the Académie Suisse whose work was unlikely to gain in popularity through the Salon therefore had to find alternative outlets. Dealers could offer some help in this respect if they were sympathetic to avant-garde art, but they did not necessarily have the means to finance major exhibitions and neither could they expect their exhibitions to receive the same amount of attention from the critics as the Salon. Yet both Courbet and Manet had set precedents by organizing private exhibitions at critical moments in their careers. During the Universal Exhibition of 1855, where Ingres and Delacroix were given places of honour, Courbet set up his own exhibition space (the Pavillon du Réalisme) opposite the main Palais des Beaux-Arts on the Avenue Montaigne.

In 1863, rejections from the Salon were so numerous and caused such a furore that the Emperor himself, Napoleon III, suggested that a special display should be made of the rejected works in an annexe to the main exhibition – in effect a Salon des Refusés. Manet, Pissarro and Cézanne participated on that occasion. When the same situation arose, however, in 1867, the idea of another Salon des Refusés was resisted, thereby once again excluding the more advanced painters, including those of the younger generation. Instead, to coincide with the Universal Exhibition of 1867 both Courbet and Manet held private exhibitions as a form of protest. They set up their temporary pavilions side by side on the Place de l'Alma, which was a location that would have been known to those visiting either the Salon or the Universal Exhibition. These private displays were disapproved of by the government, from whom of course they received no financial support, but they did create a precedent for the eight Impressionist exhibitions held between 1874 and 1886. These became the focus of an avant-garde art where contemporary subject matter, novel compositional devices and broader techniques of colour,

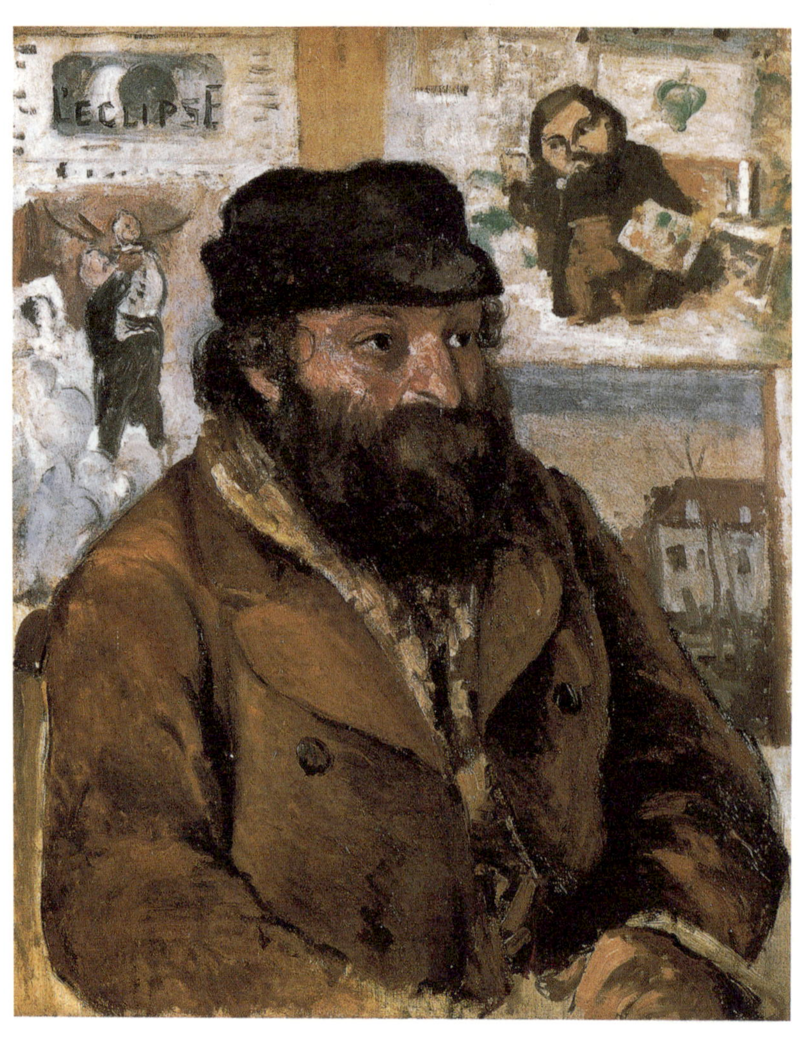

35. Camille Pissarro, *Paul Cézanne*, *c.* 1874.
Oil on canvas, 73 × 59.7 cm (28¾ × 23½ in.).
Private collection, on loan to the
National Gallery, London

drawing and facture characterized the paintings, denoting a fresh and more invigorating approach to art. This is the environment in which Cézanne instinctively belonged, but he was, in fact, included in only two of the Impressionist exhibitions – the first in 1874 and the third in 1877.

Of the three paintings shown in 1874 only one, *The House of the Hanged Man, Auvers-sur-Oise* (Musée d'Orsay, Paris), is a finished work. The other two – one an imaginary narrative scene, *Une Moderne Olympia* (Musée d'Orsay, Paris), and the other a landscape, either *Paysage à Auvers-sur-Oise* (Philadelphia Museum of Art) or *House of Père Lacroix* (National Gallery of Art, Washington, DC) – are described as 'Esquisse' or 'Etude' respectively. Three years later, there was not only a significant increase in the number of works shown by Cézanne, but also a greater variety. Not all of the sixteen items in the catalogue can be specifically identified, but there were five still lifes, four landscapes, a head of a man, a figure of a woman, a scene of bathers, an animal painting and three watercolours [34, 46, 48]. Several of these items are described simply as 'Etude'. Most came from the collection of Victor Chocquet, who emerged publicly at this moment as the artist's principal supporter. The greater variety of work by Cézanne on display at the third Impressionist exhibition was clearly intended to broaden the artist's appeal to potential buyers, but it was also a measure of his growing maturity.

The fact that Cézanne was included at all in these two Impressionist exhibitions was undoubtedly due to the progress he had made as a painter working alongside the slightly older Pissarro. Having met at the Académie Suisse at the beginning of the 1860s, the two artists became close friends from 1872 when Pissarro returned to live in Pontoise, an important medieval town nineteen miles to the northwest of Paris. At the same time Cézanne moved to the neighbouring village of Auvers-sur-Oise where Dr Paul Gachet lived. As Pissarro wrote to Guillemet on 3 September 1872, 'Our Cézanne raised our hopes and I have seen his paintings; I have with me here a painting of great force, of remarkable strength. If, as I hope, he settles for some time in Auvers where he is going to live, he will certainly surprise all those artists who have hastily condemned him.' The friendship between Cézanne and Pissarro was ostensibly a professional one, but, as a number of paintings [35], drawings and photographs illustrate, it was profound even after Cézanne left Auvers-sur-Oise in 1874. The professional and emotional security provided by Pissarro enabled Cézanne to write to his mother on 26 November 1874:

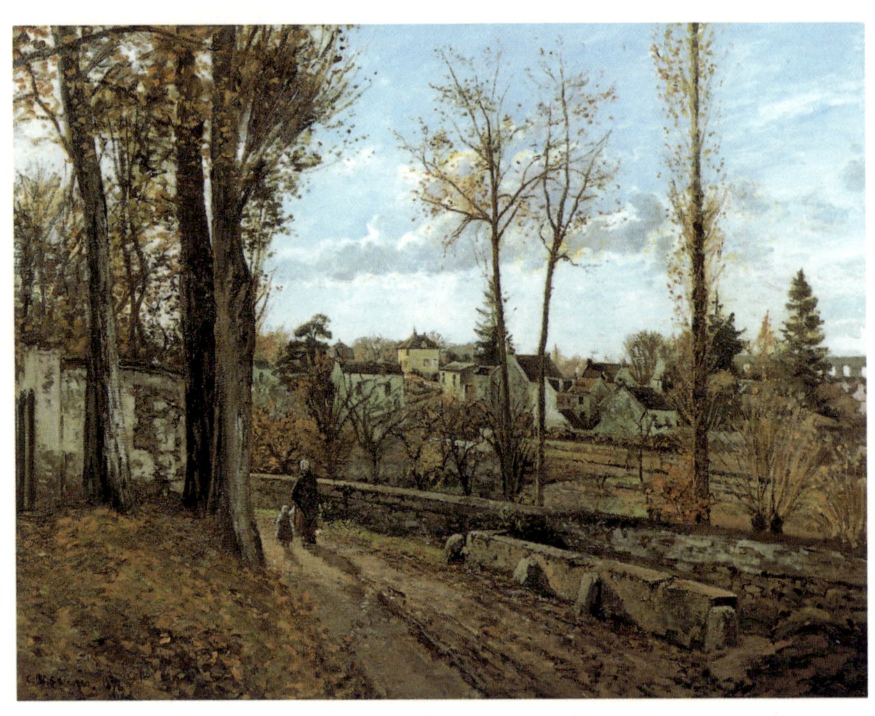

36. Camille Pissarro, *Louveciennes*, 1871.
Oil on canvas, 90 × 116.5 cm (35½ × 45⅞ in.).
Private collection

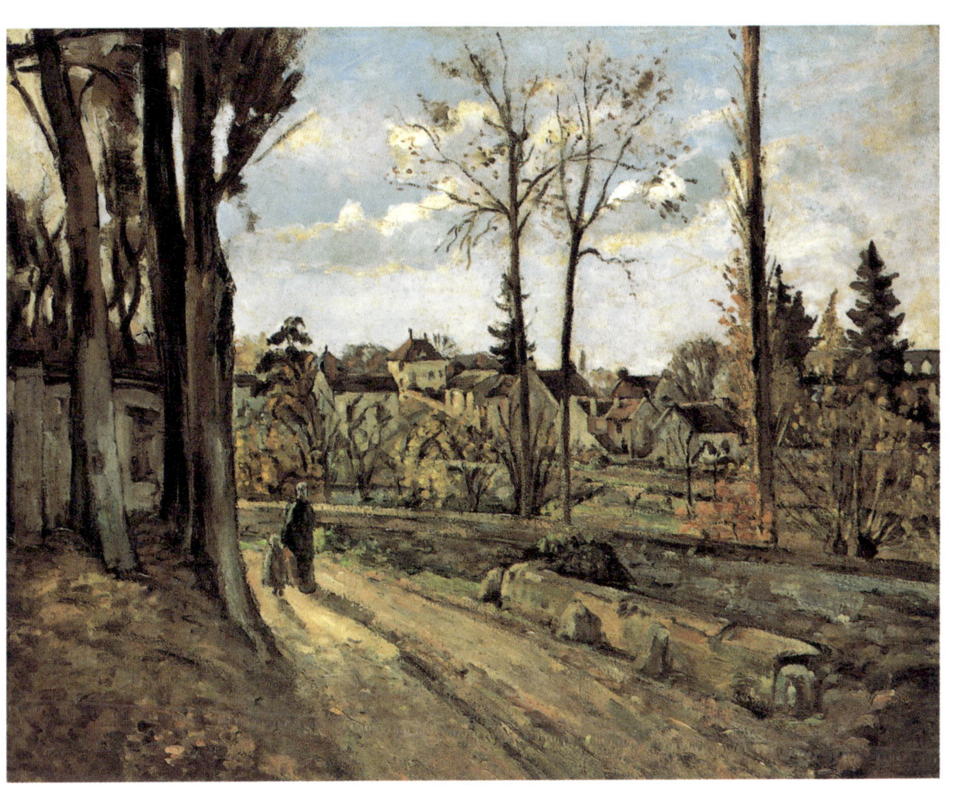

37. *Louveciennes*, 1872.
Oil on canvas, 73 × 92 cm (28¾ × 36¼ in.).
Private collection

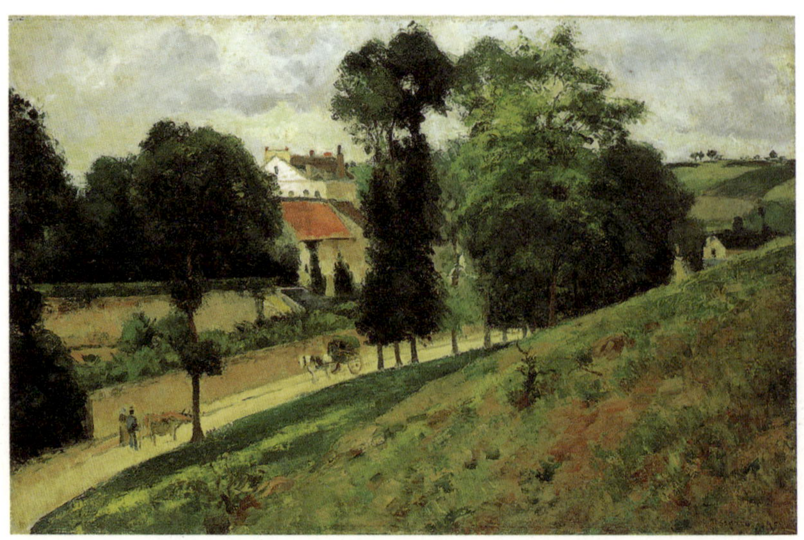

38. Camille Pissarro, *Rue de L'Hermitage, Pontoise*, 1875.
Oil on canvas, 52.5 × 81 cm (20⅝ × 31⅞ in.).
Private collection, on permanent loan to the Kunstmuseum Basel

> Pissarro has not been in Paris for about a month and a half, he is in
> Brittany, but I know that he has a good opinion of me, and I have a
> good opinion of myself. I am beginning to consider myself stronger
> than all those around me, and you know that I hold that good
> opinion advisedly. I have to work all the time, but not to achieve
> the finish that earns the admiration of imbeciles.

Close contact between Cézanne and Pissarro was maintained during
the second half of the 1870s and into the early 1880s until 1885, after
which they had less opportunity to meet.

It is no exaggeration to say that the interaction between Cézanne
and Pissarro in these years laid the foundations of modern art and are
comparable in significance with the working methods established later
between Matisse and André Derain in 1906 in the south of France at
Collioure regarding Fauvism, or Picasso and Braque in Paris in 1908–09
in the context of Cubism. Pissarro, in effect, tamed the potential
that everyone saw in Cézanne and encouraged him to work in a more
disciplined manner. He did this by example, which is why in 1902
Cézanne told Jules Borély, 'Pissarro was like a father to me: he was a
man you turned to for advice, and was something like le bon Dieu.'

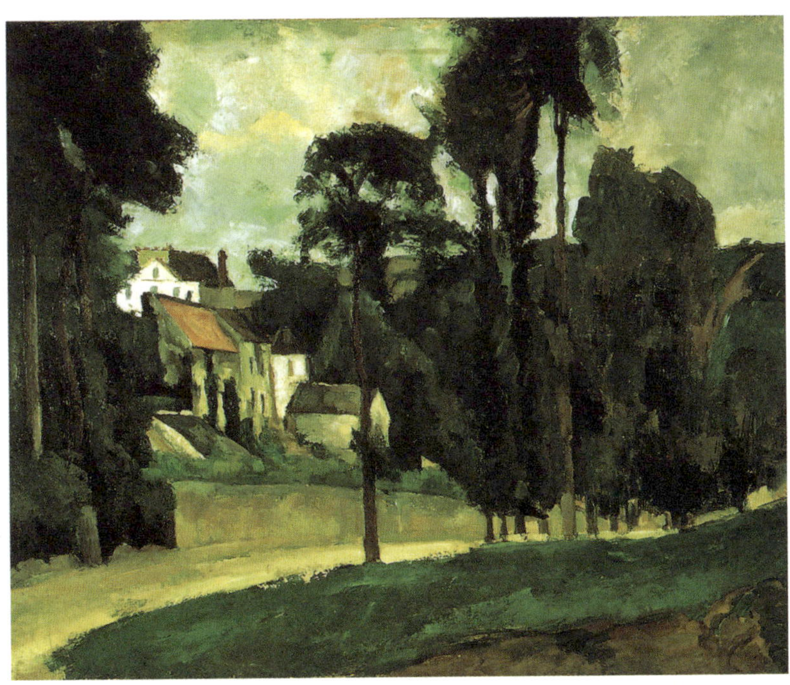

39. Road at Pontoise (Le Clos des Mathurins at Pontoise), 1875.
Oil on canvas, 58 × 71 cm (22⅞ × 28 in.).
Pushkin State Museum of Fine Arts, Moscow

Apart from discussing painting, about which they also corresponded
at intervals when they were apart, Cézanne began by making a direct
copy of one of Pissarro's paintings of Louveciennes dating from 1871
[36, 37], but later they painted identical motifs in areas around Pontoise
and Auvers-sur-Oise. As many as fifteen or so of these pairings can
be identified: for example, *Rue de L'Hermitage, Pontoise* by Pissarro
and *Road at Pontoise* by Cézanne, both of 1875 [38, 39], or *Kitchen
Garden, Trees in Flower, Spring, Pontoise* by Pissarro and *The Garden
of Maubuisson, Pontoise* by Cézanne, both of 1877 [40, 41]. Although
the motifs are identical, it is the differences of approach, style and
technique that are significant. Pissarro stands back from the motif,
favouring more of a panoramic view, and tends towards the descriptive.
He does, however, give a strong structural sense to the compositions,
which have carefully calculated spatial divisions and methodically
built up paint surfaces. By contrast, Cézanne is more analytical and

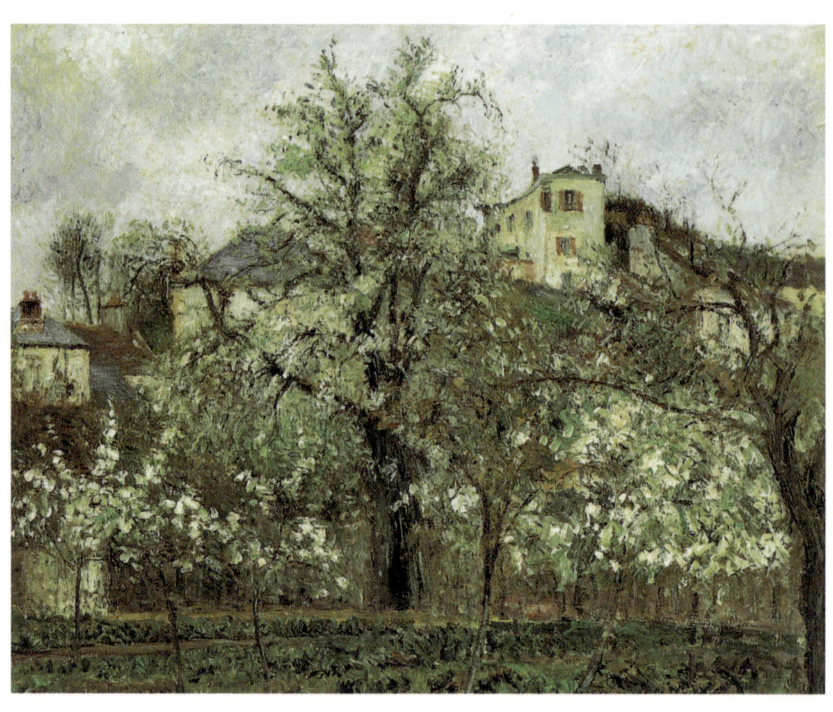

40. Camille Pissarro, *Kitchen Garden, Trees in Flower,*
Spring, Pontoise, 1877.
Oil on canvas, 65.5 × 81 cm (25¾ × 31⅞ in.).
Musée d'Orsay, Paris

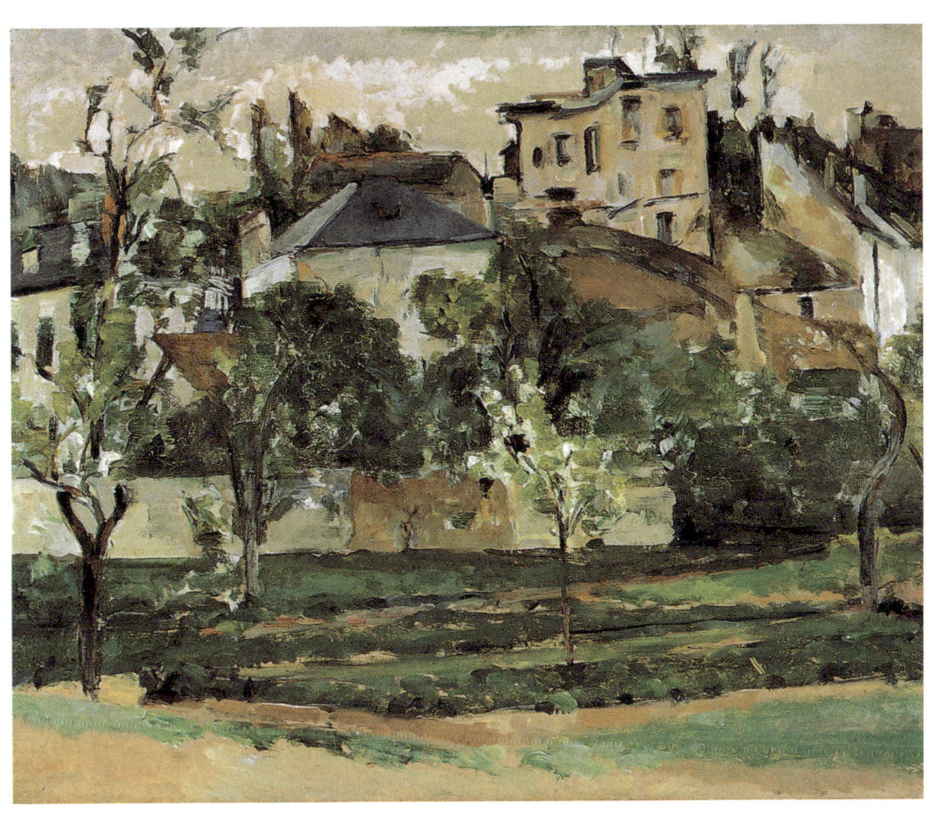

41. *The Garden of Maubuisson, Pontoise*, 1877.
Oil on canvas, 50.2 × 60 cm (19¾ × 23⅝ in.).
Collection of Mr and Mrs Jay Pack, Dallas

confrontational. He concentrates on the forms, reducing them to the essentials and consequently the final images are starker and more imposing. The paint is applied with a greater sense of deliberation with the palette knife as well as brushes.

The same differences are apparent when the artists painted similar, but not identical, motifs at separate dates: *Small Bridge, Pontoise* of 1875 by Pissarro (Kunsthalle, Mannheim) and *The Bridge at Maincy near Melun* of 1879–80 by Cézanne (Musée d'Orsay, Paris). Overall, it would seem that where Pissarro adds Cézanne subtracts. Neither, therefore, could be said to have surrendered their artistic identity while working together. They both recognized the need to retain the personal sensations that they each experienced before nature. Indeed, Pissarro emphasized this point in a letter of 22 November 1895 to his elder son, written after seeing Cézanne's exhibition at Vollard's gallery.

> People forget that Cézanne was first influenced by Delacroix, Courbet, Manet and even Legros, like all of us; he was influenced by me at Pontoise, and I by him. You may remember the sallies of Zola and Béliard in this regard. They imagined that artists are the sole inventors of their styles and that to resemble someone else is to be unoriginal. Curiously enough in Cézanne's show at Vollard's there are certain landscapes of Auvers and Pontoise that are similar to mine. Naturally, we were always together! But what cannot be denied is that each of us kept the only thing that counts, the unique 'sensation'.

While working together in Pontoise and the neighbouring region Pissarro showed Cézanne some of the motifs that he had previously examined in the semi-rural area of the town known as L'Hermitage, where he had lived in 1866–68. Here he had painted a series of large canvases for exhibition in the Salon, which prompted brilliant passages of criticism from Zola. Of the two pictures shown at the Salon of 1868 (*L'Hermitage*, Wallraf-Richartz Museum, Cologne, and *La Côte du Jallais, Pontoise*, Metropolitan Museum of Art, New York) he wrote:

> The artist only cares for the solemn truth: he places himself before a landscape resolved to depict the full grandeur of horizons without adding the slightest touch of his own invention; he is neither poet nor philosopher, but simply an observer of nature, a recorder of skies and of the earth. You may dream dreams if you want to, but this is what he has seen … The originality here is profoundly human. It is not derived from a certain facility of hand or from a falsification of nature. It stems from the temperament of the painter himself and comprises a feeling for truth resulting

from an inner conviction. Never before have paintings appeared to
me to possess such an overwhelming dignity. One can almost hear
the inner voices of the earth and sense the trees burgeoning. The
boldness of the horizons, the disdain of any show, the complete
lack of cheap tricks, imbue the whole with an indescribable feeling
of epic grandeur. Such reality is more than a daydream … Camille
Pissarro is one of the three or four genuine painters of the day.
He has solidity and breadth of touch, he paints freely, following
tradition like the old masters. I have rarely encountered a technique
that is so sure. A beautiful painting by this man is the act of an
honest man. I cannot think of a better way of describing his talent.

What Zola detected in Pissarro's paintings of L'Hermitage was
compositional clarity, a rugged but varied application of paint and a
unified sense of colour. But, more than anything else, these pictures
demonstrated the artist's remarkable degree of objectivity in front of
nature. They all have a strong horizontal emphasis with the disparate
parts related to one another through the use of diagonals often aligned
with footpaths or tilting ground. The buildings in the middle distance
play an important role in shackling together foreground and background,
and so act as the fulcrum for the whole composition. These paintings,
therefore, provided Cézanne with a lesson in how to examine a landscape
by detecting the various shapes and patterns within it and then how
to translate what was seen into a unified spatial unit. Pissarro was, in
essence, an extremely articulate painter and it is this self-assurance that
gives his pictures such an air of authority. It was this feature of Pissarro's
art, in addition to any technical considerations, that had such an appeal
for Cézanne.

Photographs of Pissarro and Cézanne taken during the mid-1870s
show them dressed like mountaineers with hats, boots, sticks, and
equipment, including watercolour boxes and easels, strapped to their
backs [see 1 and 4]. Such images imply a more determined and resolute
approach to the art of landscape painting and one that was somewhat
removed from the topographical tradition of the late eighteenth and
early nineteenth centuries in which the sublime and the picturesque
were paramount. By contrast, Pissarro and Cézanne aimed to assert
themselves over nature rather than to be seduced or overwhelmed by it.
Their approach to landscape painting was almost scientific, as though
they were conducting a geological survey.

Elisée Reclus, the most famous human geographer of the day and
an anarchist philosopher personally known to Pissarro in the 1890s,
published *The History of a Mountain* (1880). This is a book with
chapter headings such as 'Rock and Crystals', 'Fossils', 'Clouds', 'Fogs'

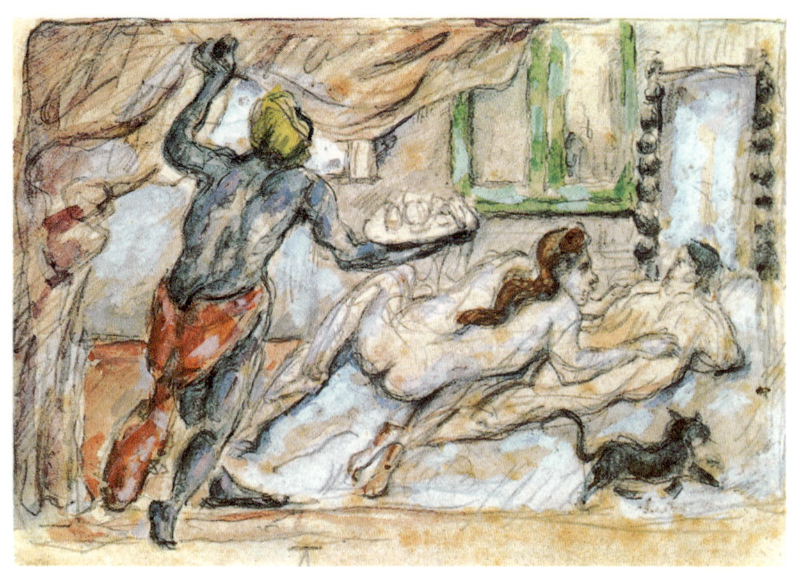

42. *Afternoon in Naples*, 1870–71.
Pencil, watercolour and gouache, 11 × 16 cm (4⅜ × 6⅜ in.).
Private collection

and 'Avalanches' that Cézanne's friend, the zoologist and palaeontologist
Fortuné Marion, might well have known and read. For Reclus the
mountain is in the first instance a place for scientific investigation, but
also a spiritual retreat. He looks down from the summit and sees that,
'the immense panorama of the country is beautiful as a whole, with its
towns, villages, and isolated houses, which here and there brighten the
scene beneath the light in which they are bathed; the dark spots blend
with all that surrounds them in one harmonious whole; the atmosphere
sheds its azure mantle over the whole plain.'

It is a utopian vision characteristic of anarchist philosophers at
the end of the nineteenth century, but the passage in many ways evokes
comparison with the landscapes painted by Pissarro and Cézanne
in Pontoise and Auvers-sur-Oise during the 1870s and early 1880s.
Furthermore, it can be read in terms of Cézanne's own pervading interest
in Mont Sainte-Victoire, which occasionally appears in one or two of his
earlier landscapes, but was to become such a focus of his attention from
the mid-1880s onwards.

These years, therefore, in which he was open to guidance from Pissarro were a vital source of inspiration for Cézanne, allowing him time to identify his strengths as an artist and to develop his own style. The fundamental shift between his work of the 1860s and the 1870s can also be traced in his drawings and watercolours, although in this transitional phase he was less prolific on paper. The pursuit of imaginative subjects with erotic overtones continued – *The Dance*, *Afternoon in Naples* [42], *Olympia* [49], *The Eternal Feminine* [50] and *Carnival Scene* – in which Cézanne, albeit with a sense of irony, seems to have been paying homage to Manet. These are tightly organized compositional drawings, but they are on a small scale, intensely rhythmical, emotionally charged and somewhat ambiguous. Cézanne also attempts contemporary subject matter inspired not just by Manet, but more in line with early works by Monet and Renoir – river scenes [52], parks [51, 53] and, exceptionally, cityscapes [54]. However, he had only a passing interest in the urban or suburban themes so closely associated with Monet, Renoir or Degas. His friendship with Pissarro, on the other hand, was firmly based on a shared love of landscape.

Nor is there any great consistency in Cézanne's watercolours inspired by the landscape of the Ile de France at this time, probably because it was an experimental phase during which the artist was not only learning about compositional practices, but also about watercolour technique. His reliance on gouache denotes that he had not yet quite gained complete mastery over such aspects of the use of watercolour as the translucency and overlaying of washes.

At the same time, Cézanne was learning to develop his powers of spatial organization, which involved the careful placement of verticals and horizontals within a firmly demarcated composition. The initial outline drawings of a landscape made in pencil vary from a series of episodic flourishes and limited areas of hatching [57] to elaborate exercises with the finest of lines stretched tautly across the paper like wire [55]. Such outline drawings without the addition of watercolour were at first presumably conceived as part of the preparatory process for a painting. But, as Cézanne's facility for watercolour rapidly became apparent, so he began to use both pencil and watercolour interdependently.

A particularly fine example of this stage in his development is *In the Valley of the Oise* [56]. Here the composition depends on interlocking verticals and horizontals that unite the foreground, middle distance and sky. The foreground, however, is dominated by the sinuous trunks of saplings with spreading branches, which screen the background and so provide a feeling of recession. Beginning with bare outlines in pencil, the composition is then developed in watercolour and gouache as the artist evolves the work with growing confidence. On completion the watercolour comprises a mesh of fine lines and parallel brushstrokes.

The screening device became one of Cézanne's favourite motifs during the late 1870s, extending well into the 1880s. However, the artist was also discovering that taut compositional discipline did not necessarily require a restricted, precisely controlled, style. The compositions of both *Jallais Hill, Pontoise* (*c.* 1877–81; Private collection) and *Landscape in Provence* (*c.* 1880; Kunsthaus Zurich) are carefully structured with the essential underlying outlines briefly delineated in pencil before being overlaid by areas of watercolour varying from clusters of hatched strokes to broader passages of free-flowing washes. The stylistic diversity that Cézanne instinctively found in the application of watercolour in combination with pencil at this intermediary stage of his development signals his instant recognition of its potential and foreshadows the achievements of his later years.

The greatest impact that Pissarro's guidance had on Cézanne is most evident in his response to the luminous landscape of Provence. *The Bay of L'Estaque* [58] is composed like one of Pissarro's canvases of L'Hermitage with the plunging diagonal of the hillside offset by the horizontals of the foreground, the sea and the horizon. *Rooftops of L'Estaque* is characterized by an even greater display of geometry and falls neatly into two halves [61]. The lower half is dominated by the architectural elements, while the upper half incorporating the bay and the distant mountains south of Marseille is left virtually blank. The pale tones and thin washes capture the fugitive effects of light and create an ethereal quality redolent of late watercolours by J. M. W. Turner.

A watercolour that may have been made in Provence, as opposed to the Ile de France, is *Village Houses* [59]. Cézanne has prepared this with a meticulous pencil drawing to which washes and gouache have been carefully added. The colour of the paper provides a warm middle tone. The foreground is in shade, which contrasts with the bright light falling on the buildings. The washes have been applied sparingly in small, clearly defined patches of colour. The gouache is used to emphasize the light striking the architecture while the grey suggests pools of dark shadow. The precision of the technique is comparable with architectural draughtsmanship at its best and it is a style that very occasionally recurs in Cézanne's graphic output, as in his drawing of *The Church of St Pierre, Avon* [60] with its insistent diagonals, made in 1892–93 when he was working in the area of Fontainebleau. Other watercolours dating from the second half of the 1870s demonstrate a similar sense of assurance in the establishment of spatial divisions within a composition [62].

This compositional strength combined with technical bravado is matched in the watercolour *Pool and Allée of Chestnut Trees at the Jas de Bouffan* [63]. The view is from the east terrace of the house looking down the long avenue of chestnut trees with a corner of the ornamental pool lower right. At first, it seems as though the composition is strictly balanced and controlled, but in fact Cézanne places the perspectival view down the avenue off-centre, cuts off the trees at the top and allows the corner of the pool to invade the space. The real centre is indicated by a small touch of light blue beyond the wall at the end of the avenue. The branches of the trees reach down like the furled wings of a large bird, forming a series of diagonals. The washes are limited to shades of green and blue for the grass and leaves, grey for the tree trunks, and darker greys and blues for the shadows. Yellow and ochre are used very sparingly among the branches. Pissarro had taught his 'pupil' well.

The friendship with Pissarro during the 1870s and early 1880s was timely and advantageous for Cézanne, but the happy childhood relationship that he had formed with Zola was coming to an end. The idyllic years spent growing up in Aix-en-Provence had resulted in many shared experiences and not least a love of literature. Separated in age by only one year, at first it seemed that Cézanne would become a poet and Zola an artist, but the roles were soon reversed. Zola's departure for Paris (where he had in fact been born) was a defining moment since he was in effect renouncing the provincial persona that he had cultivated alongside Cézanne. Aiming to establish himself as a writer, he experienced considerable poverty before becoming a highly controversial journalist and art critic. Success came quite quickly with the series of novels that not only made his name, but also his fortune. The twenty volumes published between 1871 and 1893, comprising the *Rougon-Macquart* cycle, can only be measured against Honoré de Balzac's long series of novels, known collectively as *La Comédie Humaine*, in their scope, ambition and sustained stylistic vigour. Zola used his novels to survey French society during the Second Empire. Power and money are the central themes through which the author highlights a number of political and social ills. The cycle includes some of the most famous titles in French literature: *L'Assommoir* (1877), *Nana* (1880), *Germinal* (1885), *La Terre* (1887). The author's work rate was prodigious and only equalled by the amount of research required for each title. As a mark of friendship Zola sent copies of each of his early novels to Cézanne as they were published.

Cézanne had been encouraged to come to Paris by Zola in 1861 and was supported by him both financially and emotionally during the 1860s and 1870s. The preface of Zola's short book of art criticism,

Mon Salon (1866), was dedicated to the painter. It takes the form of manifesto: 'For ten years we have been talking art and literature. We have lived together – do you remember? – and often daybreak came when we were still discussing, ransacking the past, questioning the present, seeking the truth and trying to create for ourselves a complete and infallible religion.'

Gradually, however, as Zola's reputation increased so his doubts about Cézanne began to emerge. This was caused as much by the artist's slow development as by his unwillingness to cast aside his provincial habits and enthusiasms. The personal differences between them have been summed up as the result of 'diverging lifestyles and incompatible life philosophies'. But Zola's doubts about Impressionism were also growing. The champion of Manet felt that by the end of the 1870s the Impressionists as a group had not fulfilled their promise and that as an instrument for change they were a spent force, divided among themselves and lacking cohesion. This led to Zola losing confidence in the power of art as a means of changing the world and confirmed his preference in this respect for literature.

Symbolizing the altered circumstances of the lives of Cézanne and Zola was the writer's acquisition in 1878 of a villa in the small town of Médan on the river Seine twenty miles or so to the northwest of Paris. This he filled with the trappings of success – paintings, sculpture, decorative objects such as ivories, porcelain, crystal, as well as carved furniture (including an enormous writing desk), oriental rugs, tapestries and weapons. For Cézanne Zola had now become too much part of the Establishment, like a Minister of State, and too outwardly bourgeois, pursuing an epicurean lifestyle governed by dubious taste. Nonetheless, they remained in contact during the early 1880s when Cézanne often visited Médan to paint. A watercolour, *The Château at Médan* [64], is testimony to Cézanne's increasing skill in devising a balanced symmetrical composition. Made in connection with the painting of the same title (Burrell Collection, Glasgow) once owned by Gauguin, Cézanne views the town from an island in the river Seine. By choosing this view the horizontal emphasis becomes more pronounced, moving upwards from the river and the bank to the buildings in the middle distance and then to the hillside beyond. The château is in the left half of the composition and Zola's villa is behind the wall on the far right with only its red roof visible. The trees create vertical accents extending from the bank into the sky. Broad areas of wash over pencil outlines are applied in combination with the hatched strokes that the artist was now beginning to use more frequently in his search for a more systematic mode of representation. As such, *The Château at Médan* demonstrates how Cézanne has succeeded as an Impressionist in capturing the fleeting moment while at the same time looking for a more permanent method of rendition.

The final break with Zola came in April 1886 and was occasioned by the publication of *L'Oeuvre* in the *Rougon-Macquart* series. The principal figure in the book is a painter, Claude Lantier, who undertakes a major picture for exhibition at the Salon. He regards this as his masterpiece, but on being unable to complete it Lantier suffers increasingly from self-doubt and disillusion, to the extent that he hangs himself in his studio in despair. A study in artistic impotence and failure, *L'Oeuvre* is a very personal novel and many of the places, situations and characters are recognizable. Although, in fact, according to Zola, Claude Lantier was not based solely on Cézanne, it created an atmosphere of accusation and counter-accusation. The artist – forever polite – wrote a curt note of thanks to the author for sending him a copy, but as far as is known they never met or communicated again.

Zola's final judgment on Cézanne is recorded in his last piece of Salon criticism, written in 1896, where the artist is described as 'a great painter who miscarried'. Unfortunately for Zola, this was written just at the moment when Cézanne's true abilities were beginning to be more widely recognized and at the very time when he was endeavouring, in the words he used to Denis shortly before his death, to make of Impressionism 'something solid and durable like the art of Museums'. Zola died in 1902 of carbon monoxide poisoning caused by a blocked chimney in the bedroom of his Paris apartment. On hearing the news Cézanne was inconsolable.

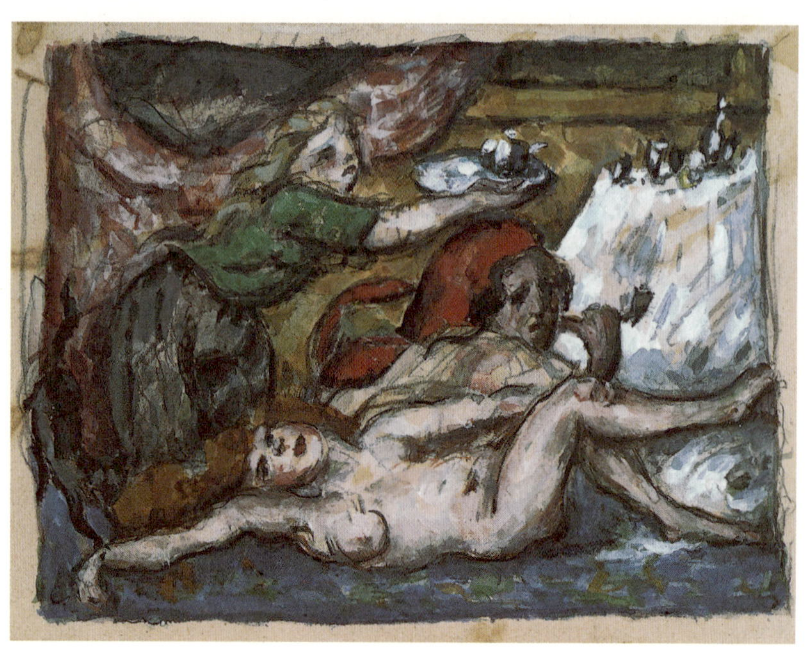

43. *The Wine Grog*, 1866–67.
Pencil, watercolour and gouache, 11 × 14.8 cm (4⅛ × 5⅞ in.).
Private collection

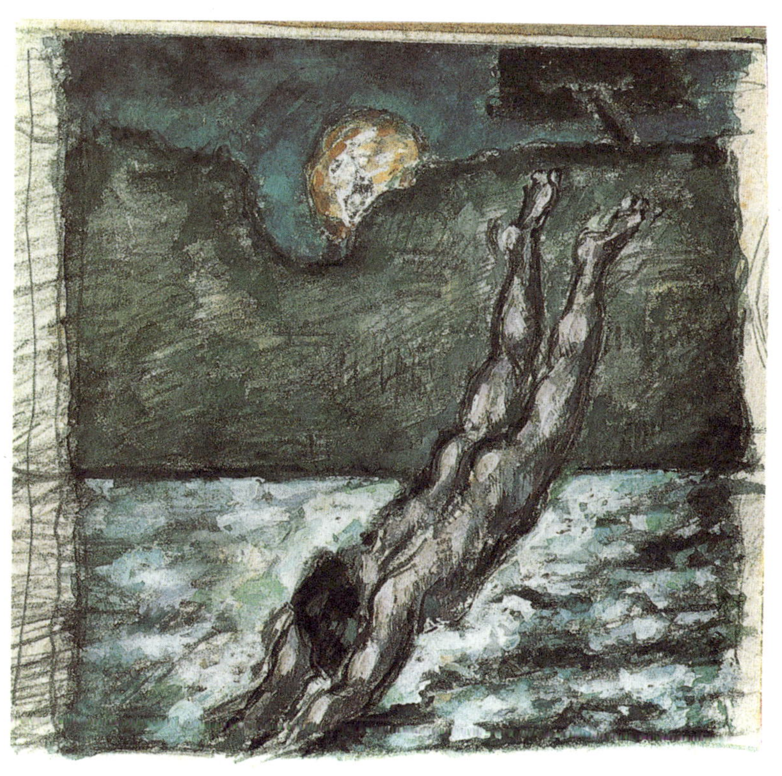

44. *The Diver*, 1866–69.
Pencil, watercolour and gouache, 12.7 × 12.1 cm (5 × 4¾ in.).
National Museum of Wales, Cardiff

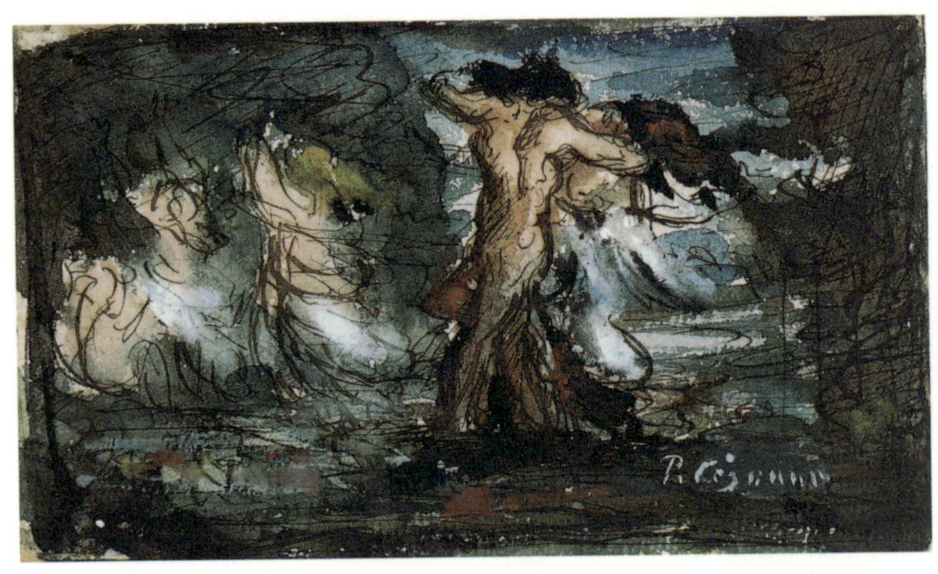

45. *The Abduction*, 1867–69.
Pen and ink, watercolour and gouache, 7 × 12.7 cm (2¾ × 5 in.).
Pierpont Morgan Library, New York

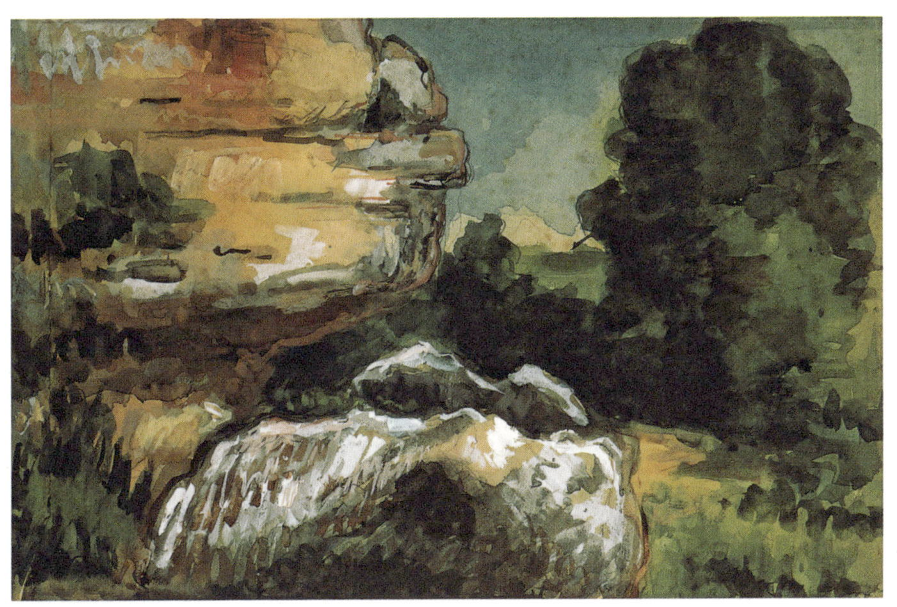

46. *Landscape with Rock*, 1866–69.
Pencil, watercolour and gouache, 23 × 34.5 cm (9 × 13⅝ in.).
Städel Museum, Frankfurt am Main

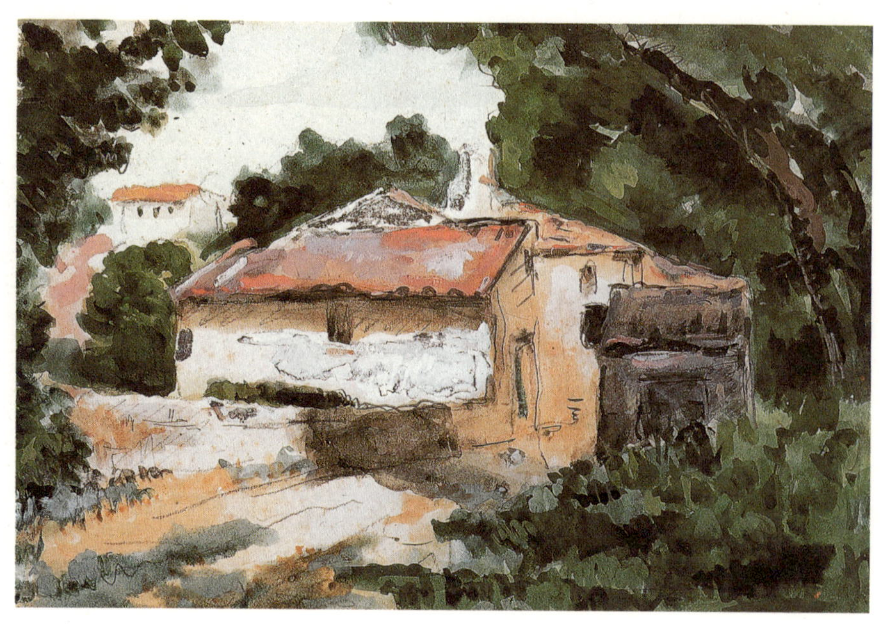

47. *House in Provence*, 1865–67.
Pencil, watercolour and gouache, 21 × 34 cm (8¾ × 13⅜ in.).
Musée du Louvre, Paris

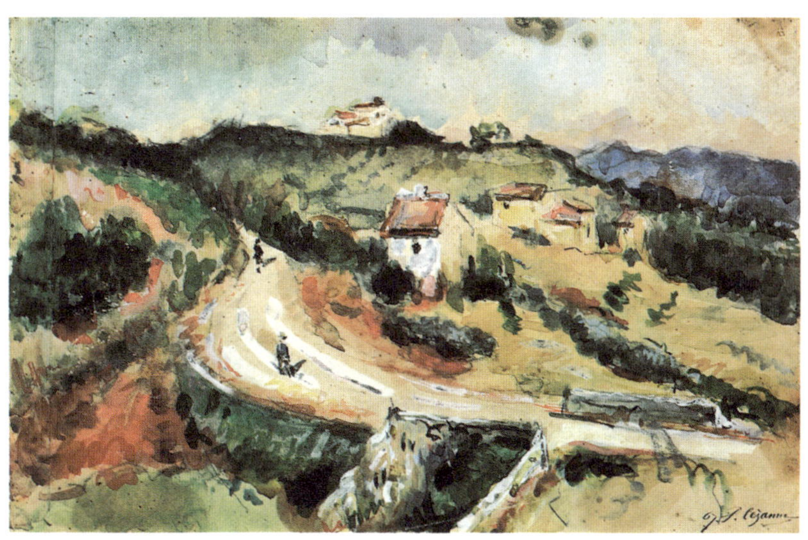

48. *The Climbing Road*, 1867.
Pencil, watercolour and gouache, 21 × 34.5 cm (8⅜ × 13⅝ in.).
Eisei-Bunko Museum, Tokyo

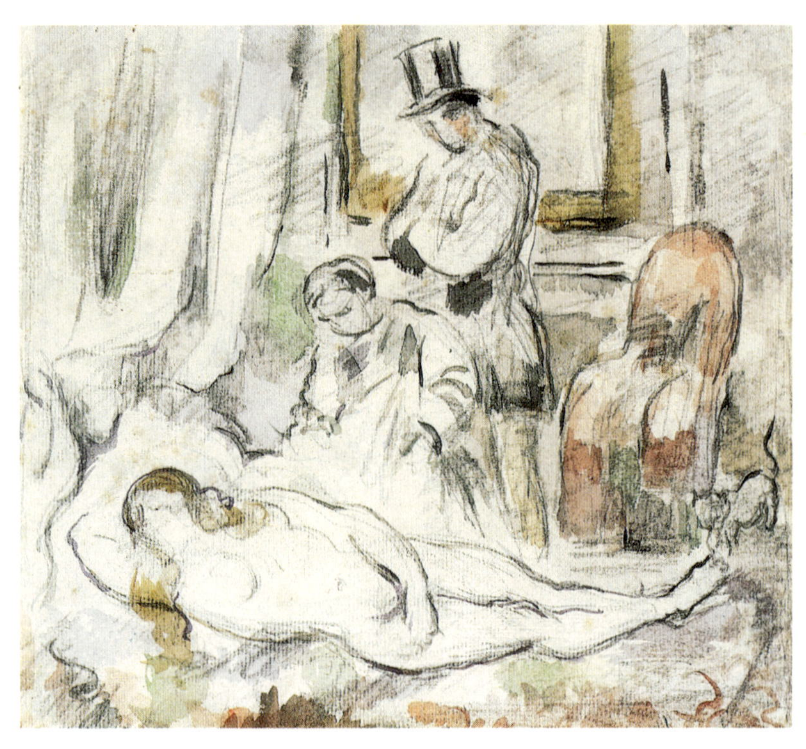

49. *Olympia, c.* 1877.
Pencil and watercolour, 24.8 × 28.6 cm (9¾ × 11¼ in.).
Philadelphia Museum of Art

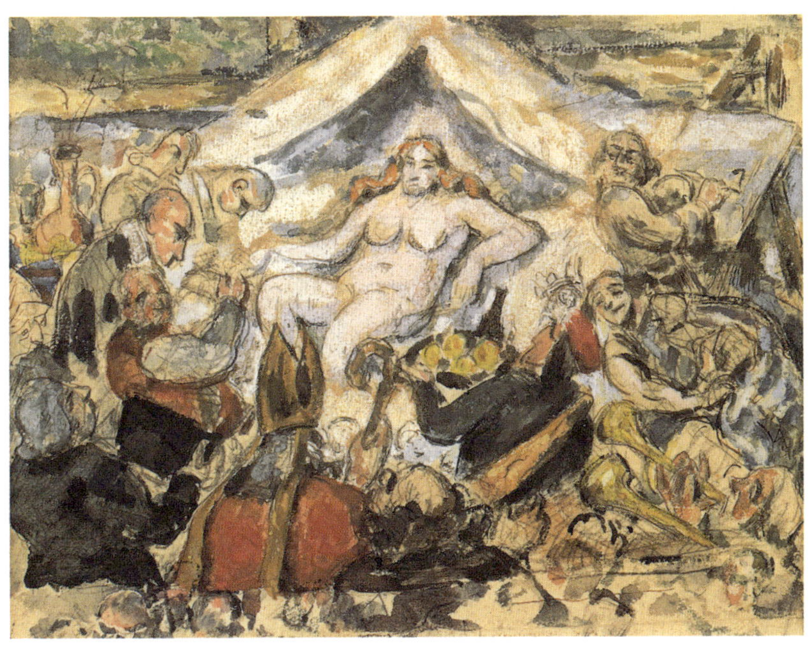

50. *The Eternal Feminine, c.* 1877.
Pencil, watercolour and gouache, 17.4 × 22.8 cm (6⅞ × 9 in.).
Private collection

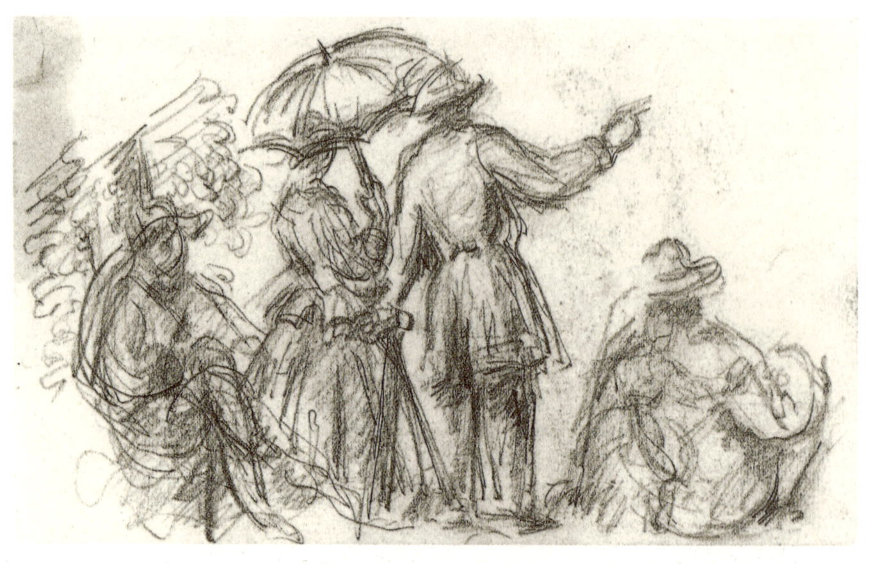

51. *Spectators*, 1886–89.
Pencil, 12.6 × 20.4 cm (5 × 8 in.).
Kunstmuseum Basel

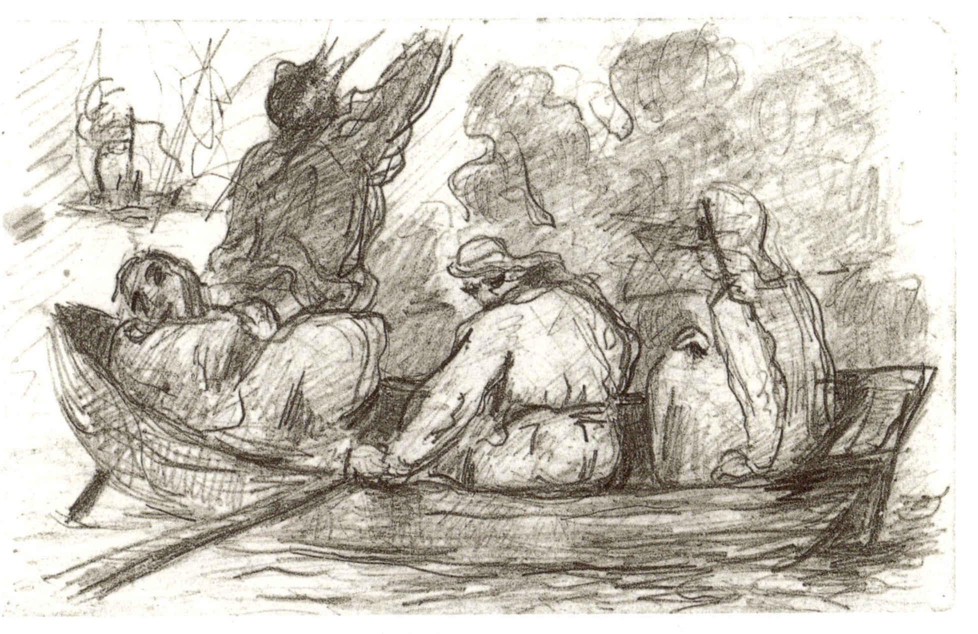

52. *Outing in a Boat*, 1871–74.
Pencil, 10.3 × 16.8 cm (4 × 6⅝ in.).
Kunstmuseum Basel

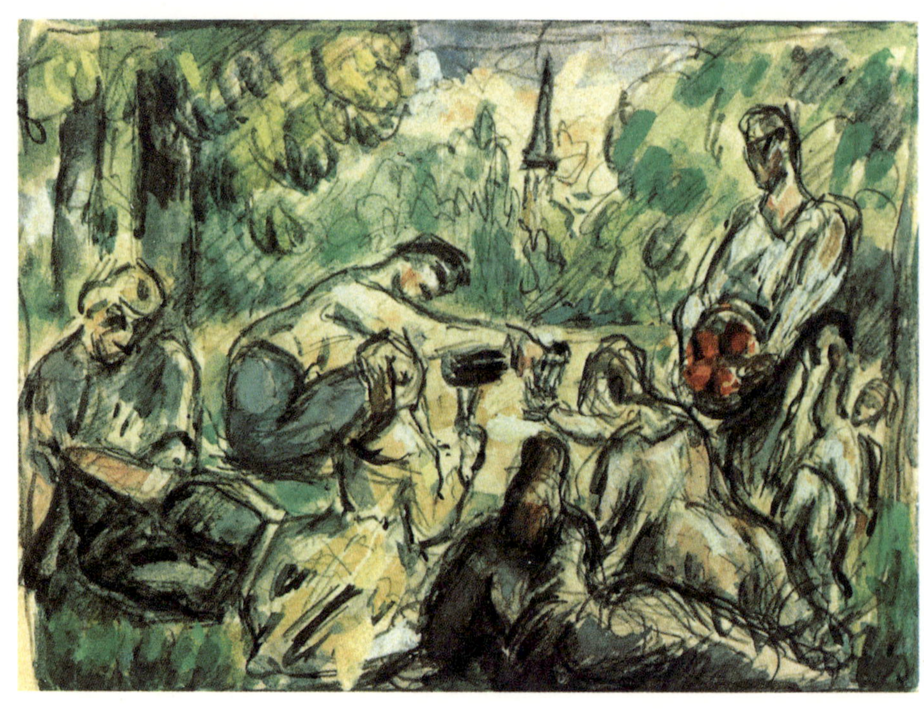

53. Déjeuner sur l'Herbe, c. 1875.
Pencil and watercolour, 9.5 × 13 cm (3¾ × 5⅛ in.).
Private collection

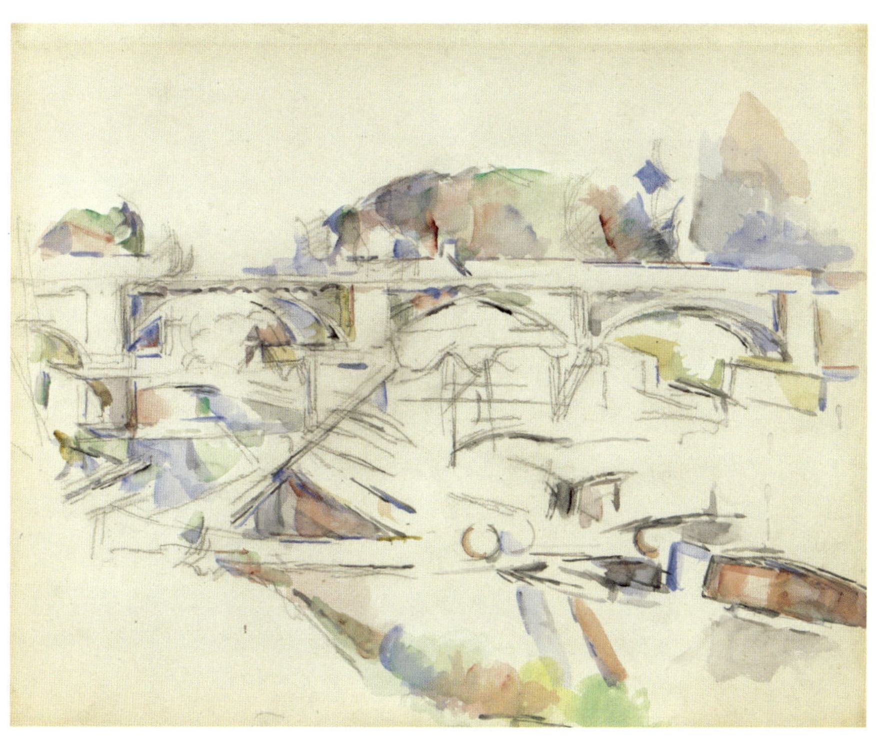

54. *Bridge over the River Seine, c. 1885.*
Pencil and watercolour, 48.9 × 60 cm (19¼ × 23⅝ in.).
Yale University Art Gallery, New Haven, Connecticut

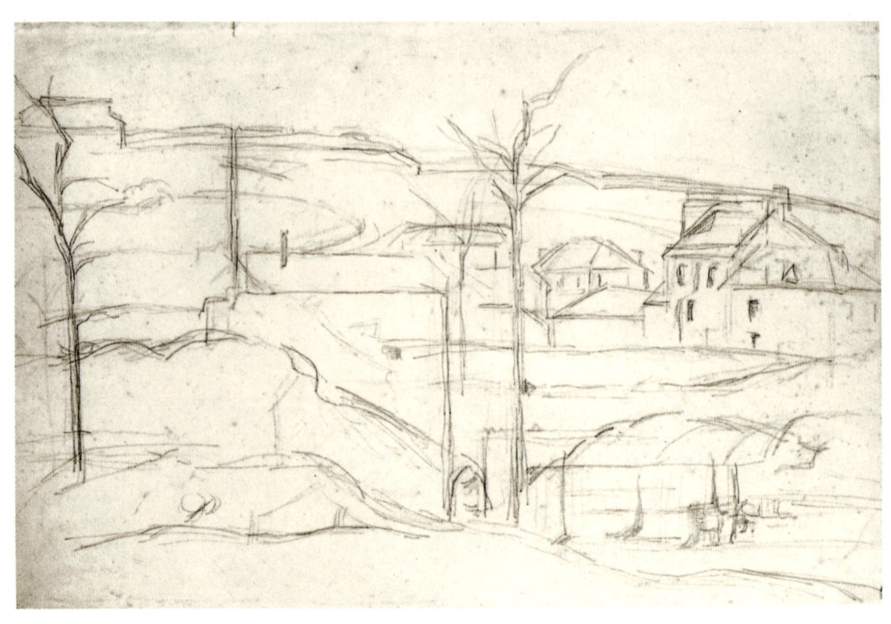

55. *Hills with Houses and Trees, c.* 1880–83.
Pencil, 20.5 × 30.4 cm (8 × 12 in.).
Kunstmuseum Basel

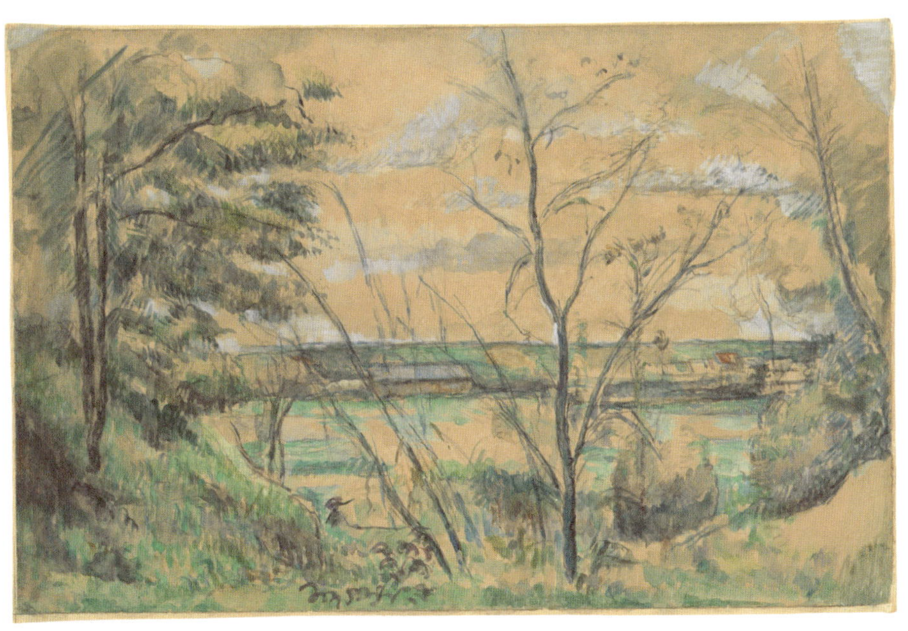

56. *In the Valley of the Oise*, 1878–80.
Pencil, watercolour and gouache, 32.4 × 50 cm (12¼ × 19¼ in.).
Metropolitan Museum of Art, New York

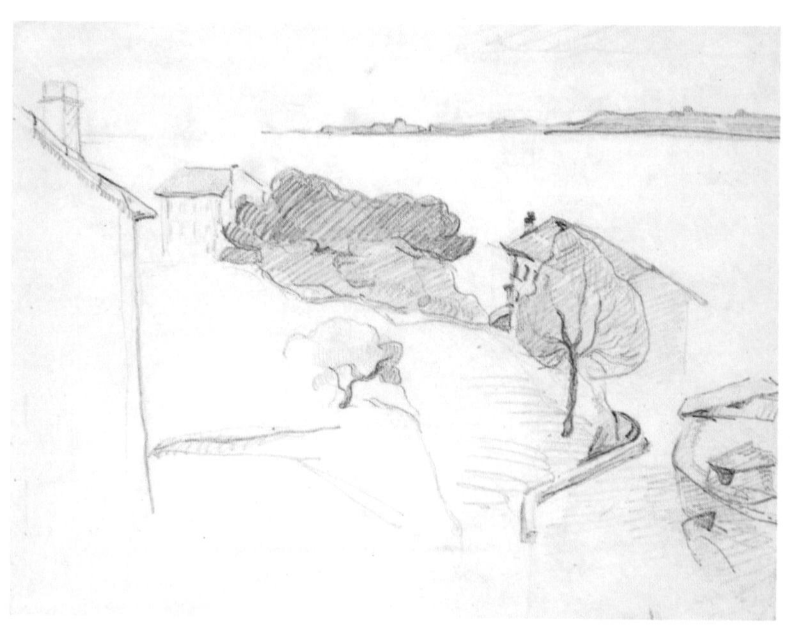

57. *Landscape at L'Estaque*, 1870 or 1871.
Pencil, 24.2 × 31.6 cm (9½ × 12½ in.).
The Art Institute of Chicago

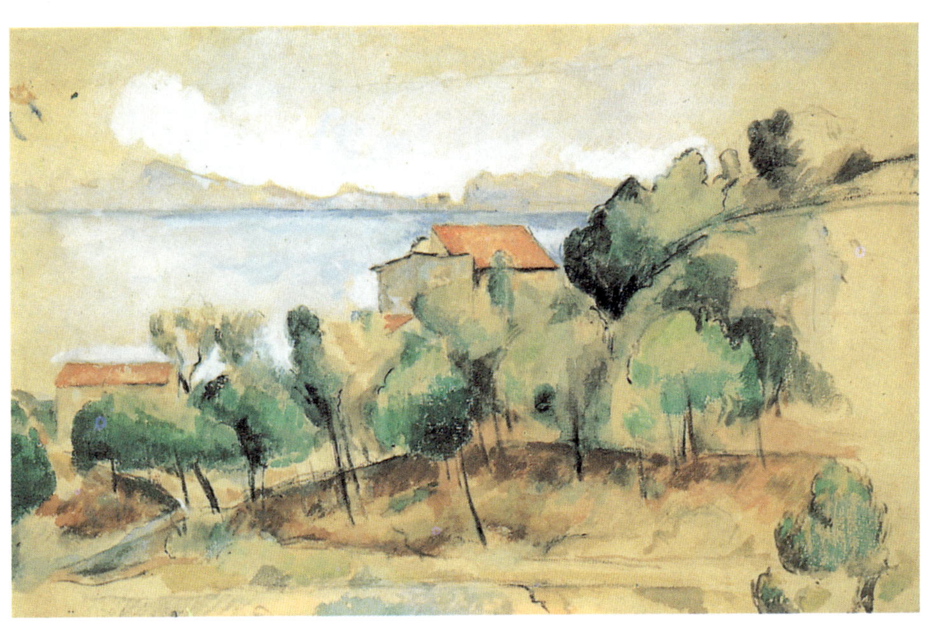

58. *The Bay of L'Estaque*, 1876–82.
Pencil, watercolour and gouache, 29.1 × 45.5 cm (11½ × 17⅞ in.).
Kunsthaus Zurich

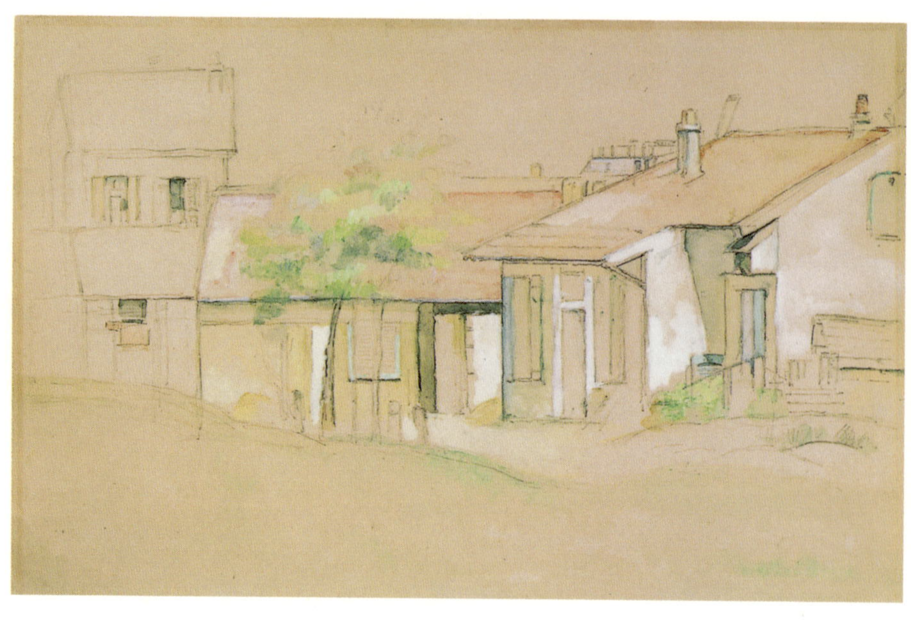

ABOVE
59. *Village Houses*, 1876–82.
Pencil, watercolour and gouache on beige paper, 32.7 × 49.9 cm (12⅞ × 19¼ in.).
Smith College Museum of Art, Northampton, Massachusetts

OPPOSITE
60. *The Church of Saint Pierre, Avon*, 1892–93.
Pencil and watercolour, 47 × 30.8 cm (18½ × 12⅛ in.).
Collection Phyllis Lambert, Montreal

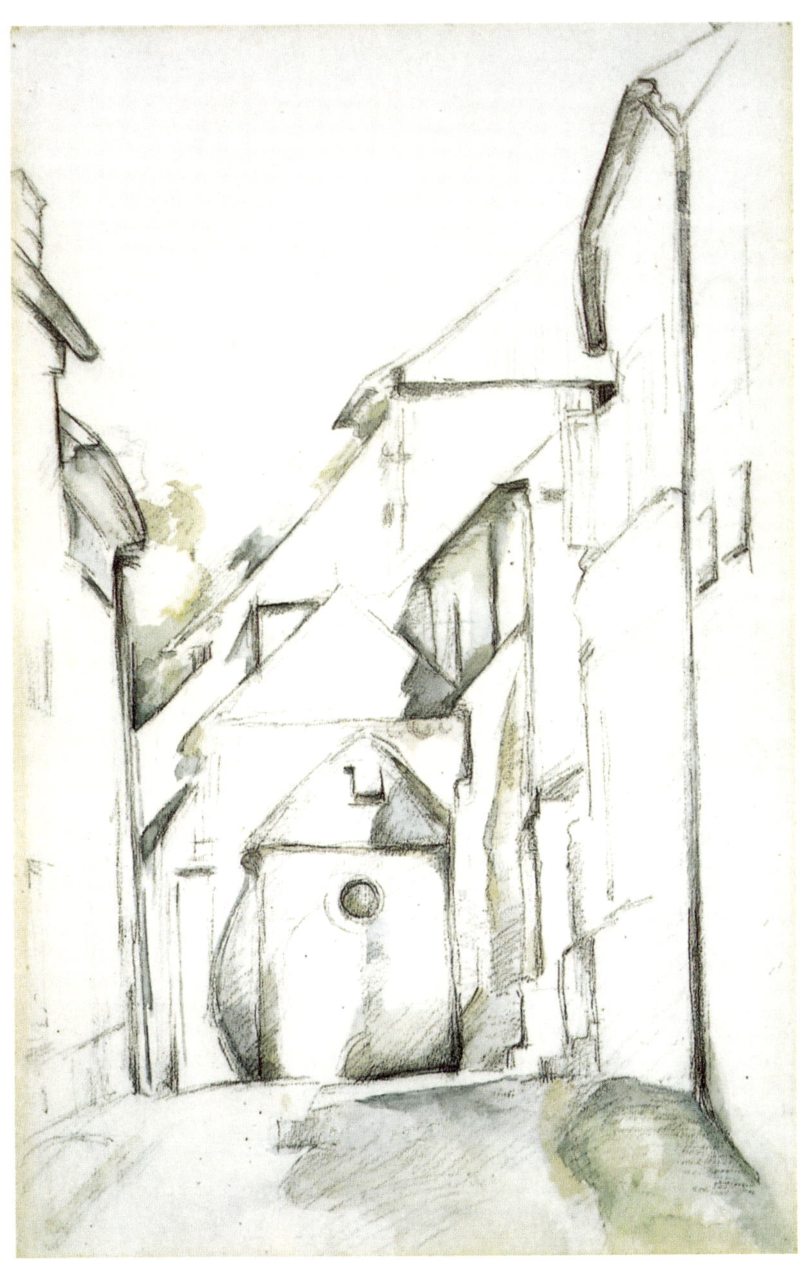

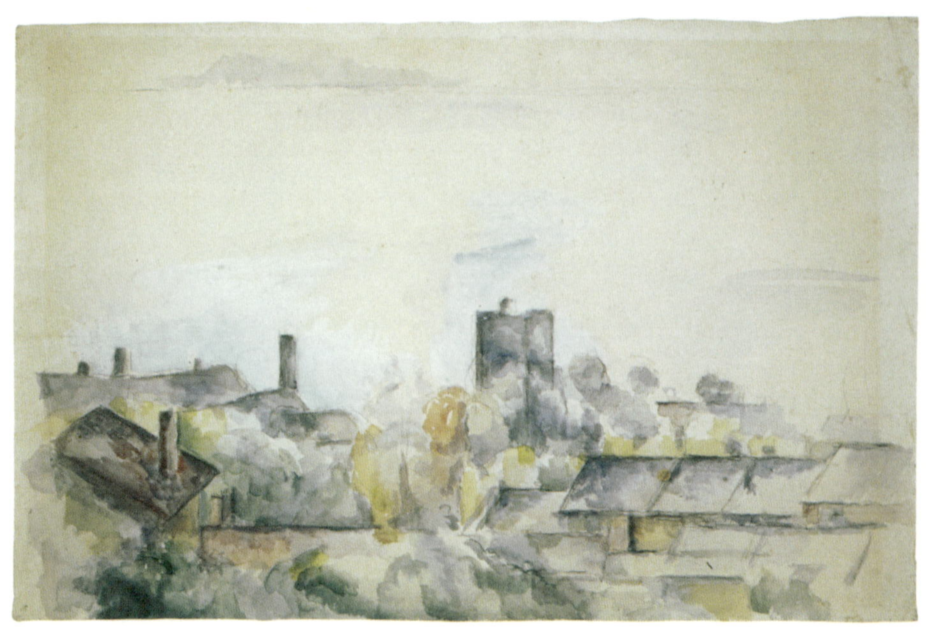

61. *Rooftops of L'Estaque*, 1876–82.
Pencil, watercolour and gouache, 30.6 × 47.2 cm (12½ × 18⅝ in.).
Museum Boijmans Van Beuningen, Rotterdam

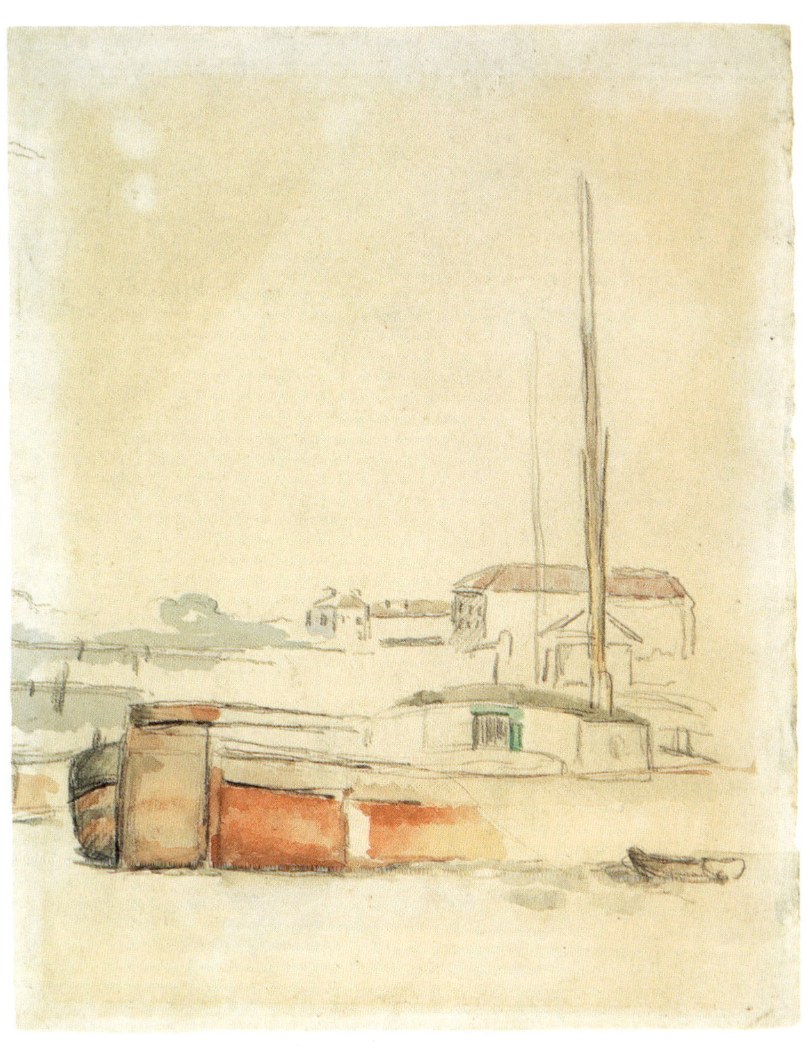

62. *Barge on a River*, 1873–77.
Pencil and watercolour, 26.7 × 21.8 cm (10½ × 8½ in.).
Jordan Schnitzer Museum of Art, University of Oregon, Eugene

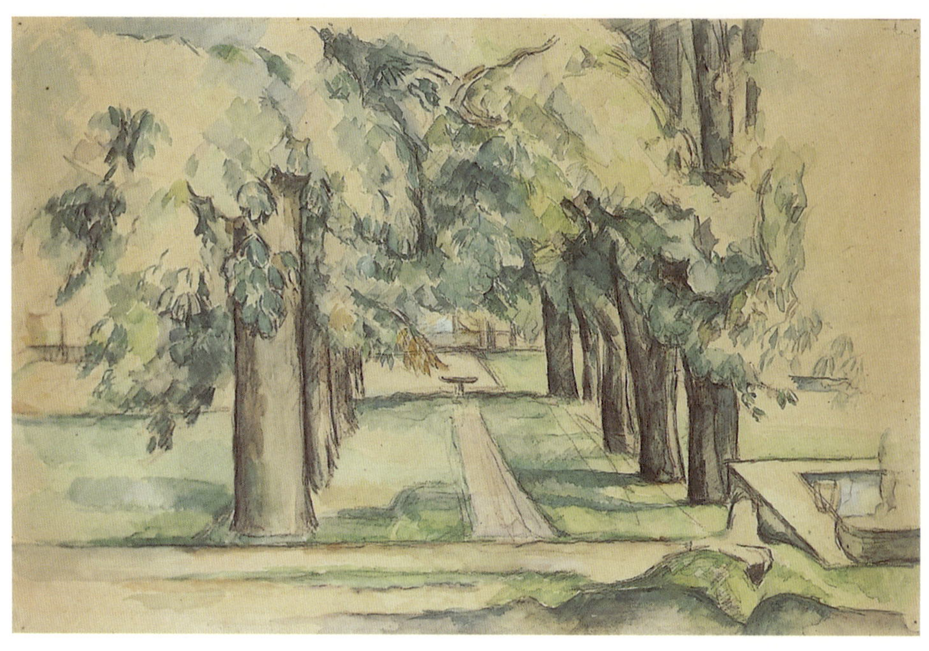

63. *The Pool and Allée of Chestnut Trees at the Jas de Bouffan,* 1878–80.
Pencil and watercolour, 30 × 47 cm (11⅞ × 18½ in.).
Städel Museum, Frankfurt am Main

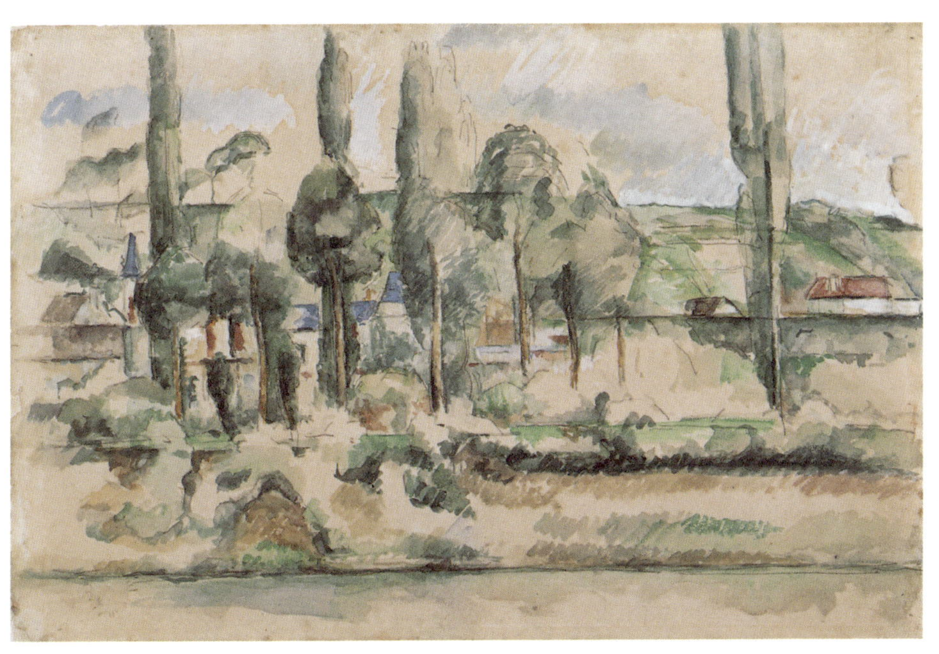

64. *The Château at Médan*, 1879–81.
Pencil, watercolour and gouache, 31.3 × 47.2 cm (12⅜ × 18⅝ in.).
Kunsthaus Zurich

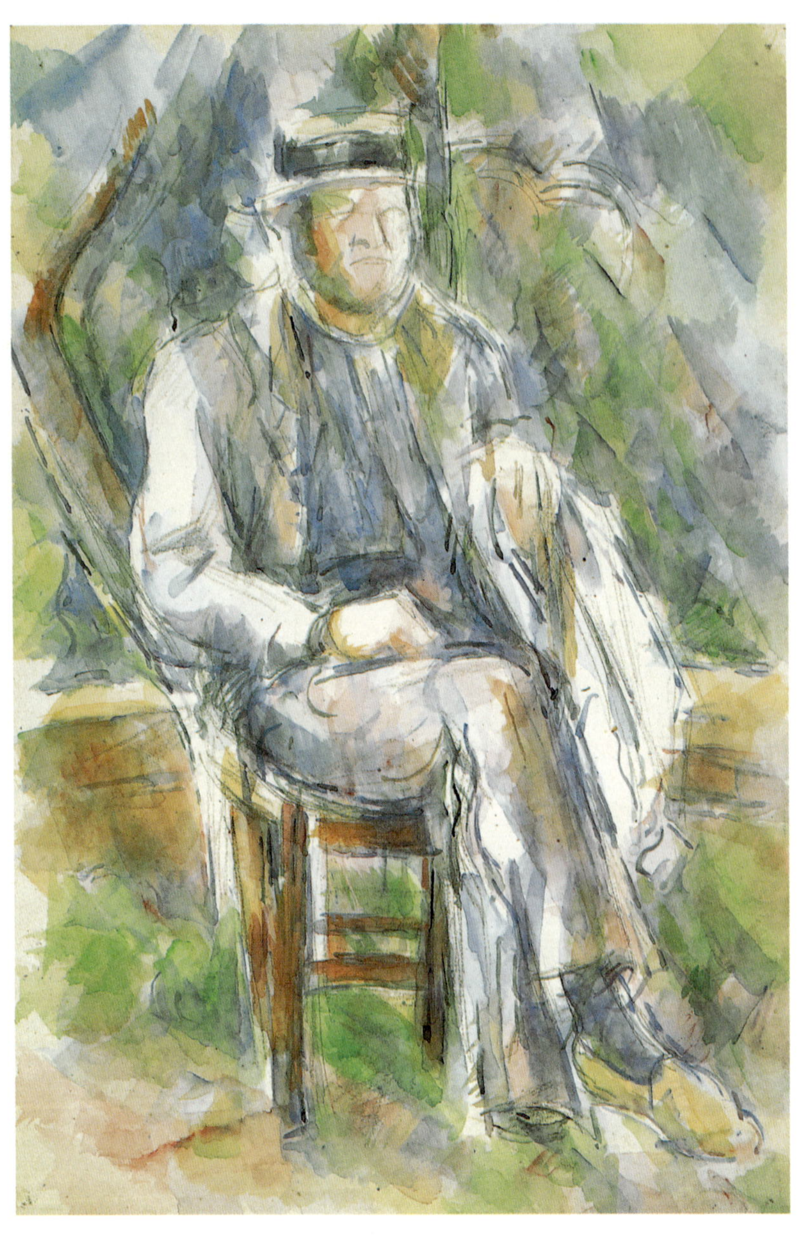

65. *Man Wearing a Straw Hat*, 1906.
Pencil and watercolour, 47.9 × 31.5 cm (18⅞ × 12⅛ in.).
The Art Institute of Chicago

CHAPTER THREE

Portraying the Individual

*'We must live in harmony, my model, my colours and I
and together catch the same passing moment.'* Paul Cézanne

At first sight it would seem as if Cézanne lacked the right attributes to be
a portrait painter. As a young man he was inclined to be too impetuous
and when older he became intensely reserved. Both these aspects
are reflected in his style, which in his early portraits is vigorous and
simplified, and in his later ones ponderous and deliberate to the point
of becoming over-elaborate.

At the back of Cézanne's mind there may have been the predicament
of the artist Frenhofer in Balzac's historical short novel *Le Chef d'Oeuvre
Inconnu* (1837). It is known that he identified closely with Frenhofer, just
as he had a particular veneration for another artist featuring in the same
novel – Poussin. For ten years Frenhofer worked on a life-size portrait of
his mistress, which he intended to be his masterpiece and an unsurpassed
contribution to the history of portraiture. 'My painting is not a painting,
but a feeling, a passion!', he declared. But in his rising anxiety to finish
the picture Frenhofer overworks the canvas, creating what Poussin
describes when he finally sees it as 'a mass of strange lines forming
a wall of paint'. Sensing his failure Frenhofer burns all his canvases,
bids farewell to his friends and the world, and dies during the night.

At no stage, in fact, was having your portrait painted by Cézanne
a pleasant experience. Concerning the early double-portrait, *Fortuné
Marion and Antony Valabrègue Setting Out for the Motif* (1866) [66],
Valabrègue wrote to Zola, 'At the present time Marion and I are posing
for him. We are arm in arm, and have hideous shapes. Paul is a horrible
painter as regards the poses he gives people in the midst of his riots of
colour. Every time he paints one of his friends it seems as though he
were revenging himself on him for some hidden injury.' Later sitters,
such as his school friend Henri Gasquet and his son Joachim, the critic
Gustave Geffroy or the dealer Ambroise Vollard, also found the task
exacting. By the 1890s any painting by Cézanne was a protracted exercise

and portraiture in particular involved numerous sittings with no clear indication as to whether the painting would ever be finished.

Vollard left a vivid account of his experience when Cézanne painted him in 1899 [67]. The sessions, which took place in the artist's studio in Paris, began at eight o'clock in the morning and lasted for over three hours. The artist preferred to work in absolute silence and ideally in an even natural light, but progress after one hundred and fifteen sittings was still 'slow and occasionally painful'. The resolution of problems that the painter encountered while the portrait was being painted necessitated anxious visits to the Musée du Louvre to make copies after the old masters as a way of finding answers. Cézanne often became frustrated. '"You understand, Monsieur Vollard, the contour keeps slipping away from me!"' Every brushstroke was carefully pondered. '"Don't you see, Monsieur Vollard, that if I put something there by guesswork, I might have to paint the whole canvas over starting from that point?"' – a prospect that the sitter naturally dreaded. The painting of the portrait, therefore, became an endurance test for both artist and sitter. The long sessions made Vollard drowsy, which caused Cézanne to instruct him, '"Do I have to tell you again you must sit like an apple? Does an apple move?"' And it is noteworthy regarding this last instruction that in two of the artist's self-portrait drawings he places his own head alongside an apple. In the end, Cézanne abandoned Vollard's portrait remarking only that, '"The front of the shirt is not bad"'.

It is clear that Cézanne found formal portrait painting challenging, but this does not mean that he ignored the genre completely. Vollard stated firmly of Cézanne that 'He loved to paint portraits', and, indeed, in addition to the paintings, the *oeuvre* includes a considerable number of drawn portraits. During the earlier decades of his working life these were predominantly of family and friends. Later, during the 1890s, he often depicted familiars or those who worked on the estate at the Jas de Bouffan or for him at his studio at Les Lauves. By no means all the sitters in these final portraits are identifiable and some were used not just in the context of straightforward portraiture but also in narrative genre paintings such as *The Card Players* [74].

From the start even Cézanne realized that portraiture was a means of winning artistic respectability and possibly gaining financial stability. It was also a way for him to demonstrate his potential as an artist to his family, thereby obtaining the all-important support of his father. Not surprisingly, therefore, his father is the subject of two early full-length portraits dating from the mid-1860s: one [see 2] where he is seated in an armchair reading the newspaper *L'Evénement* for which Zola wrote, and another where he is seen in profile reading another unidentifiable

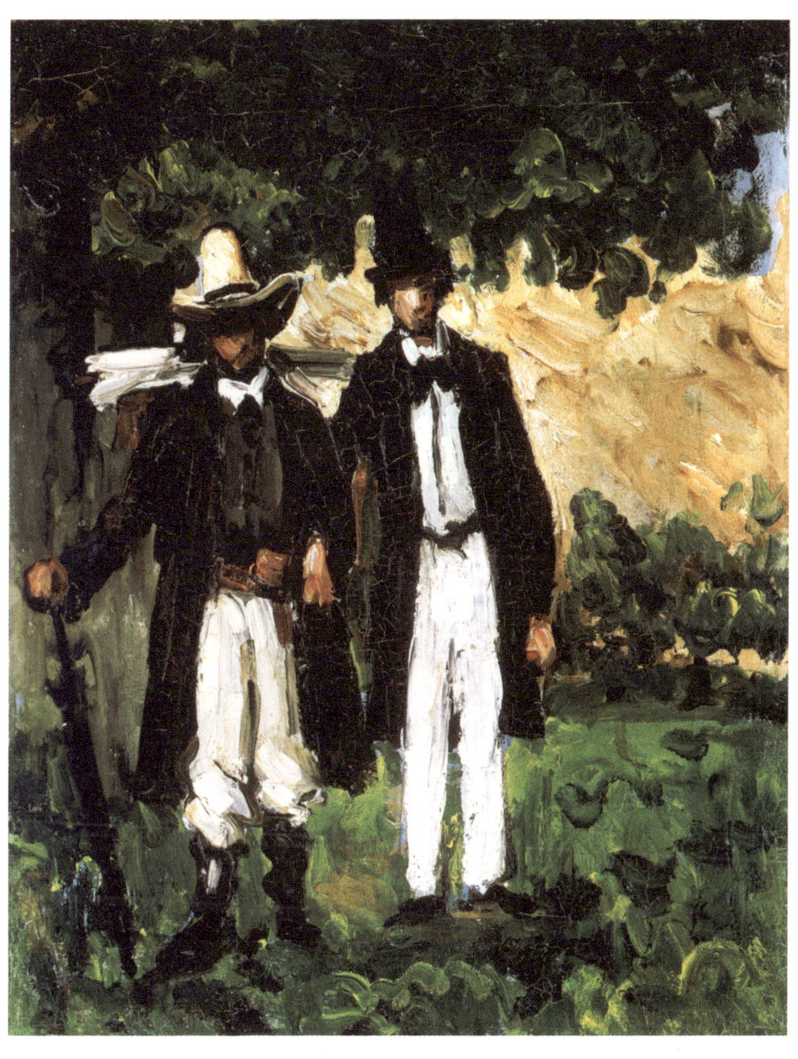

66. *Fortuné Marion and Antony Valabrègue Setting Out for the Motif*, 1866.
Oil on canvas, 39 × 31 cm (15⅜ × 12¼ in.).
Private collection

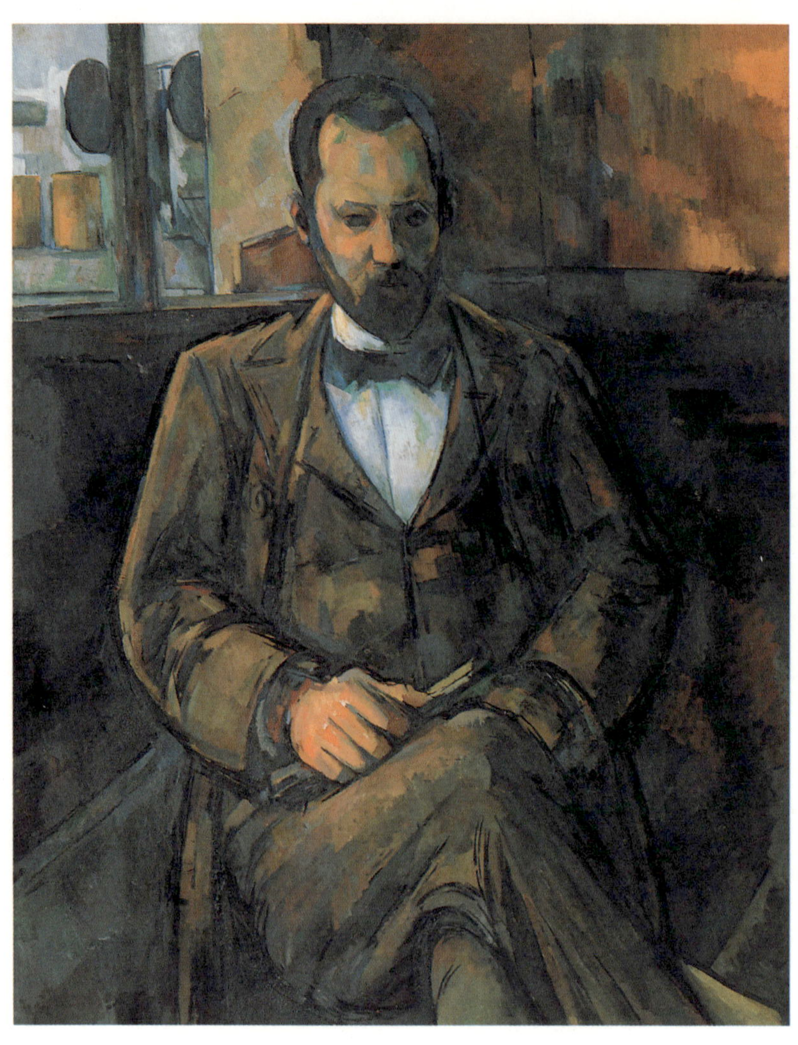

67. *Ambroise Vollard*, 1899.
Oil on canvas, 100 × 81 cm (39¾ × 31⅞ in.).
Petit Palais, Musée des Beaux-Arts de la Ville de Paris

newspaper (National Gallery, London). This second portrait hung in the grand salon of the Jas de Bouffan between the artist's allegories of *The Four Seasons* that he jokingly signed 'Ingres'. The artist's maternal uncle, Dominique Aubert, was the subject of several smaller, but powerful, portraits in bust or half-length in which he is shown in various guises such as a monk, lawyer and artisan. Female family members were painted less frequently. The head and shoulders of Cézanne's sister Marie, seen directly from the front (Saint Louis Art Museum) has a rare depiction of his mother on the back. Both these figures are almost certainly the subjects shown in the conversation piece known as *Young Girl at the Piano – Overture to Tannhäuser* (c. 1869) in the State Hermitage Museum, St Petersburg.

These earliest portraits dating from the mid-1860s, for which the palette knife has often been used, are remarkably direct and almost schematized in composition, as well as being rugged, forceful and at times even brutal in execution. Although many heterogeneous sources can be detected in these images, extending from Antonello da Messina and El Greco through Courbet and Corot to Manet, Cézanne's style is distinctive. So, too, is his general approach to portraiture, where he is less concerned at this stage with a mere likeness and more with a dramatization or impersonation of character [75–77]. This form of role playing, which applies equally to both the paintings and the drawings, had quite the opposite effect to portraits by Ingres, for example, who Cézanne cheekily dismissed as 'a minor painter', referred to as 'a stuffed shirt' and lampooned in an early copy after the master's painting of *Jupiter and Thetis* that hung in the museum at Aix-en-Provence.

If Cézanne intended his early portraits to ease his passage as a Salon painter, he met with no success. The *Portrait of Antony Valabrègue* (National Gallery of Art, Washington, DC) of 1866 was submitted to the Salon jury, but rejected. It was this rejection that led in the first place to Cézanne's appeal to the Comte de Nieuwerkerke to repeat the Salon des Refusés of 1863 and, secondly, to Zola's publication of *Mon Salon* (1868), with its dedication to the aggrieved artist. Perhaps to ingratiate himself with the jury, Cézanne laid aside the palette knife in his next portraits and opted for a broader and flatter handling with brushes. He also embarked upon more traditional compositions such as the double-portrait entitled *Paul Alexis Reading to Emile Zola* (c. 1869–70) in the Museu de Arte São Paolo, which emulates Manet in composition and style but was unfinished and therefore never submitted to the Salon. Interestingly, an earlier version of this double-portrait amounts to an exercise in the manner of Dutch seventeenth-century art with reminiscences of Vermeer and Pieter de Hooch. Such disparities reveal

not only how flexible Cézanne could be in his attitude to portraiture,
but perhaps also some uncertainty as to the direction in which he should
now move in this respect.

A greater resolve surrounded the painting of *Achille Emperaire*
(*c.* 1869–70) in the Musée d'Orsay, Paris [69]. The sitter was a painter
from Aix-en-Provence, but the portrait was undertaken in Paris after the
two friends had met up again at the Académie Suisse. Emperaire was a
dwarf of striking appearance. His high domed forehead was framed by
an abundance of hair and his face adorned with a moustache and goatee
beard. As Cézanne emphasizes in the portrait, Emperaire's legs were rather
spindly and the fingers extremely etiolated. Two outstanding preparatory
drawings make it clear that Cézanne was fascinated by the sitter's head,
but he also admired him as a person, describing him to Gasquet as 'a
burning soul, nerves of steel, an iron pride in a misshapen body, a flame of
genius in a crooked hearth, a mixture of Don Quixote and Prometheus'.

The painted portrait is full-length showing Emperaire seated in
a chair with a tall back similar to the one that Cézanne had used for
the portrait of his father reading *L'Evénement* [see 2]. The sitter is
informally dressed in what appears to be a bathrobe and he wears
slippers, a red shirt and leggings; the feet are raised on a footstool.
There is certainly an affinity with Manet, but also an echo of the *Portrait
of Innocent X* (1650) by Velázquez. Even so, the tone of the portrait is
essentially subversive, since the figure is hardly eligible for an official
portrait as if he were a head of state. Indeed, Emperaire is enthroned
against a dark background and his identity openly declared in capital
letters along the upper edge (ACHILLE EMPERAIRE PEINTRE) as
in some formal portraits dating from the sixteenth century. A further
visual allusion may also have been to *Napoleon I on his Imperial Throne*
(1806) by Ingres, in the Musée de l'Armée, Paris, which, if correct, would
amount to a visual and verbal pun on the sitter's name and would further
underscore Cézanne's satirical intentions. The Salon jury of 1870 once
more rejected his submission.

The two studies in charcoal of Emperaire's head are of outstanding
quality and notable for the care with which they have been drawn.
The sheet in Paris [78] shows the sitter looking to the left. The fall of
the light defines the principal features of the face. Offsetting the areas
of the paper that have been deliberately left blank are the sinuous but
heavily scored lines of the hair, moustache and beard. The intensity of
the expression is derived from the large eyes beneath pronouncedly long
eyebrows. This study has an immediacy and variety that suggests it was
rapidly drawn from life, concentrating on the expression of the sitter
with the clothes barely suggested.

By contrast, the second study [68] is closer to the finished painting. The eyes are half-closed but cast downwards looking to the right; the expression is calmer and more contemplative. Correspondingly, the style is less linear and the hatching more controlled with greater modulation of the surface. The finish is smoother with fewer accents. As before, it is the expression of the sitter that has absorbed the artist's attention rather than any aspect of the setting or dress. Such formal studies are testimony to Cézanne's powers as a portrait draughtsman and it is regrettable that there are hardly any comparable examples in his surviving *oeuvre* from these years of his early maturity.

During the 1870s and the 1880s the majority of Cézanne's portrait drawings were contained within his sketchbooks. A few are of his friends – Zola [79], Pissarro, Gachet [80], Chocquet [81, 82] – but the bulk are more personal, being of his parents, himself, his wife, Hortense, and their son, Paul. Of these, the portraits of his parents are more often of his father, as opposed to his mother who remains virtually invisible in Cézanne's *oeuvre*, and even the drawings of his father are not very elaborate, being more like vignettes. The self-portraits are the most sustained group, which are followed in numerical order by portraits of his son from the time he was a baby to his becoming a young man, and then of his wife.

The artist himself made numerous self-portraits at every stage of his adult life: twenty-six painted images and a further twenty made on paper. Furthermore, he included himself in at least ten imaginary compositions, such as *The Temptation of St Anthony* (c. 1870), *A Modern Olympia* (c. 1869–70 and 1873), or *The Apotheosis of Delacroix* [see 14]. It is easy to speculate on a theoretical basis as to why Cézanne depicted himself so often, but many artists have been preoccupied by their appearance. Albrecht Dürer used self-portraiture to advertise his arrival as an important artist; Rubens chose it as a way of celebrating his presence at the leading courts of Europe; Rembrandt recorded both the high points and the low points in his life in terms of self-portraiture; and Sir Joshua Reynolds charted his rise to fame as the first President of the Royal Academy of Arts in London by the same means.

Cézanne also indulges in role-playing in his painted self-portraits [see frontispiece]. Up until the mid-1870s both his wild appearance and the rough technique are calculated to call attention to his originality. The early self-portraits also stress how different he is as a result of his provincial identity. They deliberately set out to provoke, which is why Cézanne depicts himself as pugnacious, curmudgeonly, unkempt and altogether unapproachable. By the end of the 1870s and through the 1880s the painter presents himself as calmer, graver, wiser and more

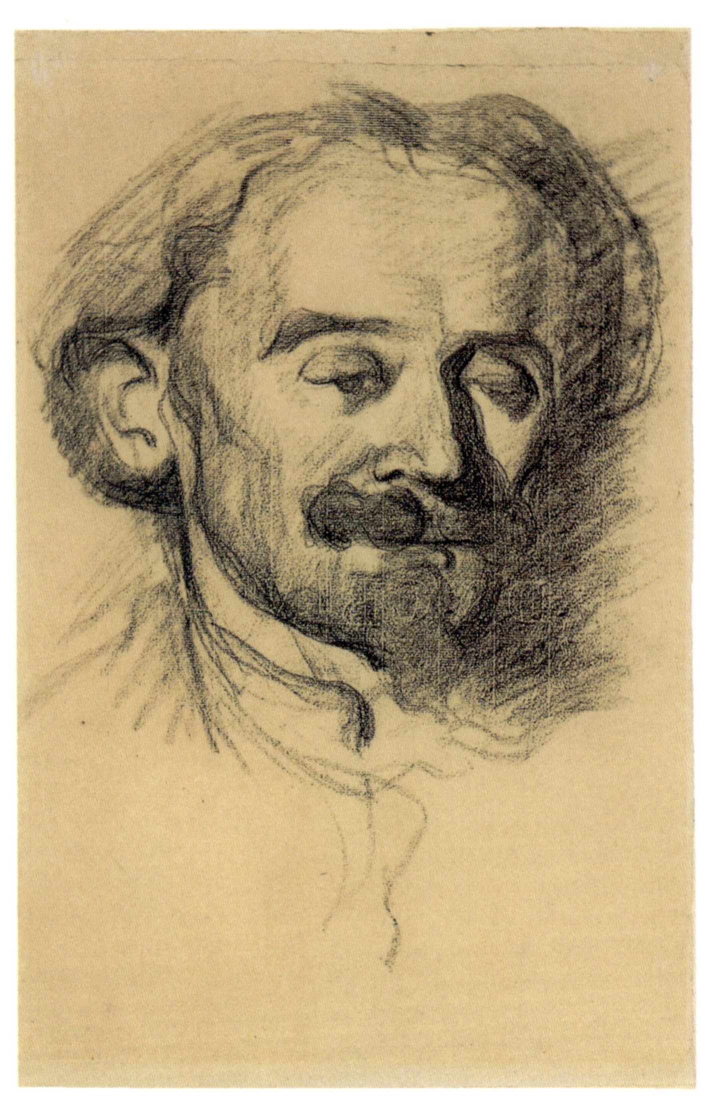

ABOVE
68. *Achille Emperaire*, 1869–70.
Charcoal, 43.2 × 31.9 cm (17 × 12½ in.).
Kunstmuseum Basel

OPPOSITE
69. *Achille Emperaire*, c. 1869–70.
Oil on canvas, 200 × 120 cm (78¾ × 47¼ in.).
Musée d'Orsay, Paris

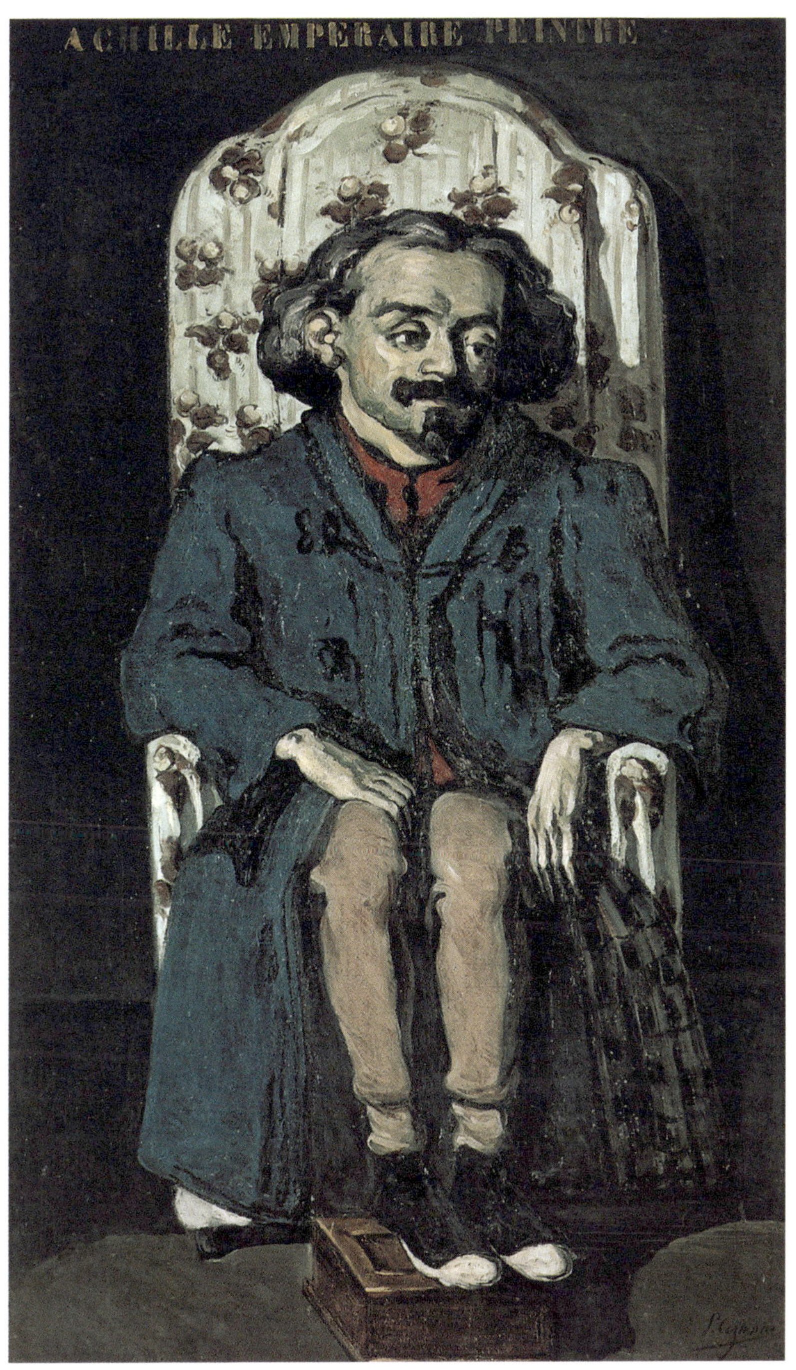
ACHILLE EMPERAIRE PEINTRE

affable. Where Rembrandt dipped into his dressing-up box to effect a transformation, Cézanne often tried on different styles of headgear as an attempt at embourgeoisement. There is considerable variety in the poses – some of them playful as when he looks over his shoulder – but significantly in only one self-portrait does he portray himself in the act of painting. Overall, there is a sense of increasing confidence and quiet satisfaction at proving to be such a successful proponent of the Provençal renaissance.

The self-portrait drawings are more introspective than the paintings [83–89]. Usually confined to head and shoulders, they emphasize the domed forehead and the closely set features of eyes, nose and mouth, which adds to the intensity of the expression. Those drawings that lack any indication of the shoulders on which the head is set have an uncanny resemblance to death masks [85]. Similarly, in a strange way the exaggerated eye-sockets and shiny cranium anticipate the skulls that appear so often in the artist's late still lifes. Often, too, the juxtaposition of a self- portrait on a page that includes compositional studies, preliminary ideas for compositions, or copies after old masters gives Cézanne's features a ghostly impression comparable with the technique of a dissolve in cinematography [88, 89]. The clumsy style of the earliest self-portrait drawings, dating from the early 1870s, with their stenographic contours and chiaroscural effects [83], gave way towards the end of the decade to a more curvilinear mode with small rectangular areas of even-faceted hatching, which seem to concentrate on the shape of the head [84–86]. This lighter, more relaxed style of drawing has the effect of elongating the face while also making it seem more monumental. In the end, as elsewhere in Cézanne's *oeuvre*, it was less the personal characterization of his head that interested the artist than its generalized formal structure.

Overall, Cézanne's self-portraits dignify his reserve and insist upon his vigilance, but in this he had an obvious advantage over the rest of his family. Since he kept his sketchbooks to hand at home he was constantly able to rely on his wife and child as models. He frequently drew his wife, Hortense, in a domestic context resting, sewing, sleeping, or in straightforward informal studies for possible portraits either of her herself or of other potential subjects. She was a captive model and while the family relaxed in the evening it was natural for Cézanne to record what he observed in his immediate presence, often randomly and intuitively [90–93]. The sketchbooks allowed for an intimacy that was not apparent on other occasions in Cézanne's life when he was always so protective of his privacy. Thus it is that he created one of the most beautiful homages ever paid by an artist to his wife.

Madame Cézanne with Hortensias [94] comprises on the right a
sketch in pencil of Hortense with her head resting on a pillow: it seems
as though she has just awakened. The delicacy of line and subtlety
of modelling in this part are spellbinding in the creation of a poetic
tenderness that is redolent of eighteenth-century sensibility or early
nineteenth-century romanticism. Equally compelling, however, is the
effulgence of the still life on the left. The mauve flower, which flourishes
in the Midi, is contained within a circlet of green leaves. The gentle
diagonal formed by the balancing of the flower with the head of
Hortense gives the whole composition an overwhelming sense of calm
as though the artist had been suddenly overcome by a moment of
unsurpassed beauty. The drawing also signifies Cézanne's own innate
artistic intelligence, since he has here devised a visual pun on his wife's
name and the French word for hydrangeas. The quality of this drawing is
such that there is every justification in comparing Cézanne's achievement
with representations by other artists of their wives: Agnes Frey by Dürer;
Saskia van Uylenbergh by Rembrandt [70]; or Isabella Brant by Rubens
[71]. In this single sheet Cézanne fuses the two main strands of French

70. Rembrandt van Rijn, *Saskia Asleep in Bed, c.* 1635.
Pen and brush in bistre ink, 13.7 × 20.3 cm (5⅜ × 8 in.).
Ashmolean Museum, Oxford

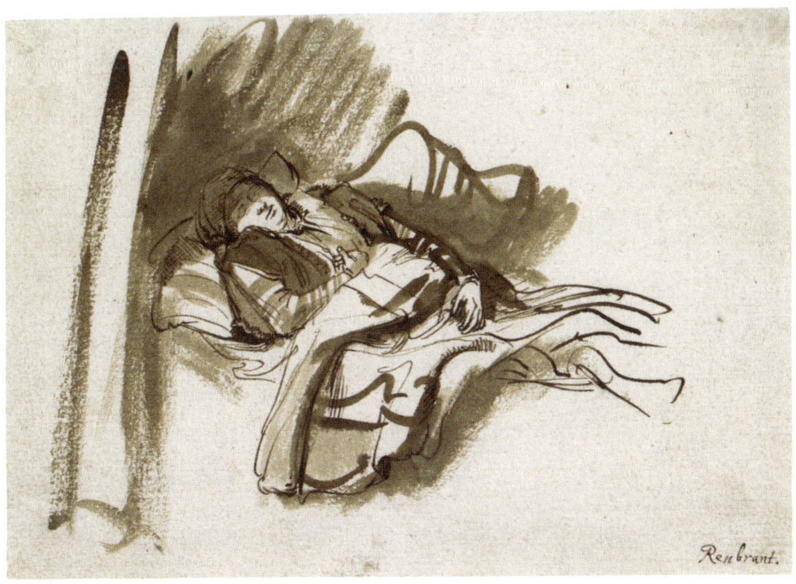

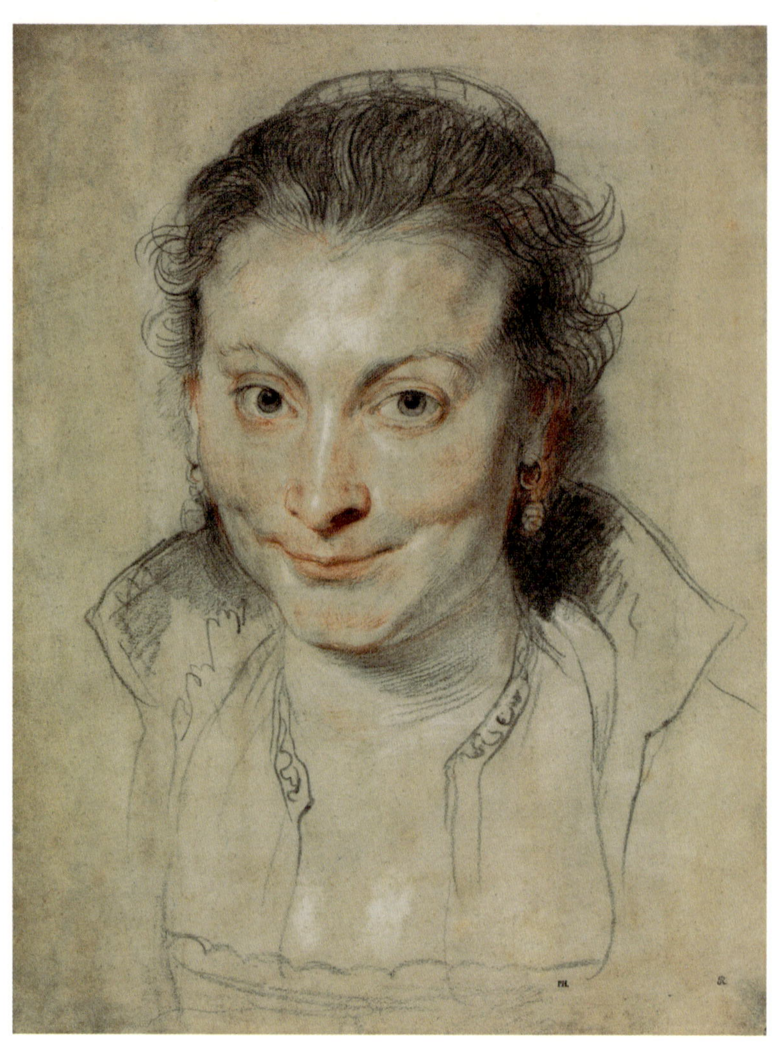

71. Peter Paul Rubens, *Isabella Brant*, c. 1622.
Black, red and white chalk with some pen and ink lightly
washed on beige paper, 38.1 × 29.4 cm (15 × 11⅝ in.).
British Museum, London

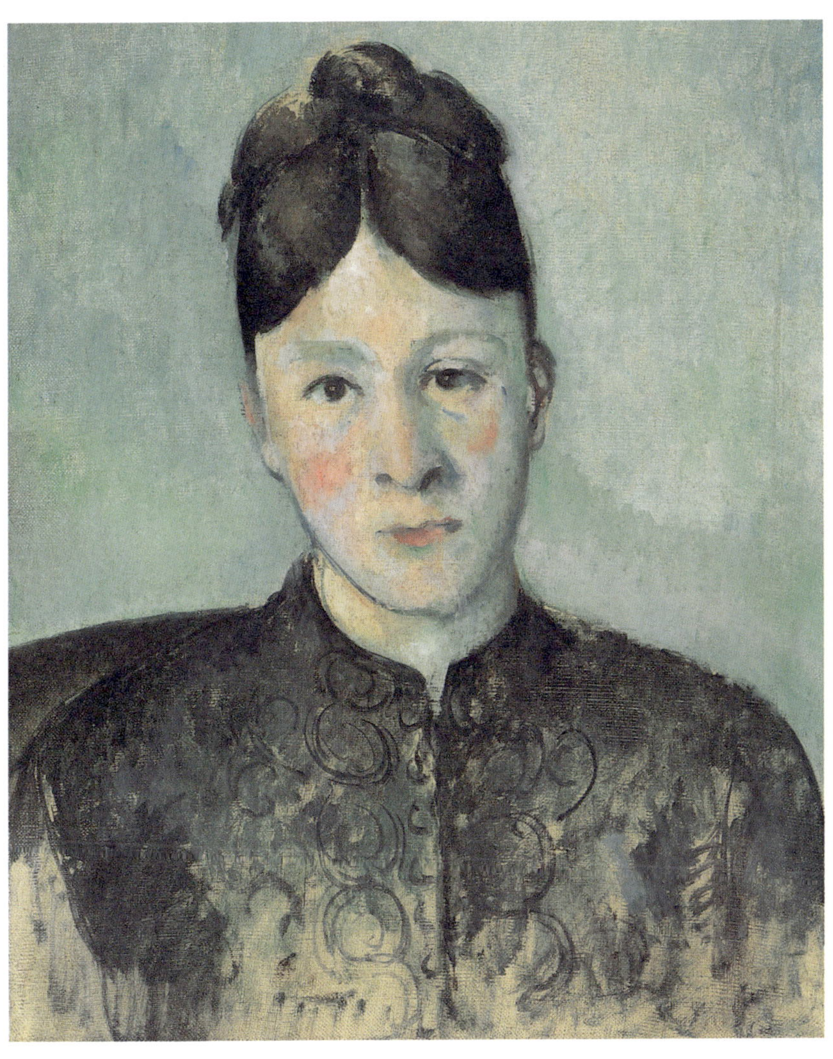

72. *Madame Cézanne, c. 1885.*
Oil on canvas, 46 × 38 cm (18⅛ × 15 in.).
Museum Berggruen, Berlin

nineteenth-century art: the Neoclassicism of Ingres in the pencil drawing
of Hortense and the Romanticism of Delacroix in the watercolour of
the flower.

Cézanne honoured his wife in other ways, too, producing as many
as twenty-six painted portraits of her dating from between 1877 and
1894. These portraits are notable for their variety of mood, setting and
execution. As a group they ultimately proved to be more influential
than the artist's own self-portraits. Both Picasso and Matisse were
clearly impressed by the compositional complexity and the range of
colour occurring, for example, in *Madame Cézanne in a Red Armchair*
(c. 1877) [see 5], *Madame Cézanne* (c. 1885) [72], *Portrait of the Artist's
Wife* (c. 1867–82; E. G. Bührle Collection, Zurich), *Madame Cézanne
in a Yellow Chair* (c. 1888–90; Foundation Beyeler, Basel), *Madame
Cézanne in a Red Dress* (c. 1888–90; Metropolitan Museum of Art,
New York), *Madame Cézanne in a Conservatory* (1891–92; Metropolitan
Museum of Art, New York), or *Woman with a Green Hat* (c. 1891–92;
Barnes Foundation, Philadelphia). The elongated oval face, brown hair
parted in the middle, the large eyes and the sallow complexion suggest
an imperturbable personality that on depiction appears sometimes as
serenity, sometimes as impassivity and sometimes even as docility.

Two drawings of Hortense have a similar impact to the paintings.
One in Rotterdam [95] shows the sitter leaning back against a cushion
dressed in a brocaded jacket, stiff collar, and a hat decorated with an
ornament, as though about to leave the house. Rapidly sketched with
flurries of lines, sporadic hatching and pronounced accents, in this
drawing Cézanne affectionately emphasizes this fashion-conscious
element in his wife's personality. The face is lit from the left with the
features deftly picked out. The second drawing is in the National Gallery
of Art in Washington, DC [96], and is more sculptural by being reduced
to the essentials, almost in the manner of Amedeo Modigliani. At the
same time, it emphasizes the curvilinear aspects of Hortense's face. The
outline indicating the top-knot in the hair forms an oval with the outline
of the jaw. The tilt of the head requires that the eyes and the mouth are
set on shallow diagonals, which are repeated in the sloping shoulders.
Cézanne's skill in conveying arrested movement instantaneously and
fixing it permanently on the page is here brilliantly manifested.

The artist's much loved son, Paul, spent a great deal of his time with
his mother while he was growing up, but when the family was together,
which was mostly in Paris rather than Aix-en-Provence, Cézanne drew
him regularly. The drawings show him being nursed as a baby [97]
and as a small boy growing up [98, 99]. Paul *fils* was described by his
father in a letter to Charles Camoin, written on 22 February 1903, as

'a *great philosopher*', but he added, 'By that I don't mean the equal or
the emulator of Diderot, Voltaire or Rousseau … he is rather touchy,
incurious, but a good boy'. Towards the end of Cézanne's life his son
acted as an intermediary negotiating or making arrangements with
dealers who wanted to exhibit or buy his father's work or handling
encounters with artists who wanted to consult him. The letters written
by Cézanne to his son during his final years are uncharacteristically open
and engaging.

A particularly fine portrait drawing of Paul is a full-length
study made in *c.* 1885 when he was aged about thirteen and on the
threshold of manhood [100]. Dressed in a waistcoat with culottes he
is nonchalantly posed in an interior with hand on hip and his left leg
thrust forward. There are echoes of Cézanne's academic studies, as
well as of his copies after antique sculpture. Although this study does
not appear to have been developed any further, the artist did use his
son as a model for the painting made in Paris entitled *Mardi Gras* of
1888 (Pushkin State Museum of Fine Arts, Moscow) where two boys
wear *commedia dell'arte* costumes. They are pictured on a stage having
emerged from behind a looped curtain. Paul is on the right dressed in red
as Harlequin while his friend Louis Guillaume is in white in the role of
Pierrot. Cézanne took immense trouble over this composition, making
detailed studies of the curtain and the individual heads of the two boys
[101–103].

He reduced the original painting with two figures to the single
Harlequin in three further canvases, for which additional studies were
required: one in pencil [104] and one in watercolour. In both of these
it is the sense of rhythmical movement that is being examined with
the body tilted slightly backwards as though to suggest an uncertain
forward movement. This results in a somewhat mannerist pose, which
is enlivened by the pattern of the lozenges on the costume. The loss of
monumentality that is such a feature of the painted *Mardi Gras* is now
replaced by a rag-doll image.

At the start of the 1890s Cézanne began to use models beyond
his family. He could now afford to hire professionals when in Paris,
such as the Italian boy, Michelangelo di Rosa, who features in four
paintings entitled *Boy in a Red Waistcoat*. Seeing his son growing up,
Cézanne may suddenly have felt confident to tackle a similarly youthful
adolescent subject. The two watercolours of Michelangelo di Rosa
show the seated model seen from the front. The composition in both
examples is based on a pyramid, recalling Raphael's treatment of the
Virgin and Child, but here Cézanne goes further and positions the boy's
arms with jutting elbows so that they form a diamond shape. One of the

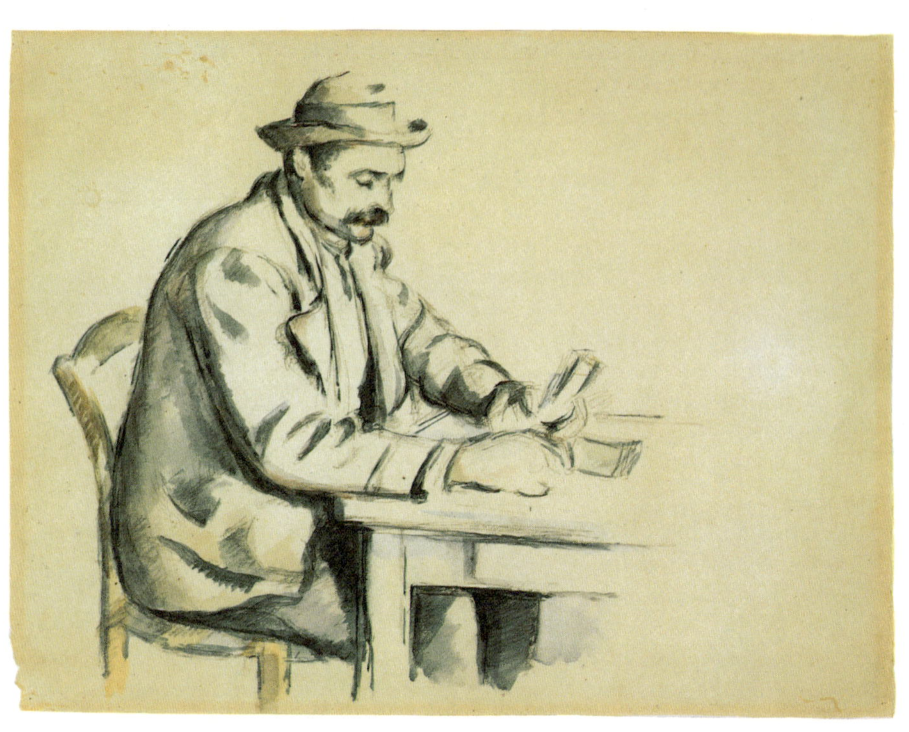

73. *Card Player*, 1890–92.
Pencil and watercolour, 36.2 × 48.5 cm (14¼ × 19⅛ in.).
Private collection, on loan to The Art Institute of Chicago

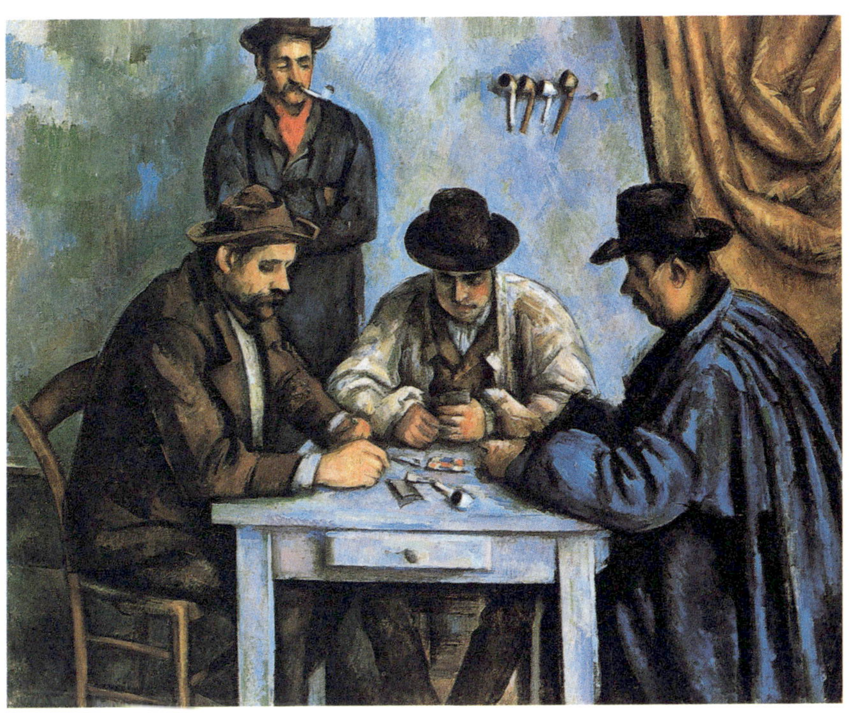

74. *The Card Players*, 1890–92.
Oil on canvas, 65 × 81 cm (25⅝ × 31⅞ in.).
Metropolitan Museum of Art, New York

drawings is done in pencil with watercolour [106] and the other (surely made subsequently) is in pure watercolour, executed with remarkable fluidity [105]. The white paper plays a dominant part in the system of highlighting, which falls across different areas of the front of the body and the clothes. Even without undue emphasis being put upon the physiognomy, the viewer readily appreciates the virtual presence of the figure.

Many of the models chosen by Cézanne in Aix-en-Provence during his final years were people who worked on the family property at the Jas de Bouffan before its sale in 1899. They are sometimes directly observed as portraits and at others deliberately posed for use in a narrative composition. The prime instance of this transference occurs in *The Card Players*, of which there are five versions. The most complex in composition is the one in the Barnes Collection in Philadelphia of 1890–92, which has five figures. There is a reduced version of this design with four figures in the Metropolitan Museum of Art in New York [74]. Later, between *c.* 1892 and 1896, Cézanne repeated the subject in a simpler pattern with only two figures (examples are in the Courtauld Gallery, London, and Musée d'Orsay, Paris). Cézanne made separate studies of the figures used in these pictures from life before incorporating them into the paintings [73, 107–110]. In doing this the figures lose some of their individuality and liveliness as the artist strives to give the forms a monumentality that some writers have compared with paintings by Giotto. More realistically, it is apparent that Cézanne was, in fact, hoping to emulate such predecessors as the Le Nain brothers in the seventeenth century and Chardin in the eighteenth, who had treated the subject of card players. The choice of a theme with rural overtones also aligned him with painters of his own time such as Courbet and Jean-François Millet, who often fused genre scenes with portraiture and still life as a way of undermining the hierarchy of preferred subject matter exemplified by the academic tradition. Furthermore, Cézanne probably intended his paintings of *The Card Players* to be seen in the context of the Provençal renaissance as though ennobling local people in the court of humanity. In addition, it is perhaps significant that his friend Antony Valabrègue wrote the first monograph on the Le Nain brothers (published posthumously in 1904).

Cézanne's late portraiture, therefore, is dominated by those people in Provence with whom he felt most at ease and with whom he was in daily contact. He could observe them first at work and then invite them into the Jas de Bouffan to pose. The titles of these late pictures tend to be generic (*The Smoker, Peasant in a Blue Smock, Woman with a Coffee Pot, Old Woman with a Rosary* or *Woman in Blue*), but the sitters are certainly not to be designated merely as types and mostly they defy classification. Rather, as with Vincent van Gogh, they reflect the artist's respect for the dignity of his fellow human beings.

After the sale of the Jas de Bouffan Cézanne carried out most of his portraiture on the shaded terrace of the studio he built at Les Lauves in 1902 on the outskirts of Aix-en-Provence. Here he undertook such watercolours as *Man Wearing a Straw Hat* [65], *Seated Peasant* [111] and *Seated Woman* [112]. Portraits of the gardener Vallier exist in two different compositions, both especially moving as at the very end of Cézanne's life Vallier acted as factotum and on occasions even as nurse. The figures are seen either directly from the front, where the positioning of the jutting elbows and the angle of the arms form rhomboidal shapes [113], or in profile [114]. The pencil and the brush are used in close harmony. Only *Seated Peasant* in this group of late portraits is in pure watercolour. Many of the outlines in the others have been reinforced several times with the point of the brush even after the broader washes have been applied. The colours seem to quiver in the atmosphere and the lines appear to tremble. The figures are defined well enough just as the artist's intentions are clear, but the febrile, restless style with so many repeated strokes and such a dense network of overlapping brushstrokes belies the calm of the sitters, who were no doubt pleased to be out of the hot Mediterranean sun. The untouched areas of the paper provide the highlights, but the features of each of the sitters are kept to the minimum and only barely suggested. Rivière likened Cézanne's watercolours to stained-glass windows that 'give off light, it seems, as if the sun had penetrated them'. These late figure studies in watercolour are so suffused with light that they are imbued with a spectral quality.

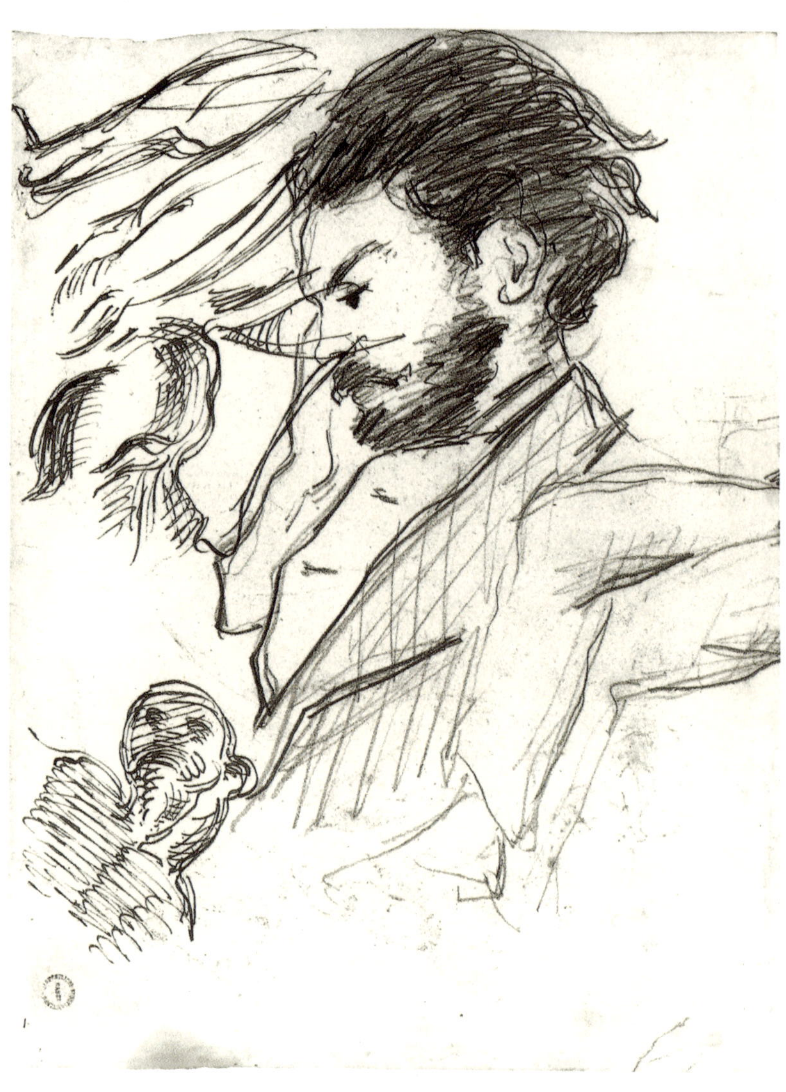

75. *Fortuné Marion*, 1869–73.
Pencil and pen and ink, 23 × 17.7 cm (9 × 7 in.).
Kunstmuseum Basel

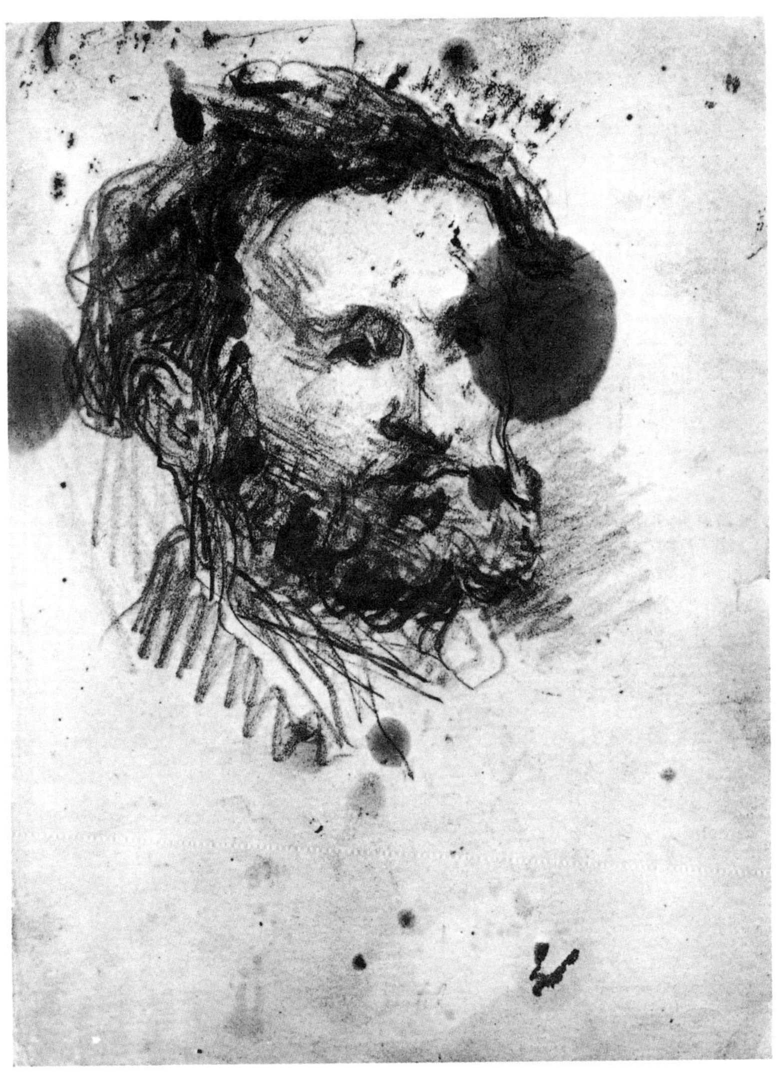

76. *Armand Guillaumin*, 1866–68.
Pencil and black chalk, 23.6 × 17.2 cm (9¼ × 6¾ in.).
Museum Boijmans Van Beuningen, Rotterdam

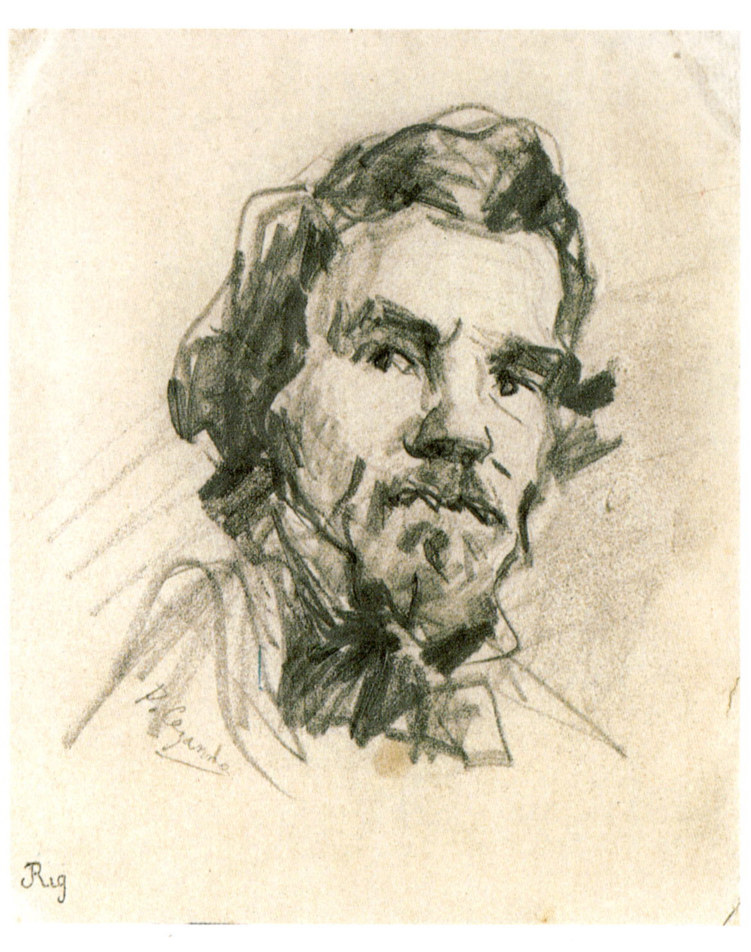

ABOVE

77. Eugène Delacroix
(after a photograph by Durrieu), c. 1870.
Pencil with some indications of wash, 14 × 13 cm (5½ × 5⅛ in.).
Musée Calvet, Avignon

OPPOSITE

78. Achille Emperaire, 1869–70.
Pencil and charcoal, 48.2 × 30.8 cm (19 × 12⅛ in.).
Musée d'Orsay, Paris

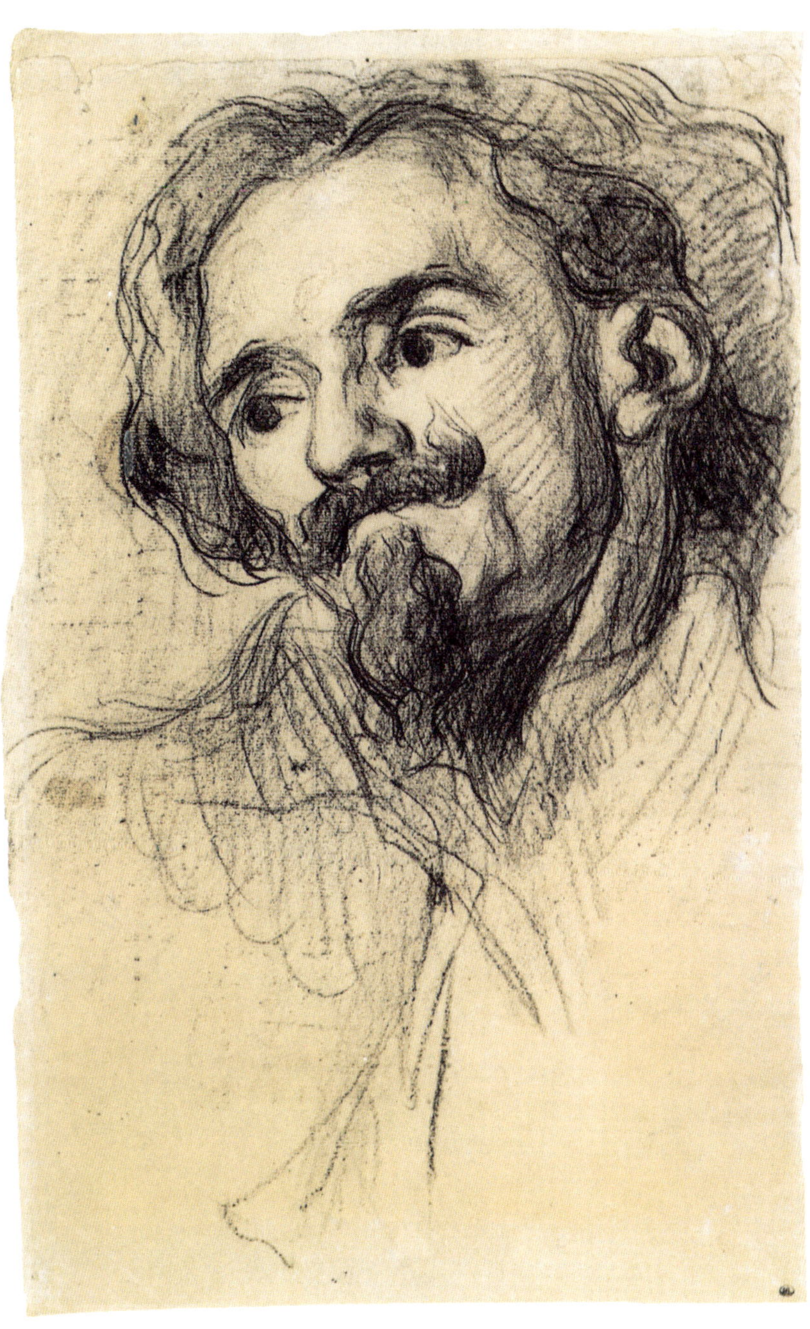

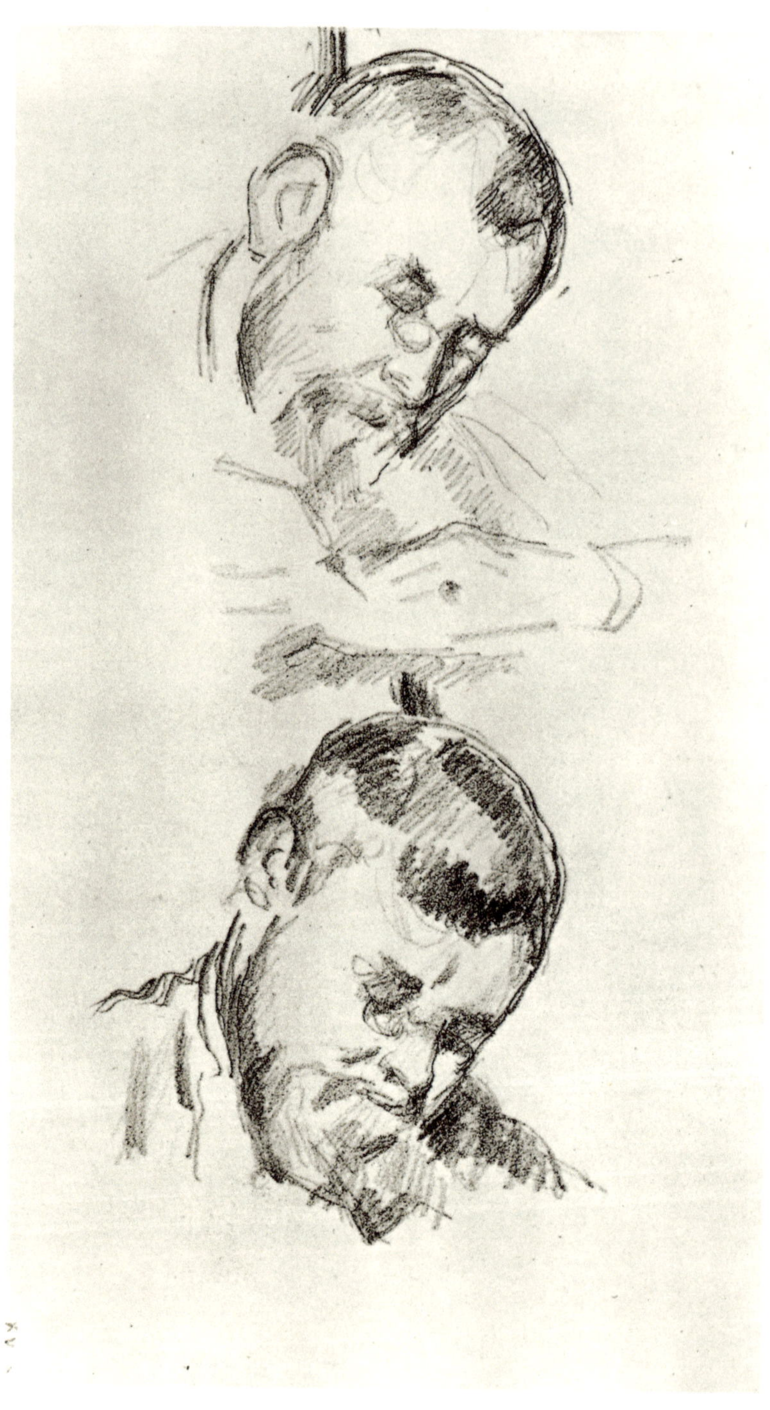

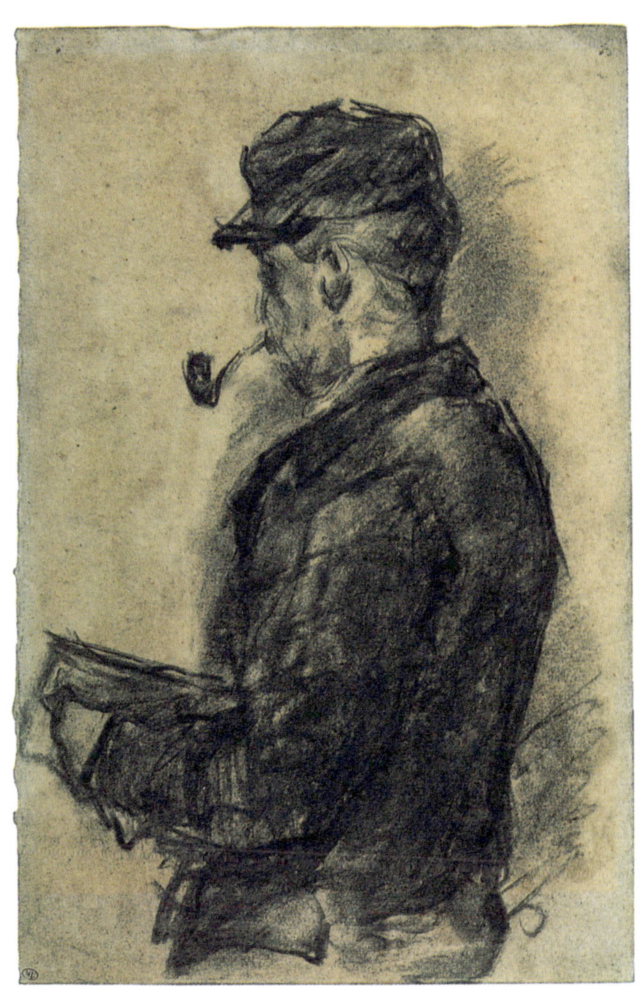

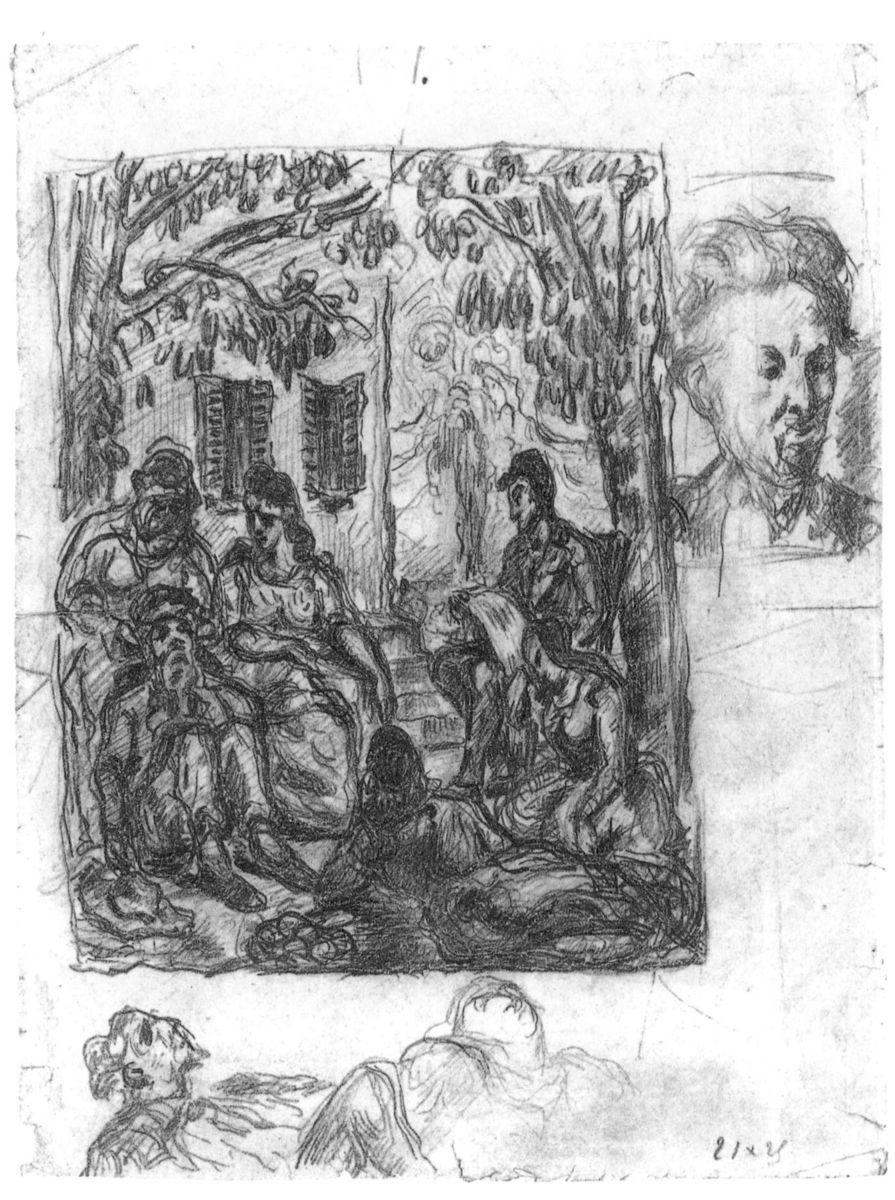

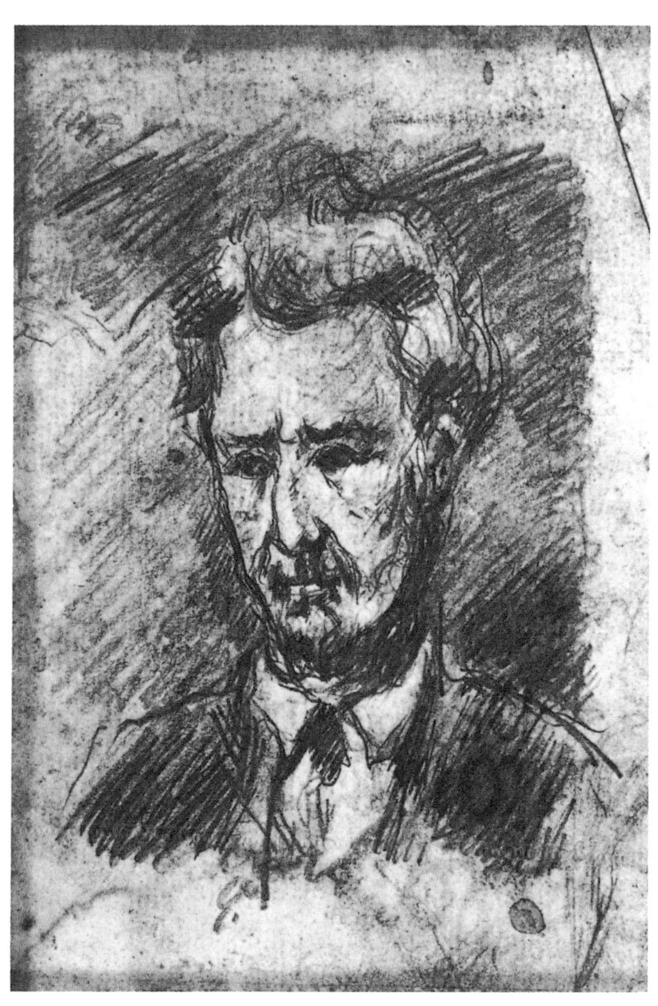

81. *Family in a Garden with Portrait of Victor Chocquet*, 1870–73.
Pencil, 25 × 21 cm (9⅞ × 8¼ in.).
Kunstmuseum Basel

82. *Victor Chocquet, c. 1872*.
Pencil, 14 × 10 cm (5½ × 3⅞ in.).
Private collection

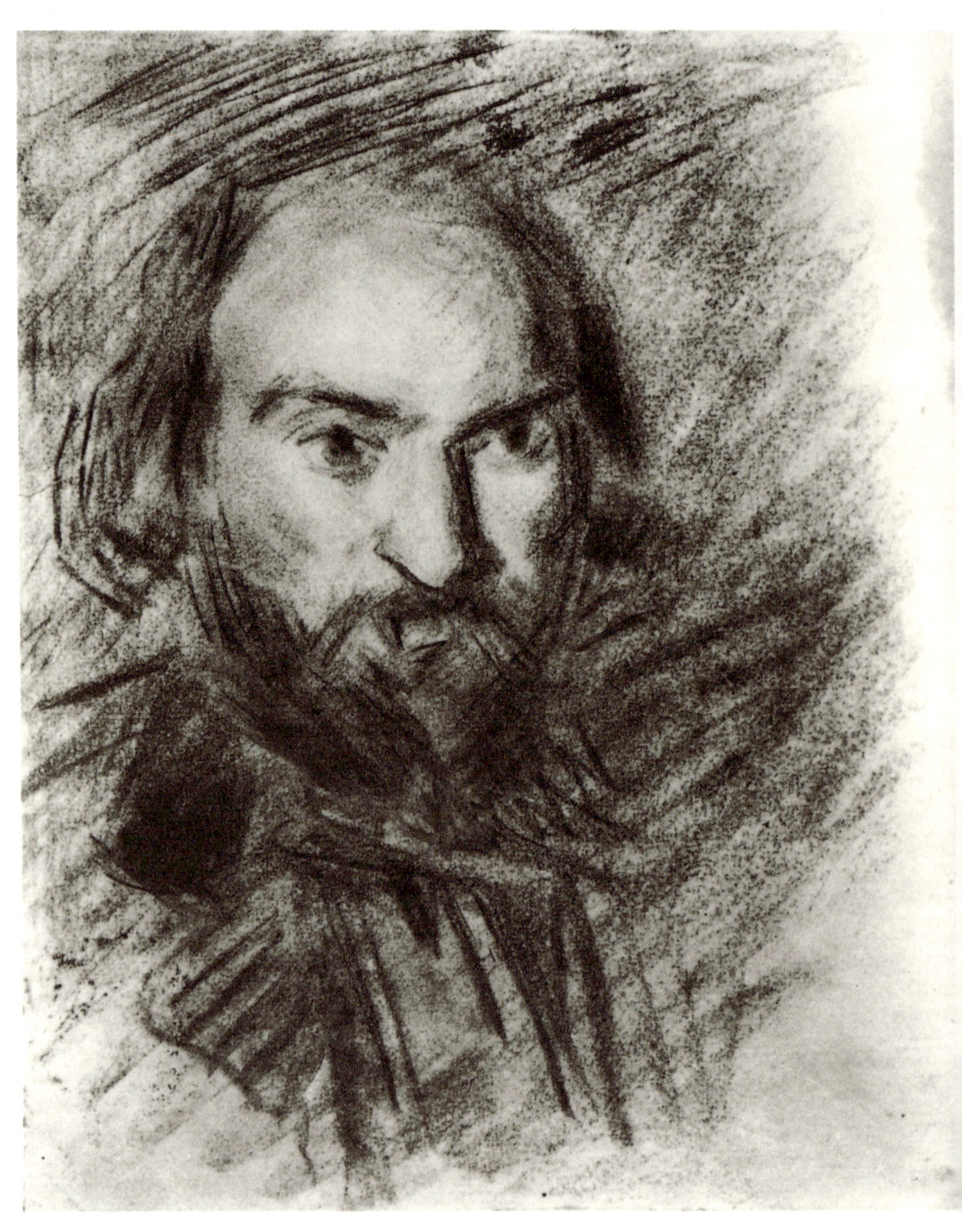

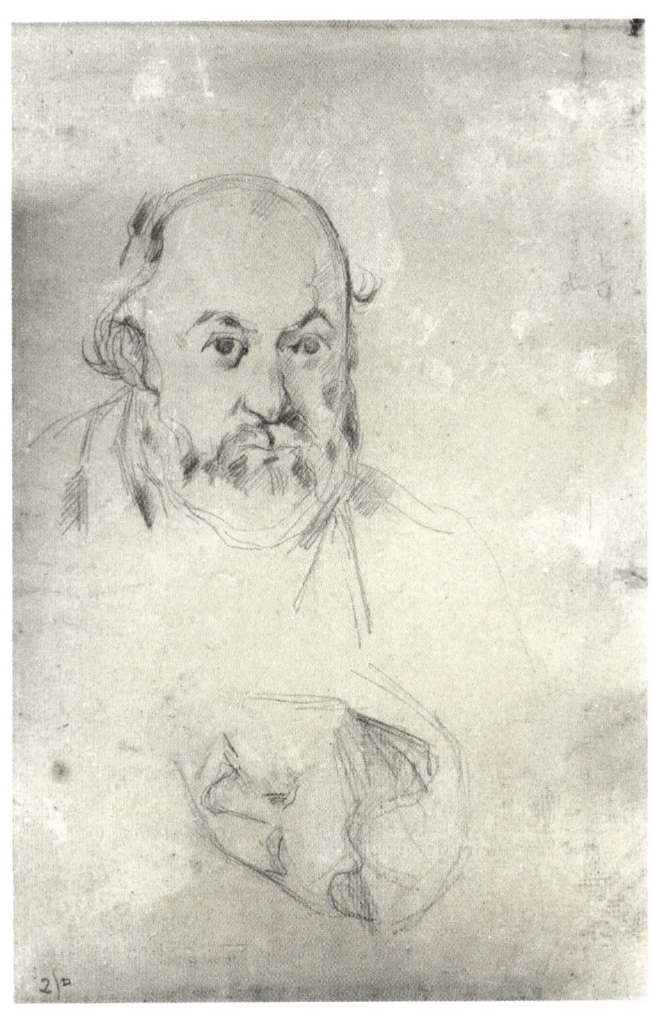

OPPOSITE

83. *Self-Portrait, c.* 1875.
Charcoal heightened with white chalk, 30.2 × 24 cm (11⅞ × 9⅜ in.).
Private collection

ABOVE

84. *Self-Portrait, c.* 1880.
Pencil on beige paper, 30.4 × 20.5 cm (12 × 8⅛ in.).
Kunstmuseum Basel

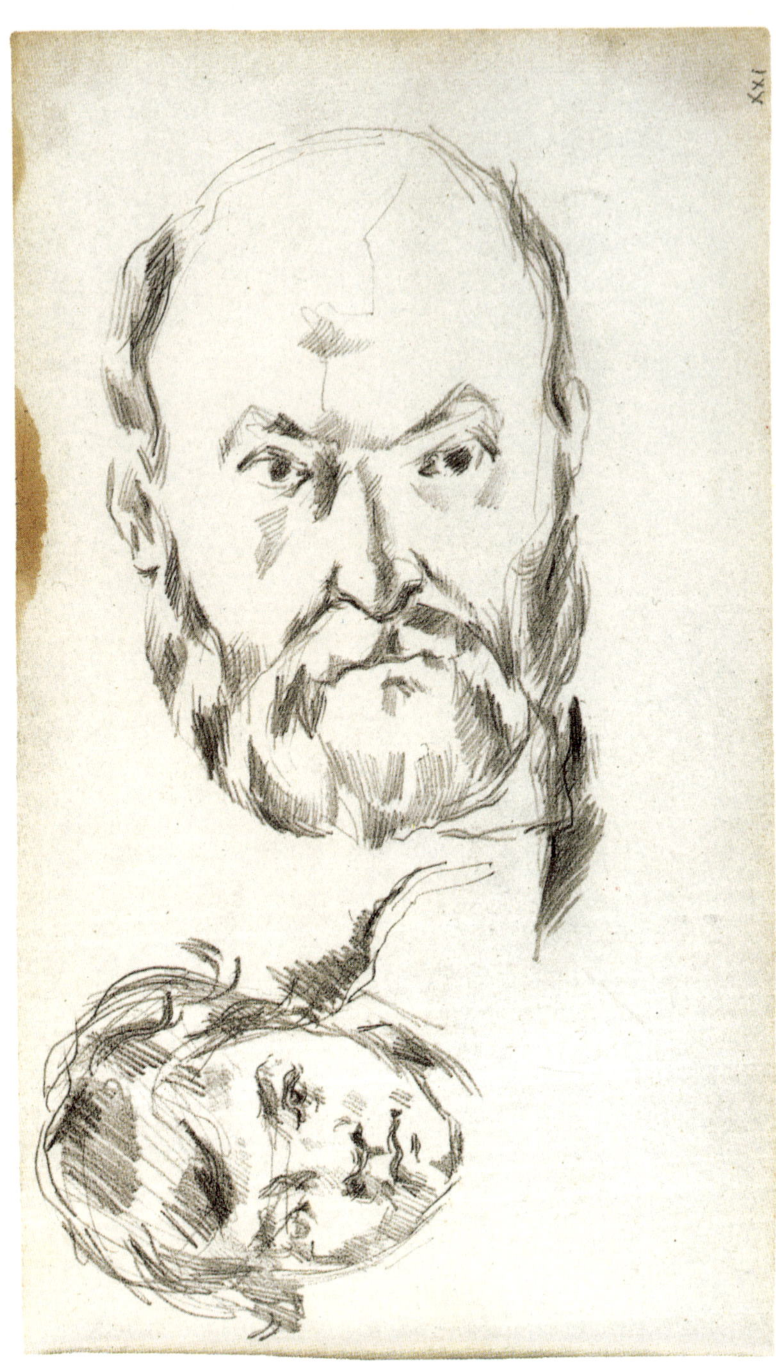

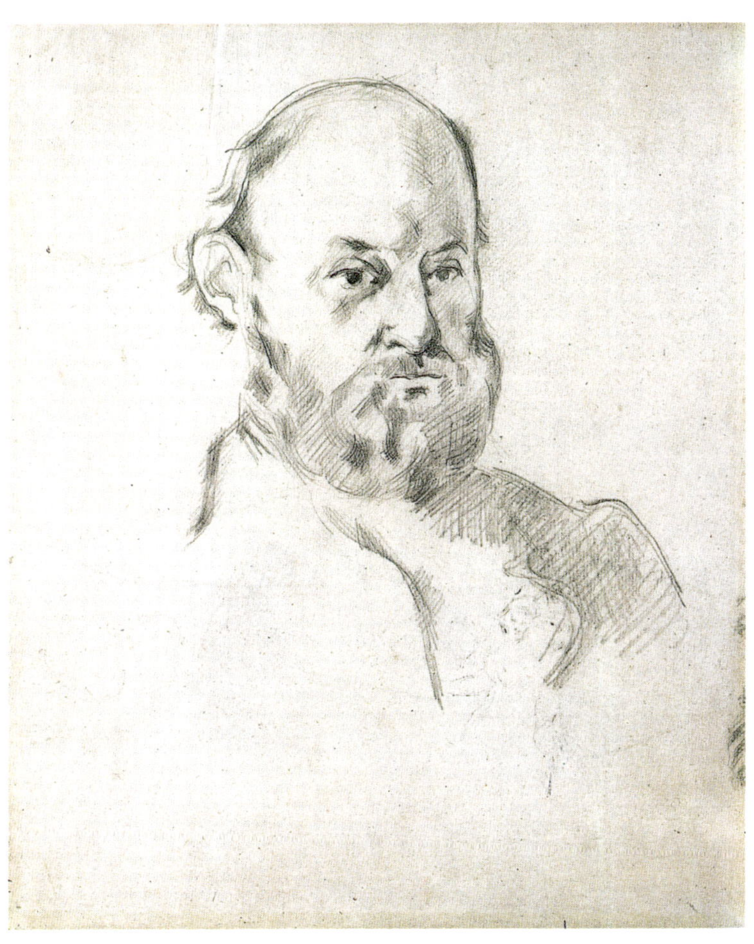

OPPOSITE
85. *Self-Portrait*, c. 1878–82.
Pencil, 21.7 × 12.4 cm (8½ × 4⅞ in.).
The Art Institute of Chicago

ABOVE
86. *Self-Portrait*, c. 1880.
Pencil, 30 × 25 cm (11⅞ × 9⅞ in.).
Museum of Fine Arts, Budapest

87. *Self-Portrait, c.* 1895.
Pencil and watercolour, 28.2 × 25.7 cm (11¼ × 10⅛ in.).
Private collection

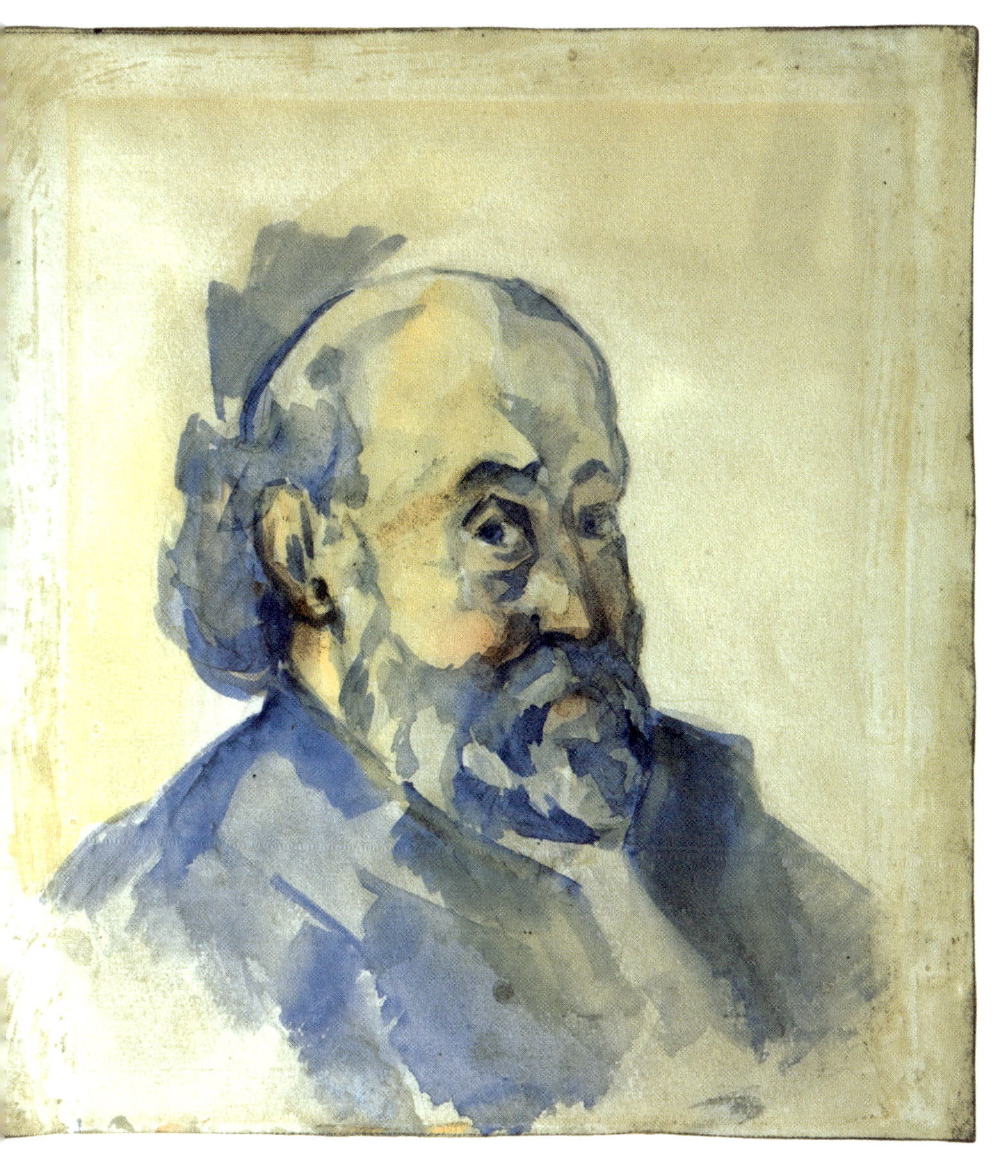

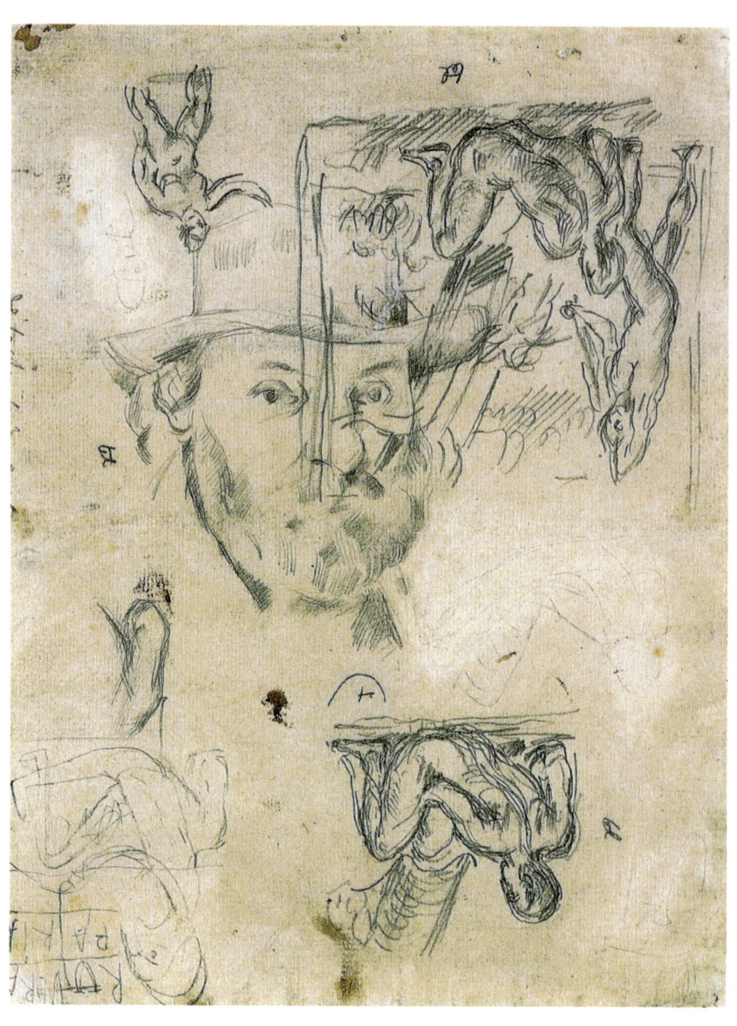

ABOVE
88. *Page of Studies with Self-Portrait*, c. 1875–78.
Pencil, 30 × 23 cm (11⅞ × 9 in.).
Metropolitan Museum of Art, New York

OPPOSITE
89. *Page of Studies with Self-Portrait*, 1881–82.
Pencil and black chalk, 48.5 × 32 cm (19⅛ × 12⅝ in.).
Museum Boijmans Van Beuningen, Rotterdam

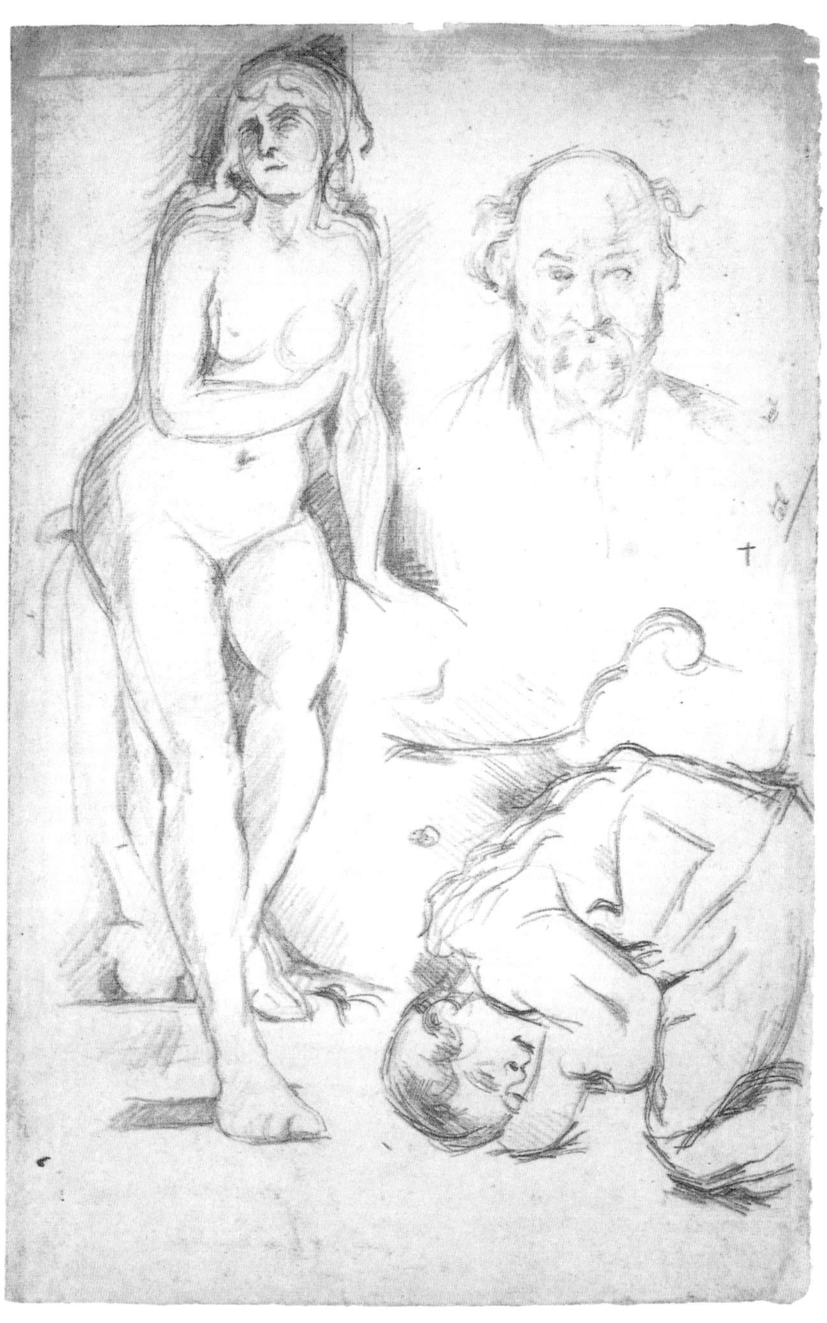

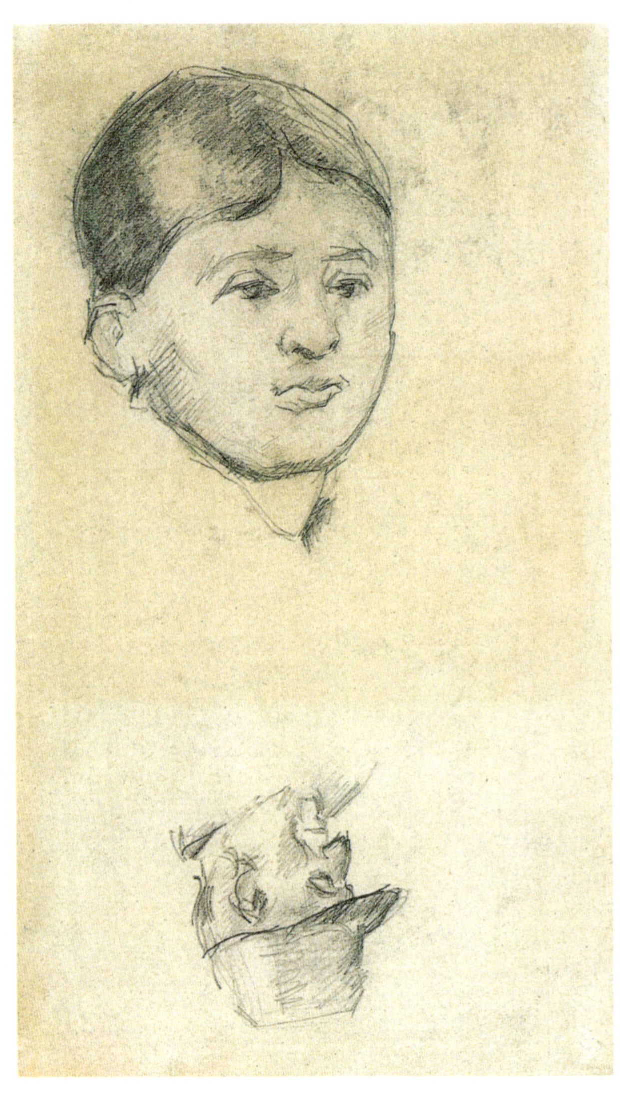

90. *Madame Cézanne with Head of Louis-Auguste Cézanne, c. 1878–81.*
Pencil, 21.4 × 12.5 cm (8⅜ × 4⅞ in.).
Fogg Museum, Cambridge, Massachusetts

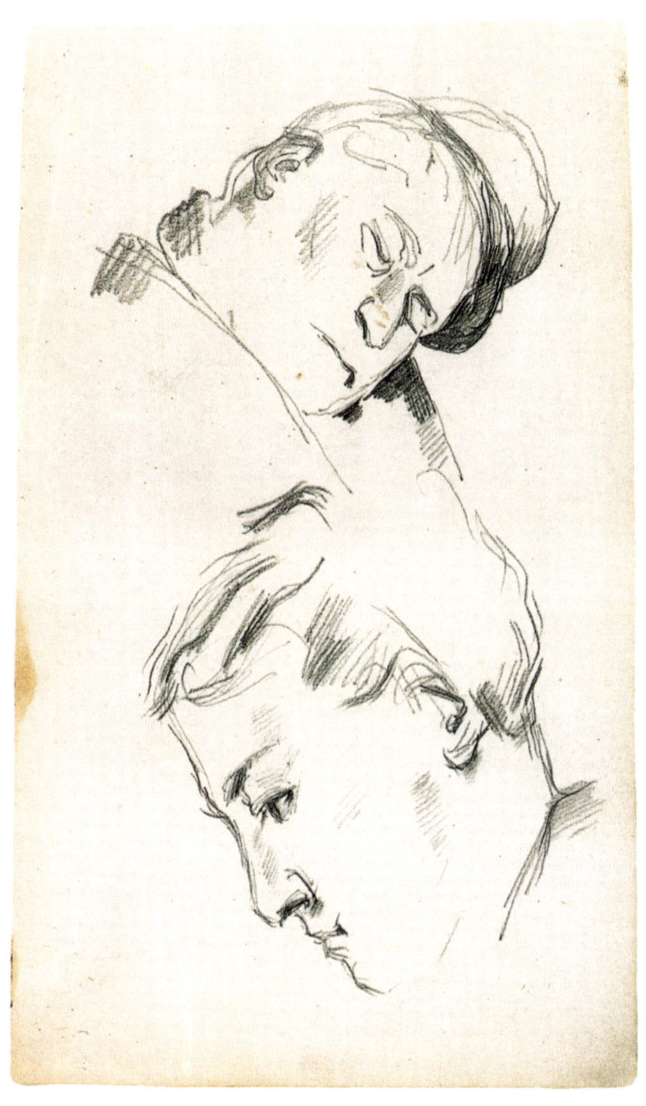

91. *Louis-Auguste Cézanne and Head of a Female*
[probably Madame Cézanne], *c.* 1882–85.
Pencil, 21 × 12 cm (8¼ × 4⅞ in.).
The Art Institute of Chicago

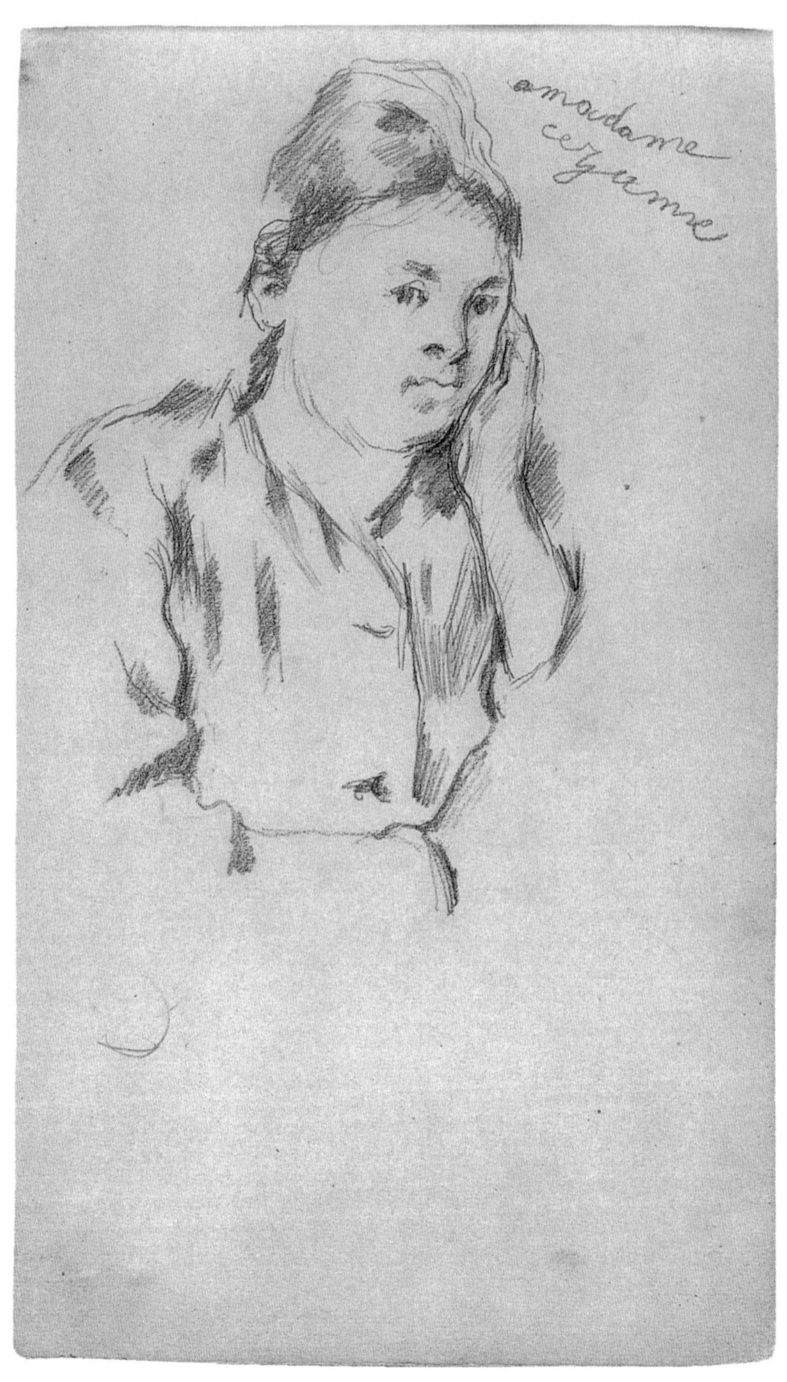

a madame
cézanne

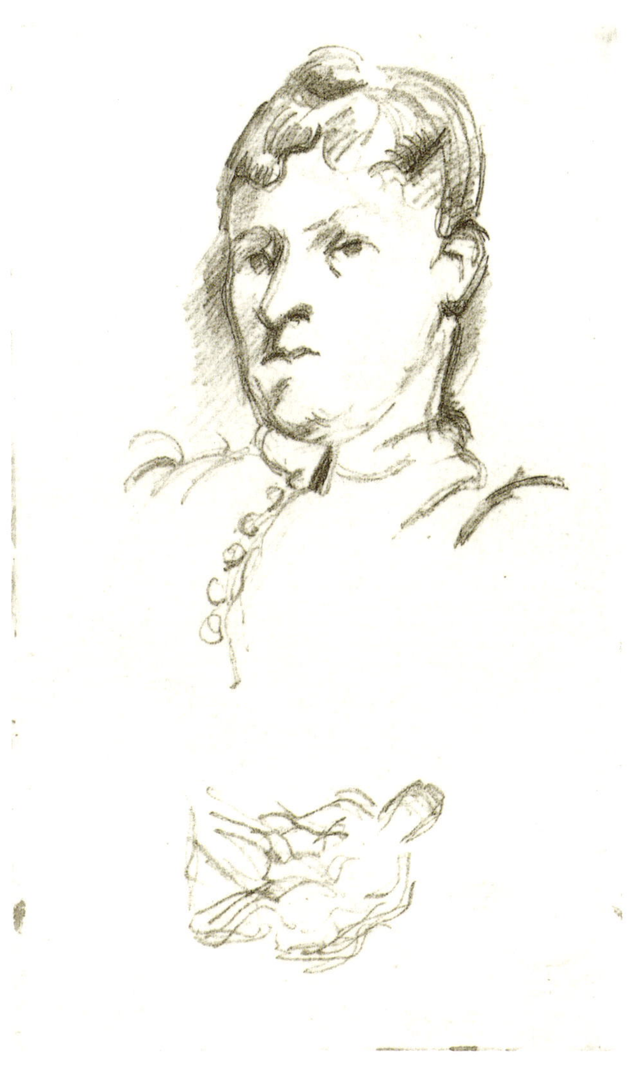

OPPOSITE
92. *Madame Cézanne*, c. 1865.
Pencil [inscribed by another hand], 21 × 12 cm (8¼ × 4¾ in.).
The Art Institute of Chicago

ABOVE
93. *Madame Cézanne*, c. 1887–90.
Pencil, 20.6 × 12.6 cm (8⅛ × 5 in.).
Kunstmuseum Basel

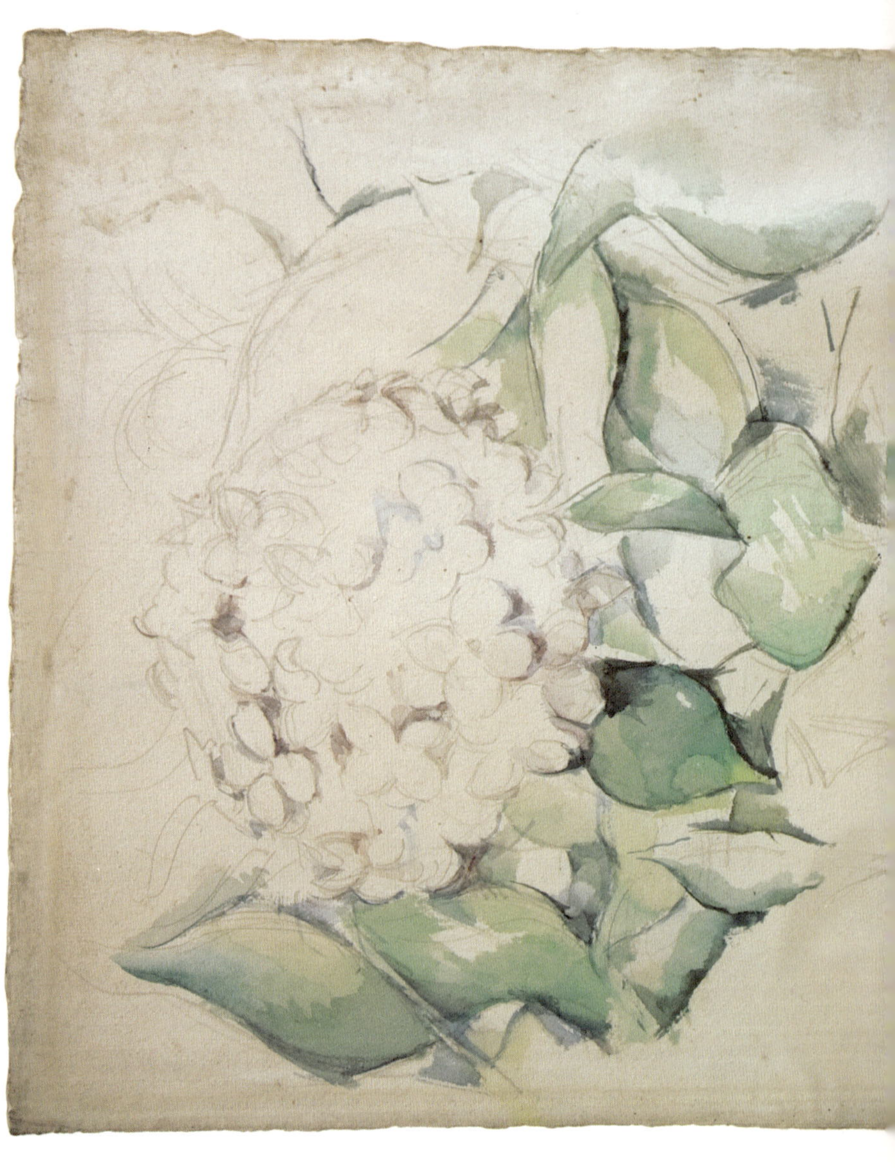

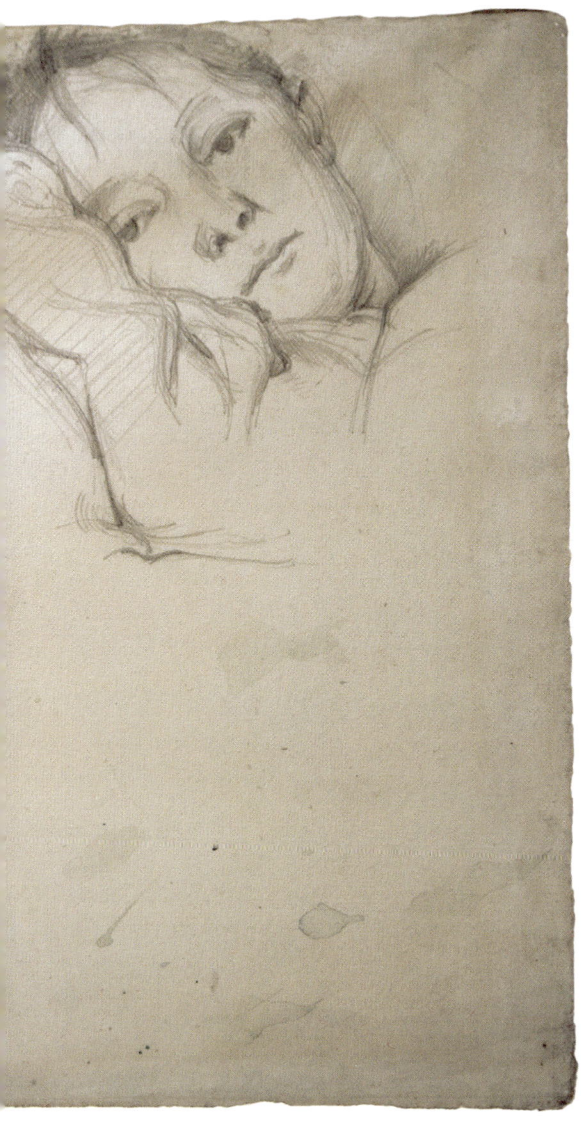

94. *Madame Cézanne
with Hortensias, c.* 1885.
Pencil and watercolour,
30.5 × 46 cm (12 × 18⅛ in.).
Private collection

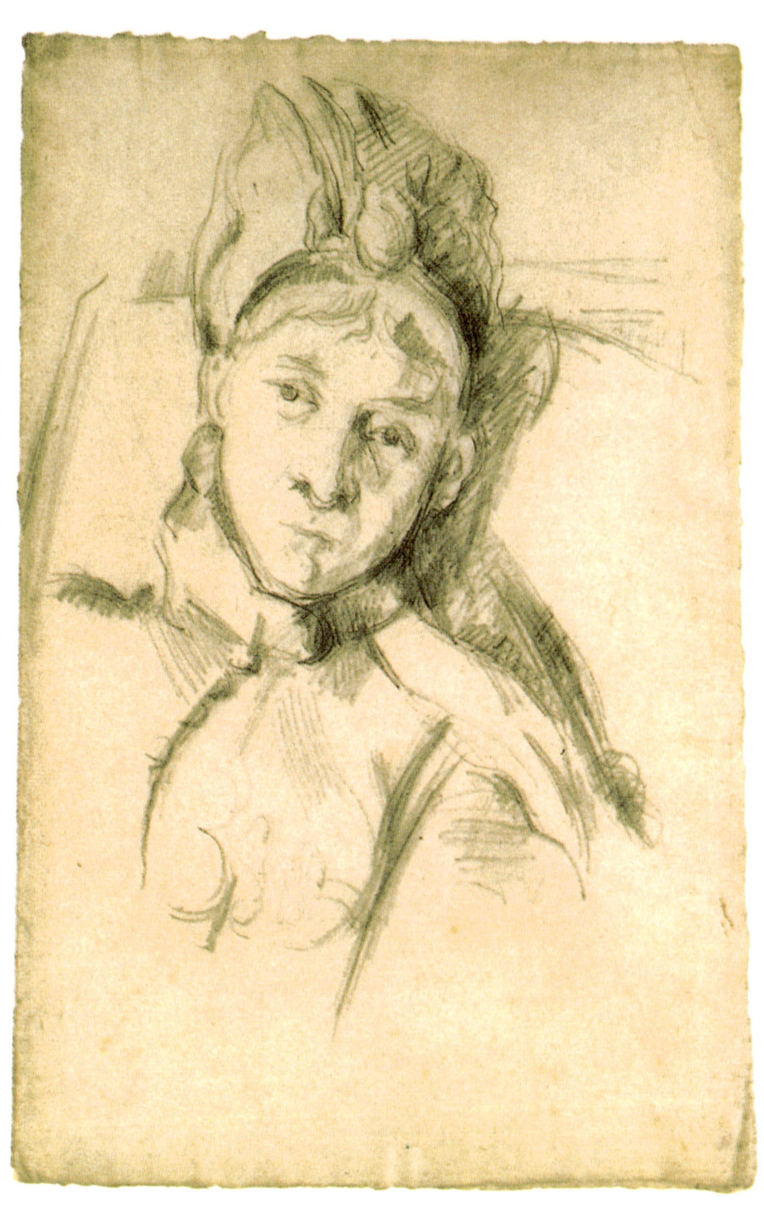

95. *Madame Cézanne, c.* 1887–90.
Pencil, 48.5 × 32.2 cm (19⅛ × 12⅝ in.).
Museum Boijmans Van Beuningen, Rotterdam

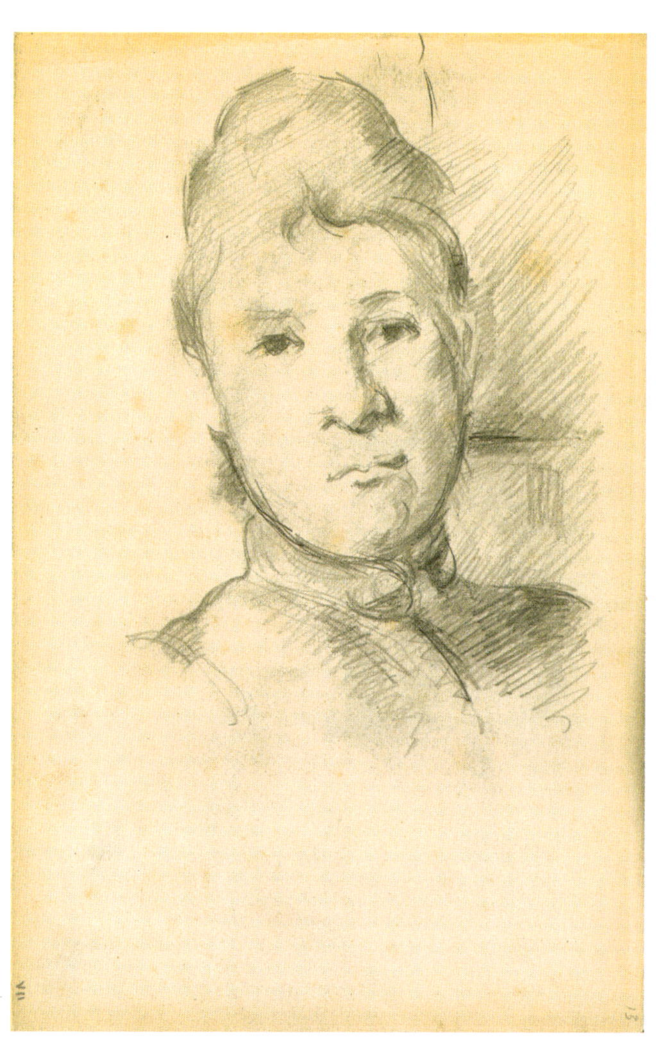

96. *Madame Cézanne, c. 1891–92.*
Pencil, 23.7 × 15.2 cm (9⅜ × 6 in.).
National Gallery of Art, Washington, DC

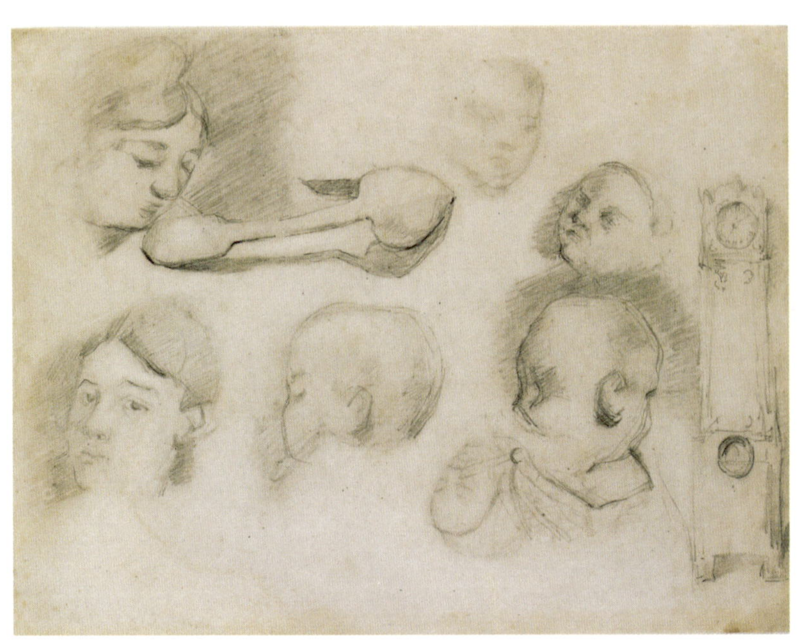

97. *Page of Studies with Head of a Child,
a Woman's Head, a Spoon and a Long Clock*, 1872.
Pencil with touches of black crayon,
23.8 × 31.4 cm (9⅜ × 12⅜ in.).
Ashmolean Museum, Oxford

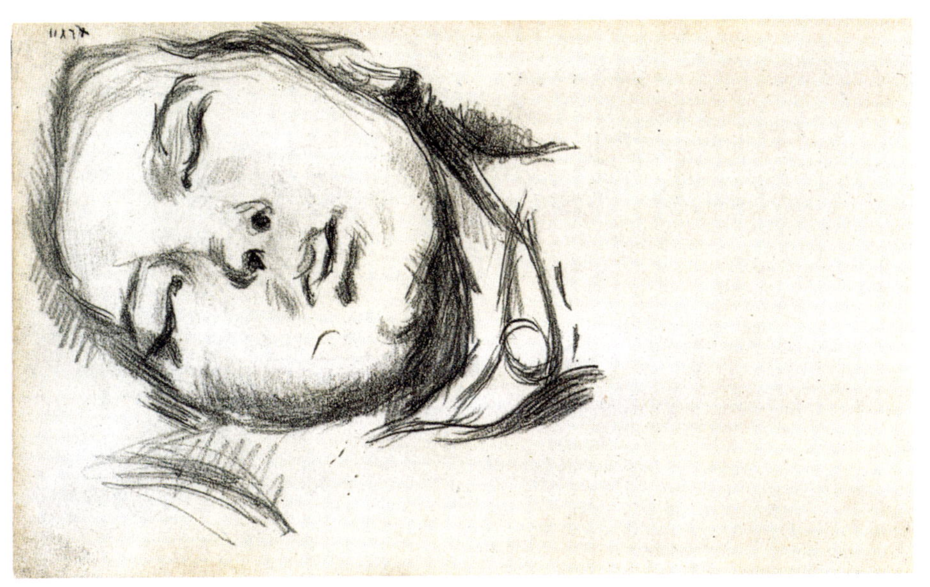

98. *The Artist's Son Asleep*, c. 1875–76.
Pencil, 12 × 21 cm (4¼ × 8¼ in.).
The Art Institute of Chicago

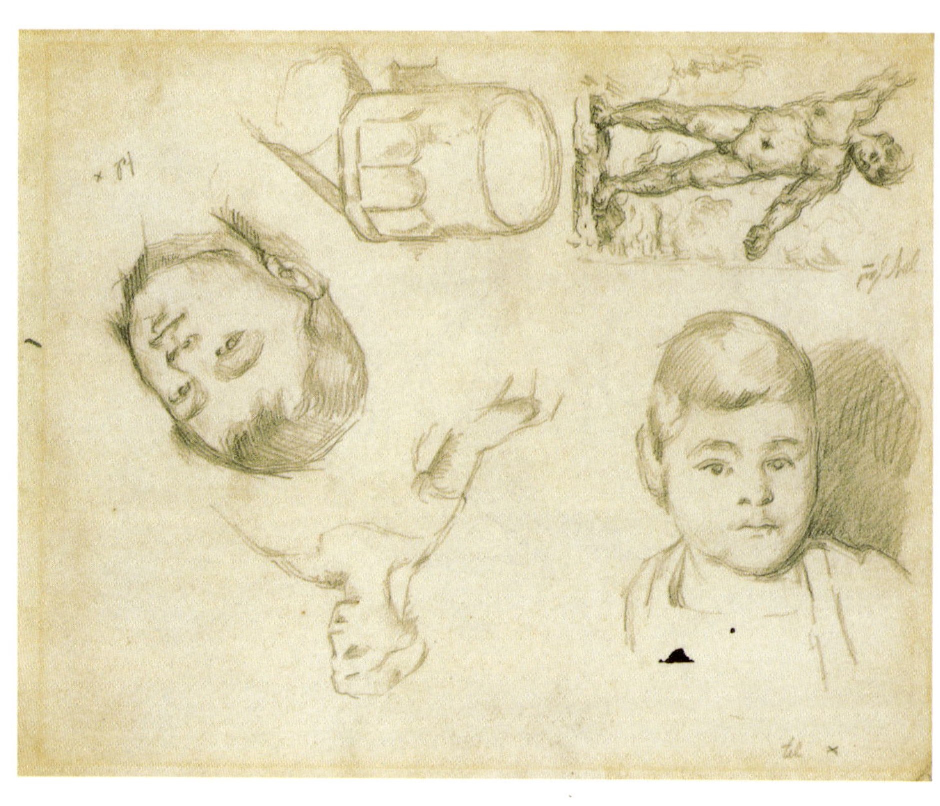

99. *Page of Studies with Portraits of the Artist's Son, c.* 1878.
Pencil, 24.8 × 30.8 cm (9¾ × 12⅛ in.).
Albertina, Vienna

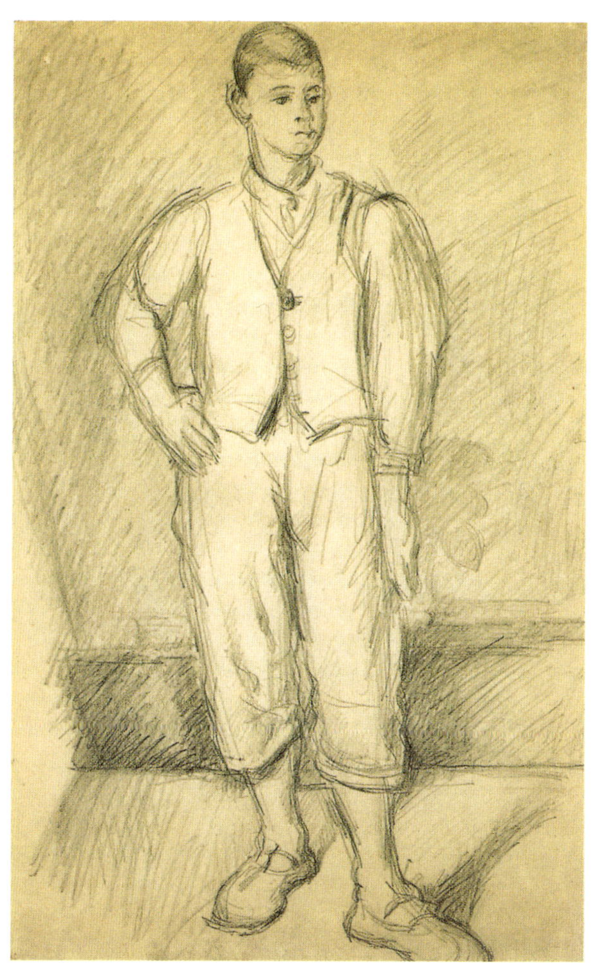

100. *The Artist's Son, c. 1885.*
Pencil, 50.2 × 31.7 cm (19¾ × 12½ in.).
Private collection

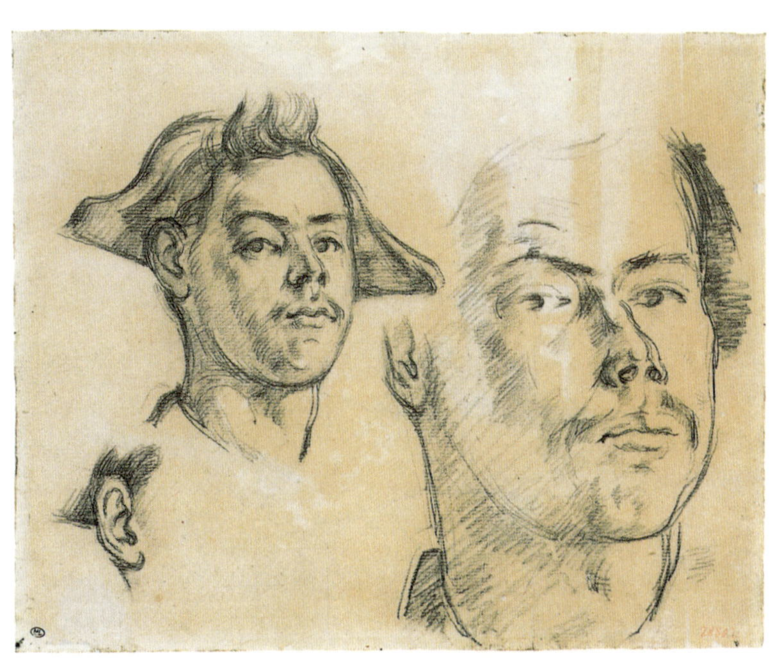

101. *Studies for 'Mardi Gras', c.* 1888.
Pencil with highlights in white chalk, 24.5 × 30.6 cm (9⅝ × 12 in.).
Musée du Louvre, Paris

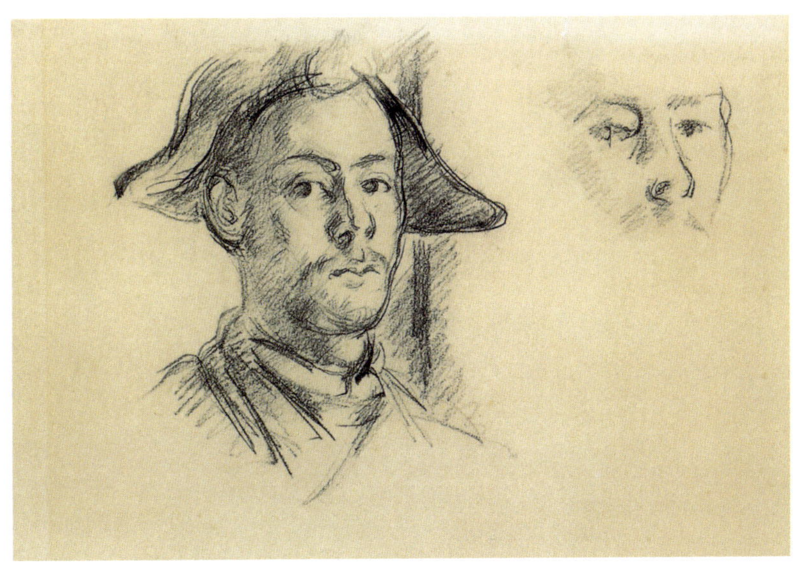

102. *Studies for 'Mardi Gras'*, *c.* 1888.
Pencil, 20.1 × 27.2 cm (7⅞ × 10¼ in.).
Kunstmuseum Basel

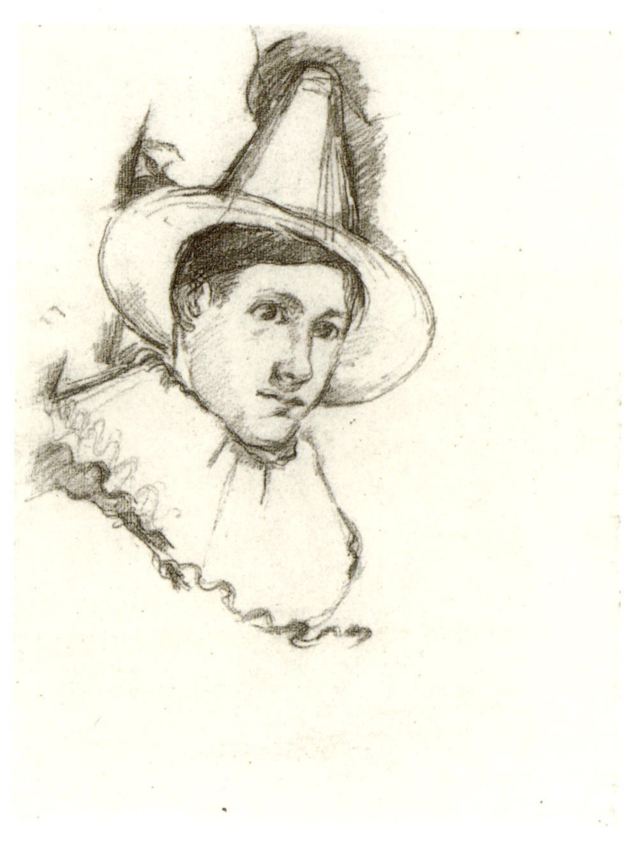

103. *Louis Guillaume in Pierrot Costume, c.* 1888.
Pencil, 31.4 × 24.3 cm (12⅛ × 9½ in.).
Kunstmuseum Basel

OPPOSITE

104. *Harlequin, c.* 1888.
Pencil, 47.3 × 30.9 cm (18⅝ × 12⅛ in.).
The Art Institute of Chicago

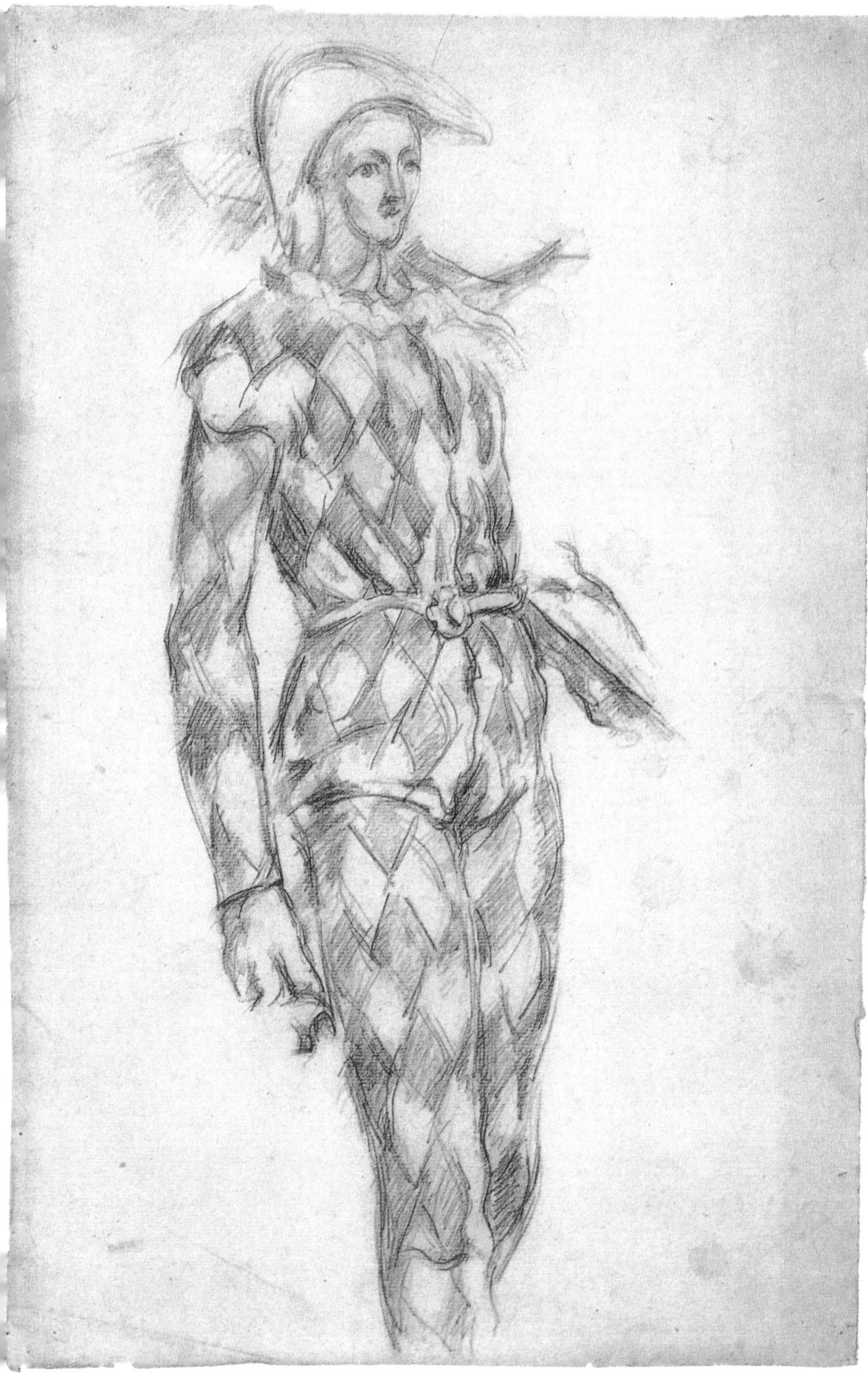

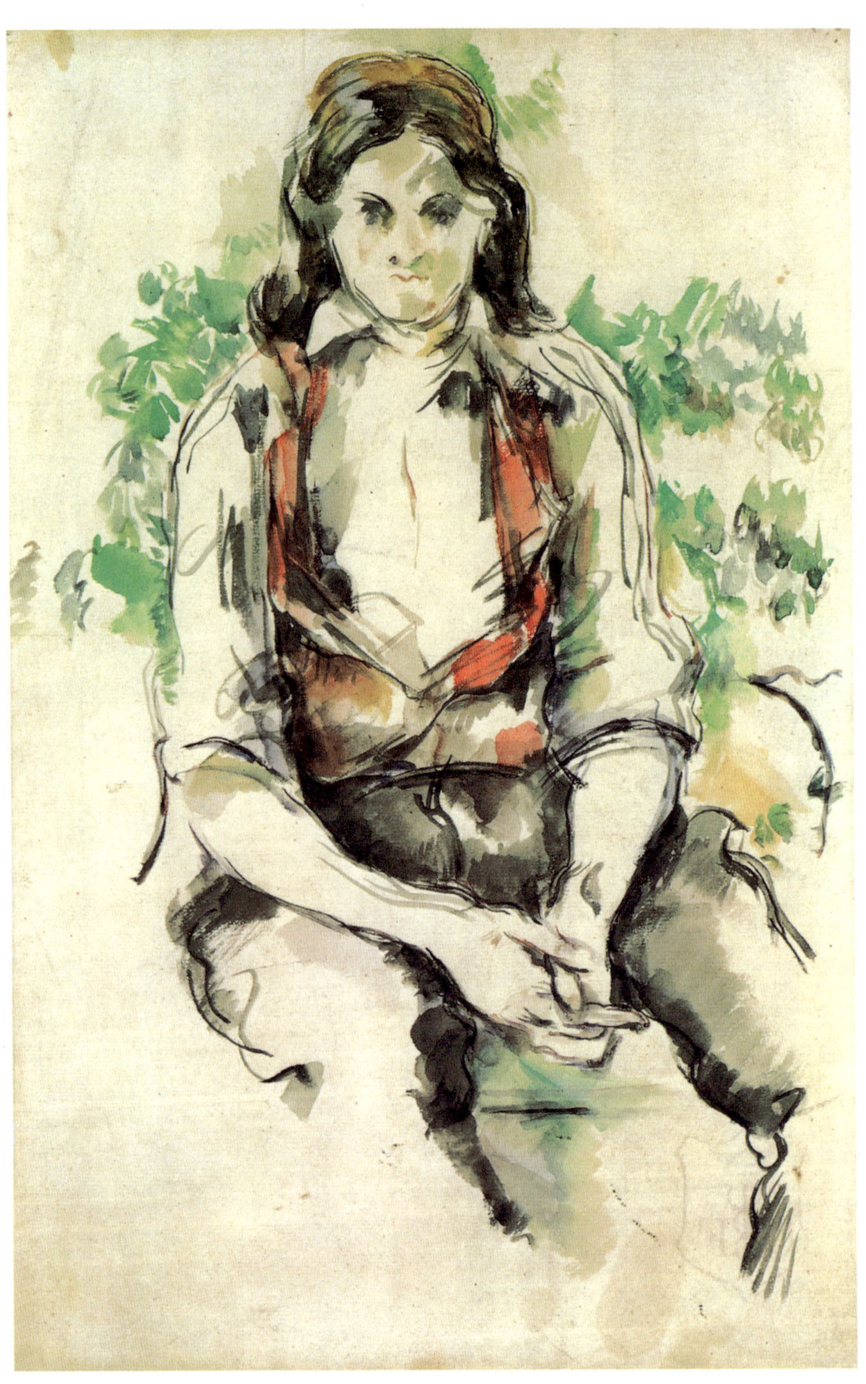

158   *Portraying the Individual*

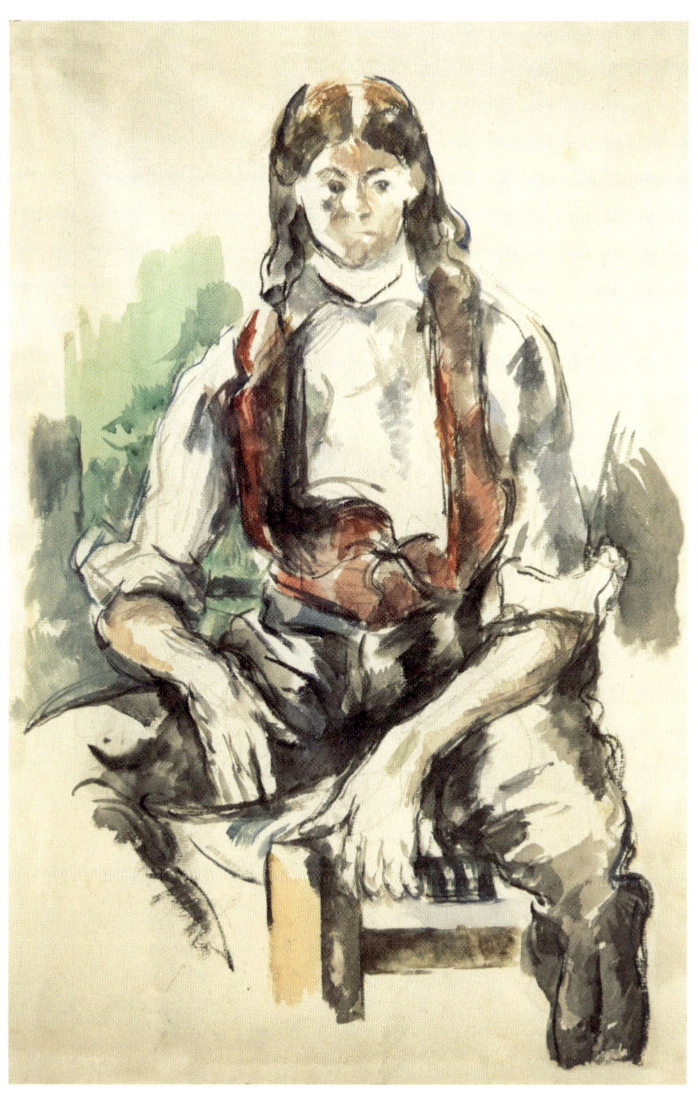

OPPOSITE
105. *Boy in a Red Waistcoat*, 1889–90.
Watercolour, 46.5 × 31 cm (18½ × 12¼ in.).
Private collection

ABOVE
106. *Boy in a Red Waistcoat*, 1889–90.
Pencil and watercolour, 46 × 31 cm (18⅛ × 12¼ in.).
Private collection

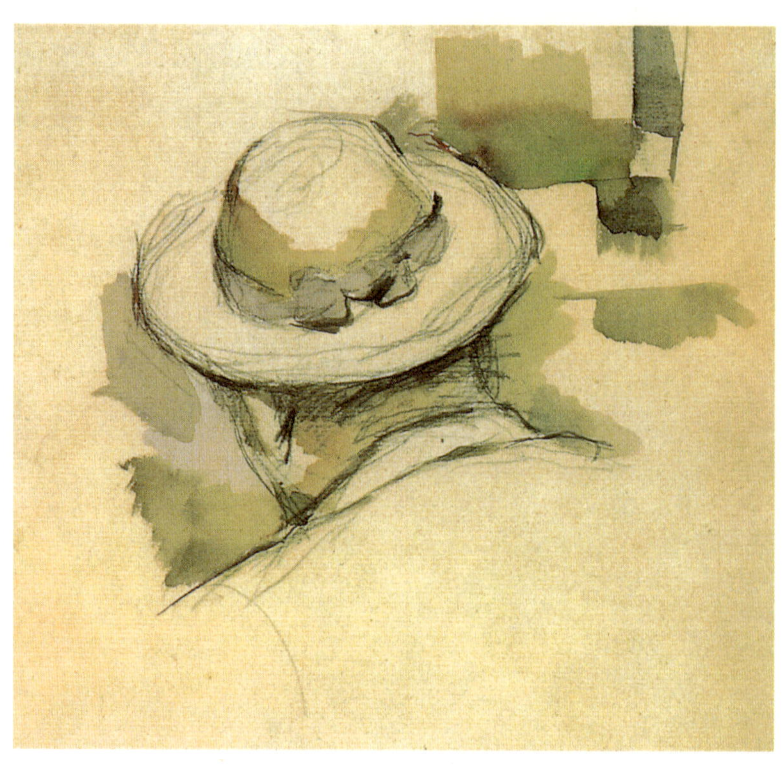

107. *Man Wearing a Hat Seen from the Back, c.* 1880.
Pencil and watercolour, 27 × 31 cm (10⅝ × 12¼ in.).
Private collection

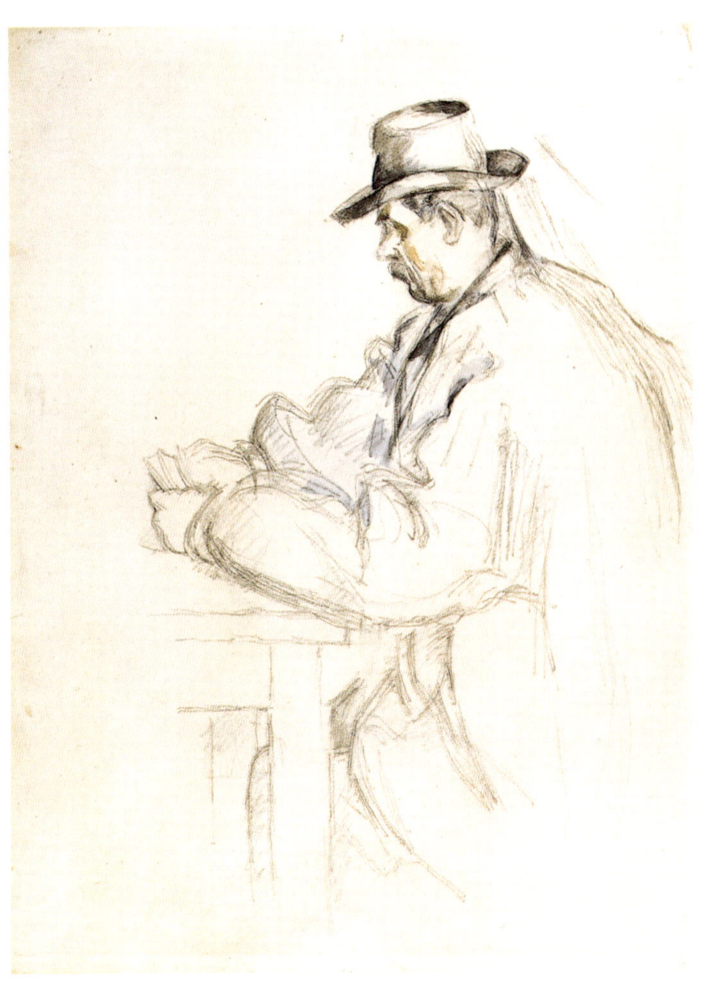

108. *Card Player in a Blue Smock*, 1890–92.
Pencil and watercolour, 51.4 × 37 cm (20¼ × 14½ in.).
Museum of Art, Rhode Island School of Design, Providence

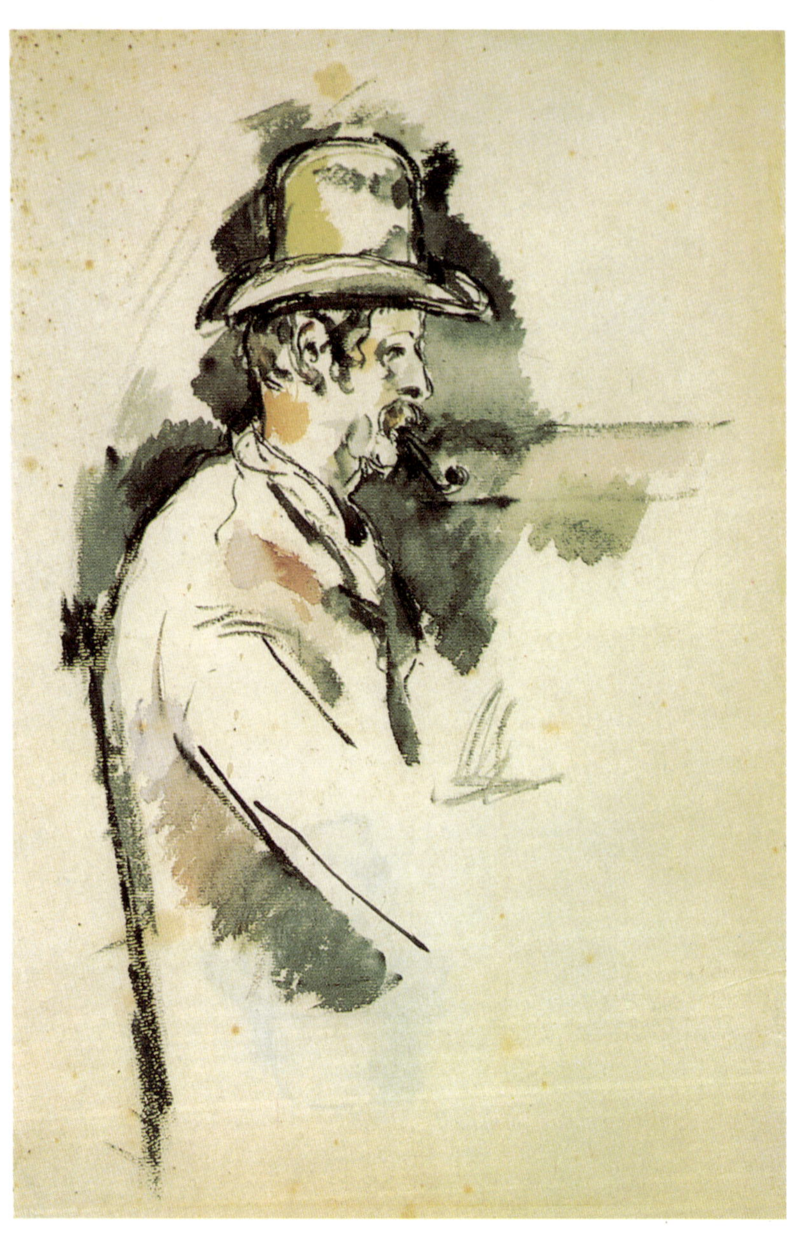

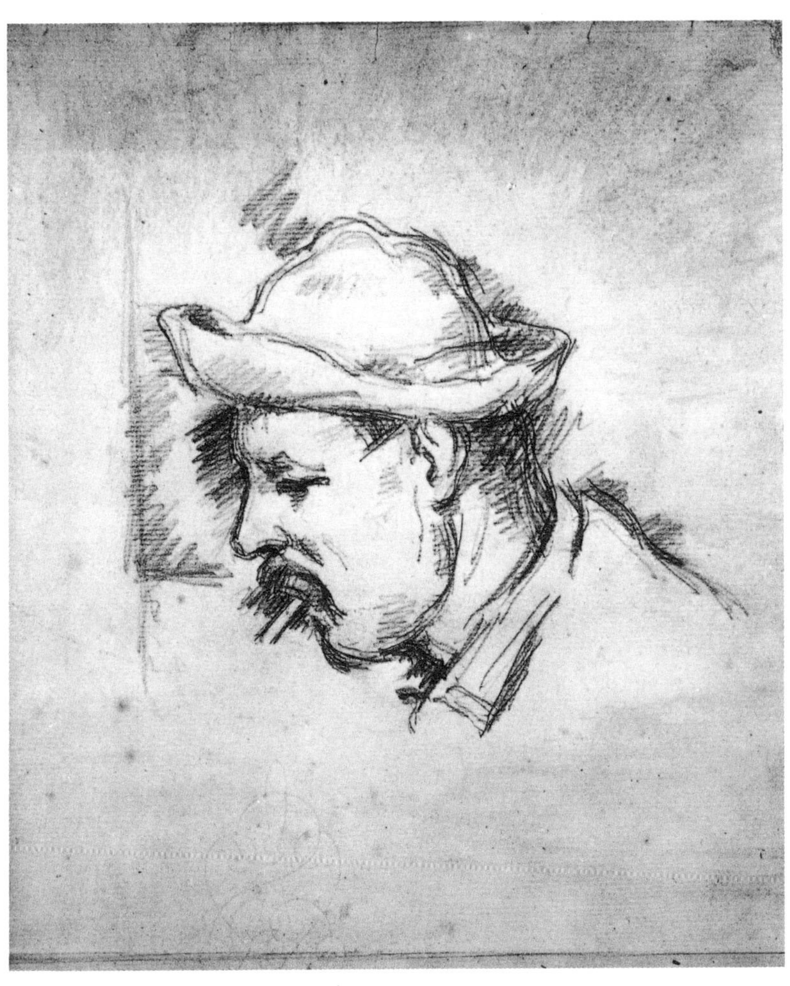

OPPOSITE
109. *Man Smoking a Pipe*, 1892–96.
Watercolour, 51 × 32 cm (20⅛ × 12⅝ in.).
Private collection

ABOVE
110. *Man Smoking*, 1892–96.
Pencil, 50.8 × 31.9 cm (20 × 12½ in.) [whole page].
Museum Boijmans Van Beuningen, Rotterdam

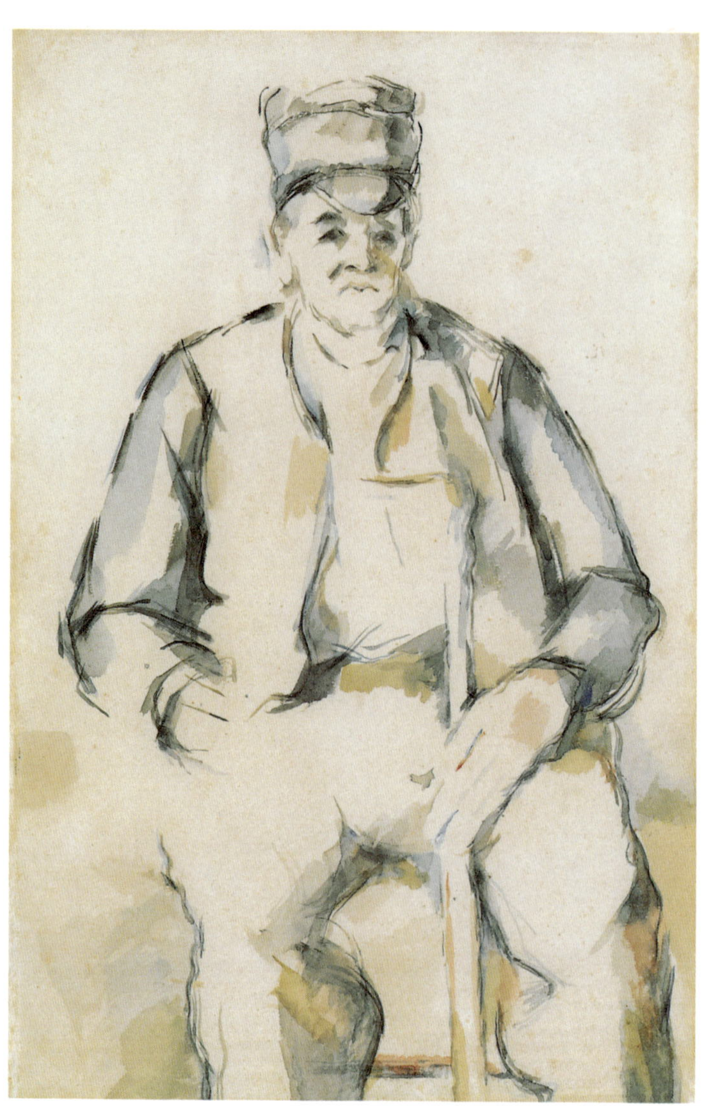

III. *Seated Peasant*, c. 1900.
Watercolour, 45.8 × 31 cm (18 × 12¼ in.).
Kunsthaus Zurich

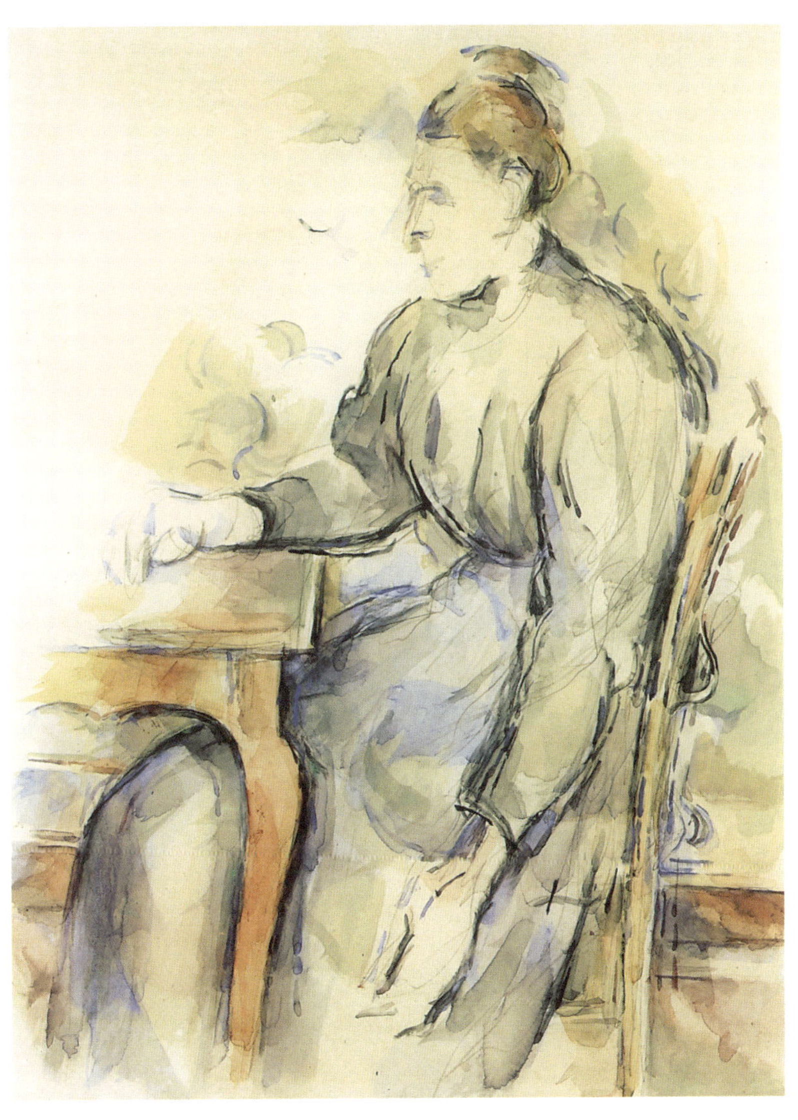

112. *Seated Woman*, 1902–04.
Pencil and watercolour, 49 × 37.2 cm (19¼ × 14⅝ in.).
Private collection

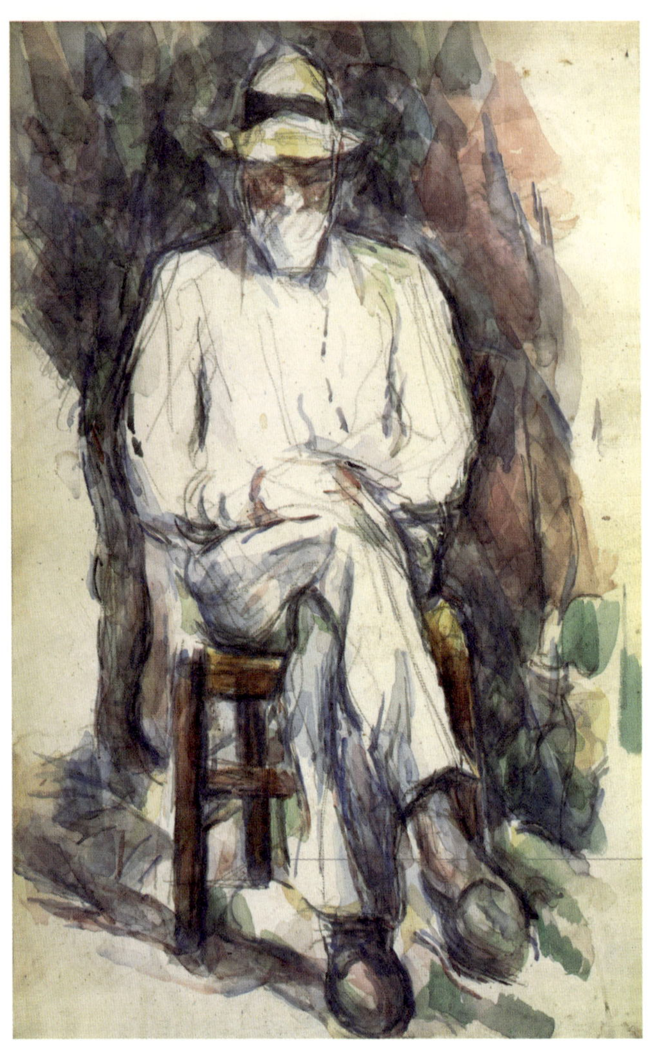

113. *The Gardener Vallier, c.* 1906.
Pencil and watercolour, 48 × 31.5 cm (18⅞ × 12⅜ in.).
Museum Berggruen, Berlin

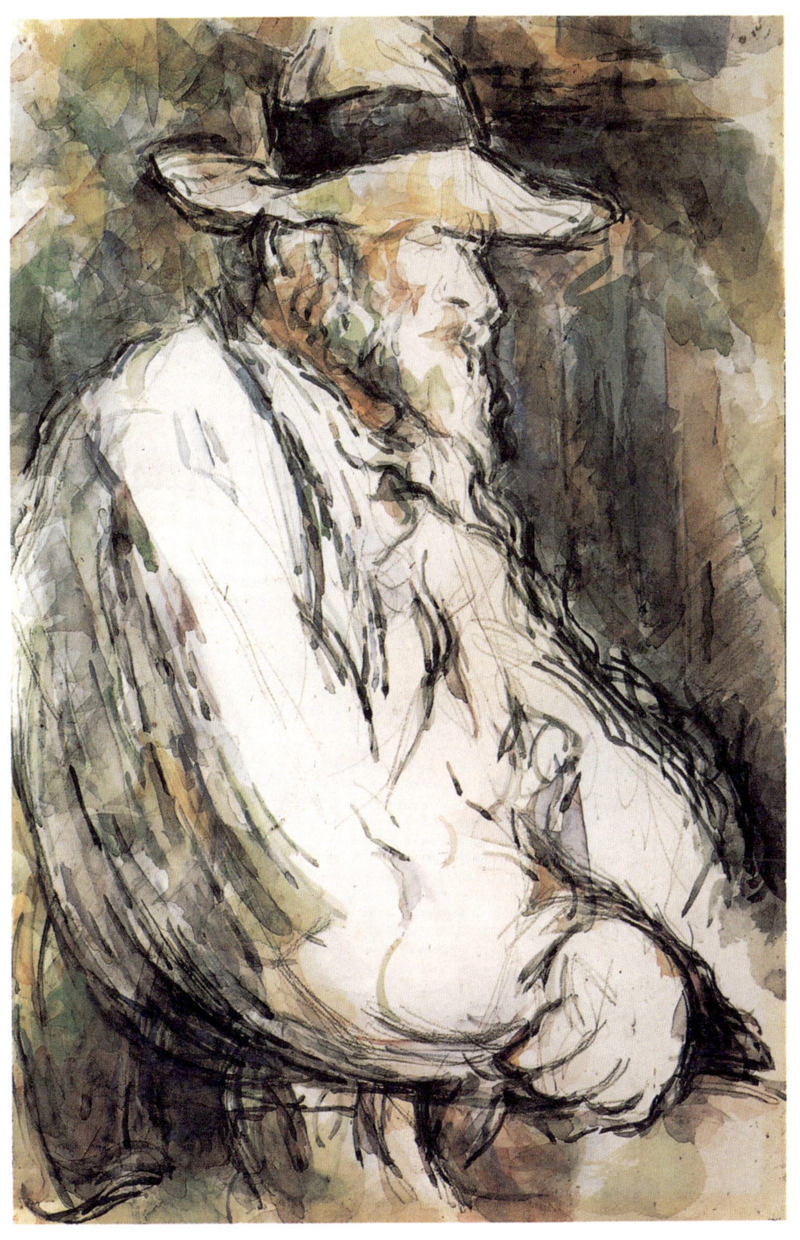

114. *The Gardener Vallier in Profile*, 1906.
Pencil and watercolour, 48 × 32 cm (18⅞ × 12⅝ in.).
Private collection

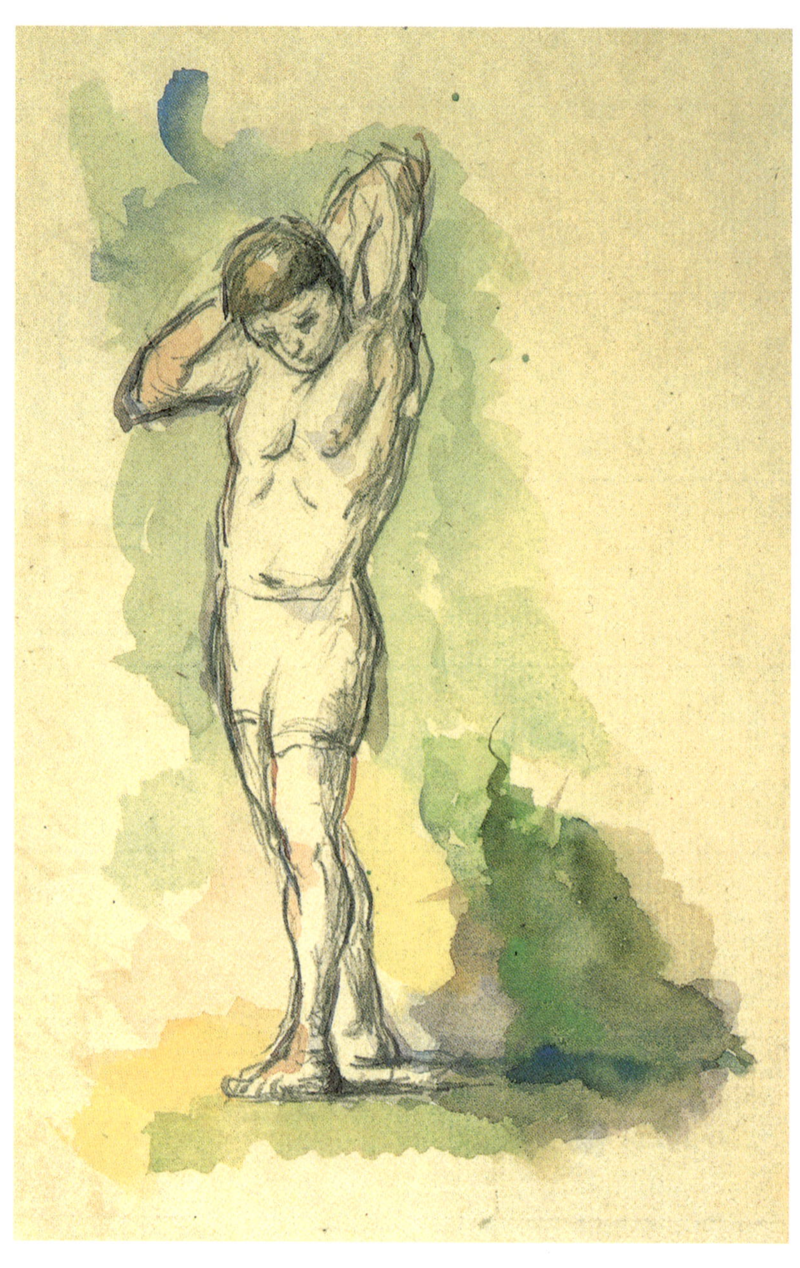

115. *Standing Male Bather with Arms Raised behind his Neck, c.* 1880.
Pencil and watercolour, 29.7 × 25.1 cm (11¾ × 9⅞ in.).
Albertina, Vienna

CHAPTER FOUR

In Pursuit of the Human Figure

'Q. What leisure activity do you enjoy most?
A. Swimming.' Paul Cézanne

Cézanne's interest in the human figure as a subject found its fullest expression in his paintings of bathers. His earliest attempts at such compositions date from the mid-1870s and culminate in the three large-scale versions known as *The Large Bathers*, now divided between Philadelphia (Barnes Foundation and Philadelphia Museum of Art) and London (National Gallery), that preoccupied him from the mid-1890s until the end of his life. It is widely believed that *The Large Bathers* in the Barnes Foundation was begun first (*c.* 1895) and was followed by the version in London before concluding in 1906 with the painting in the Philadelphia Museum of Art. Cézanne painted and drew numerous scenes of male and female bathers, but there can be no doubt that the compositions known as *The Large Bathers* are the most ambitious works he ever conceived, not only in terms of their scale, but also as feats of his imagination.

The significance of Cézanne's paintings of bathers can be measured by the role that they have played in the development of modern art. It is impossible to imagine, for instance, either *The Joy of Life* (1905–06) by Matisse or *Les Demoiselles d'Avignon* (1907) by Picasso being painted without the example of Cézanne – or, indeed, the many nudes that can be counted among the mature work of both these artists. Matisse, in fact, owned *The Three Bathers* (1879–82), which he acquired in 1899 from Vollard and gave to the Petit Palais (Musée des Beaux-Arts de la Ville de Paris) in 1936 [116]. At that time he wrote a covering letter to the curator, Raymond Escholier, expressing his 'admiration for this work, which has grown increasingly greater ever since I have owned it'. Matisse explained that the painting 'has sustained me morally in the critical moments of my venture as an artist; I have drawn from it my faith and my perseverance'. For the generation of Matisse, Derain, Picasso and

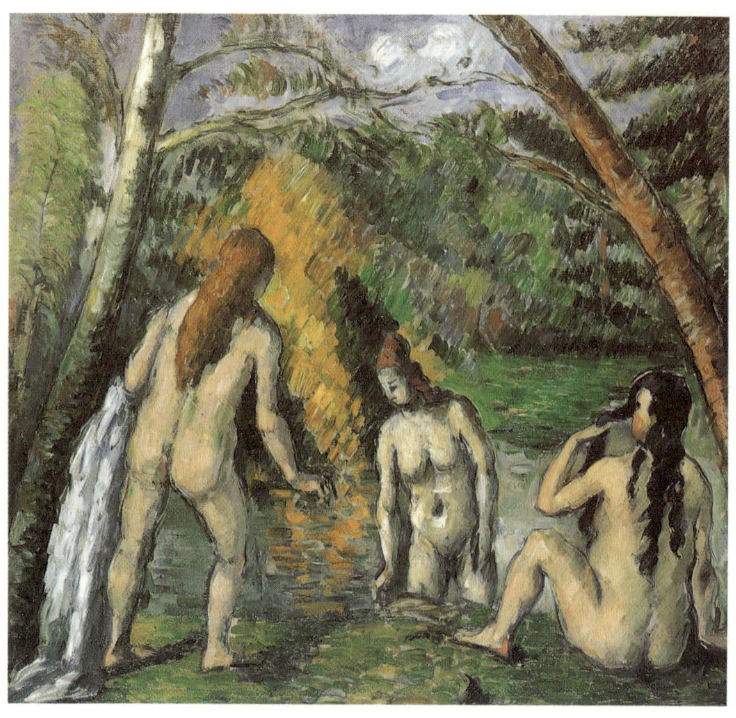

116. *The Three Bathers*, 1879–82.
Oil on canvas, 52 × 55 cm (20½ × 21⅝ in.).
Petit Palais, Musée des Beaux-Arts de la Ville de Paris

Braque, the exhibitions of Cézanne's work held at the Salon d'Automne, particularly the commemorative exhibition of 1907, were a revelation, just at the time when they were searching for ways in which to move art forward beyond Impressionism and Post-Impressionism.

Picasso's friendship with Matisse meant that he knew *The Three Bathers* well, but it was not until the late 1950s that he acquired his own version of the subject – *The Five Bathers* (1877–78), now in the Musée Picasso in Paris [117].

A decade later the sculptor Henry Moore also purchased one of Cézanne's scenes of bathers – the slightly earlier *Three Bathers* (c. 1875). This is looser in style, resembling a sketch in its technique, but the figures are no less monumental [118]. Indeed, their dance-like movements make them seem even more aggressively monumental, which is exactly what Moore admired about the picture. Accordingly, he was inspired to make both drawings and sculpted figurines after it, beginning with

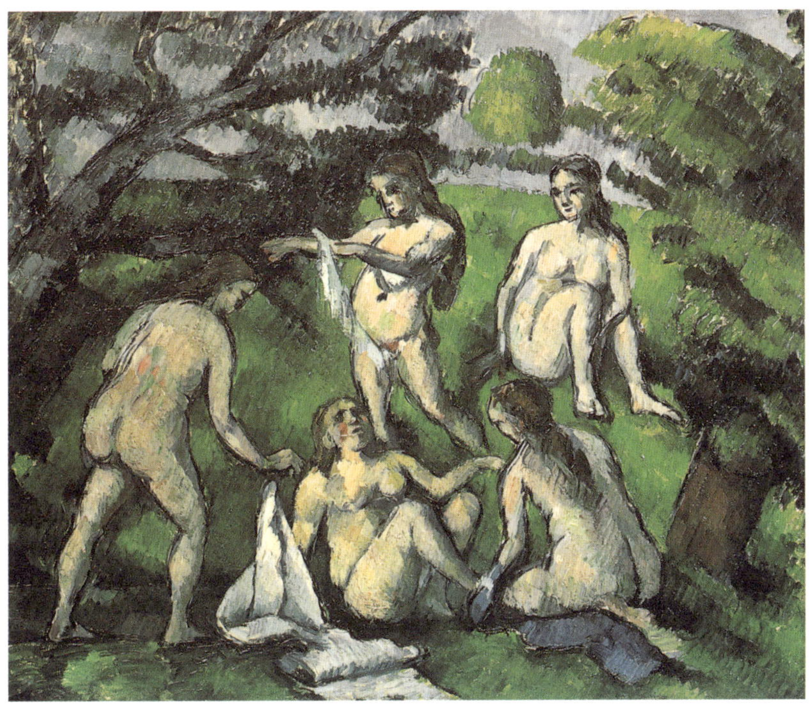

117. *The Five Bathers*, 1877–78.
Oil on canvas, 45.8 × 55.7 cm (18 × 21⅞ in.).
Musée Picasso, Paris

independent sculptures after the principal figures, which he could then
arrange in different positions. Later Moore united the sculpted figures
on a single base as Cézanne had arranged them. Moore's attraction to
the *Three Bathers* he owned stemmed from the exaggerated freedom
of Cézanne's style, which he thought reflected the painter's struggle to
devise a satisfactory composition and interpreted as being comparable
with the process of sculpture itself. He also appreciated Cézanne's honest
treatment of the female nude, combining matronly proportions with
romantic traits, such as the long tresses of hair.

The interest taken in Cézanne's bathers by Matisse, Picasso and
Moore reveals how protean his influence was even if it was only a passing
phase in the careers of each of these artists. Picasso spoke for them all
when much later he told the photographer Brassaï, '[Cézanne] was my
one and only master. It was the same with all of us – he was like our
father. It was he who protected us.'

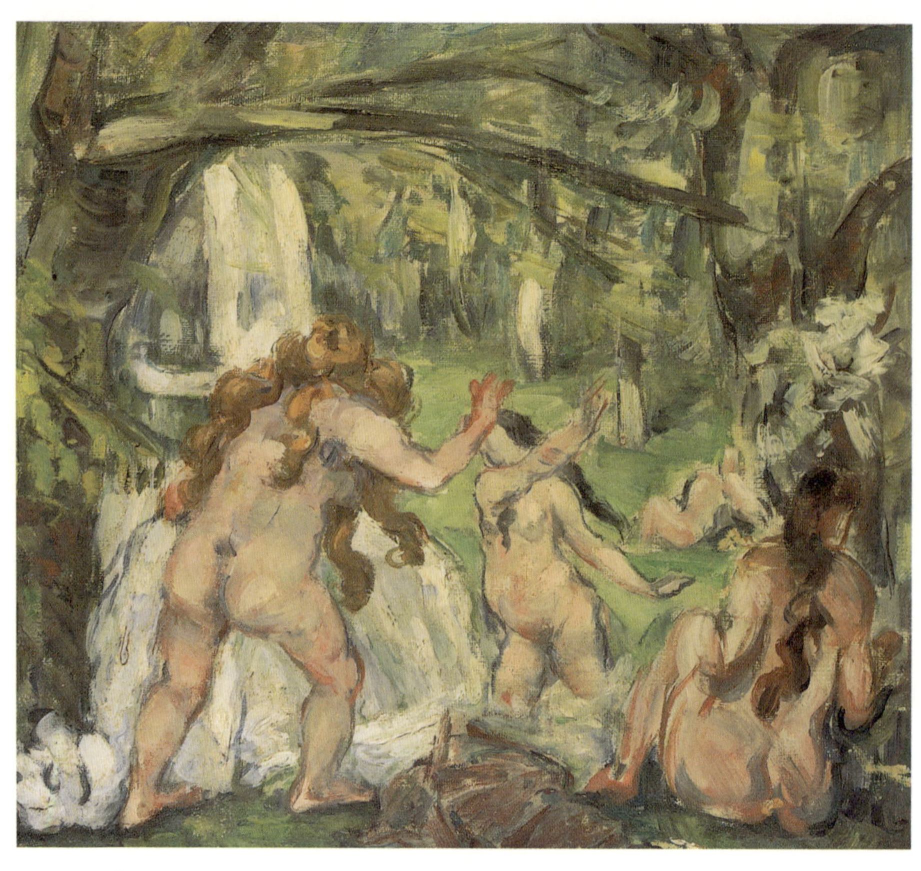

118. *Three Bathers, c.* 1875.
Oil on canvas, 28.8 × 31.2 cm (11⅛ × 12¼ in.).
Private collection

Cézanne's skill at depicting the human figure was apparent from an early stage during his attendance at the classes conducted by Joseph Gibert at the Ecole Spéciale et Gratuite de Dessin in Aix-en-Provence between 1857 and 1862. Here he learnt to draw from live models and antique sculpture according to academic principles with clear outlines and neatly demarcated passages of smooth, velvety hatching [125]. Such drawings were made for the purposes of gaining a better understanding of human anatomy and how the various parts of the body fitted together, as opposed to how they actually worked or moved. Cézanne was reluctant to repeat the experience when he went to Paris in 1861 and again in 1862, and so perhaps his failure to secure a place at the Ecole des Beaux-Arts was not too disappointing in this respect. Instead, he studied the human figure at the Académie Suisse where the rules were not so strict, the teachers were more open-minded, the models given greater freedom in their poses, and unorthodox procedures, such as working from memory, were encouraged.

The studies made by Cézanne at the Académie Suisse reveal his potential for drawing the human figure: they are strong, dynamic, carefree, full of bravura [126–128]. The strength of these works derives in part from the use of softer media – chalk and charcoal – that allowed for a greater suppleness in the lines and firmer shading, as well as stronger contrasts between light and shade. An apposite example of Cézanne's blending of the past and the present occurs in the drawing *Male Nude* [130] made from a model at the Académie Suisse and his copy of the *Dead Christ* after Fra Bartolommeo, combined for use as the corpse in the painting *The Autopsy* (*c.* 1868; Private collection). Significantly, when Bernard visited Cézanne in Aix-en-Provence in 1904 he was shown drawings made by the artist when at the Académie Suisse and was told, 'I have always made use of these drawings, they are hardly sufficient, but at my age one must make do' [129].

Although Cézanne's direct engagement with the academic tradition was short-lived, he never completely eschewed its influence. After all, the basis of academic art was the nude and Cézanne's compositions of male and female bathers are predominantly an exacting and exhaustive exploration of a practice central to the development of European art that he pursued for over three decades. But, whereas the multi-figured compositions of bathers differed enormously from anything preceding them, the single figure paintings, *Bather with Outstretched Arms* (1877–78) and *The Large Bather* (*c.* 1885), have more than a lingering echo of the system of academic practice that Cézanne so rapidly transcended [119, 120]. Indeed, *The Large Bather*, in particular, has played a significant part in an interpretation of modern art that leads straight from Cézanne to Picasso.

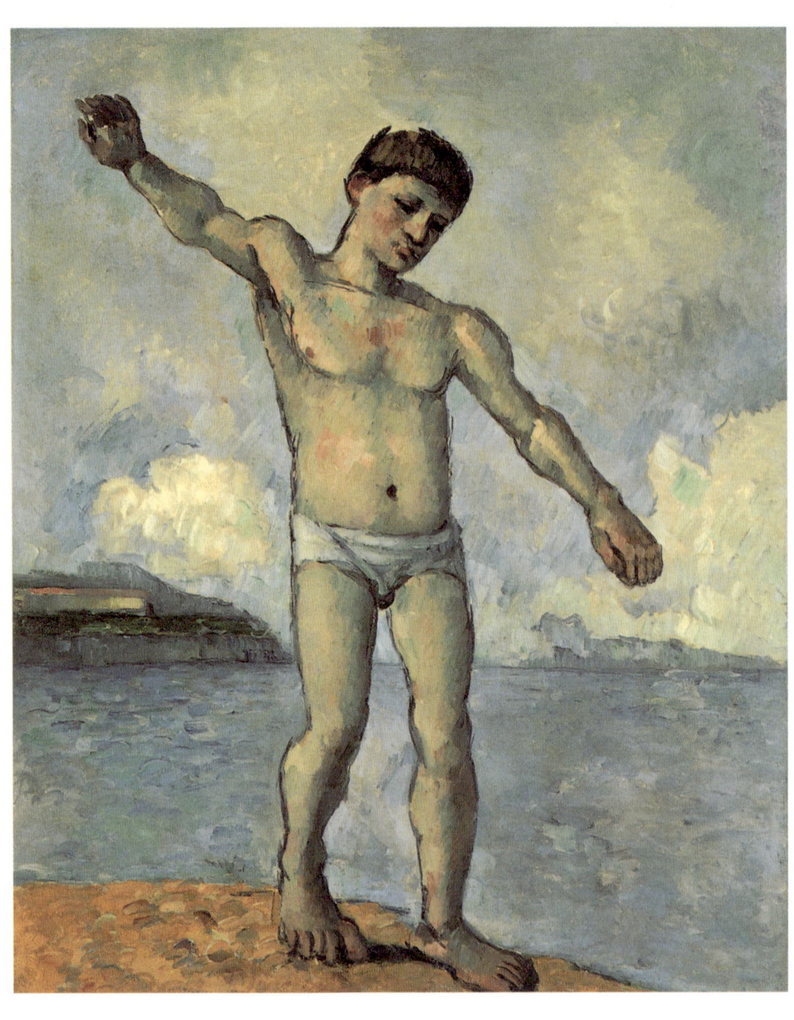

119. *Bather with Outstretched Arms*, 1877–78.
Oil on canvas, 73 × 60 cm (28¾ × 23⅝ in.).
Private collection

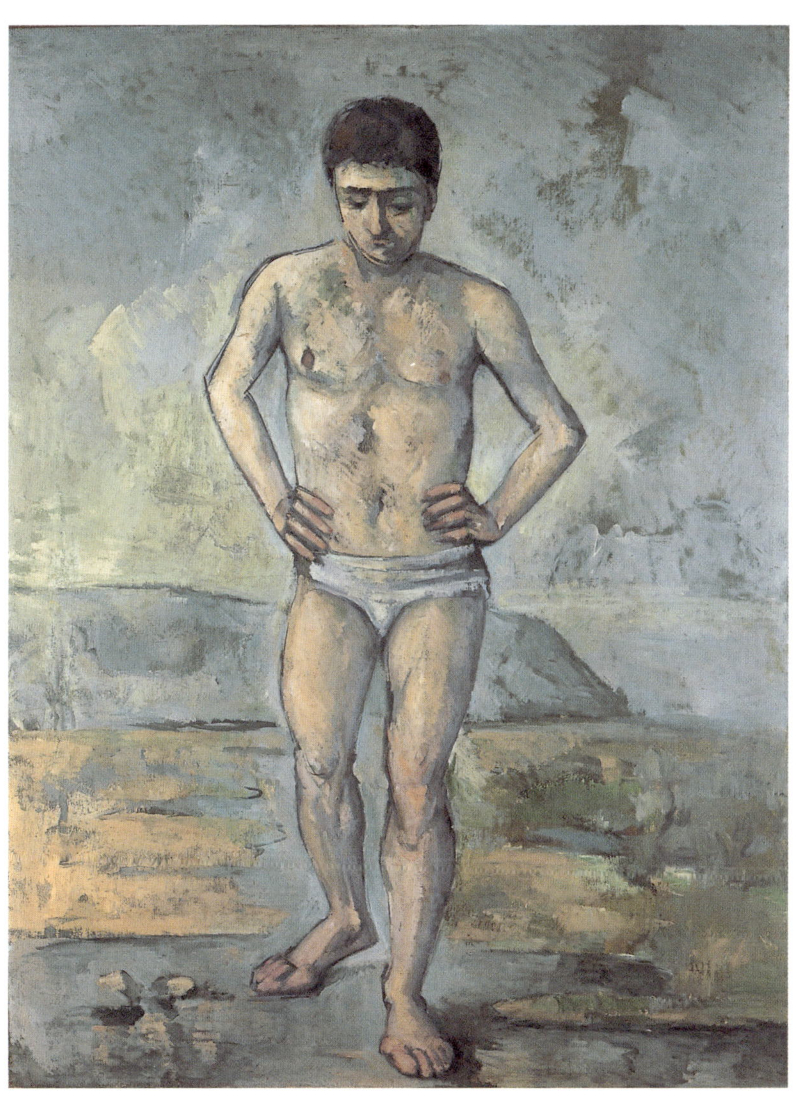

120. *The Large Bather*, c. 1885.
Oil on canvas, 127 × 96.8 cm (50 × 38⅛ in.).
Museum of Modern Art, New York

The origin of the single figure found in *Bather with Outstretched Arms* and *The Large Bather* lies in the centrally placed male bather wearing swimming trunks in *Bathers at Rest* (1875–76) in the Barnes Foundation, Philadelphia, which was shown at the third Impressionist exhibition of 1877 and was admired by Degas who made a brief copy of it. Common to both the paintings of the single bather is the sense of monumentality accentuated by the downwards direction of the gaze and the outlines of the bodies silhouetted against the sky. So striking are these paintings within Cézanne's *oeuvre* it is hardly surprising that they have generated a great deal of discussion as regards their date, finish and meaning, which in the final analysis remains enigmatic. To a certain extent these figures do not belong to the real world – a response reinforced by the carefully considered poses and wide-open backgrounds. *Bather with Outstretched Arms* has a threatening air, while *The Large Bather* is more reflective. But, both 'bestride the narrow world/Like a Colossus' and indeed it is not unlikely that Cézanne used classical sculpture as his starting point (for example, *The Roman Orator* of 40–30 BC, *The Borghese Mars* [see 26], or *The Dancing Satyr* [see 28] of the 3rd century BC – all in the Musée du Louvre). A number of related drawings or watercolours demonstrates how the idea of a single male bather dominated Cézanne's mind during the late 1870s and into the 1880s, which were in turn later incorporated into compositions with several bathers [115, 123].

Cézanne's examination of the female nude as a subject began early in his career. Many of the highly wrought, often over-crowded, narrative compositions of the 1870s include naked female figures of different types in secular and religious contexts: *Afternoon in Naples* [see 42], *The Orgy* (c. 1870; Private collection), *Olympia* [see 49], *Modern Olympia* (c. 1869–70; Private collection, and 1873; Musée d'Orsay, Paris), *The Temptation of St Anthony* (c. 1873–75; Staatliche Museen, Berlin), *Pastoral* (c. 1870; Musée d'Orsay, Paris), *The Eternal Feminine* [see 50]. Such pictures, both in terms of their narrative and technique, illustrate not only Cézanne's continuing search for his own style, but also his concern to be seen as a painter of contemporary subjects in the same way as Manet. Yet these early works can hardly be described as Realist. They are, in fact, the opposite, namely highly imaginative, and Cézanne's scenes of male and female bathers were conceived in a similar vein. Comparison of his bathing subjects with the more literal depictions of recreation places, such as the restaurant and bathing establishment known as La Grenouillère on the river Seine portrayed in 1869 by Monet and Renoir, reveals how far removed Cézanne's paintings were from more popular contemporary social conventions. The modernity of Cézanne's bathing pictures lies not so much in any specific references to time or place as in their universality. For, in attempting pictures of this subject and in this manner with such persistence and determination, Cézanne was aligning himself with some of the greatest practitioners of painting the nude in European art. A list of such artists would extend from Giorgione, Titian, Veronese and Tintoretto in the Renaissance, through Annibale Carracci, Rubens, Poussin and Domenichino in the seventeenth century, to Boucher, Fragonard and Delacroix in the eighteenth and nineteenth centuries.

Understandably, therefore, confronted with this challenge Cézanne began by approaching the theme of bathers with a certain caution. He seems at first to have been reluctant to forego identifiable subjects inspired by classical or religious sources such as *Bathsheba* [131], *Diana and Actaeon* [132], *Venus and Cupid* (c. 1875; Private collection), *Leda and the Swan* (*Reclining Female Nude*, 1882–90; Barnes Foundation, Philadelphia), *The Amorous Shepherd* (or *The Judgement of Paris*, c. 1883–85; now lost) and *The Battle of Love* [133], as though somewhat mockingly inviting direct comparison with his predecessors. Of these it is *The Amorous Shepherd* and *The Battle of Love* that come closest to the bathing scenes in their imaginative interpretation of subject matter, which is distinctly Virgilian, and in their narrative treatment, which recalls the reliefs on the sides of antique sarcophagi.

The paintings of female bathers, at first during the 1870s, are usually depicted in broad settings where the emphasis is as much on the landscape as the figures. By the 1880s, when Cézanne generally reduced the number of figures to three, four or five, the square, or almost square, compositions impress by the care with which they have been devised. The positions of each of the figures and the way in which they relate to one another while disporting themselves on the river bank in a leafy forest glade were seemingly carefully plotted in detailed preparatory compositional drawings. One such study [134] in Rotterdam relates to *Four Bathers* (1879–82) in the Barnes Foundation in Philadelphia and another of *Five Bathers* [121] made for the painting of 1885–87 in the Kunstmuseum Basel [122] is the only surviving drawing by Cézanne squared for enlargement. Any kind of compositional drawing is rare in Cézanne's *oeuvre* and these two examples are indicative of how seriously he regarded his pictures of female bathers. Most of the existing drawings explore a variety of poses involving reclining, stooping, striding, squatting, sitting, leaning, swimming, drying, combing, dressing and undressing. These are drawn at random in sketchbooks as if the poses are suddenly recollected by the artist. They are jotted down in the same way as a composer writes out a theme ripe for embellishment.

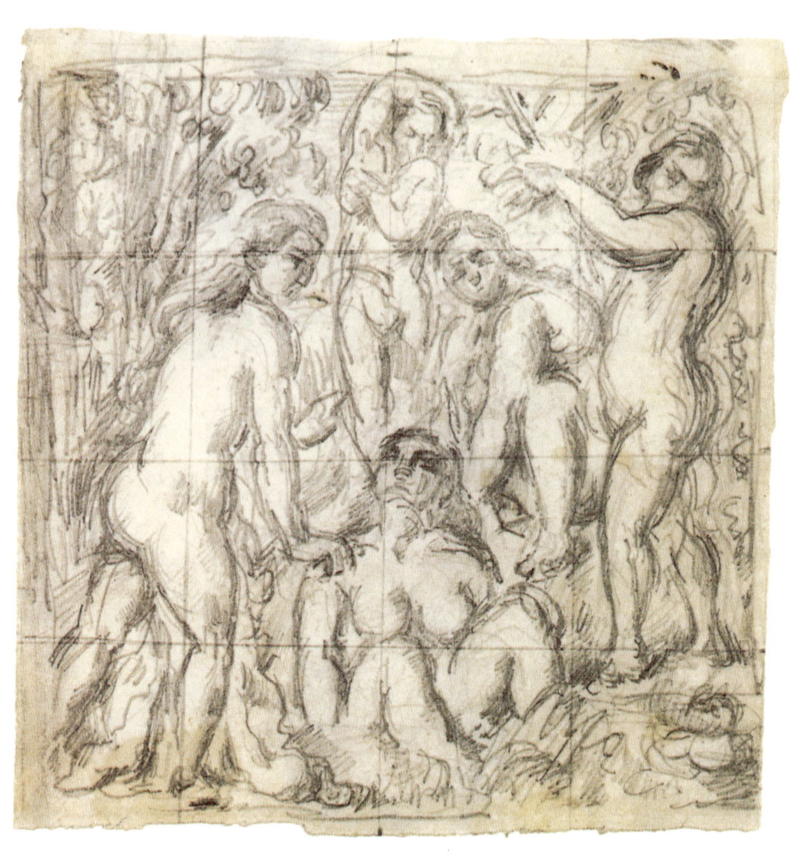

121. *Five Bathers*, 1885–87.
Pencil, squared for enlargement, 13.3 × 13.3 cm (5¼ × 5¼ in.).
Private collection

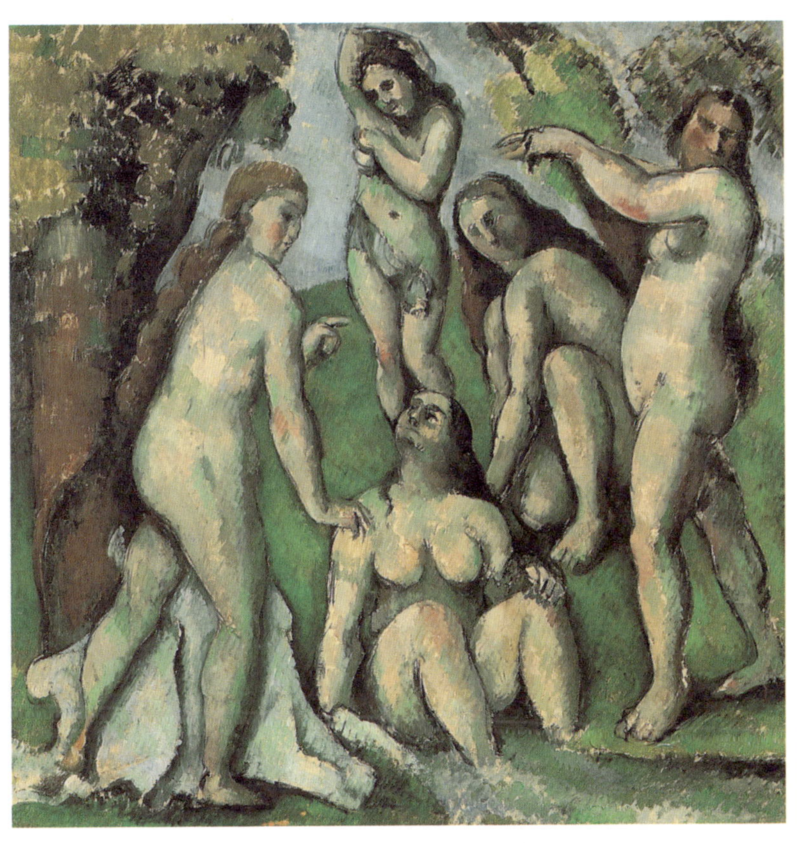

122. *Five Bathers*, 1885–87.
Oil on canvas, 65.3 × 65.3 cm (23¾ × 25¾ in.).
Kunstmuseum Basel

Essentially, Cézanne's paintings of female bathers are based on a repertoire of figures lodged in the artist's mind and each composition has the air of an improvisation or variation on a theme. Hardly any studies of female nudes made from life are known and those that were done were executed more in homage to Rubens or Delacroix than as preparatory exercises for pictures [135]. Cézanne told Bernard that he refrained from using female models in his studio for reasons of propriety, but, in fact, there were specific artistic reasons for this decision. In the paintings of female bathers ideal forms are avoided at all costs and Cézanne's preference is for the ungainly, the ponderous and the distorted. In his keenness to be expressive he is prepared to go so far as to embrace the grotesque. Whatever shapes the figures might assume, however, the most important aspect is the concern that Cézanne shows for their arrangement. This was most apparent during the mid- to late 1880s when the figures are made to dominate the foreground in pyramidal configurations that are contained within landscapes notable for their lack of recession, thereby emphasizing their monumentality, which is in turn enhanced by the glimpses of white flesh tones offset against lush greens, aqueous blues and sharp yellows [122]. Cézanne also buttresses each composition at the sides with standing or seated figures, often aligned with trees that stretch overhead like a vault. The visual effect is unquestionably architectonic and it is at once apparent that in these carefully thought-out compositions the emotional turmoil so typical of the artist's narrative paintings of the 1860s and early 1870s has now been overtaken by the exercising of his organizational powers.

Towards 1900, while working on the three versions of *The Large Bathers*, Cézanne's watercolours of the theme become more elaborate [136]. He increased the number of figures, which now flow freely across the page in less well-organized groups and altogether have more energy. Correspondingly, the compositions are much more open and the backgrounds less confining. This even applies in a very late watercolour, *Bathers by a Bridge* [137], which is a rare example of imaginary figures being shown in a specific location well known to the artist and where he often took refuge from the summer heat in the last year of his life – the Trois Sautets bridge on the river Arc to the south of Aix-en-Provence. It is amazing how Cézanne to the very end managed to sustain the energy exuded by these 'Rubensian' bathers, which are so reminiscent of the barely contained figures occurring in his early narrative drawings. Here the swimmers are twisting and turning in the foreground, like caught fish writhing in the bottom of a boat, almost spilling over the lower edge of the composition.

Also, in these late watercolours there is less concern for anatomical correctness and many of the figures appear to be androgynous with their actions less clearly defined. Such confusions are reflected in the style of these late watercolours, which are intensely rhythmical and constantly lively. The suppleness of the agitated brushstrokes when seen in conjunction with the flowing pencil lines suggests the vibrancy of the rural surroundings as well as the vitality of the bathers. Here the constantly redrawn outlines imitate the rustling of the foliage and the writhing of the limbs in a blur of activity that heightens the shimmering effect like a mirage.

The paintings of male bathers exhibit many of the same characteristics as those of the female bathers, although the compositions are often horizontal in format and comprise many more figures. Cézanne's starting point is also slightly different in so far as he seems to have had a greater confidence in his ability to draw the male nude following his examination of the work of Italian Renaissance artists such as Signorelli [see 10] and also Michelangelo's *Battle of Cascina*. This last was the famous scene planned in 1504 for the Sala di Gran Consiglio in the Palazzo Vecchio in Florence in competition with Leonardo da Vinci's *Battle of Anghiari*. Although the *Battle of Anghiari* was completed, but suffered during Leonardo's lifetime from his unorthodox working methods, Michelangelo never even began his painting. He did, however, finish the cartoon for it and the fame of this version was such that the sculptor Benvenuto Cellini dubbed it 'The School of Art'. Nonetheless, it was destroyed during Michelangelo's lifetime by artists and souvenir hunters eager to own a part of it. About ten of Michelangelo's preparatory drawings have survived, but the whole composition of *The Battle of Cascina* is known only through the copy of the cartoon made (*c.* 1542) by Aristotile da Sangallo that is now at Holkham Hall, Norfolk.

Apart from respecting Michelangelo's skill at drawing the male nude, Cézanne must surely have been aware that his Renaissance predecessor had chosen as his subject the moment before the battle when the Florentine soldiers shed their armour to swim in the river Arno. There is, therefore, a direct correlation between the copies made by Cézanne of figures appearing in *The Battle of Cascina* and his own scenes of male bathers. Possibly he was conflating the recollection of Michelangelo's masterpiece with personal observations of soldiers from the local garrison at Aix-en-Provence relaxing on the banks of the river Arc.

Fully incorporated into his *oeuvre* by the late 1870s, the compositions of male bathers are less varied than those of the female counterparts [124]. The foregrounds are usually dominated by two standing figures seen from the back flanked by seated or bending figures

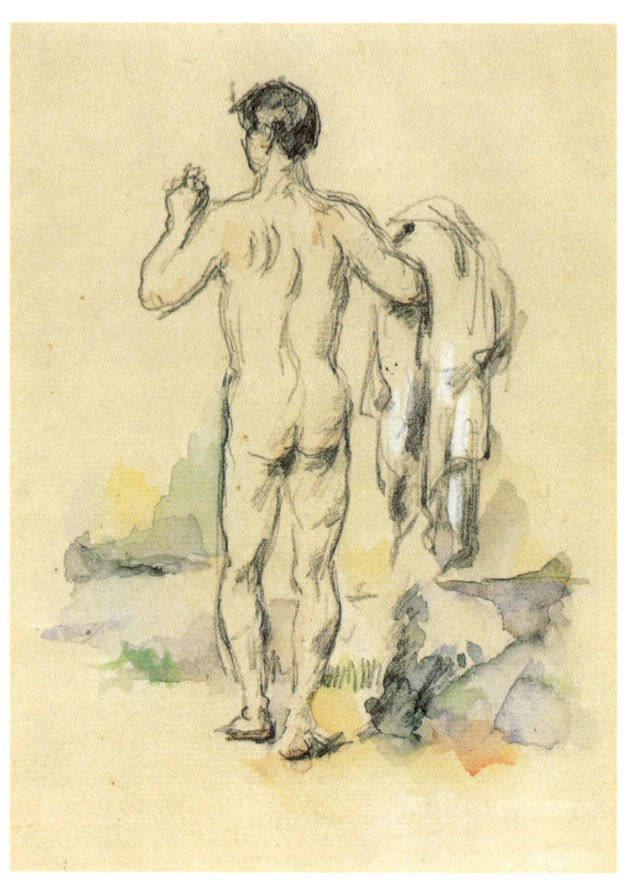

123. *Standing Bather Seen from the Back*, c. 1885.
Pencil and watercolour, 22.3 × 17.1 cm (8¾ × 6¾ in.).
Wadsworth Atheneum, Hartford, Connecticut

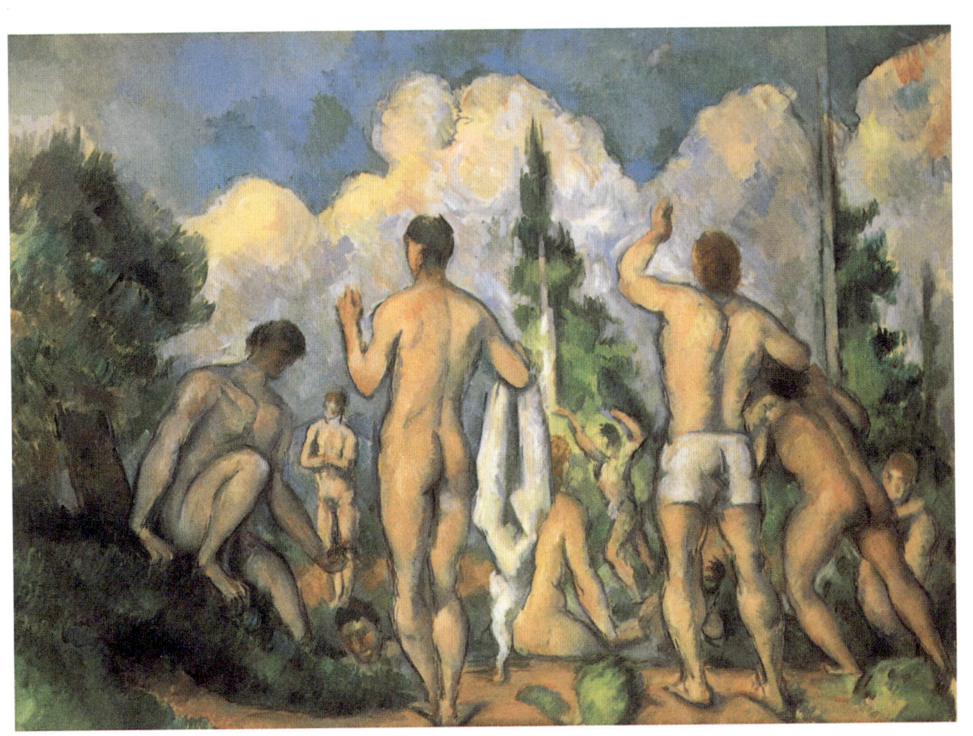

124. *Bathers*, c. 1890.
Oil on canvas, 60 × 82 cm (23⅝ × 32¼ in.).
Musée d'Orsay, Paris

with others in the water placed in the middle distance or on the opposite
bank. Because the format tends to be horizontal, as opposed to square,
the visual effect is closer to low-relief sculpture. The backgrounds
are more open and spacious with more of the sky visible. In the
compositions of female bathers Cézanne compresses the constituent
elements, but in those of male bathers a greater degree of articulation is
required, which the artist manages by dividing the space vertically using
a combination of the standing figures and trees.

From 1900 the number of figures increases with poses reversed,
groups rearranged and spatial intervals rethought. There is also a
greater dynamism, too, as the range of riparian activities now includes
wrestling and frolicking, in addition to swimming. The intensely busy,
all-over style of the late watercolours of male bathers fuses with that of
the female bathers, suggesting that the representation of the enveloping
atmosphere of light, air and water was now more important for Cézanne
than any compositional or structural interests [138–141]. The full
force of Cézanne's technique in watercolour is here evident, combining
curvilinear outlines, vertical striations and scattered blotches.

Cézanne, however, did not pursue the theme of male bathers as
far as he did that of female bathers. On the other hand, when he was
approached by Vollard in 1896 to make colour lithographs for exhibition
and sale the artist chose two of his compositions of male bathers:
Large Bathers after the painting *Bathers at Rest* (Barnes Foundation,
Philadelphia) of 1875–76 and *Small Bathers* comparable with the
painting *Seven Bathers* (Foundation Beyler, Basel) of *c.* 1897. By the
mid-1890s, *Bathers at Rest* had probably become Cézanne's best-known
painting, following its controversial reception at the third Impressionist
exhibition of 1877 and its eventual rejection from the highly significant
Caillebotte Bequest to the French nation in 1894. On the latter occasion
the critic Geffroy used the picture to describe Cézanne's particular
qualities as a painter – his rugged technique, brilliant light, strength of
drawing – emphasizing the awkward grandeur of his figures as a result
of the influence of Michelangelo and comparing the visual effect of the
finished work to faience pottery.

Cézanne's paintings of male and female bathers hold a special
position within his *oeuvre* as well as within the history of European
painting. The arcadian world of female bathers – almost a Garden of
Eden – evokes comparison with Titian's mythological poesie (*Diana and
Actaeon* and *Diana and Callisto*) painted for Philip II, whereas the more
muscular world of the male bathers brings to mind religious themes such
as St John the Baptist preaching in the desert or the baptism of Christ.
But, there is nothing retardataire about Cézanne's bathers. As Boris

Pasternak's eponymous hero in his novel *Doctor Zhivago* (1958) writes in his diary, "'Forward steps in art are made by attraction, through the artist's admiration and desire to follow the example of the predecessors he admires most.'"

Detractors of Cézanne's images of bathers point to their composite nature or their sheer repetitiveness; they might also refer to the odd proportions of the figures or the lack of variety in the settings. But such observations miss the point. Cézanne is not so much interested in the particular as in the general. Like Degas, who during the 1880s withdrew more and more into his studio, Cézanne relied on memory and a supply of drawings for inspiration as a way of devising compositions that in their novelty stand at the threshold of modern art. Cézanne's originality lies in his personal combination of strength, distortion and repetition, which, when seen as virtues rather than weaknesses, liberated those artists such as Gauguin onwards who were searching for an escape from the restrictions of the past. In terms of the history of art, and with regard to their place in his art, the sequence of Cézanne's bathers taken as a whole is tantamount to one of the great programmes of sculpture adorning the façade of a Romanesque or Gothic cathedral.

There can be no doubt that Cézanne was partly reliving his youth in his depictions of bathers and turning Provence into an Arcadia populated by a cast of Virgilian nymphs and shepherds in enchanted settings of bowers, glades and water. At the same time, however, he was able to pull back and observe the landscape of Provence as a panorama with Mont Sainte-Victoire crowning the distant vista. This landscape, too, was to give rise to yet other groups of distinguished paintings and watercolours.

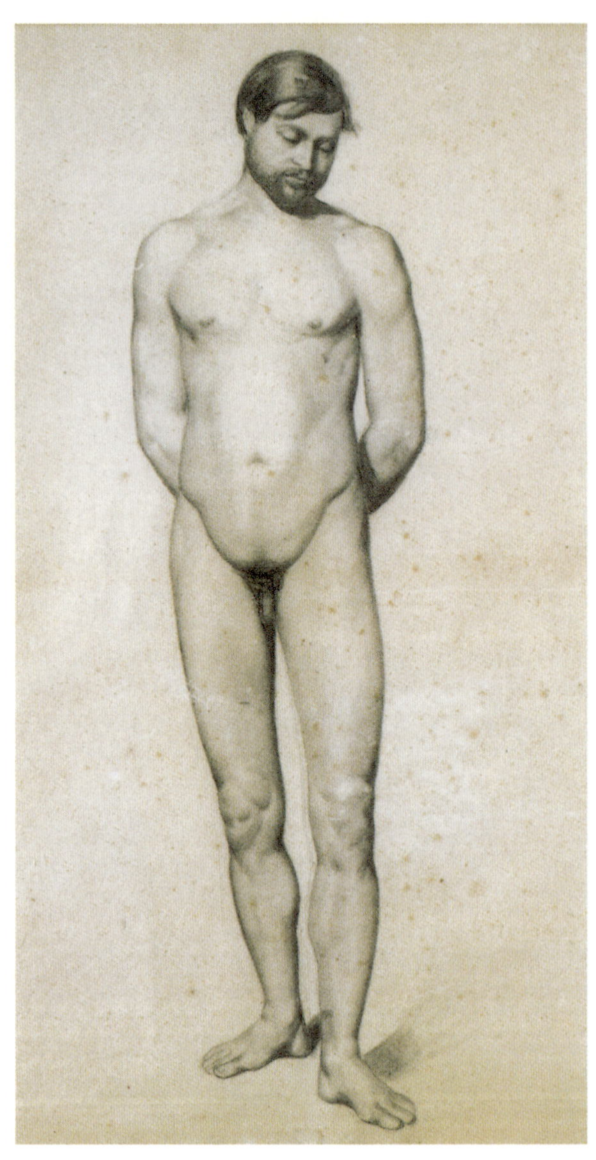

125. *Male Nude*, 1863.
Pencil, 61 × 47 cm (24 × 18½ in.).
Musée Granet, Aix-en-Provence

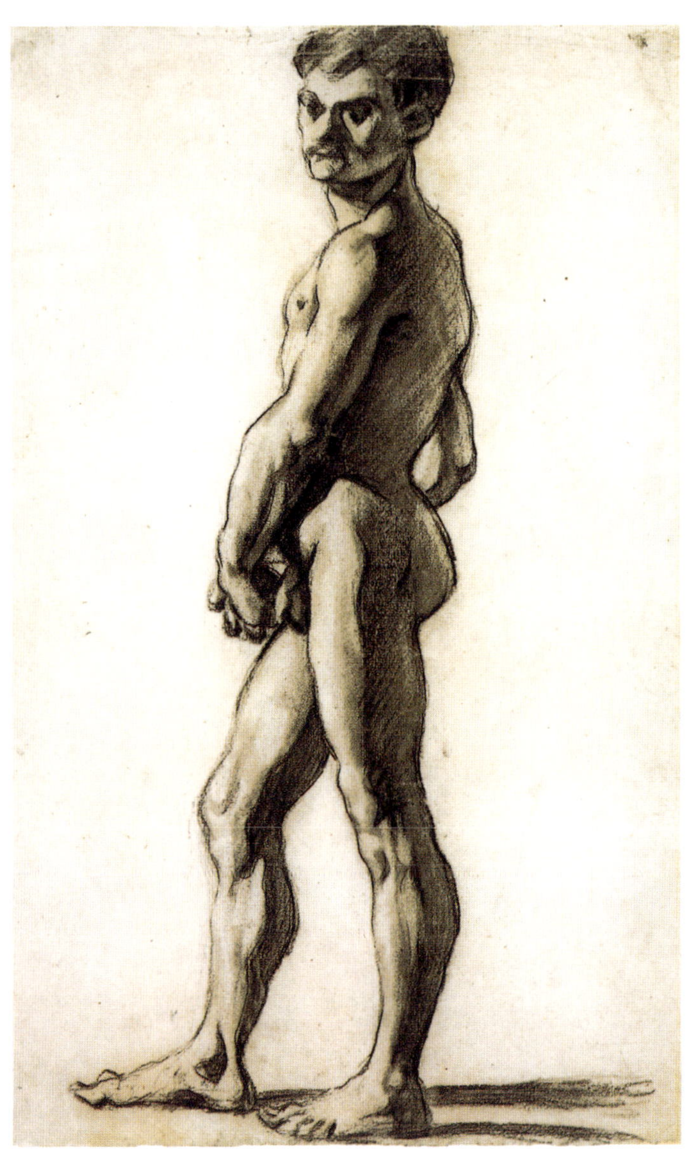

126. *Male Nude, c. 1863–66.*
Charcoal heightened with white, 49 × 31 cm (19¼ × 12¼ in.).
Fitzwilliam Museum, Cambridge

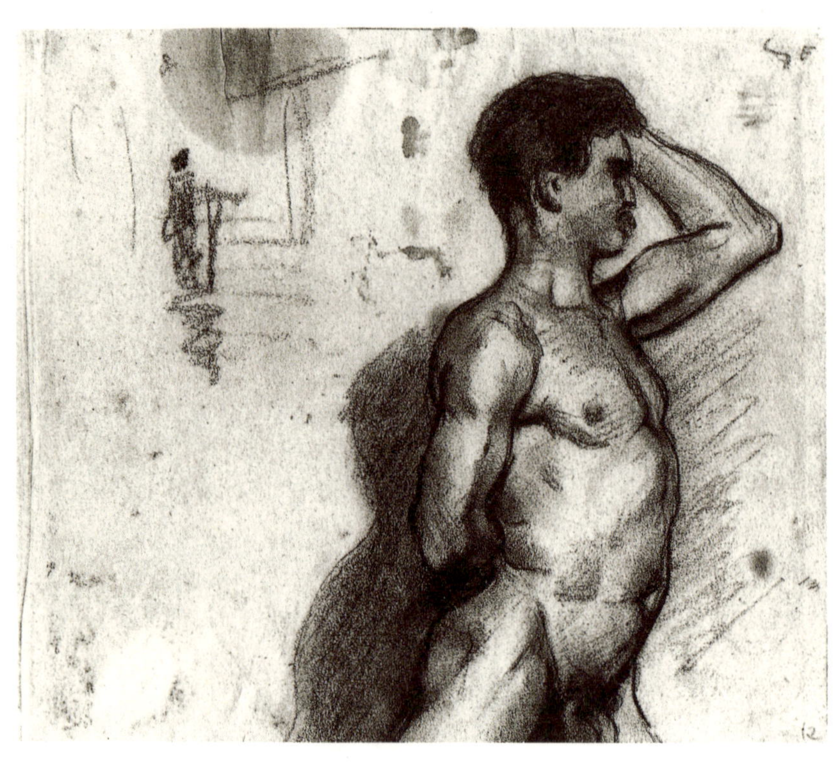

127. *Male Nude*, *c.* 1865.
Charcoal and gouache, 24.9 × 28.9 cm (9⅛ × 11⅜ in.).
Kunstmuseum Basel

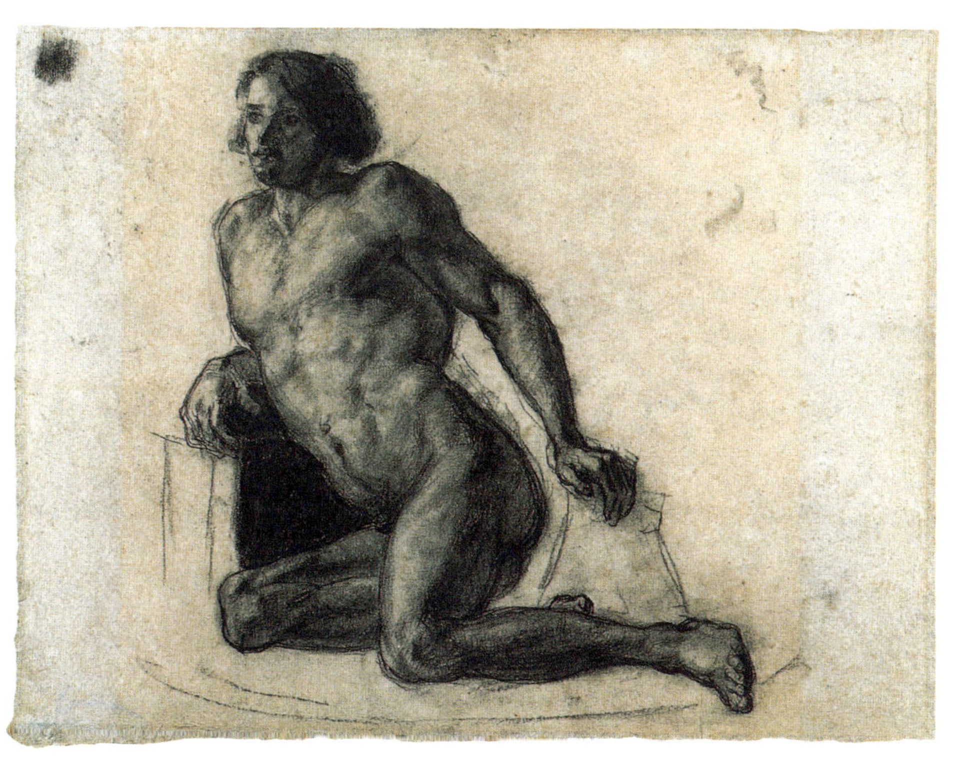

128. *Male Nude Leaning on his Elbow*, 1863–66.
Pencil on faded blue paper, 31 × 40 cm (12⅜ × 15⅞ in.).
Bridgestone Museum of Art, Tokyo

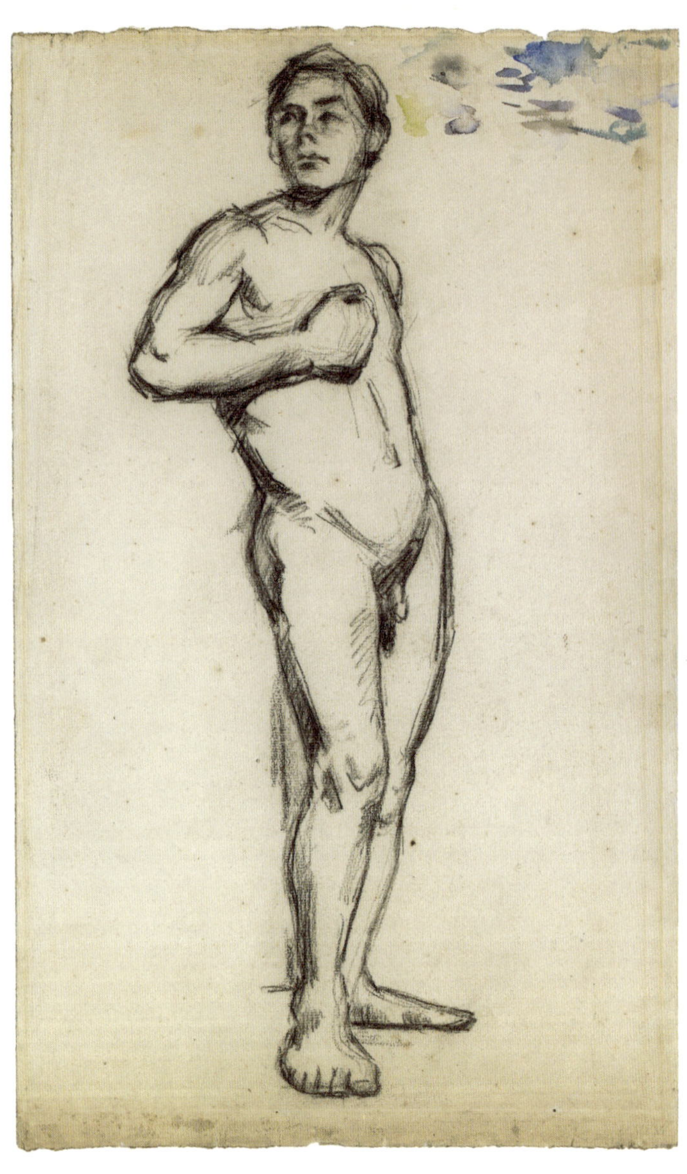

129. *Study of a Male Nude with Right Hand Clenched across the Chest,*
c. 1867–70. Black chalk and black crayon with some trial touches in watercolour
top right, 48.2 × 29.5 cm (19 × 11⅝ in.).
Ashmolean Museum, Oxford

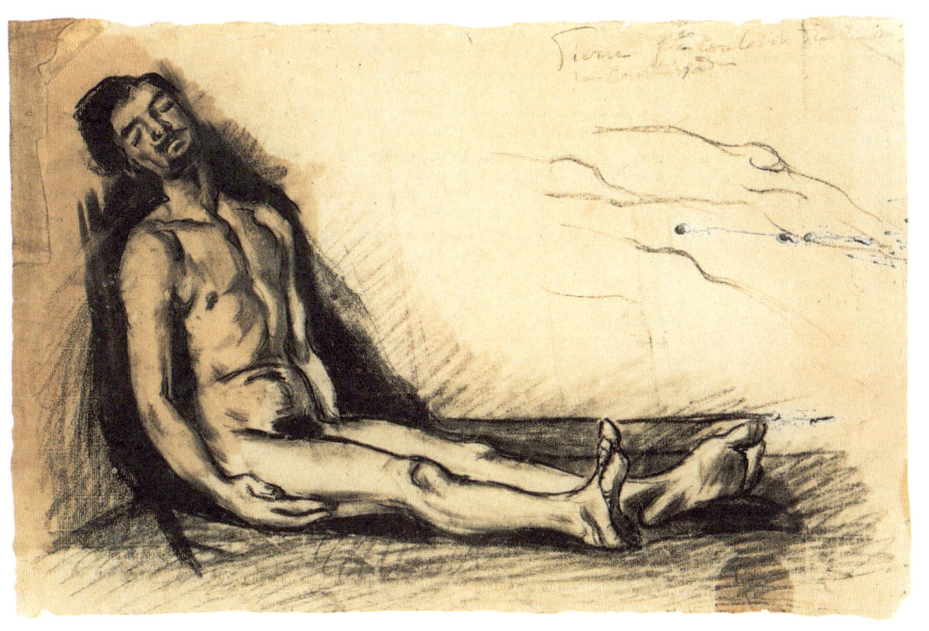

130. *Male Nude, c.* 1865.
Charcoal on light brown paper, 31 × 47.5 cm (12¼ × 18¾ in.).
The Art Institute of Chicago

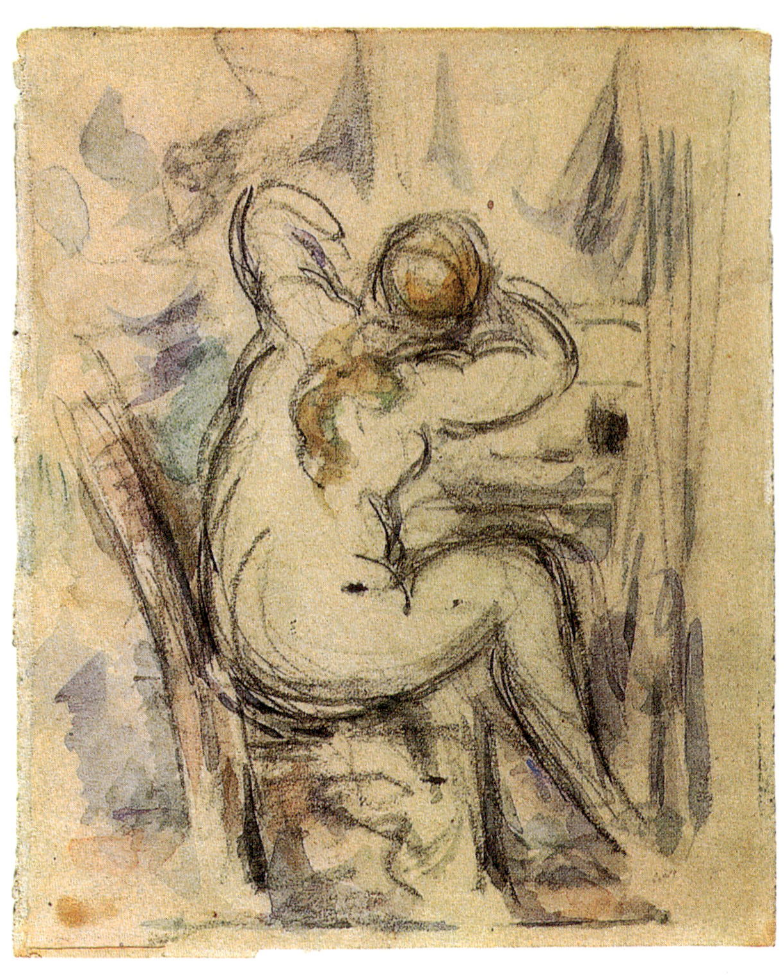

131. *Woman at her Toilette [Bathsheba], c. 1895.*
Pencil and watercolour, 15.8 × 13.3 cm (6¼ × 5¼ in.).
Hood Museum of Art, Dartmouth College, Hanover, New Hampshire

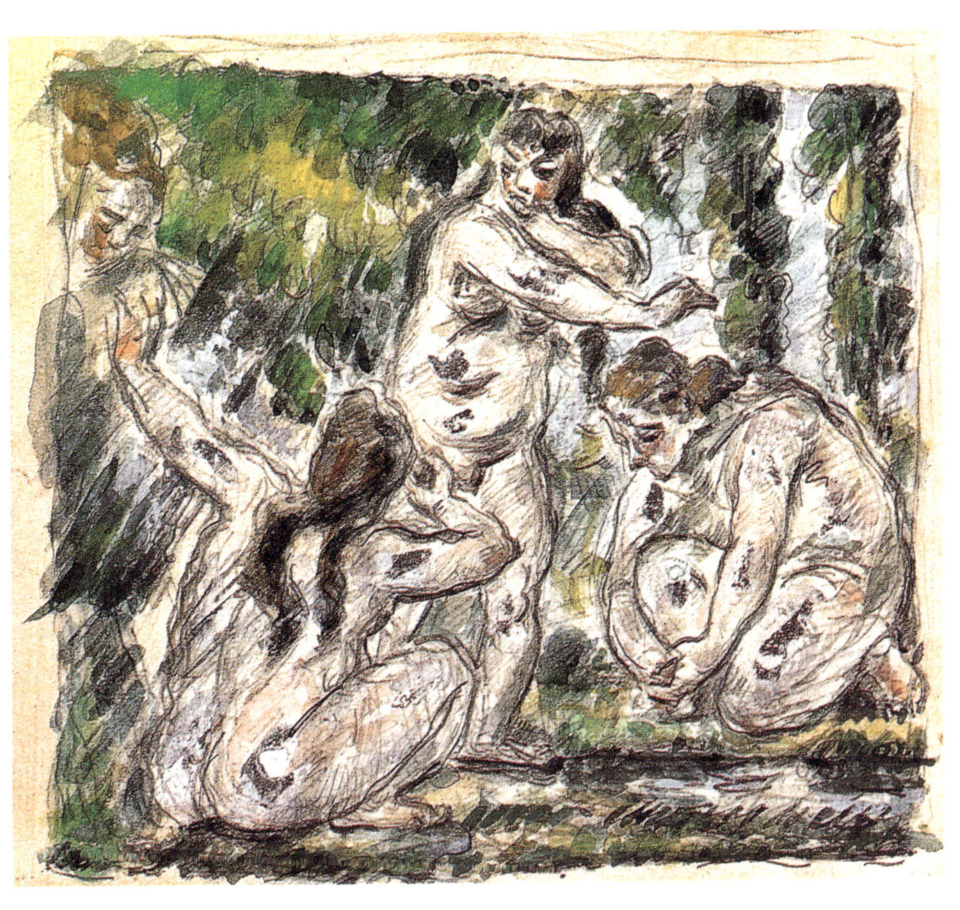

132. *Three Bathers [Diana and Actaeon]*, 1874–75.
Pencil, watercolour and gouache (with slight oxidization),
11.4 × 12.7 cm (4½ × 5 in.).
National Museum of Wales, Cardiff

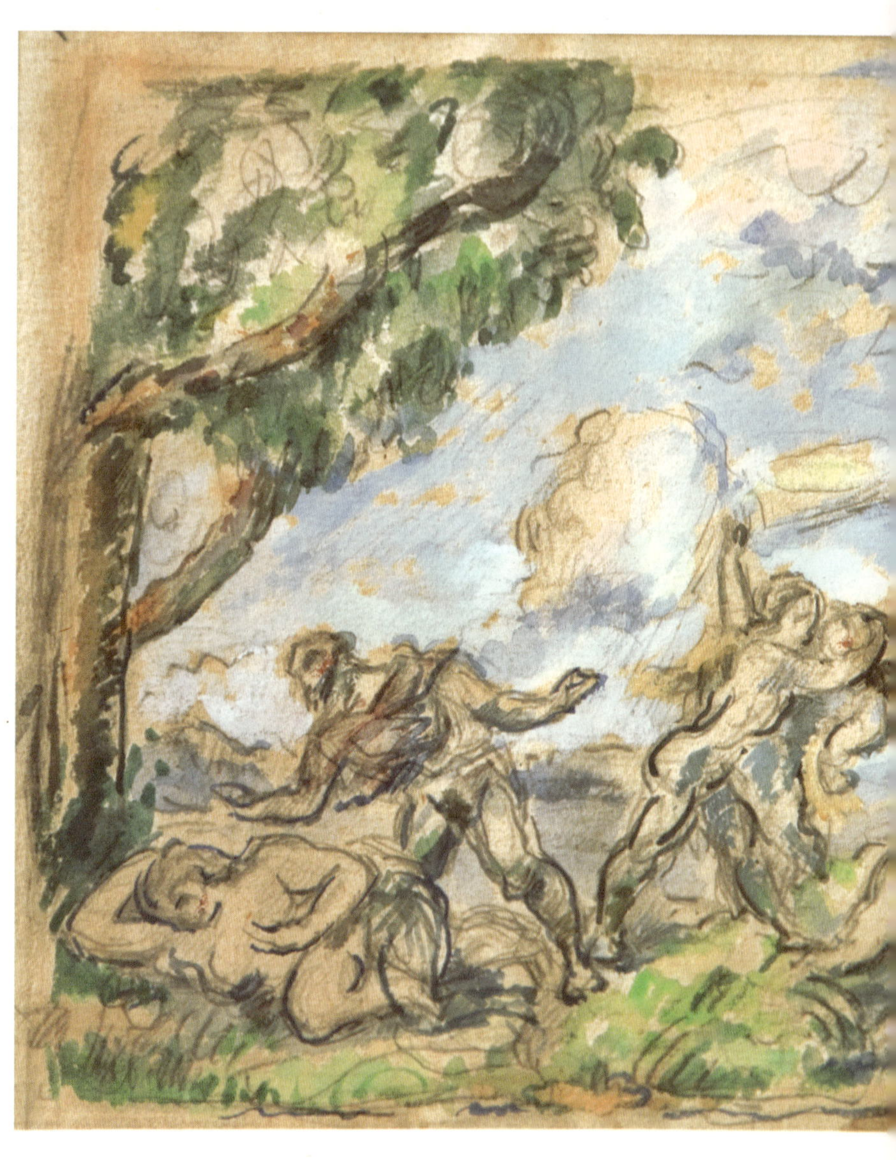

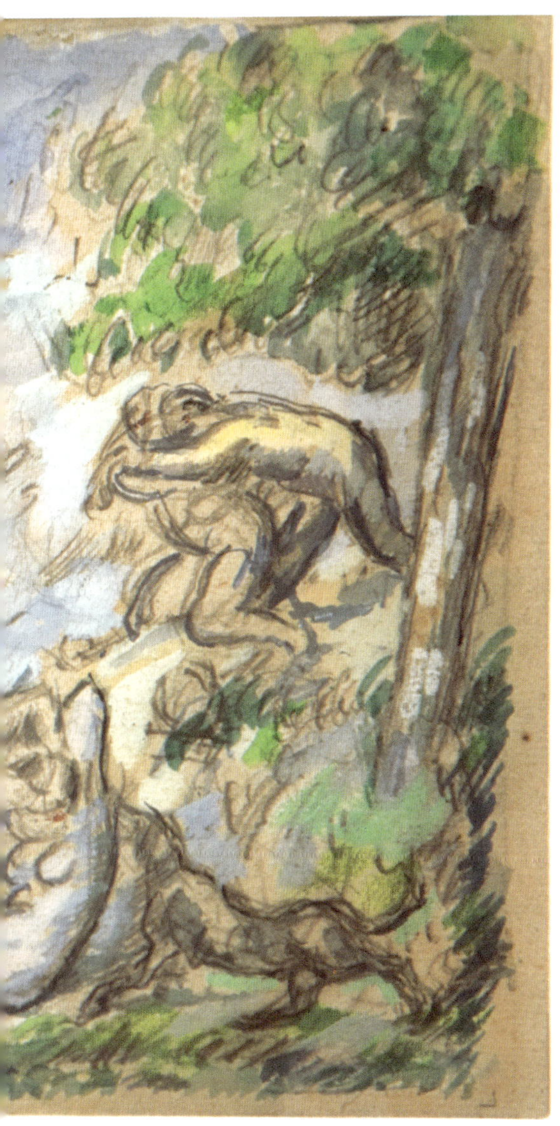

133. *The Battle of Love*, 1875–76.
Pencil, watercolour and gouache,
19 × 24.5 cm (7½ × 9⅝ in.).
Private collection

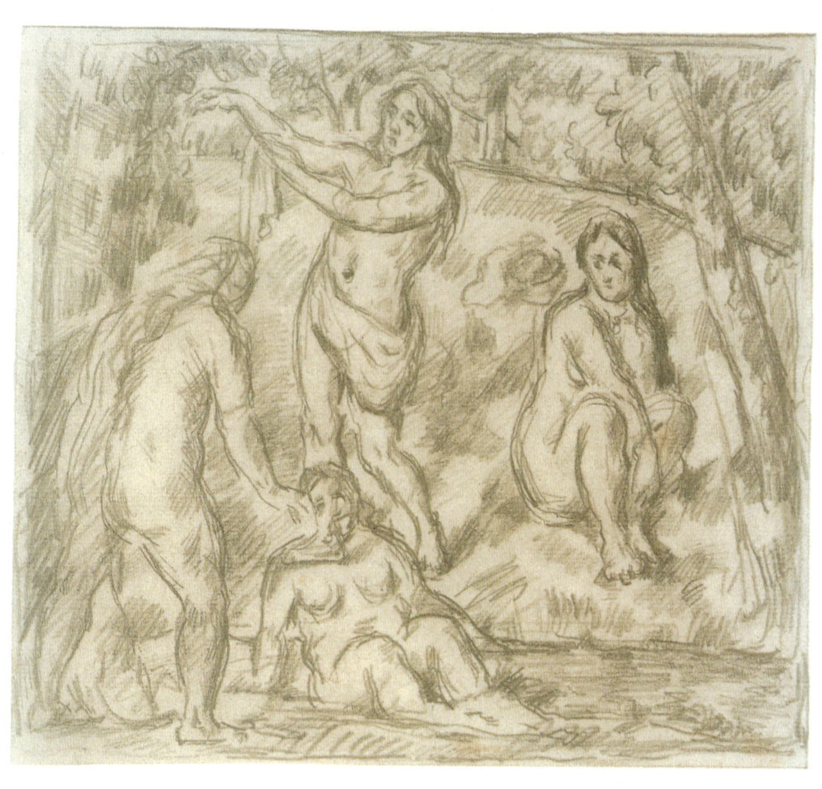

134. *Four Female Bathers*, 1879–82.
Pencil and black chalk, 20.3 × 22.3 cm (8 × 8¼ in.).
Museum Boijmans Van Beuningen, Rotterdam

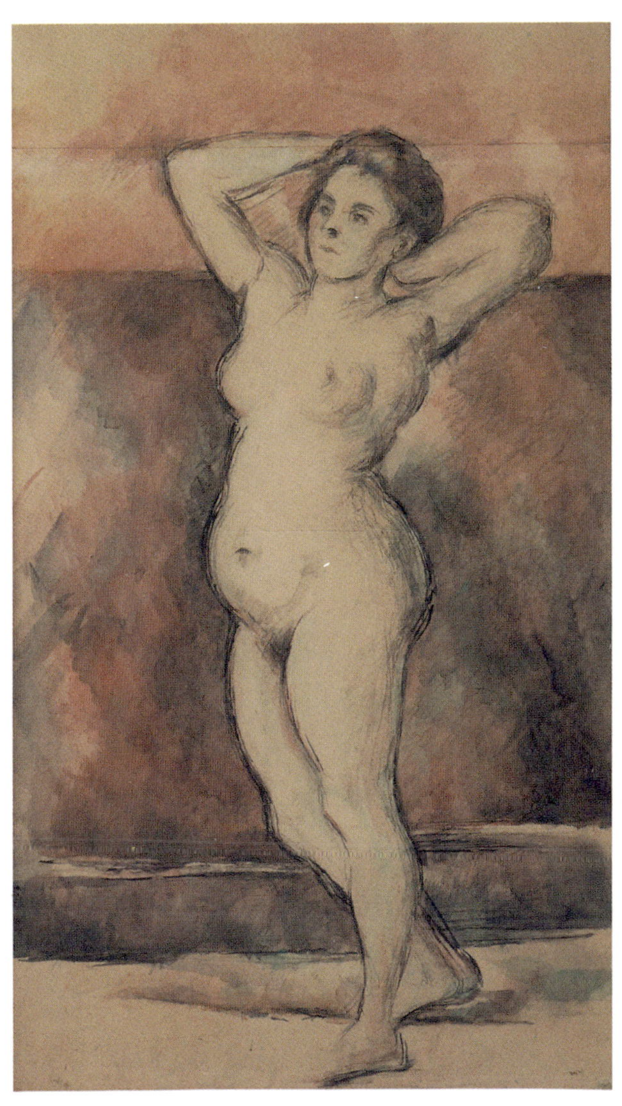

135. *Standing Female Nude*, 1900.
Pencil and watercolour, 89 × 53 cm (35 × 20⅞ in.).
Musée d'Orsay, Paris

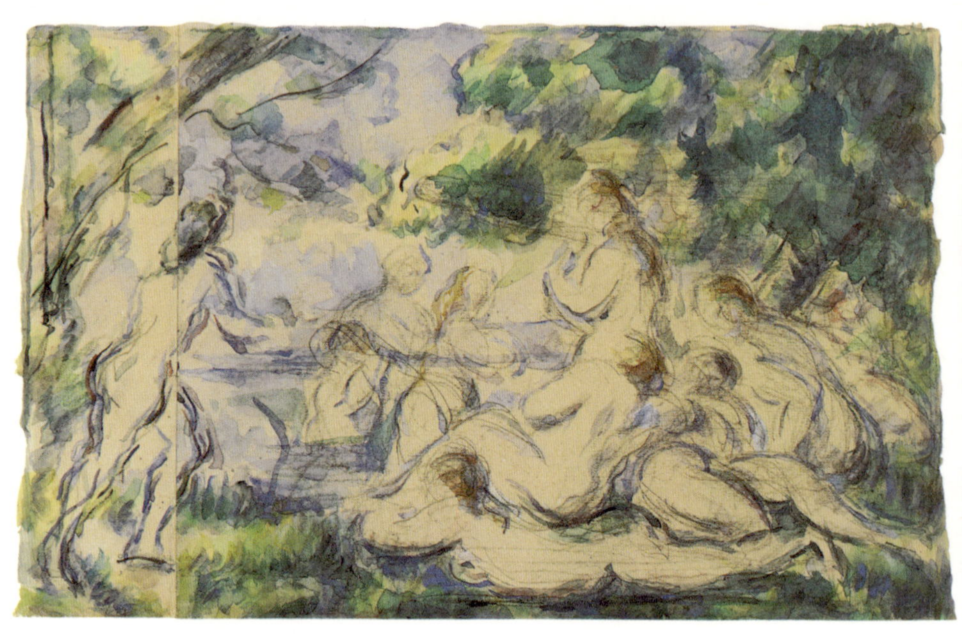

136. *Bathers*, 1894–1906.
Pencil and watercolour, 17 × 27 cm (6¼ × 10⅝ in.).
Private collection

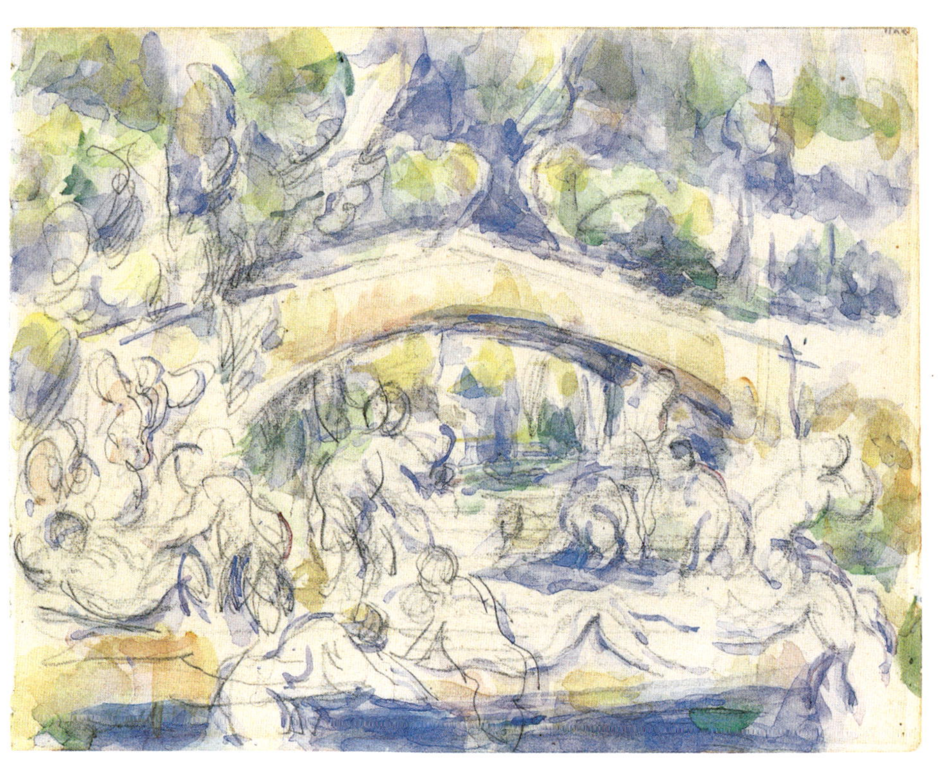

137. *Bathers by a Bridge*, 1906.
Pencil and watercolour, 21 × 27.2 cm (8¼ × 10¾ in.).
Metropolitan Museum of Art, New York

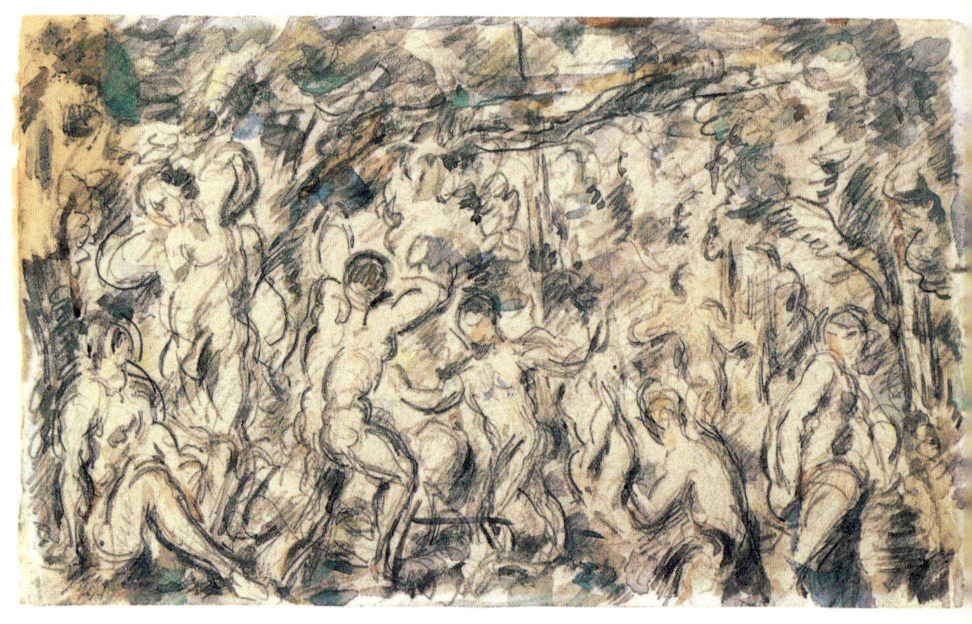

138. *Bathers, c.* 1890.
Pencil and watercolour, 12.6 × 20.8 cm (5 × 8¼ in.).
Bridgestone Museum of Art, Tokyo

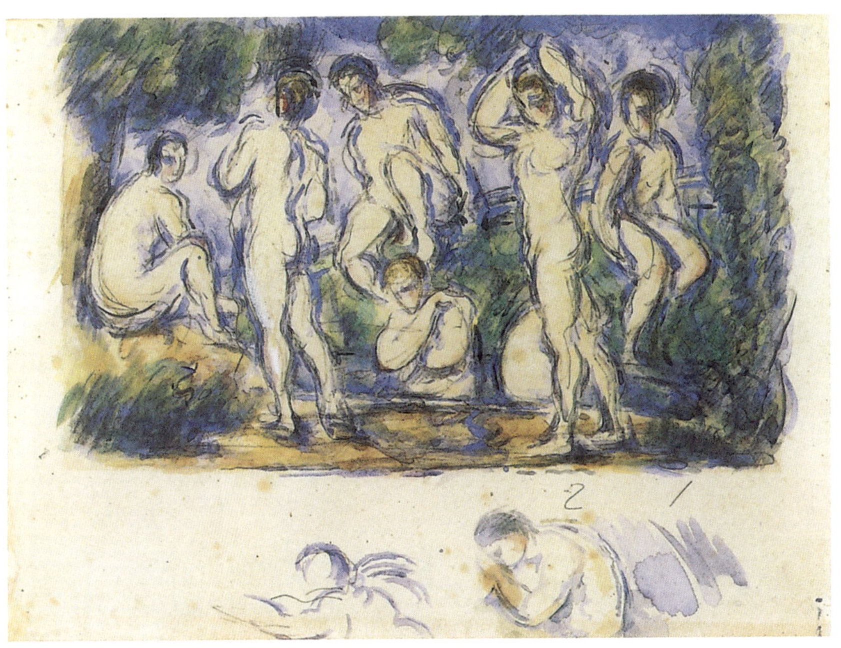

139. *Group of Bathers*, c. 1900.
Pencil and watercolour on buff paper, 20 × 27.3 cm (7⅞ × 10¼ in.).
Pierpont Morgan Library, New York

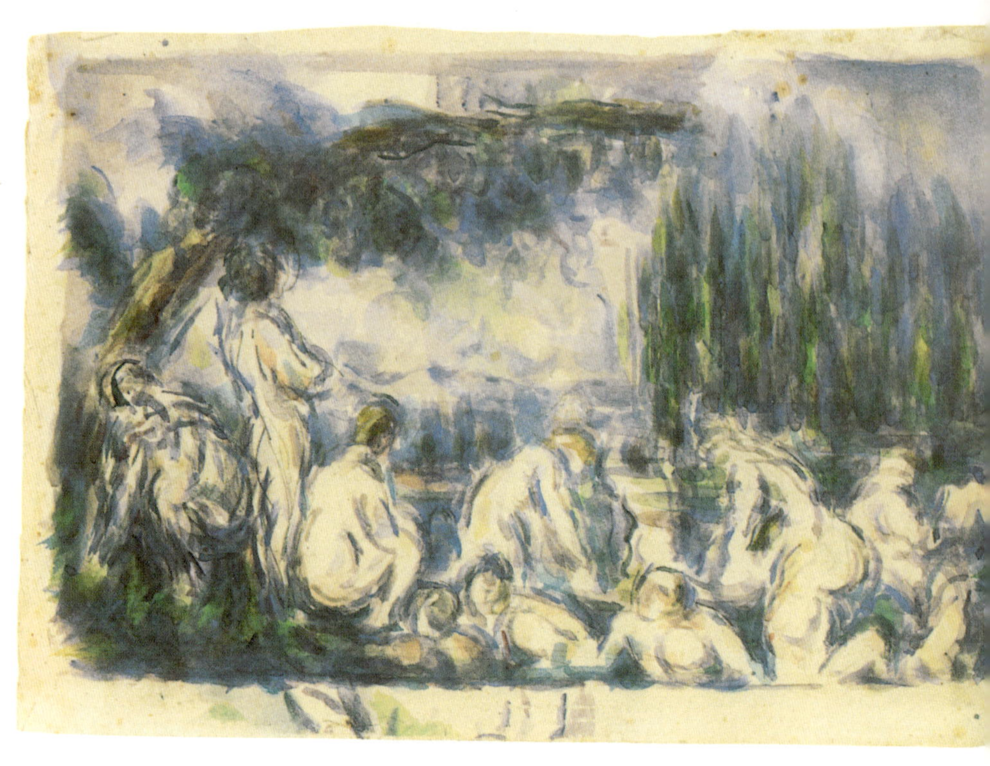

140. *Bathers*, *c.* 1903.
Pencil and watercolour, 22.4 × 31.5 cm (8⅞ × 12⅛ in.).
Private collection

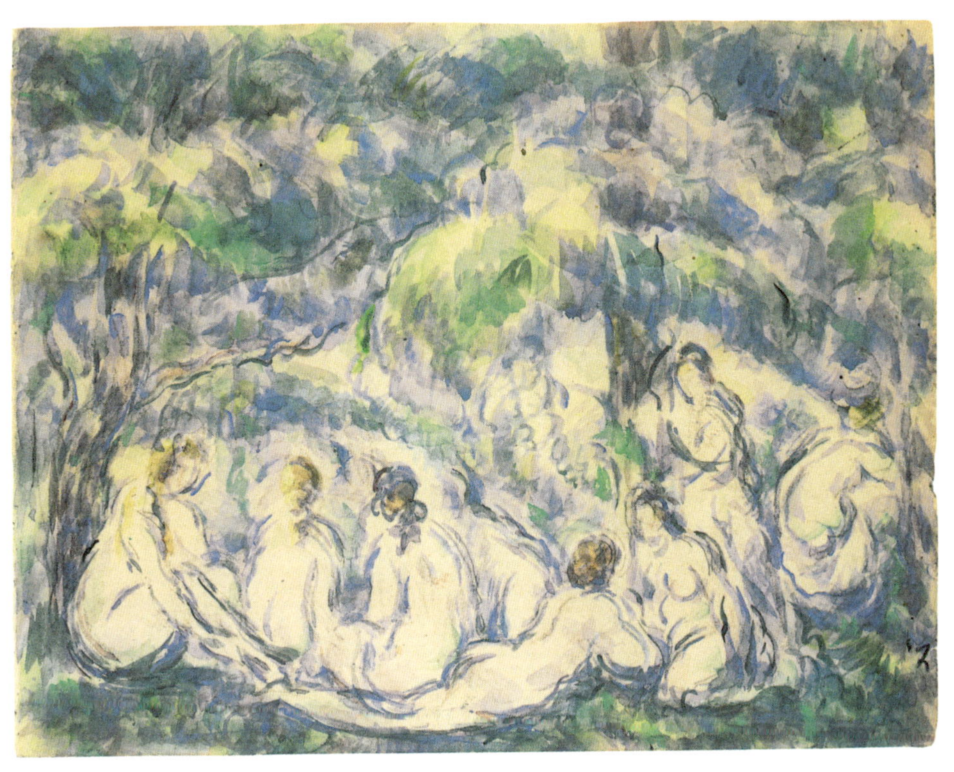

141. *Bathers*, 1902–06.
Pencil and watercolour on buff paper, 21 × 27 cm (8¼ × 10⅝ in.).
Private collection

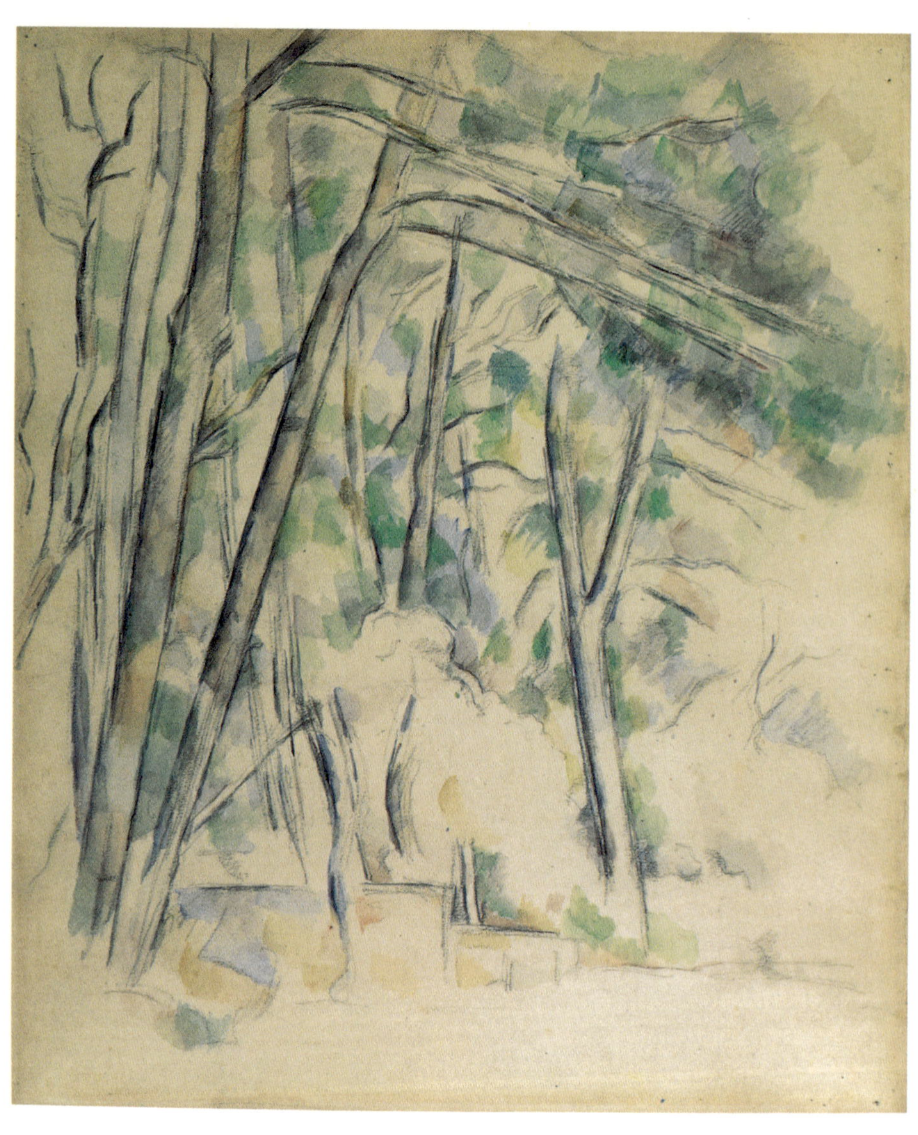

142. *Cistern in the Park of Château Noir*, 1895–1900.
Pencil and watercolour on pale buff paper, 50.6 × 43.4 cm (19⅞ × 17⅛ in.).
The Henry and Rose Pearlman Foundation, on loan to Princeton University
Art Museum, New Jersey

CHAPTER FIVE

Searching for the Ideal in the Landscape

'Q. What do you consider nature's masterpiece?
A. Her infinite diversity.' Paul Cézanne

Neither the human figure in its various manifestations nor objects in their wide variety challenged Cézanne as much as nature. He told Joachim Gasquet, 'Nature is always the same, and yet its appearance is always changing. It is our business as artists to convey the thrill of nature's permanence along with the elements and the appearance of all its changes. Painting must give us the flavour of nature's eternity.' This was Cézanne's dilemma: how to combine the fugitive with the durable and nowhere in his art was this more pressing than in his treatment of landscape. For him nature was the basis of all his art, as he wrote to Charles Camoin on 22 February 1903, 'Everything, *art above all*, is theory developed and applied through contact with nature.'

Cézanne's personal contact with nature began early in the company of his childhood friends. The experience is described in the second chapter of Zola's *L'Oeuvre* where the author reminisces about the escapades of the 'Inseparables' in the countryside around Aix-en-Provence, which in the novel is identified as Plassans:

> While they were still in the junior school the three inseparables had developed a passion for long walks. Not even a half-holyday went by without their covering a good few miles and, as they grew older and more venturesome, their rambles covered all the surrounding district and even on occasion took them away from home for days at a time. They would spend the night wherever they happened to be, under a hollow rock, on the hot, flagged threshing-floor of a barn, with the new-made straw for bedding, or in some deserted hut where they would make themselves a couch of lavender and thyme. In their unthinking, boyish worshipping of trees and hills and streams, and in the boundless joy of being alone and free, they found an escape from the matter-of-fact world, and instinctively let themselves be drawn to the bosom of Nature … In the summer especially their dream was the Viorne, the mountain torrent that waters the low-lying meadows of Plassans. They could swim

when they were scarcely twelve, and they loved to splash about
in the deeper parts of the stream; they would spend whole days,
stark naked, lying on the burning sand, then diving back into the
water, endlessly grubbing for water-plants or watching for eels.
They practically lived in the river, and the combination of clear
water and sunshine seemed to prolong their childhood, so that
even when they were already young men they still sounded like
a trip of laughing urchins as they ambled back into Plassans on a
sultry July evening after a day on the river … The memory of those
country walks always brought tears to their eyes. They went along
the white roads once more, roads covered with dust like a thick
fall of snow and ringing with the tramp of their heavy boots; they
cut across the fields again and roamed for miles where the soil was
rusty-red with iron deposits, and there was not a cloud in the sky,
not a shadow, and nothing but a few stunted olive trees and sparse
foliage of almonds. They recalled their homecomings, the delicious
sense of weariness, their boasting about having walked even farther
last time, the thrill it gave them to feel they were carried over the
ground by sheer momentum, their bodies spurred into action and
their minds lulled into numbness by some dreadful troopers' song.

Zola had renounced Aix-en-Provence for Paris and his account is
therefore tinged with nostalgia, but for Cézanne such recollections of
his youth remained a reality and grew in significance after he returned
permanently to the south after his father's death in 1886 and associated
himself more closely with the Provençal renaissance. Even in his early
paintings, Mont Sainte-Victoire makes an appearance in the backgrounds
of works as different in subject as *The Abduction* (*c.* 1867; Provost
and Fellows of King's College, Cambridge, on loan to the Fitzwilliam
Museum), *The Railway Cutting* (*c.* 1869; Neue Pinakothek, Munich),
and *Factories near Mont de Cengle* (*c.* 1869–70; Private collection). It
lurks in the distance very much in a supporting role, but it would not
be long before the mountain gained a far greater prominence both in
Cézanne's life and in his work.

Whatever impulses Cézanne may have had towards landscape
painting when he started out to become an artist they were not effectively
explored until after he arrived in Paris. Here at the Académie Suisse,
alongside Pissarro, Monet and Guillaumin, he began to look at motifs
presented by the environs of the city, particularly on the western
side along the banks of the river Seine. Such places as Louveciennes,
Bougival, Argenteuil and Chatou were becoming increasingly popular
as destinations for city dwellers, offering recreation, fresh air and
relaxation, especially at weekends. More accessible now as a result
of regular services provided by trains and steamers, the opening of

restaurants, boatyards and bathing establishments in turn revived the local economies in these districts and led to the acknowledgment of their suburban status. Any previous historical associations that places such as Louveciennes or Bougival might have had owing to their proximity to Louis XIV's palaces at Versailles or Marly were swiftly overtaken by the process of modernization.

Monet, Renoir, Pissarro and Sisley all responded in varying degrees to these changes in the suburbs of Paris, but Cézanne seems to have avoided the more popular venues. Probably already conscious of Pissarro's proclivities, his preference appears to have been for the quieter hamlets and reaches further down river nearer to Rouen than to Paris. Even though the few landscapes Cézanne painted during the 1860s are robust and powerfully executed, sometimes with a palette knife, as in the *View of Bonnières* of 1866 (Musée Faure, Aix-les-Bains), they are more reminiscent of works by the artists of the Barbizon school such as Jean-Baptist-Camille Corot or Charles-François Daubigny, as opposed to the Impressionists. Perhaps the nearest Cézanne approaches Monet and Renoir in the interpretation of modern leisure is in *The Picnic* of *c.* 1874 (Museum of Fine Arts, Boston), which is a decidedly eccentric representation of a river scene.

Similarly, other works of the 1870s reveal only a passing interest in the depiction of rural life (*The Harvest*, 1875–77; Private collection, or *Life in the Fields*; 1876–77, Private collection), and also seem to refer back, again probably through Pissarro, to works by Millet dating from mid-century. Although *The Harvest* was admired by Gauguin and Van Gogh, Cézanne himself desisted from taking the theme of rural labour further, preferring to make his own highly individual analysis of the landscape.

The artist's arrival in Paris not only exposed him to a whole new type of landscape that he could not possibly have observed in the south, but also to a different light. The intensity of the bright, relatively even light of Provence, which cast such deep shadows, was exchanged for the shifting, duller, sometimes overcast weather of the Ile de France. As has been argued in Chapter 2, it was Pissarro who turned Cézanne into a fully-fledged landscape painter by showing him how to rationalize space in forming convincingly unified compositions. But, added to this, was Pissarro's understanding of colour. Having been born in the Virgin Islands and having travelled to Venezuela where he worked for two years, Pissarro himself in 1855 had had to make the considerable change from painting in the tropics to the fluctuating conditions of northern France. He therefore had a sophisticated appreciation of colour and its application under changing conditions, which Cézanne readily absorbed at Pontoise and Auvers-sur-Oise during the 1870s and early 1880s. Yet in spite of his preference for the south, it is, nonetheless, notable how often Cézanne did return during the second half of his life to paint in the environs of Paris and specifically along the banks of the river Seine, with its tributaries of the Oise to the northwest, the Loing to the southeast, and the Marne to the east and more extensively to the southeast.

A salient example of this geographical diversity is the attention paid by the artist to the village of La Roche-Guyon on the north bank of the Seine, roughly halfway between Paris and Rouen. This part of the river is overlooked by steep cliffs and a number of chalk outcrops, as depicted by Monet when he was living at nearby Vernon during the early 1880s. La Roche-Guyon itself is dominated by a château and a medieval tower rising from the riverbank. Pissarro worked here in the mid-1860s and on one occasion with Cézanne, who returned twenty years later to paint *A Turn in the Road at La Roche-Guyon, c.* 1885 (Smith College Museum of Art, Northampton, Mass.). What attracted both artists were the different levels of terrain, the contrast between geological deposits and architectural forms, and the twisting road weaving around the outcrops. The vertical emphasis of a hillside punctuated by buildings was examined by Cézanne again in the mid-1880s in three paintings of the village of Gardanne in Provence, but, interestingly, it is La Roche-Guyon that not only once more links Pissarro and Cézanne, but also Georges Braque. The younger artist had started out by emulating Cézanne at L'Estaque in 1908 before discovering La Roche-Guyon, where a year later he began to paint several pictures, including *The Château at La Roche-Guyon* (Moderna Museet, Stockholm), in the Cubist style by using the steep vertical axis to fuse together the buildings with the landscape.

In addition to his excursion to La Roche-Guyon, Cézanne also worked at different times during the second half of his life at Hattenville in Normandy, where Chocquet owned property, and at Pontoise, Melun, Fontainebleau, Giverny, Marlotte and Chantilly. The choice of places is revealing because it is based on a mixture of personal, historical and artistic associations. He was undoubtedly intrigued by the technical challenges of working in northern France and he was just as aware of the tradition of landscape painting established by the artists of the Barbizon school based at Fontainebleau as of the recent advances made by the Impressionists. Yet for Cézanne it was an alien landscape and not one for which he developed a particularly close emotional attachment. Instead, when he combined the technical skills acquired in Paris through contact with avant-garde artists with the deep, pent-up feelings he had for the countryside around Aix-en-Provence the result was a revolution in the art of landscape painting.

The experience of Paris and the principles inculcated by Pissarro came to fruition during the decade from the mid-1870s to the mid-1880s, first at L'Estaque and then at the family home of Jas de Bouffan. By positioning himself in the pine woods behind the town of L'Estaque Cézanne could look down on the rooftops and across the expansive Bay of Marseille with its islands to the jutting promontory known as the Marseilleveyre, enclosing the gulf [see 57 and 58]. The paintings of L'Estaque – one of which Picasso owned – combine a broad sweep in the background with an accumulation of detail in the foreground. Surprisingly little preparatory material for these paintings survives, revealing the artist's instinctive skill in reducing complex viewpoints to unified images of great clarity with an immediate visual impact. The notable lack of interest in any human aspects of the landscape, which is reflected in the marked absence of figures, also rapidly became a hallmark of Cézanne's depiction of Provence. The underlying geometry of the views of L'Estaque is balanced by the vibrancy of the colours – blue, green, red, ochre – denoting the intensity of the light, the heat of the sun and the proximity of the sea. Later, in a letter of 15 April 1904 to Bernard, Cézanne could almost be recalling this moment in his development:

> Allow me to repeat what I told you here: to treat nature in terms of the cylinder, the sphere and the cone, everything put in perspective, so that each side of an object, of a plane, leads to a central point. Lines parallel to the horizon give breadth, be it a section of nature or if you prefer, the spectacle that Pater Omnipotens Oeterne Deus spreads before our eyes. Lines perpendicular to this horizon give depth. Now, we men experience nature more in terms of depth than surface, whence the need to introduce into our vibrations of light, represented by reds and yellows, a sufficient quantity of blue tones, to give a sense of atmosphere.

The Jas de Bouffan, which Zola described in *L'Oeuvre* as looking 'as white as an oriental mosque in the centre of its enormous fields', was a place of retreat for Cézanne and was of such personal significance that his approach to the motifs found there was bound to be different. The house, farm buildings, trees, pathways and ornaments seem cut off from the rest of the world [see 63 and 150]. The overriding effect of the paintings and watercolours of the family home is one of privacy and self-protection. The chestnut trees stand like sentinels, the stone lions prepare to give chase, while the gateways, fences and walls encircle the house where the shutters stand ready to be closed. There is great variety in Cézanne's concluding depictions of the Jas de Bouffan in which he continues to test out his ideas of spatial organization and his reductive processes, as well as refining his treatment of light, his knowledge of colour and his application of paint. This is where traditional landscape motifs such as *sous-bois* [149] are suddenly elevated to a new level of closely integrated forms leading to a greater unified whole. As the artist told the poet Léo Larguier, 'To paint something does not mean making a servile copy of it. It means seizing a single harmony out of all the interconnections one has observed; transposing these into a formal series with its own validity by means of working them up according to a new and original logic.' Occasionally, in the works done at the Jas de Bouffan, Cézanne allows us a glimpse of the world beyond. For example, visible from the house over the wall and through the screen of trees there looms the outline of Mont Sainte-Victoire, which would soon become a symbol of such personal significance for the artist [150].

During the 1880s and through the 1890s until his death in 1906 Cézanne became more adventurous in his approach to landscape as he rediscovered the Provence of his childhood. Although restricted geographically, his outlook extended from panoramic views of the valley of the river Arc to close studies of the buildings, forests, woods, glades and rocks of the region. Even before the sale of the Jas de Bouffan Cézanne had begun to use his sister's house at Bellevue as a base for scouting out and examining new motifs and this practice was followed successively at the unfinished neo-Gothic Château Noir (1887–1904), the abandoned quarry at Bibémus (1897–1904) and finally his studio at Les Lauves (1902–06). These places are situated at different points of the compass around Aix-en-Provence, but all are within view of Mont Sainte-Victoire. As Gasquet wrote:

> From every point Sainte-Victoire dominated the landscape, in
> the morning as blue as a virgin's prayer, at noon ablaze, at sunset
> flushed after drinking so much light, under a cap of clouds or
> a crown of sun, spreading on its slopes at night an altar-cloth
> fragrant with incense, or erecting at dawn the stone horses of an
> Assyrian bas-relief – everywhere, at the horizon of every plain, at
> the end of every road, from one hill to another, the sight of Sainte-
> Victoire entered Cézanne's fresh eyes.

The views of the mountain undertaken by Cézanne fall into two groups. The first, dating for the most part from the second half of the 1880s, are panoramic and include the valley of the river Arc seen from Bellevue. The essential elements of the scene are laid out in a slight drawing in Rotterdam followed by a more elaborate watercolour in Vienna [151]. In both of these compositional drawings a pine tree on the left serves as a repoussoir motif uniting the viaduct in the middle

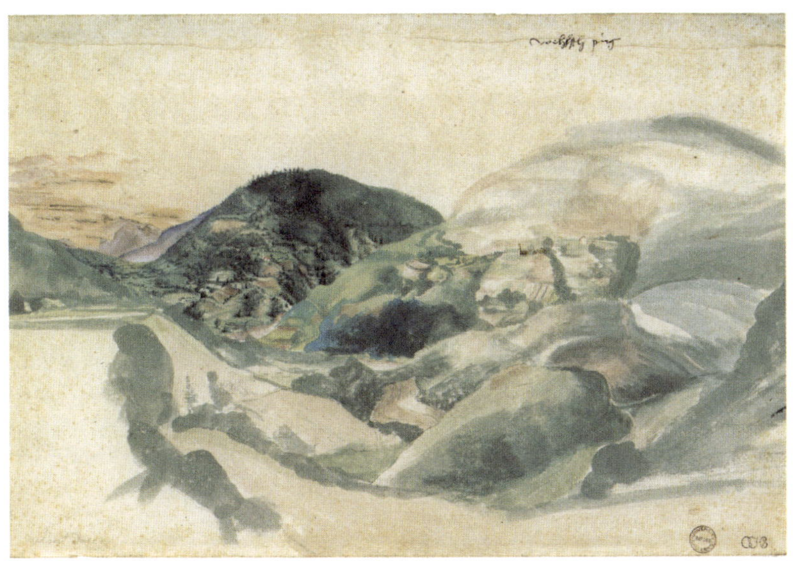

143. Albrecht Dürer, '*Welsch Pirg*', 1494.
Watercolour, 21 × 31.2 cm (8¼ × 12¼ in.).
Ashmolean Museum, Oxford

distance and a lightly indicated Mont Sainte-Victoire in the distance.
By the time of the watercolour in Chicago a great deal more of the
composition is revealed [152]. Here the trunk of the tree and its branch
frame the view, which includes houses and fields, in addition to the
viaduct that snakes across the countryside like a zip in a dress. The
mountains beyond include Mont Sainte-Victoire just to the left of centre
and the ridge leading to Mont du Cengle to the right. The serenity
of these first panoramic views of Mont Sainte-Victoire [153, 154] by
Cézanne is often compared with the work of Poussin, to whom the artist
frequently referred in his correspondence and conversation. 'Imagine
Poussin completely repainted from nature. That's what I call classical',
he remarked to Gasquet. But, more than that, Cézanne detected a feeling
of melancholy in the Provençal landscape that he felt only Poussin would
have been able to capture. 'I'd like to put reason in the grass and tears in
the sky, like Poussin', he went on to say to Gasquet. In fact, though, so
immersed in the tradition of European painting are these views of Mont
Sainte-Victoire that the names of other artists come to mind: Albrecht
Dürer for his pantheistic response to the mountains and pine trees that he
saw as he crossed the Alps on his way to Italy in 1494 [143] and Claude

Lorrain for the structural coherence and ethereal tonal subtleties that
he brought to his narrative compositions, which were so often inspired
by Virgil's poetry.

For most of the works belonging to this first series of Mont Sainte-
Victoire Cézanne kept his distance and viewed the mountain from afar,
but there are some watercolours of the same date where he shrinks the
space between himself and the mountain, virtually ignoring the valley
[155, 156]. These views are almost telescopic and show the mountain
from a slightly lower vantage point. Mont Sainte-Victoire now looms
much larger on the horizon and seems more transcendental as befitted its
emblematic status. Far from being of personal significance for Cézanne
alone the mountain had also now become a symbol for the political
and cultural aspirations of Provence as a whole. Its position within the
landscape provided sufficient credibility for such a choice, but also both
historically and geologically Mont Sainte-Victoire epitomized the unique
geophysical features of the region. Furthermore, Cézanne had climbed
the mountain on several occasions, often with his friend the scientist
Marion, and so was as aware of its geological importance as of its
spiritual resonance.

The second series of panoramic views of Mont Sainte-Victoire was
done later, between 1902 and 1906, from the studio at Les Lauves and is
more varied owing to Cézanne's tendency to experiment more with the
axis and viewpoint [157–162]. From this angle the shape of the mountain
forms an irregular triangle with its long ridge ending abruptly in a cliff
edge that drops down before the gentle ascent to the neighbouring Mont
du Cengle begins. The mountain resembles a flying buttress that seems to
spring from a strong pattern of recurring fields and buildings stretched
like a tapestry across the expansive foreground. The eye is led across
this foreground as if partaking in a game of visual hopscotch until it is
suddenly confronted by the mountain itself that towers upwards with
an elemental and talismanic force.

An aspect of Cézanne's treatment of landscape during his later years
was his closer engagement with nature. During the 1890s he suddenly
became much exercised by the motif a single pine tree. Such trees had
of course appeared in his earlier paintings, but now the pine is treated in
the vein of portraiture. While the paintings concentrate on the setting of
the pine tree seen against a bright azure sky and the parched earth, the
drawings and watercolours balance the strength of the trunk against
the delicate tracery of the interlocking branches [144, 163, 164]. Many of
the images of the pine tree made on paper by Cézanne have the precision
of botanical illustration and are reminiscent of works of this type by
contemporary artists from different schools, such as John Ruskin [145].

Like Mont Sainte-Victoire, the pine tree was an immensely evocative image for Cézanne, partaking both of the innocence of his childhood as much as of the regenerative qualities of nature, or the history of Provence. As early as 9 April 1858 he wrote to Zola, 'Do you remember the pine that stood on the bank of the Arc, lowering its leafy head over the chasm that opened at its feet? That pine that protected our bodies with its foliage from the heat of the sun, ah! May the Gods preserve it from the fatal blow of the woodcutter's axe!' Such a threat was all that was required to give the image of the pine tree the potency of a personal emblem in Cézanne's work.

The artist's close association with all aspects of the history of Provence, combined with his local knowledge of the rugged and arid countryside around Aix-en-Provence, resulted in some of the most remarkable watercolours in his *oeuvre*. Many of the sites he explored, or the motifs he chose, were abandoned. Cézanne favoured places where habitation, or signs of human intervention, were hardly evident or else were slowly being reclaimed by nature [165]. Deserted buildings, often unfinished, dilapidated or falling down, and without any sign of activity, particularly appealed to him for historical reasons as much as for formal considerations. It is as if the countryside of Provence was an architectural graveyard. Farmhouses (*mas*), country houses (*bastides*) and rural cottages (*cabanes*) frequently feature in his work [166]. Only occasionally is a working building represented, as in the lime kiln near the Pont des Trois Sautets [167].

The Château Noir, however, was a building of particular significance for Cézanne. This was an ambitious building project reputedly undertaken by a local coal merchant, but was left unfinished. It comprised two buildings with a courtyard and undeveloped grounds. Blocks of masonry, pillars and building materials intended for the installation of cisterns and mills were left strewn about the place, adding to its air of mystery and becoming the stuff of sinister legends [142, 168]. Cézanne was fascinated by the building seen from afar [169, 170], but he also chose to concentrate on the surrounding terrain extending above the château, including the caves, thick forested areas, dense foliage, rocky ridges and large boulders. The contrast with the well-kept grounds of the Jas de Bouffan must have been stark. At the Château Noir Cézanne was confronting nature in the wild. Traditional landscape motifs such as *sous-bois* are balanced by detailed studies of the irregular shapes and surfaces of rocks and boulders [146, 171]. Deep sunk shadowed crevices and running grooves are contrasted with protruding plants and foliage. So intensely observed are these watercolours made by Cézanne that at times they again resemble the more detailed scientific studies of rocks

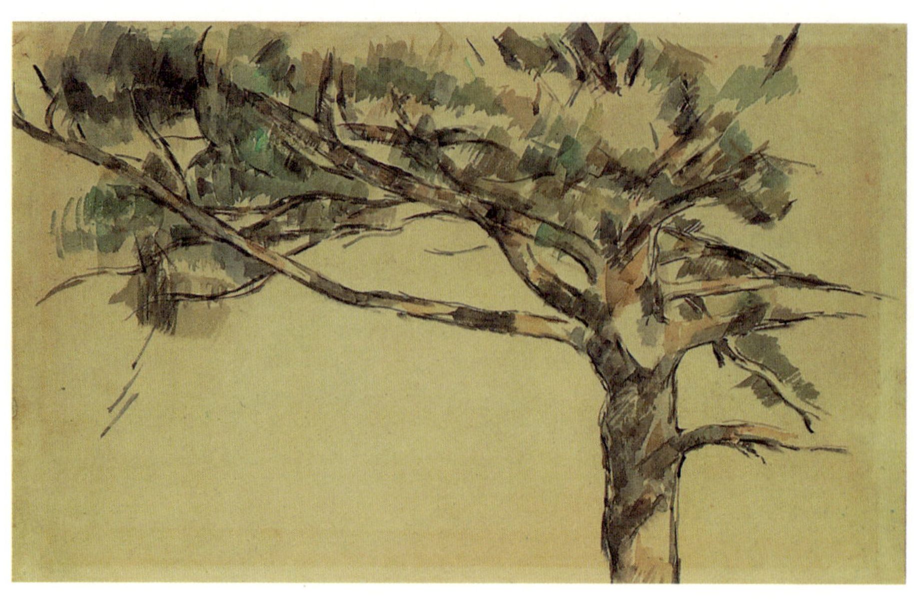

144. *The Great Tree, c.* 1890.
Watercolour, 27.7 × 43.7 cm (10⅞ × 17¼ in.).
Kunsthaus Zurich

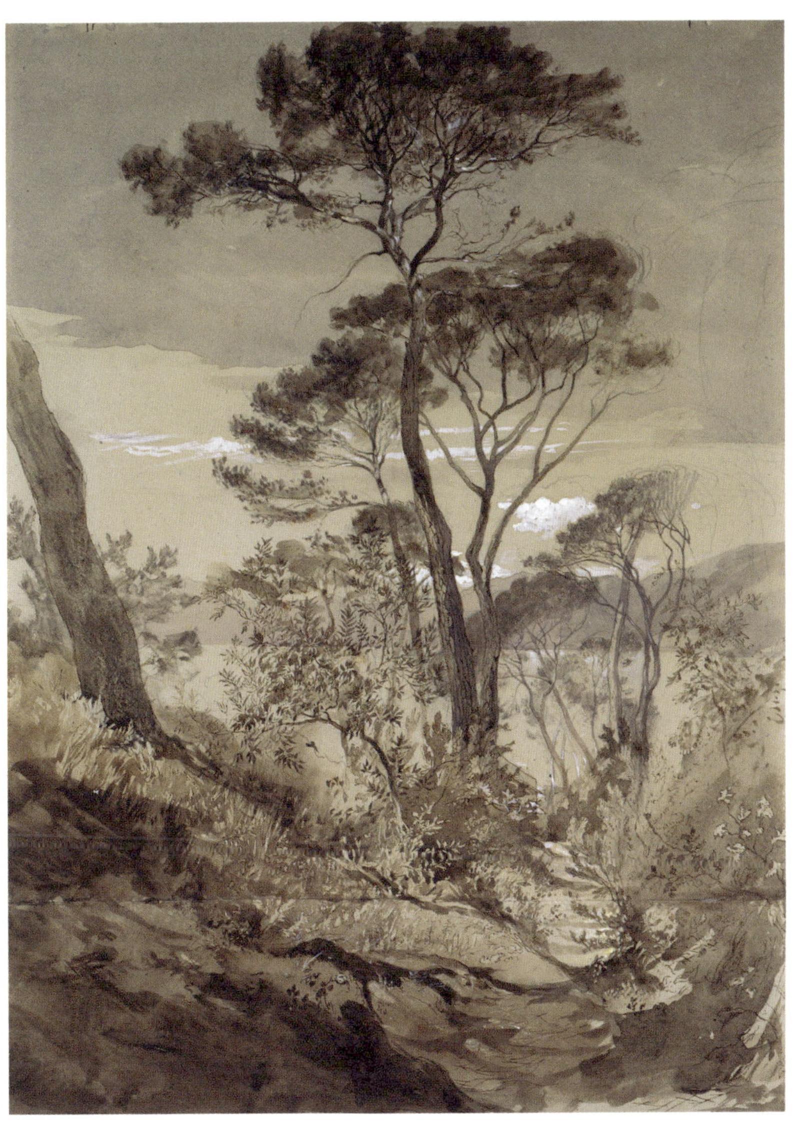

145. John Ruskin, *Stone Pines at Sestri*, 1845.
Pencil and pen with washes and white gouache on off-white paper,
44.2 × 33.4 cm (17⅜ × 13⅛ in.).
Ashmolean Museum, Oxford

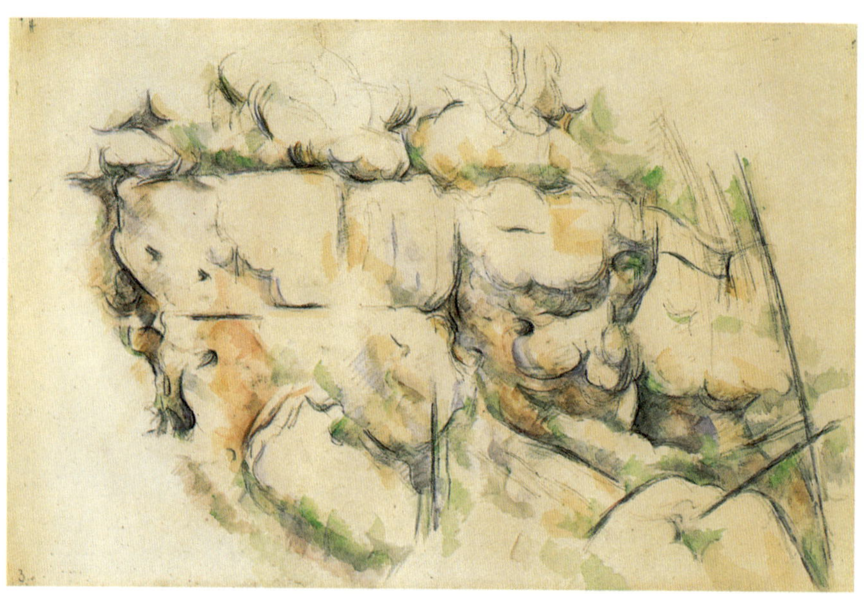

146. *Rocky Ridge above Château Noir*, 1895–1900.
Pencil and watercolour, 31.7 × 47.5 cm (12½ × 18¾ in.).
Museum of Modern Art, New York

and foliage drawn by Ruskin [147] in connection with his research for the fourth volume of *Modern Painters* (1856), where there occurs the following passage that may be said to anticipate Cézanne's interests:

> There are no natural objects out of which more can be thus learned than out of stones. They seem to have been created especially to reward a patient observer … For a stone, when it is examined, will be found a mountain in miniature. The fineness of Nature's work is so great, that into a single block, a foot or two in diameter, she can compress as many changes of form and structure, on a small scale, as she needs for her mountains on a large one; and taking moss for forests, and grains of crystal for crags, the surface of a stone … is more interesting than the surface of an ordinary hill; more fantastic in form and incomparably richer in colour.

Occasionally, however, unlike in Ruskin's case, the exact subject of these watercolours by Cézanne is difficult to discern at first and it is in this sense that the artist here begins to move beyond visual description and reaches out towards the abstract.

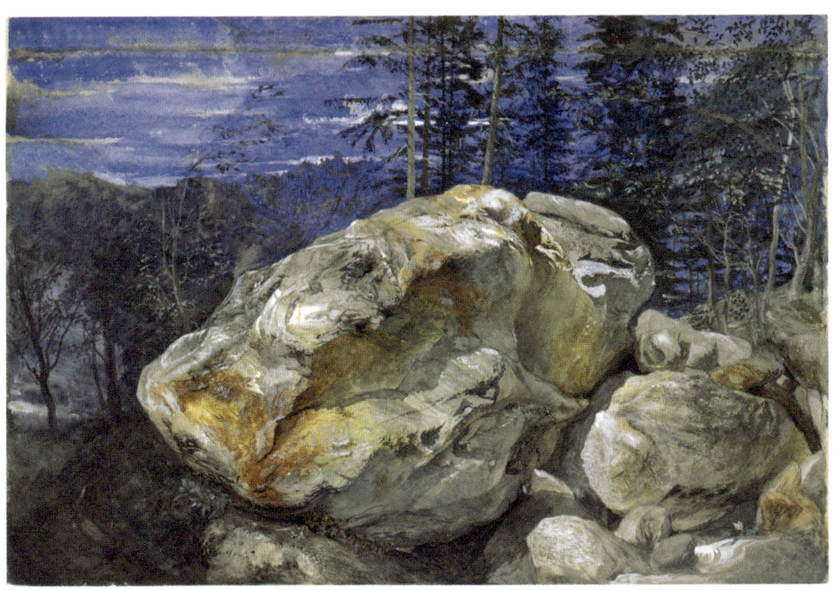

147. John Ruskin, *Fragment of the Alps*, *c.* 1854–56.
Watercolour and gouache over pencil, 33.5 × 49.3 cm (13¼ × 19⅜ in.).
Fogg Museum, Cambridge, Massachusetts

The quarry at Bibémus was appreciated by Cézanne for similar reasons. Abandoned during the 1830s, isolated and difficult to access, this inhospitable site is located in more open ground than the Château Noir. It was buffeted by winds and more exposed to the sun. The stone quarried there was an ochre-coloured sandstone, which turns orange after rain. According to legend, this effect was due to the blood spilt by the troops commanded by Gaius Marius in 102 BC. Cézanne was fascinated by the striations and fissures visible in the rock faces as a result of the quarrying and it is possible that he saw in such marks a metaphor for his own artistic techniques [172–174]. Furthermore, it could be said that the strange shapes and forms of the rocks concealed by a camouflage of overgrown plants and foliage created a visual paradox demonstrating how human endeavour has been undone by the resurgence of nature. In short, Cézanne regarded Bibémus quarry in the same way as others contemplated the ruins of antiquity. A famous example is Poggio Bracciolini's lament for the loss of the buildings of ancient Rome in his *Historia de varietate fortunae* (1448), as quoted by Edward Gibbon in the final chapter of *The History of the Decline and Fall of the Roman Empire*

(1776–88), 'This spectacle of the world, how it is fallen! How changed! How defaced! The path of victory is obliterated by vines and the benches of the senators are concealed by a dunghill … The public and private edifices that were founded for eternity lie prostrate, naked and broken like the limbs of a mighty giant.' To a certain extent, Cézanne's choice of motifs in isolated places such as the Château Noir or the Bibémus quarry can be likened to a withdrawal from the world by an anchorite monk, inducing in the artist the desire to contemplate the passing of time.

At the same time, Cézanne's instinctive reaction to the Château Noir and the Bibémus quarry was matched by an advance in his technical skills as a watercolourist [175–177]. The traditional method of making a watercolour involved an elaborate compositional underdrawing that was then developed as it was overpainted by the application of washes. This process was dependent upon an acknowledgment of the hierarchical distinction between different types and separate attributes of media. Cézanne made no such distinction. He alternated his use of pencil and wash by applying each according to his needs while also allowing the paper a positive role in the creation of the image. The tonal emphasis derived from the flurries of lines and hatched strokes in pencil provided him with a sense of form or spatial organization; the almost abstract patches of colour, which are abutted either as single splashes or in sequences that are sometimes overlaid, were modulated in such a way as to enhance the sense of form through colour. As Fry wrote in 1917, Cézanne 'arrived at the contour by a study of the interior planes; he was always plastic before he was linear'.

The placement of the patches of colour also operates as a system of aerial, or sensory, perspective free of the mathematical principles that had been applied from the Renaissance onwards. It is apparent, therefore, that neither the pencil nor the brush had precedence as Cézanne developed his technique in watercolours: one could be used without the other or both could be worked together at different stages of the creative process. Often he would return at a later stage to give added linear emphasis by strengthening the outlines of the principal forms using the pencil or point of the brush with a darker colour. The surface of many of the watercolours often reads like a palimpsest.

In effect, Cézanne combines two notational methods to make a single image, which is so strictly controlled that it often teeters on the edge of abstraction. Bernard once saw him working on one of these watercolours and recorded that, 'His method was unique, excessively complicated, and different from usual techniques. He began on the shadows with a single patch, which he then overlapped with a second, larger one; and then with a third one, until these patches, which produced screens, modelled the object by way of colouring it.' Adopting a similar technique in his paintings from the mid-1880s, Cézanne's ultimate intention was to amalgamate systems of drawing and colouring. He told Gasquet, 'The drawing and the colour are no longer distinct; as soon as you paint you draw; the more the colours harmonize, the more precise the drawing becomes … When the colour is at its richest, the form is at its fullest. Contrast and relationship of colours – that's the secret of drawing and modelling…' – a maxim that he expounded to Bernard and Larguier.

The accuracy and aplomb that Cézanne brought to the use of the brush in his watercolours was never the result of self-confidence or bravura; rather, it was derived from intense concentration brought about by self-doubt and uncertainty. There can be little wonder that a technique from which so much emerged out of such concision amazed his contemporaries. As Renoir asked of Denis, 'How does he do it? He can't put two strokes of colour on a canvas without it already being very good' – a remark echoed by Picasso, who is reported as saying of Cézanne, 'As soon as he begins to make the first stroke, the picture is already there.'

As Cézanne's energies began to fail he was forced to rely on others to transport him to and from the motifs that preoccupied him. The intense heat, the threat of sudden rain and the force of the mistral were all dangers for an ageing artist who liked to walk and spend hours in the open air. On occasion he was content to depict the terrace of his studio at Les Lauves [178] or the views that he could see from there. These were not just of Mont Sainte-Victoire [157–162], but also topographical motifs overlooking the town of Aix-en-Provence with the cathedral of Saint-Sauveur [179]. The most revealing aspect of Cézanne's very latest watercolours is their vibrancy in spite of signs of tiredness and frustration. This is due in part to the greater intensity of the drawing derived from the rhythmical almost splashing nature of the brushwork, which so effectively combines the physicality of the objects with the motion of flickering light and the quivering atmosphere [180–185]. It is also due in part to the lighter palette where ochre, violet, grey, blue and green are applied in ever brighter hues. But, Cézanne was never satisfied and he kept trying to the very end. On 8 September 1906, seven weeks before he died, he wrote to his son, Paul,

> Finally, I must tell you that as a painter I'm becoming more clear-sighted in front of nature, but the *réalisation* of my *sensations* is still very laboured. I can't achieve the intensity that builds in my senses, I don't have that magnificent richness of colour that enlivens nature. Here on the riverbank the *motifs* multiply, the same subject from a different angle provides a fascinating subject for study, and so varied that I think I could occupy myself for months without moving, leaning now more to the right, now more to the left.

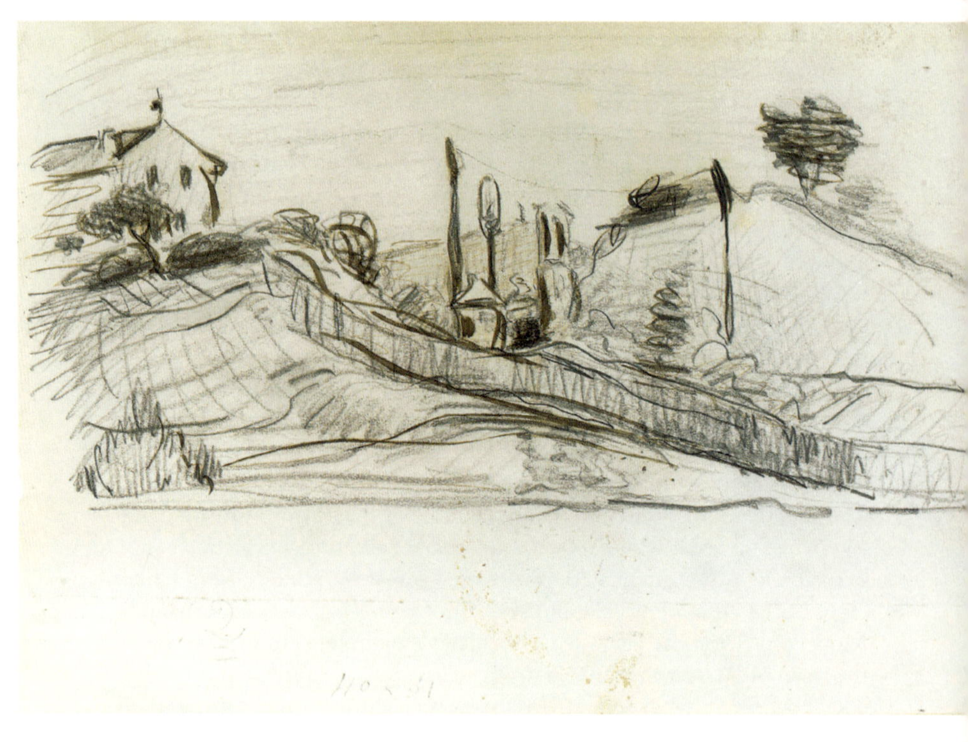

148. *The Railway Cutting, c.* 1870.
Pencil, pen and ink, 17.2 × 24.1 cm (6¼ × 9½ in.).
Private collection

149. *Trees,* 1882–84.
Pencil and watercolour, 47 × 30.5 cm (18½ × 12 in.).
Private collection

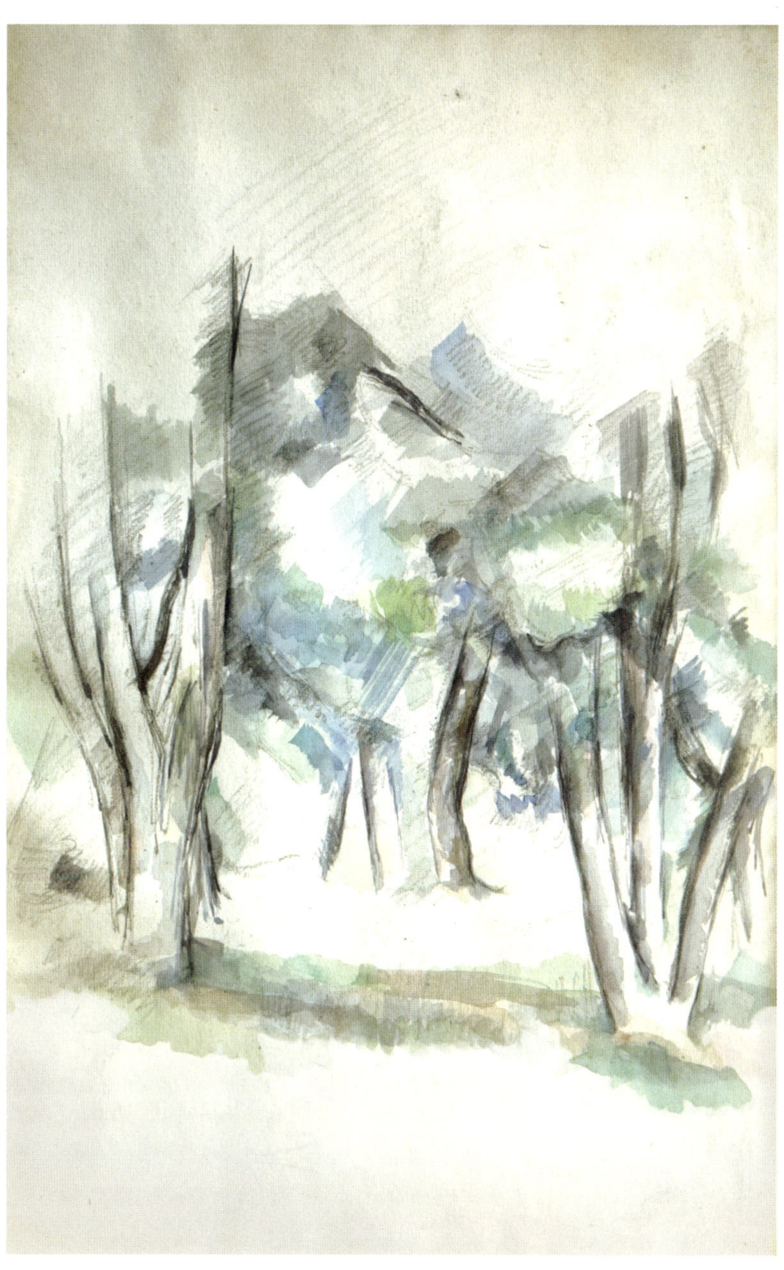

150. *Mont Sainte-Victoire Seen beyond the Wall of the Jas de Bouffan*, 1885–88.
Pencil and watercolour, 45.5 × 30 cm (18 × 11⅞ in.).
National Gallery of Art, Washington, DC

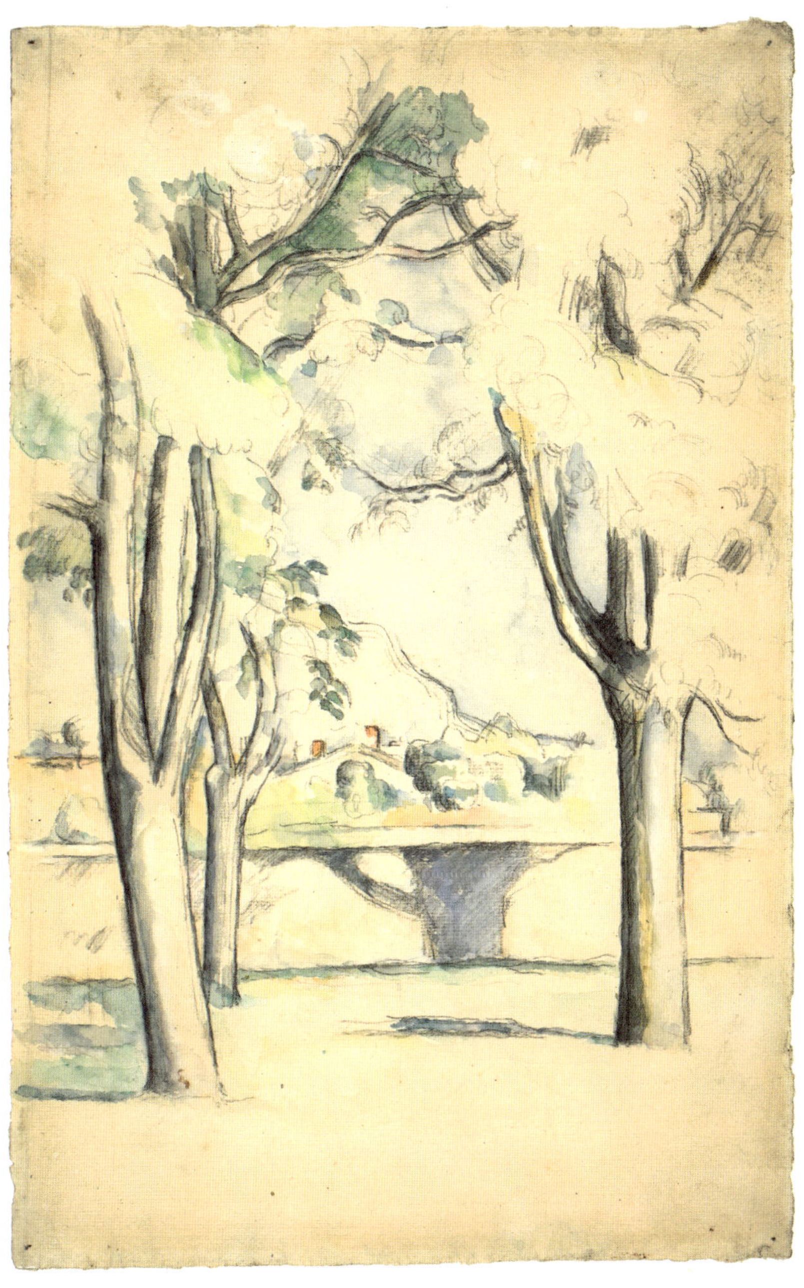

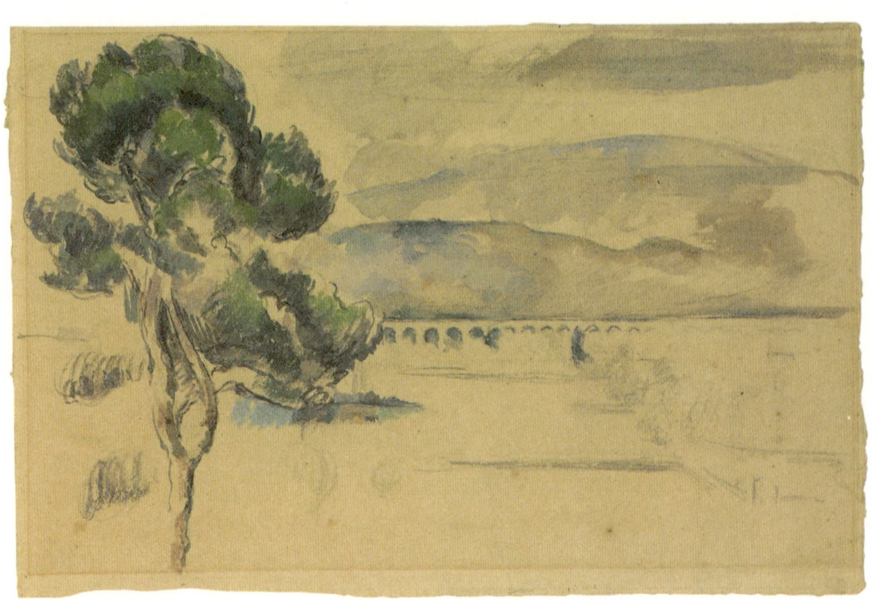

151. *Pine Tree in the Arc Valley*, 1883–85.
Pencil and watercolour, 29.6 × 47 cm (11⅝ × 8½ in.).
Albertina, Vienna

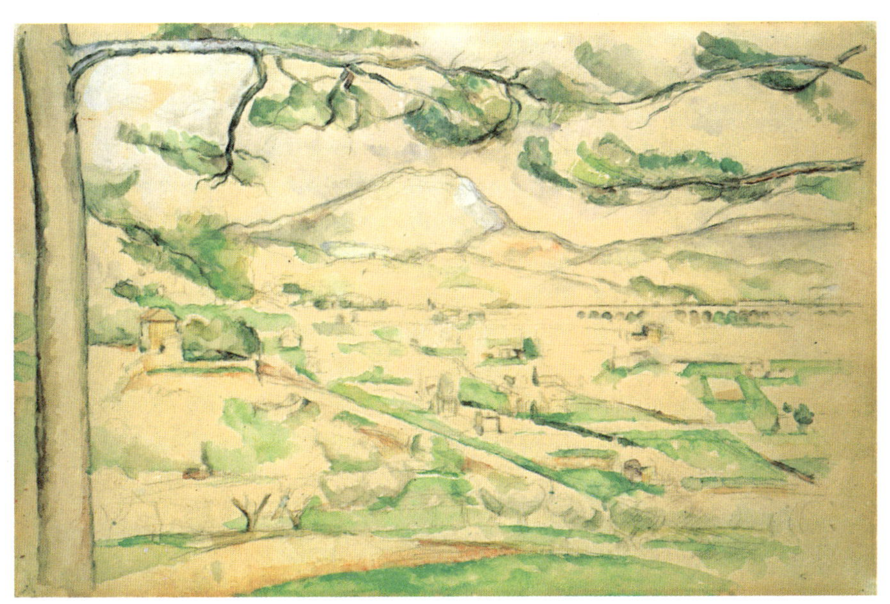

152. *The Arc Valley, c.* 1885.
Pencil and watercolour with white gouache, 35.4 × 53.7 cm (13⅞ × 21⅛ in.).
The Art Institute of Chicago

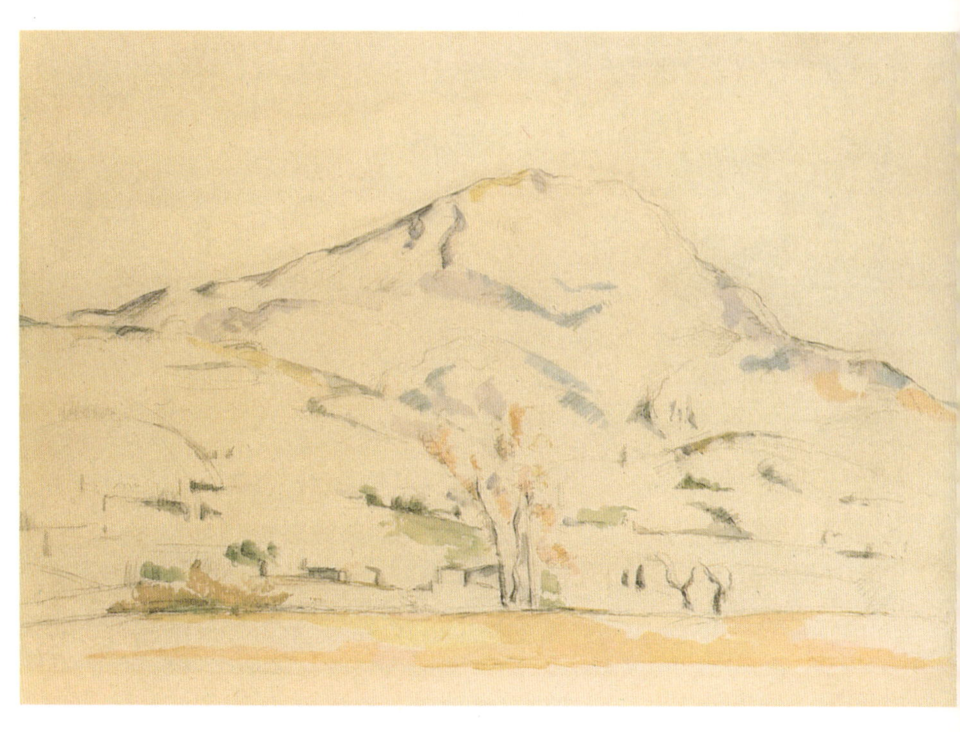

153. *Mont Sainte-Victoire*, 1885–87.
Pencil and watercolour, 38.8 × 50 cm (15¼ × 19⅝ in.).
Fogg Museum, Cambridge, Massachusetts

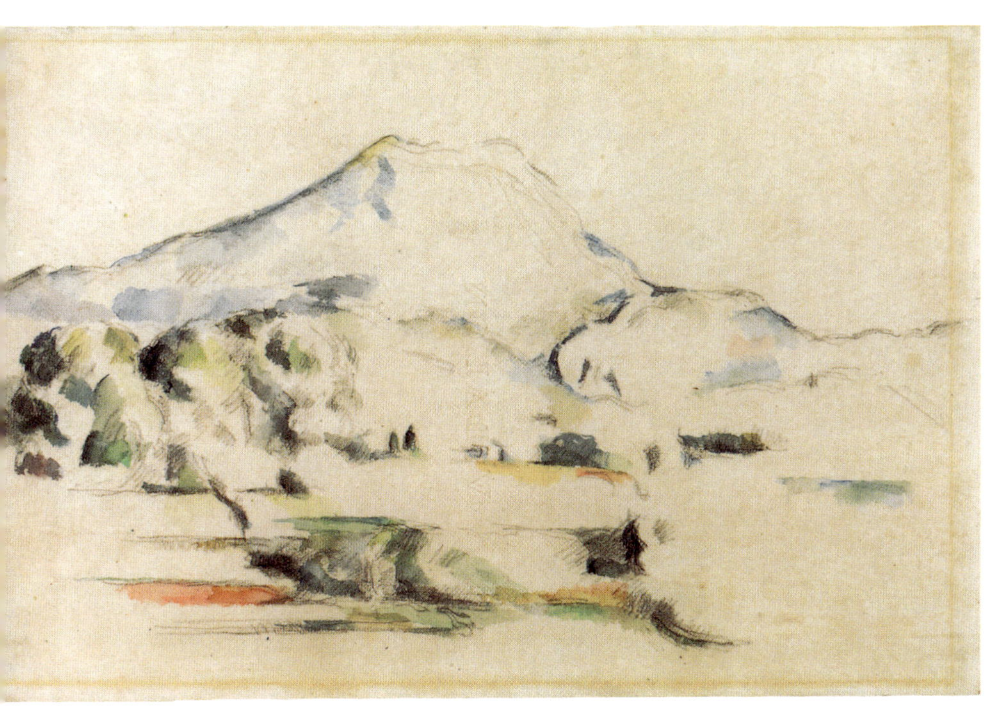

154. Mont Sainte-Victoire, 1885–86.
Pencil and watercolour, 31.5 × 47.5 cm (12⅜ × 18¾ in.).
The Courtauld Gallery, London

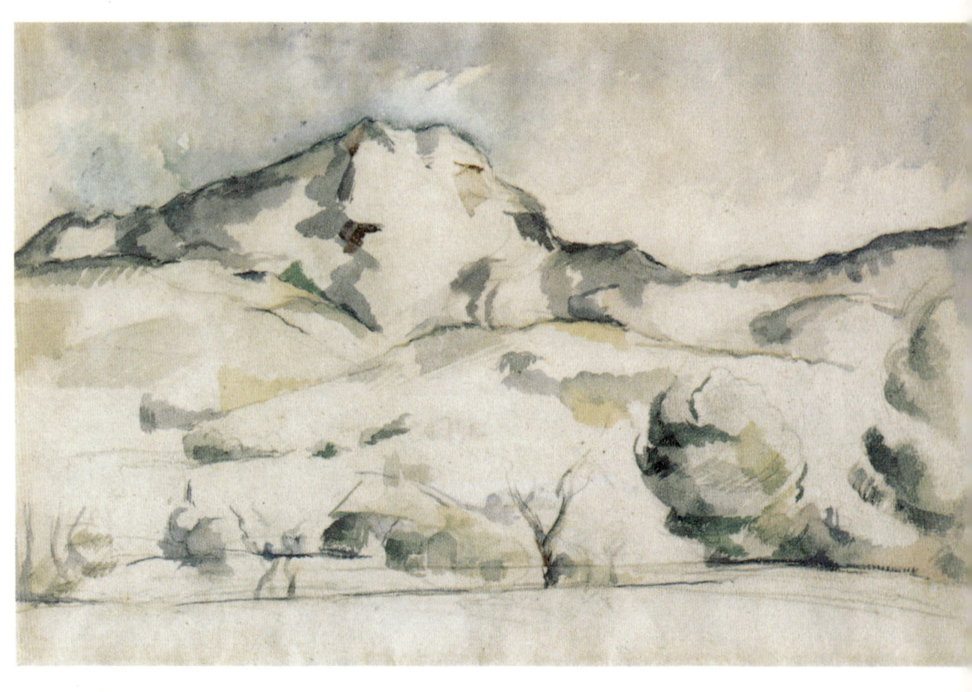

155. *Mont Sainte-Victoire*, 1885–86.
Pencil and watercolour, 30.9 × 46.7 cm (12⅛ × 18⅛ in.).
Fogg Museum, Cambridge, Massachusetts

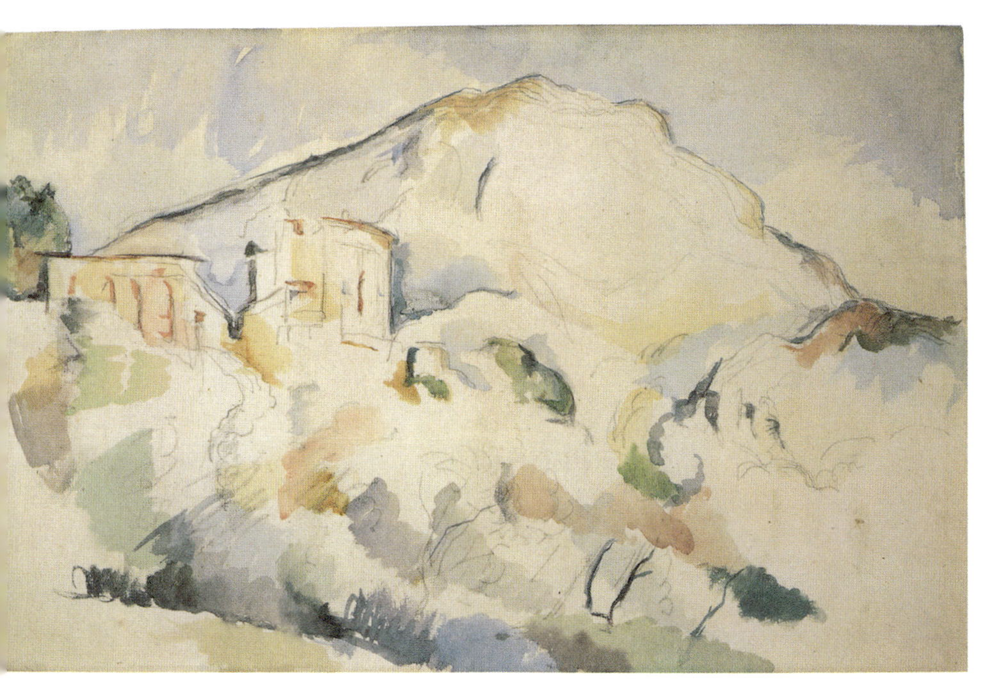

156. *Château Noir with Mont Sainte-Victoire*, 1890–95.
Pencil and watercolour, 31 × 48.3 cm (12¼ × 19 in.).
Albertina, Vienna

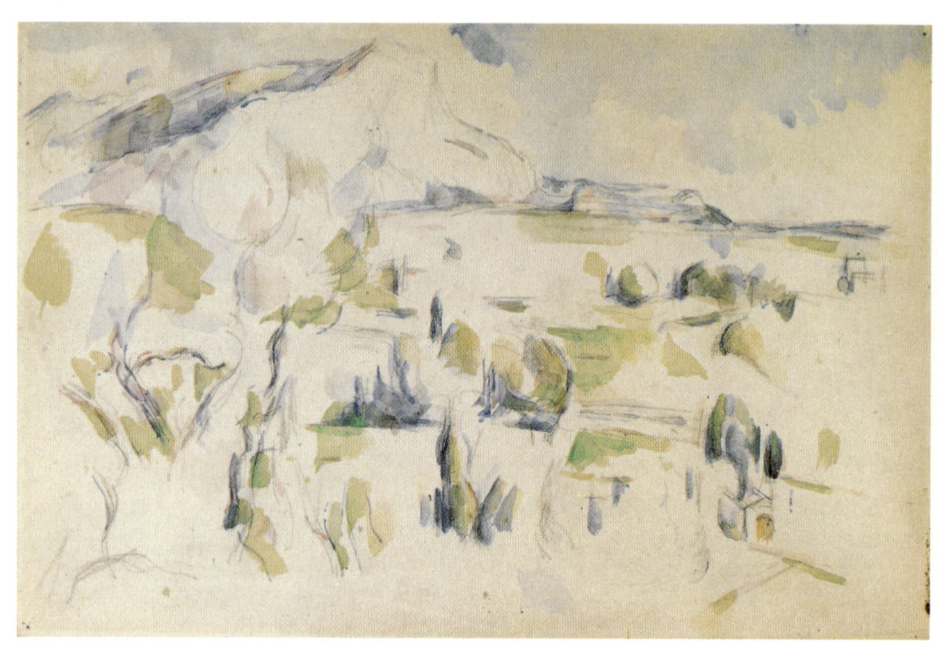

157. *Mont Sainte-Victoire from Les Lauves*, 1900–06.
Pencil and watercolour on pale buff paper, 31.9 × 47.6 cm (12¼ × 18¾ in.).
The Henry and Rose Pearlman Foundation, on loan to Princeton University
Art Museum, New Jersey

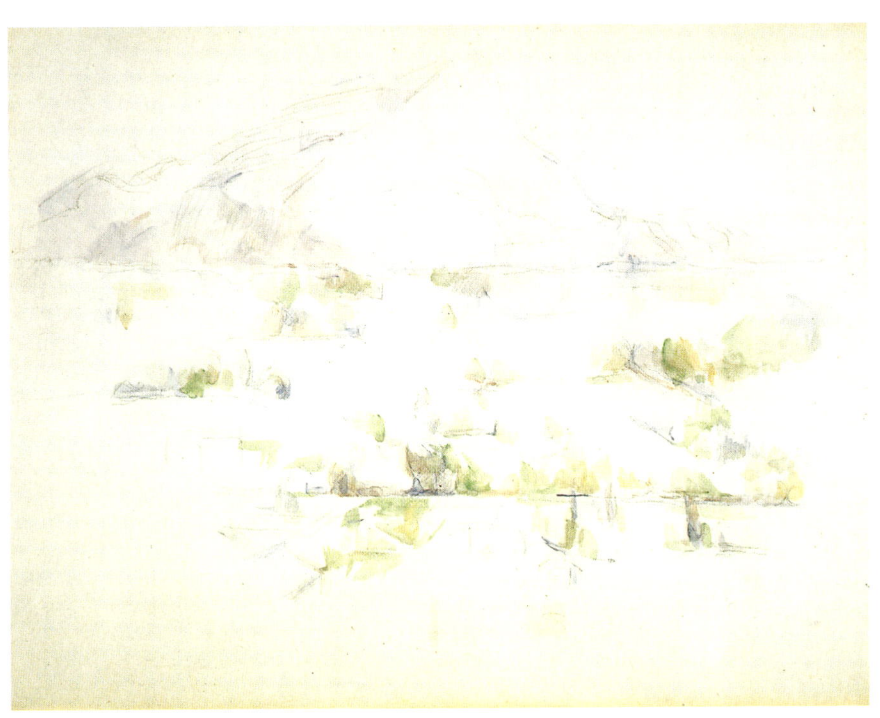

158. *Mont Sainte-Victoire from Les Lauves*, 1901–06.
Pencil and watercolour, 47.5 × 61.5 cm (18⅝ × 24¼ in.).
National Gallery of Ireland, Dublin

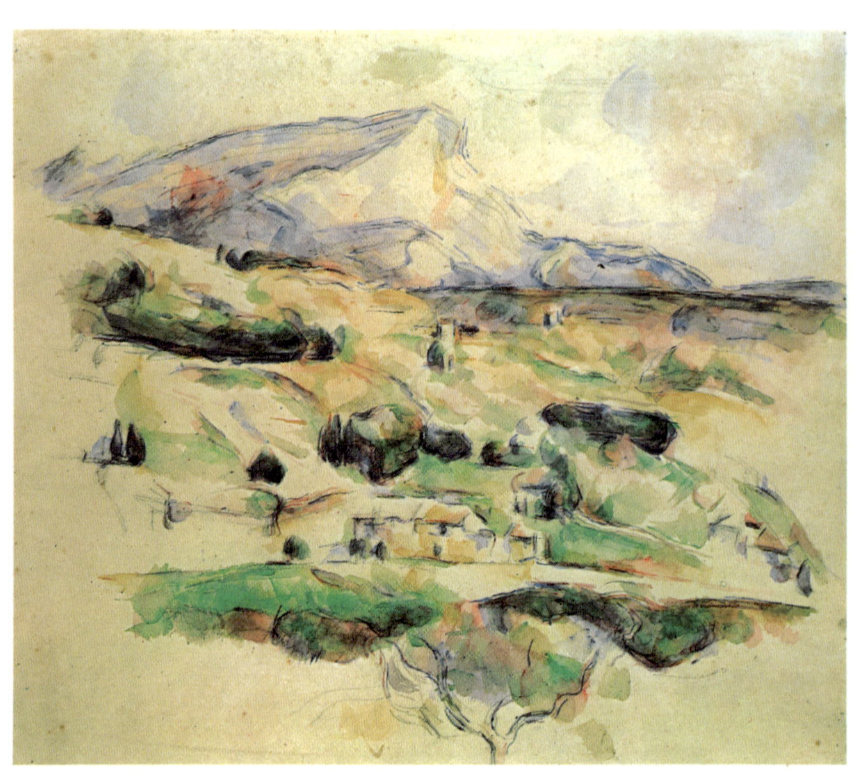

159. *Mont Sainte-Victoire from Les Lauves*, 1902–06.
Pencil and watercolour, 47.5 × 53.5 cm (18¾ × 21 in.).
Private collection

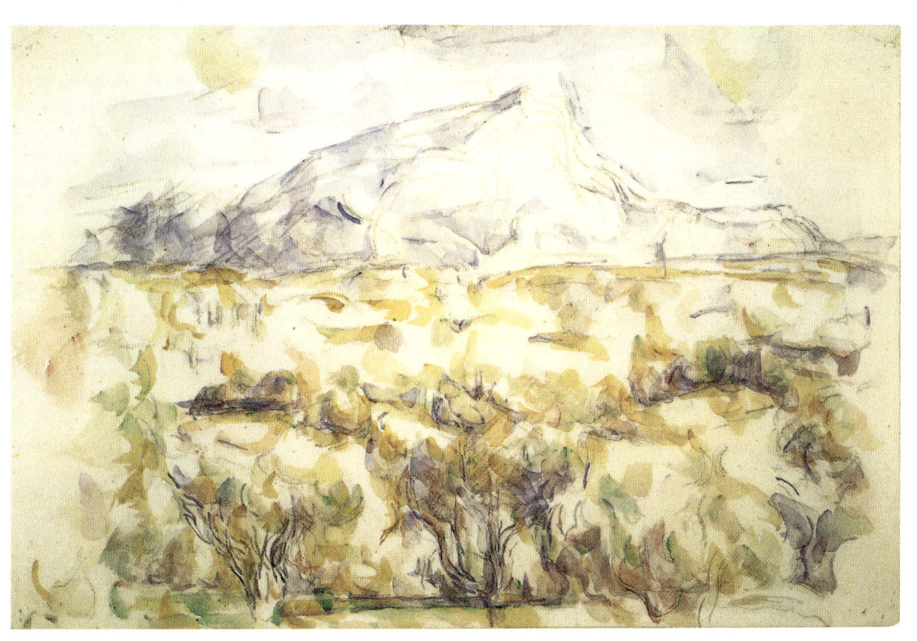

160. *Mont Sainte-Victoire from Les Lauves*, 1902–06.
Pencil and watercolour, 36 × 55 cm (14¼ × 21⅝ in.).
Tate, London

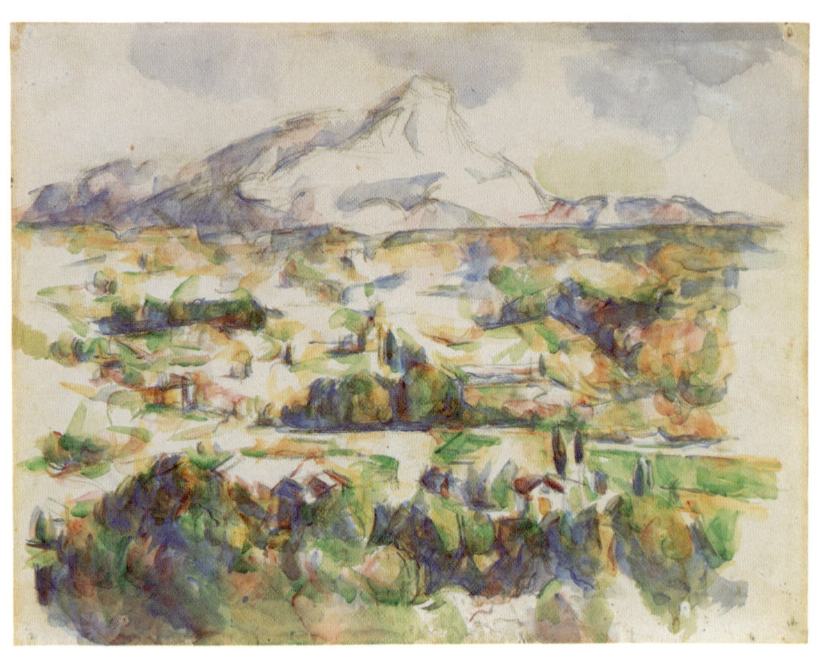

ABOVE
161. *Mont Sainte-Victoire from Les Lauves*, 1902–06.
Pencil and watercolour, 48 × 63.2 cm (18⅞ × 25 in.).
Oskar Reinhart Collection 'Am Römerholz', Winterthur

OPPOSITE
162. *Mont Sainte-Victoire from Les Lauves*, 1902–06.
Pencil and watercolour, 48 × 31 cm (18⅞ × 12¼ in.).
Philadelphia Museum of Art

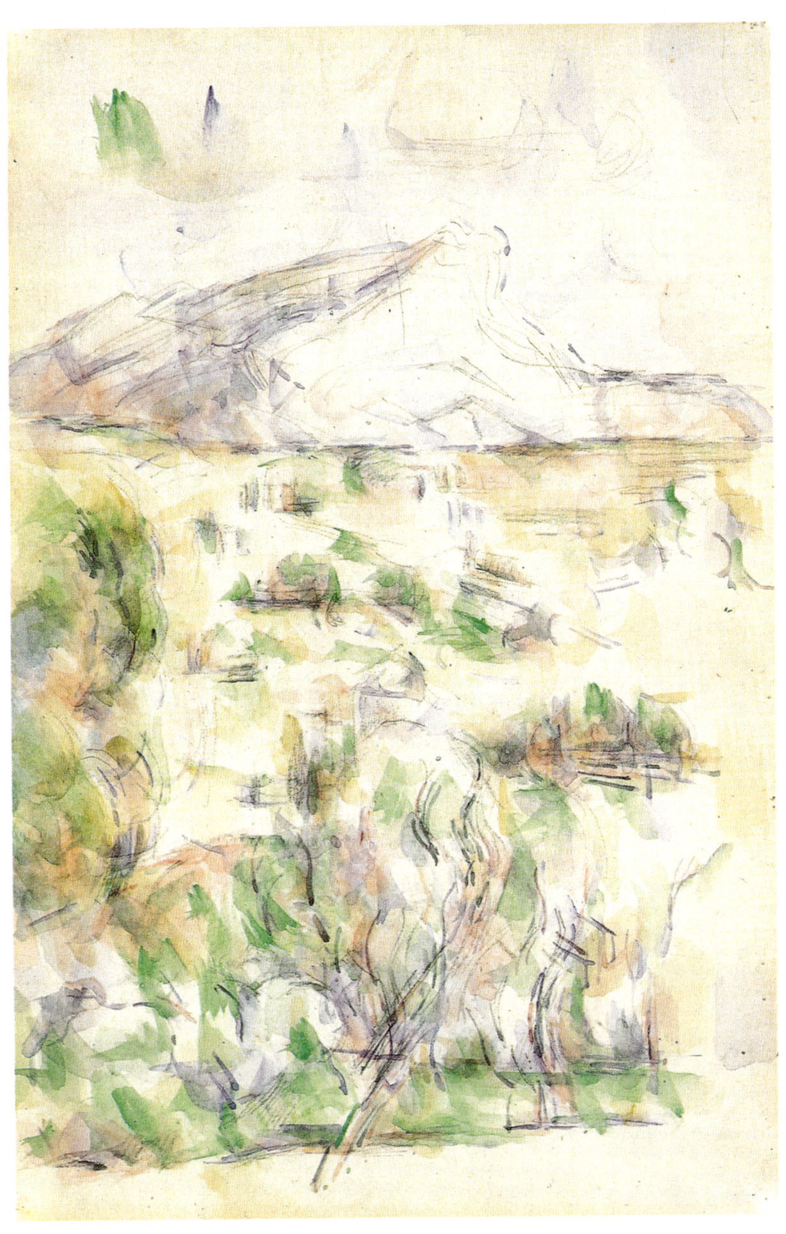

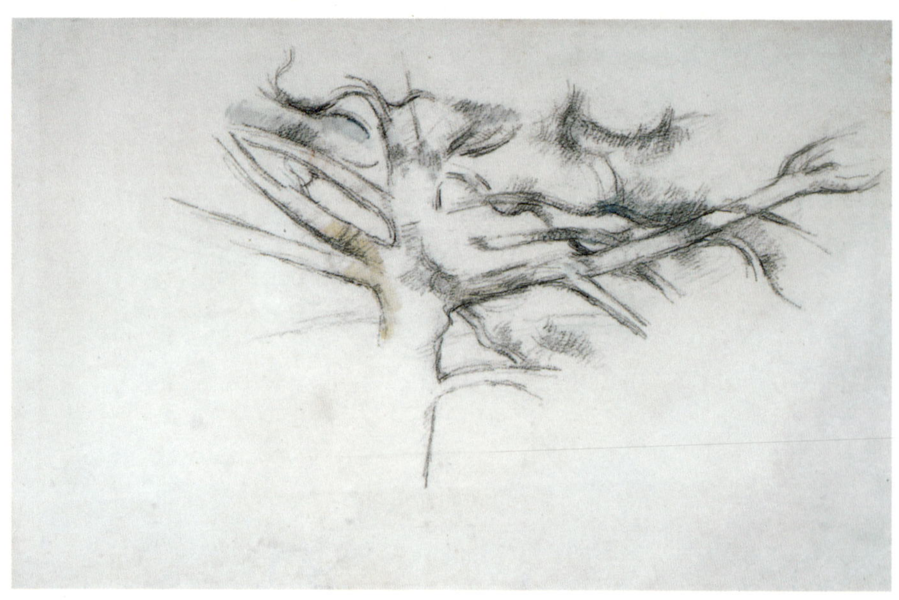

163. *The Large Pine, c.* 1890.
Pencil and watercolour, 24.6 × 40.6 cm (9¾ × 16 in.).
Virginia Museum of Fine Arts, Richmond

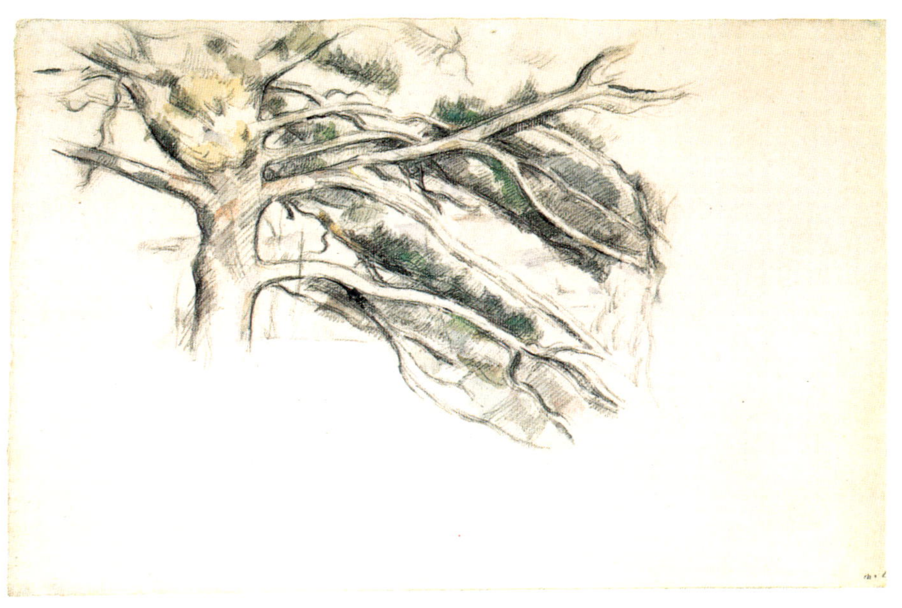

164. *The Large Pine*, 1890–95.
Pencil and watercolour, 30.5 × 46 cm (12 × 18⅛ in.).
Metropolitan Museum of Art, New York,
and Fogg Museum, Cambridge, Massachusetts

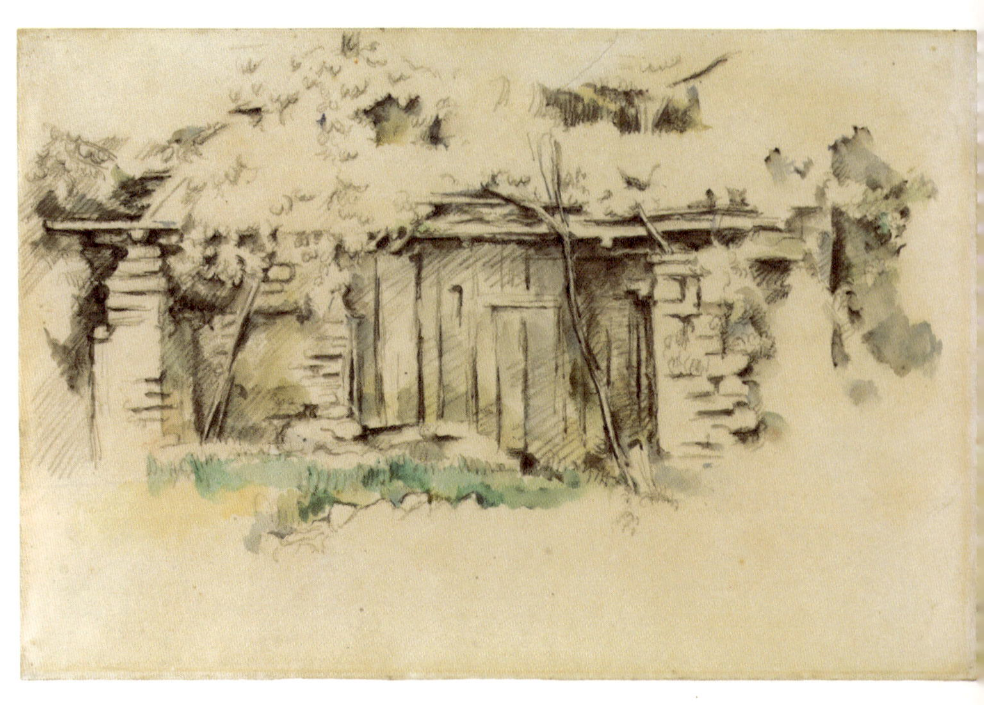

165. *A Shed, c.* 1880.
Pencil and watercolour, 31 × 47.5 cm (12¼ × 18¾ in.).
The Courtauld Gallery, London

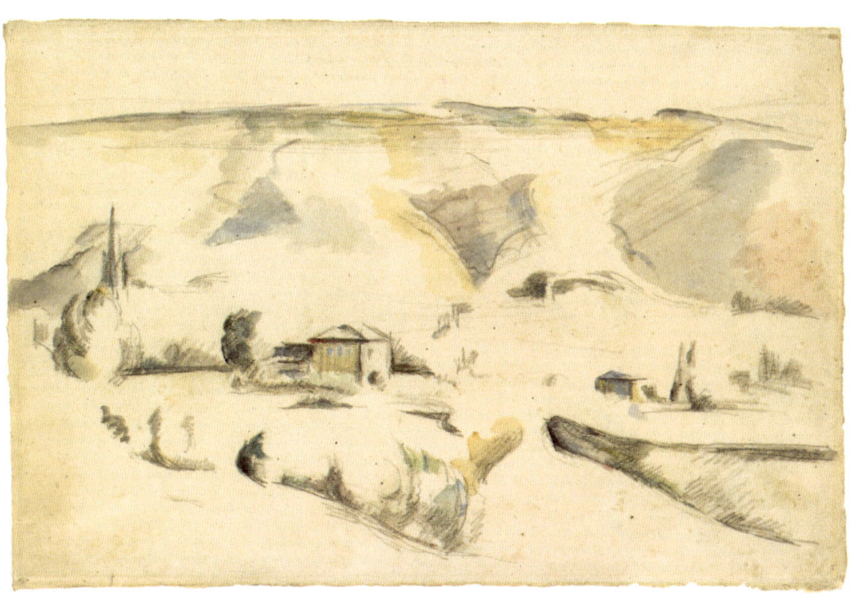

166. *Provençal Landscape*, 1885–90.
Pencil and watercolour, 32 × 48.3 cm (12⅝ × 19 in.).
Ashmolean Museum, Oxford

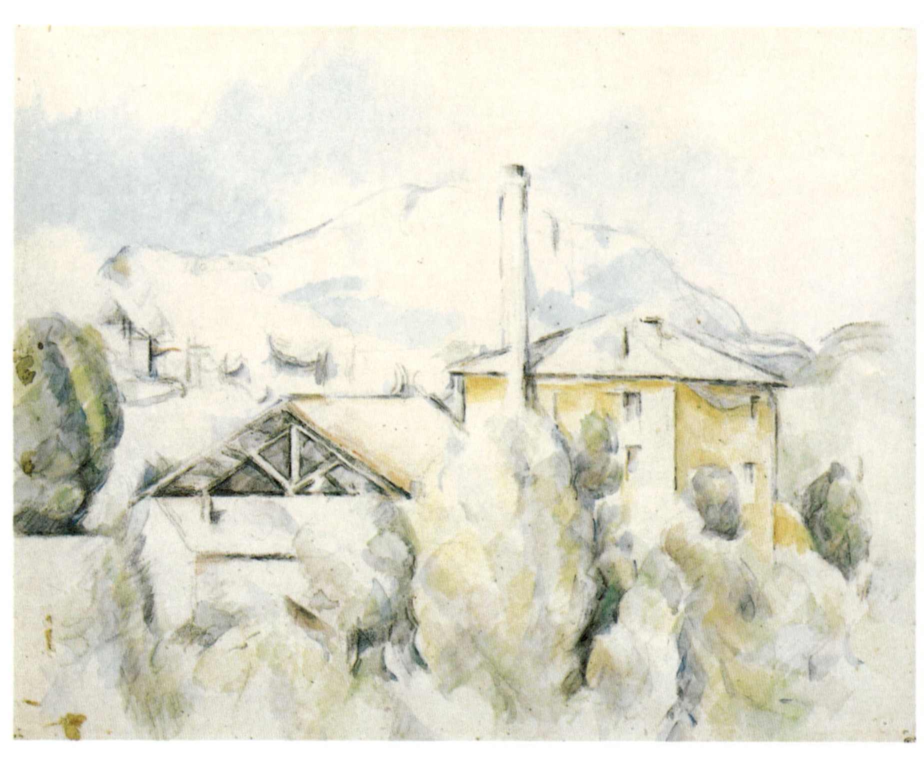

167. *The Lime Kiln at the Pont des Trois Sautets*, 1890–94.
Pencil and watercolour, 42 × 53 cm (16½ × 20⅞ in.).
Musée d'Orsay, Paris

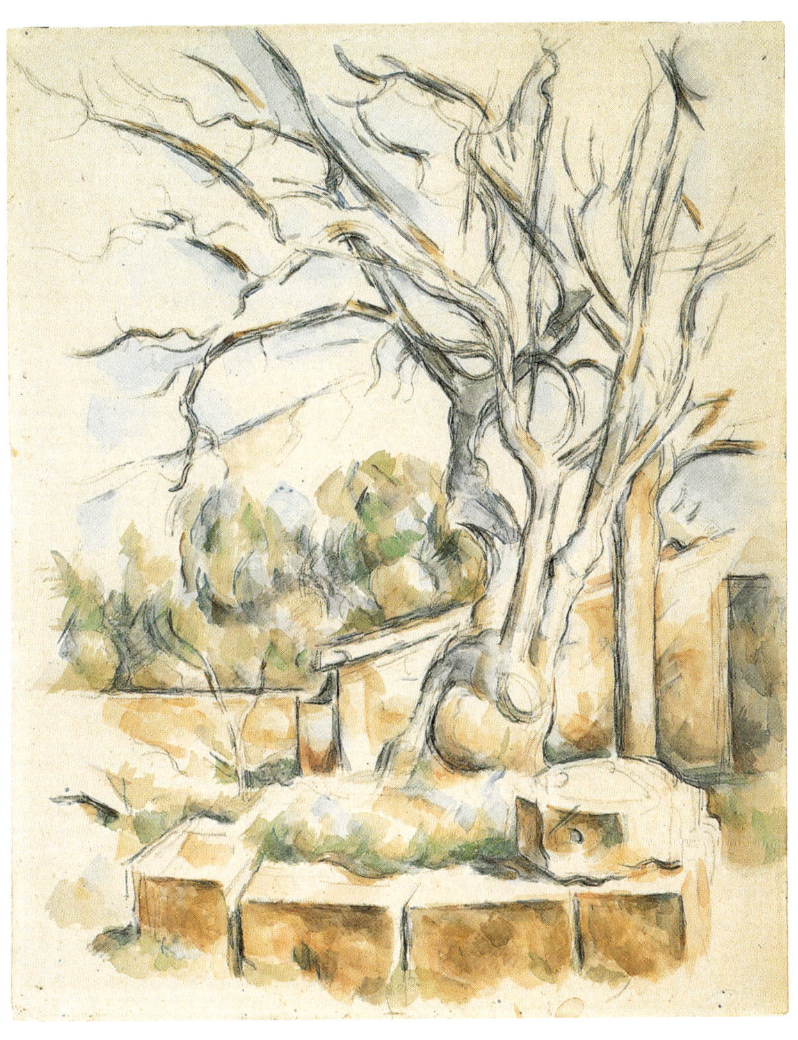

168. *Pistachio Tree in the Courtyard of the Château Noir*, 1900.
Pencil and watercolour, 54 × 43 cm (21¼ × 16⅞ in.).
The Art Institute of Chicago

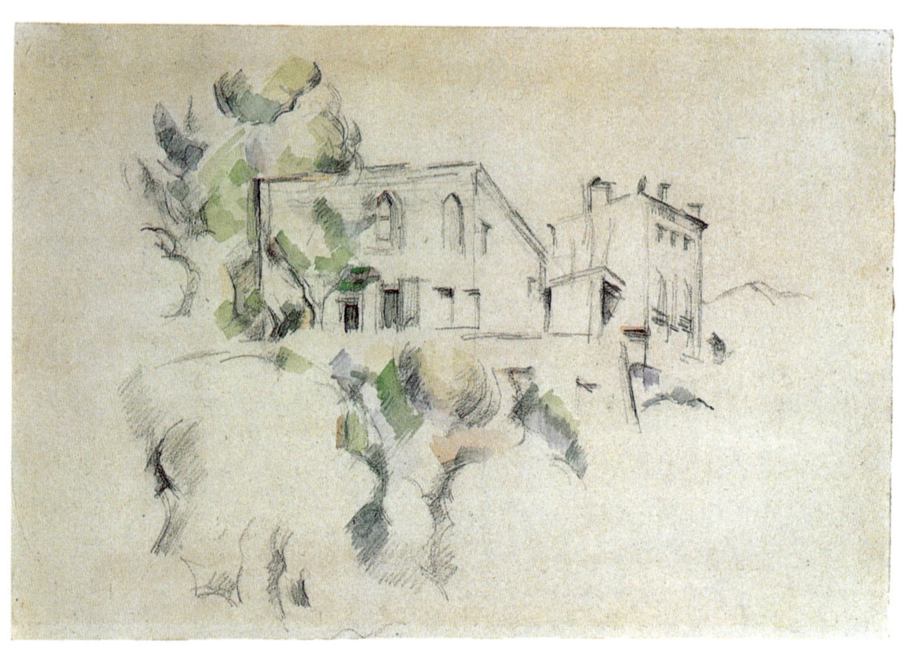

169. *The Château Noir*, 1890.
Pencil and watercolour, 36 × 52.6 cm (14½ × 20¼ in.).
Museum Boijmans Van Beuningen, Rotterdam

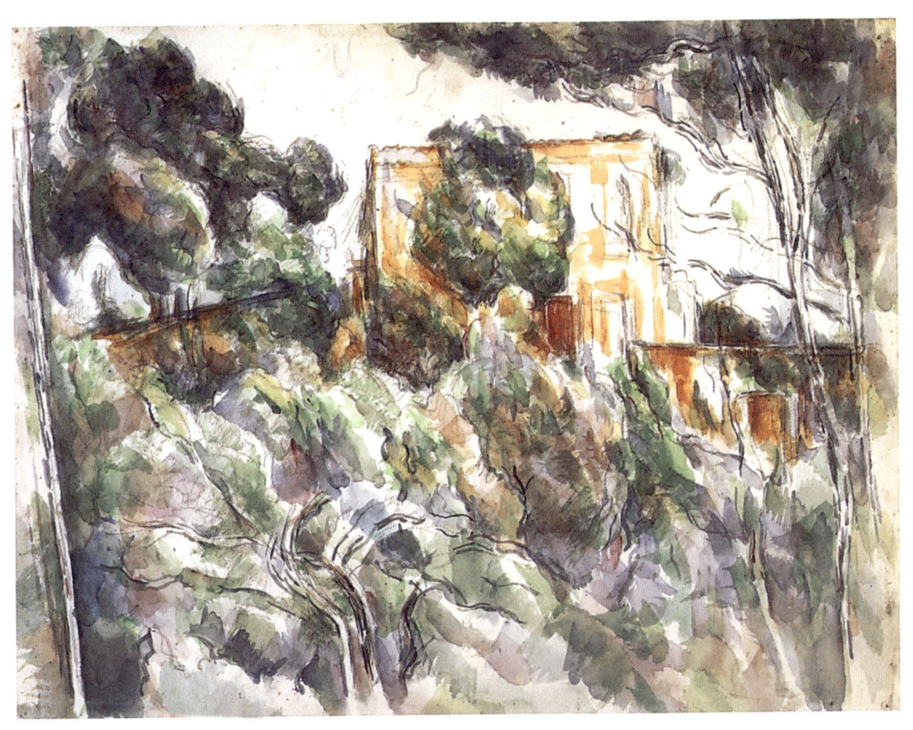

170. *The Château Noir*, 1904.
Pencil and watercolour, 41.9 × 55.2 cm (16½ × 21¾ in.).
Private collection

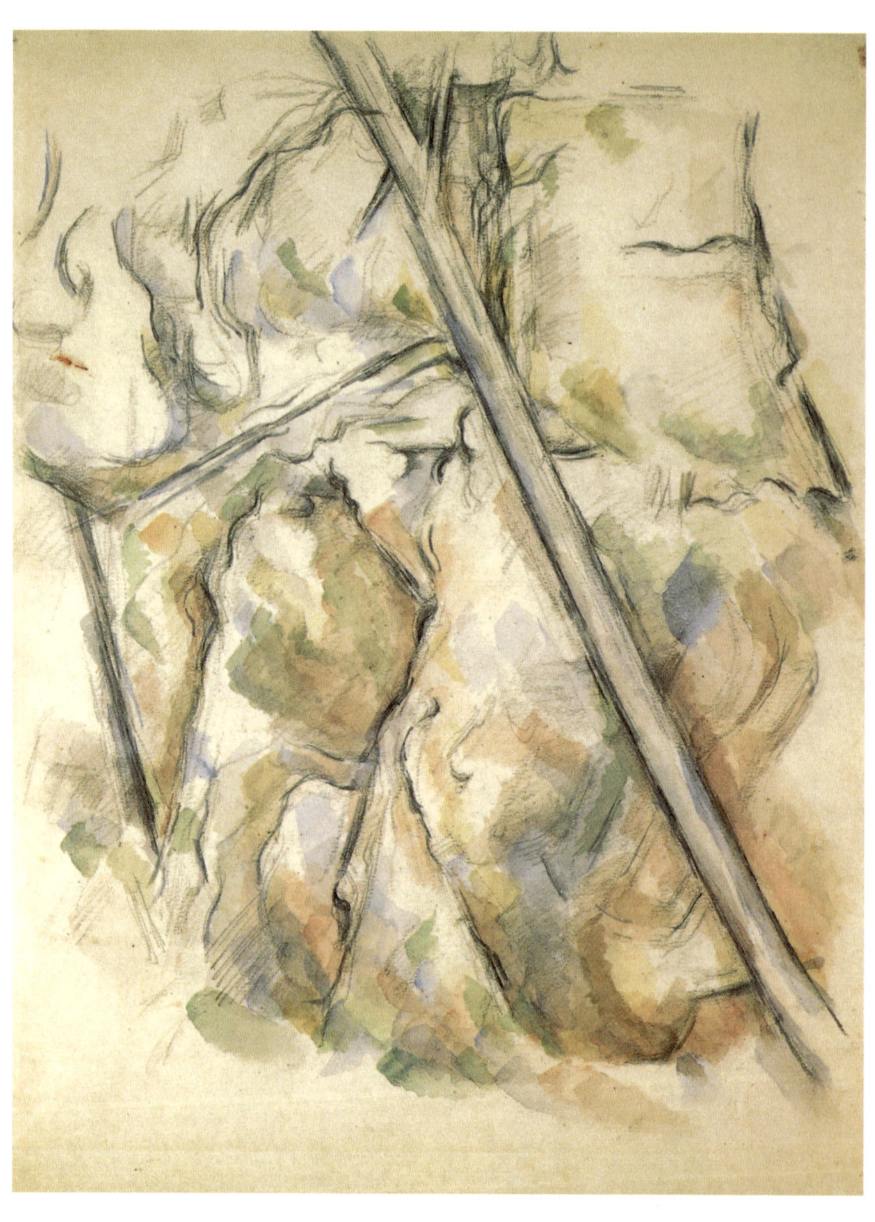

171. *Pine Trees and Rocks above the Château Noir, c.* 1900.
Pencil and watercolour, 46.5 × 35.5 cm (18¼ × 14 in.).
Princeton University Art Museum, New Jersey

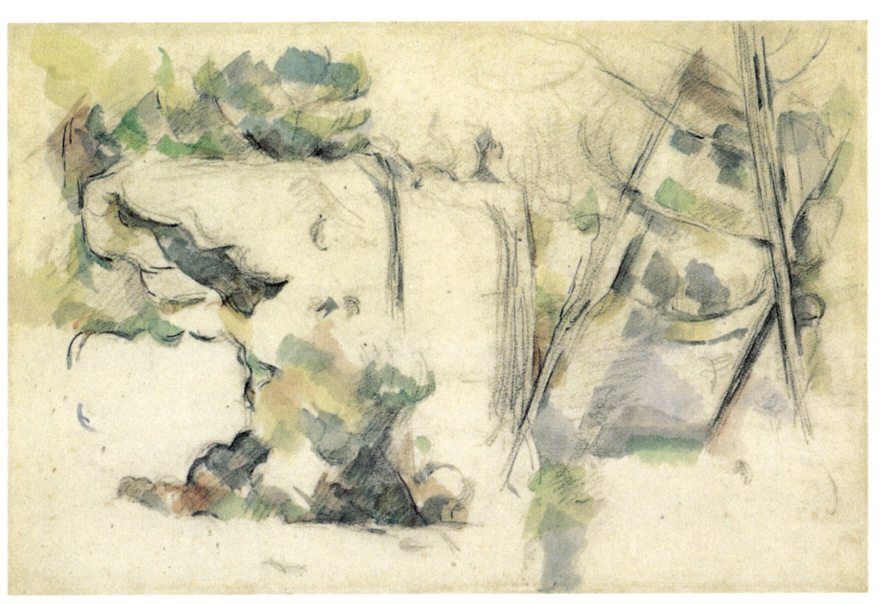

172. *Rocks at Bibémus*, 1895–1900.
Pencil and watercolour, 31 × 48 cm (12⅛ × 18⅞ in.).
Staatliche Graphische Sammlung, Munich

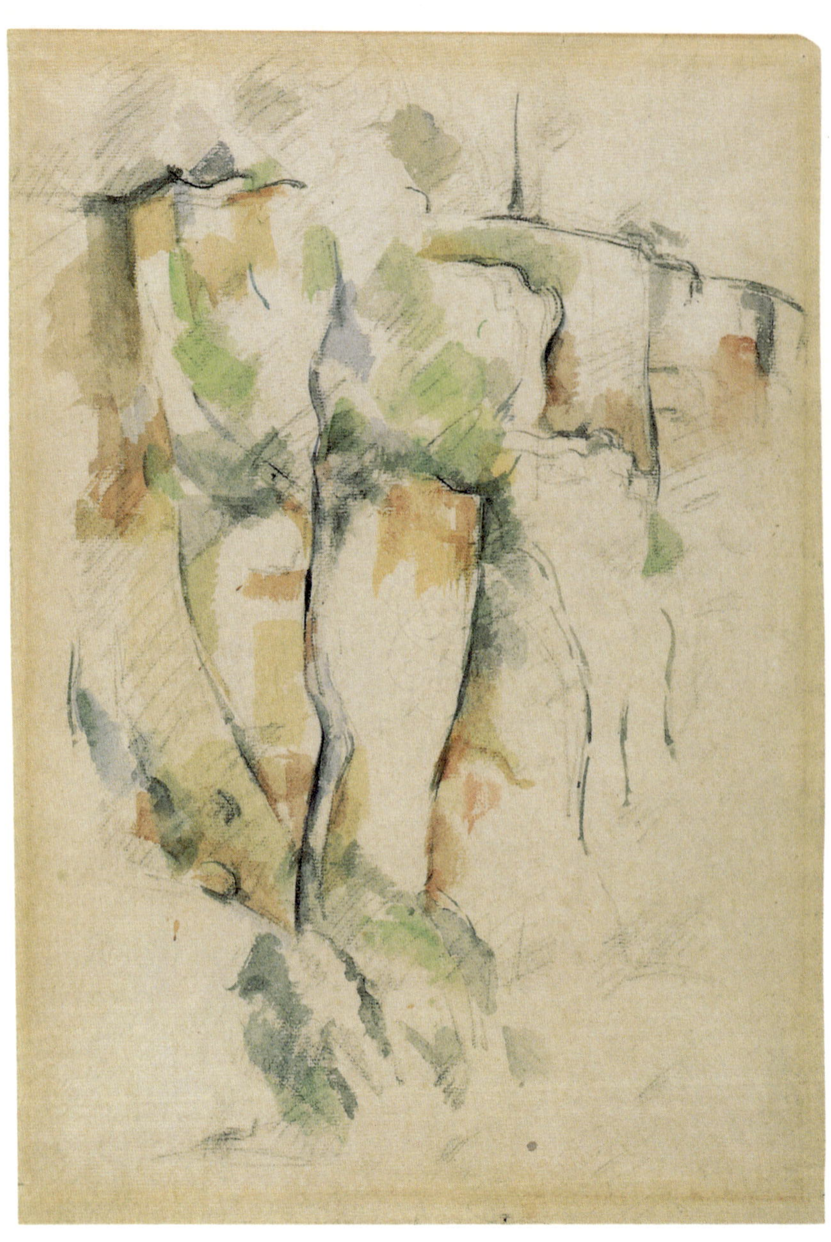

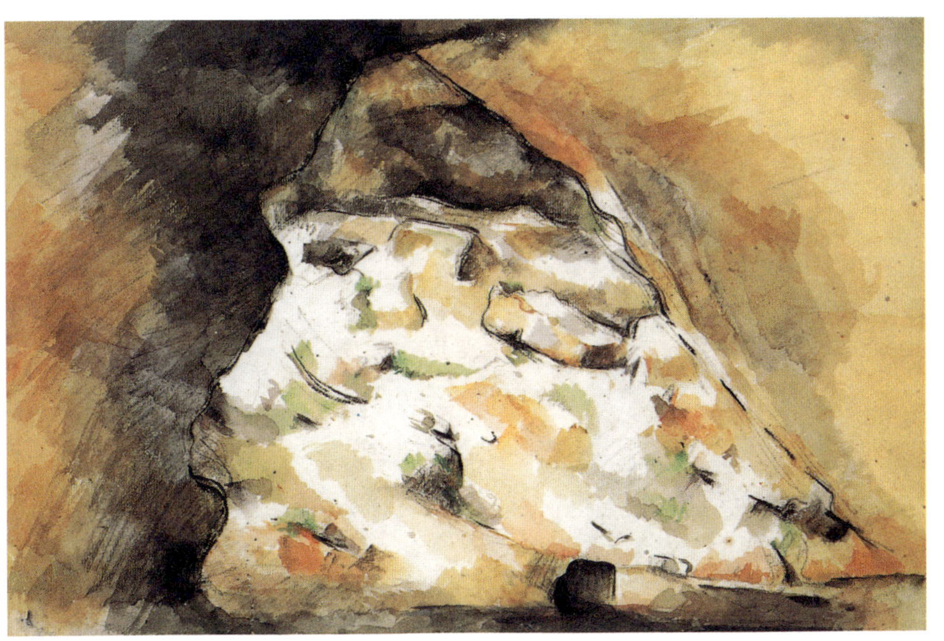

OPPOSITE
173. *Rocks at Bibémus*, 1887–90.
Pencil and watercolour on off-white paper, 45.9 × 31.8 cm (18⅛ × 12½ in.).
The Henry and Rose Pearlman Foundation, on loan to
Princeton University Art Museum, New Jersey

ABOVE
174. *Rocks and Cavern*, 1895–1900.
Pencil and watercolour, 31.9 × 48.5 cm (12½ × 19⅛ in.).
Private collection

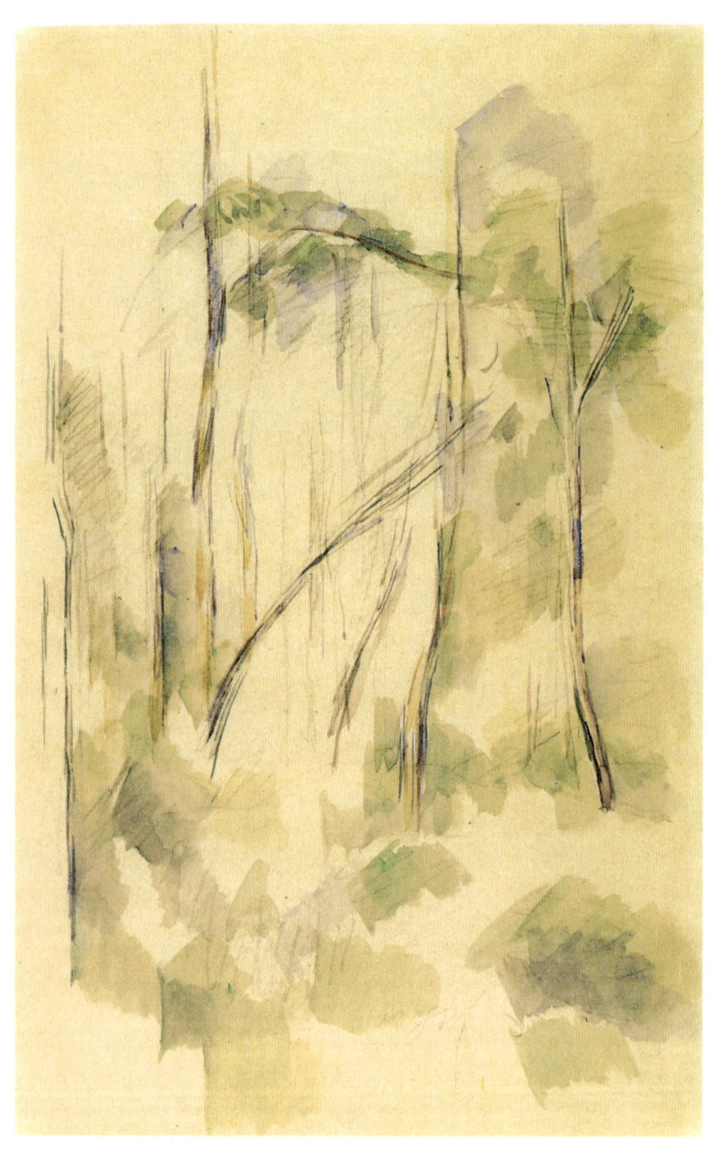

175. *Sous-Bois*, 1887–89.
Pencil and watercolour, 49.6 × 32 cm (19½ × 12⅝ in.).
Victoria & Albert Museum, London

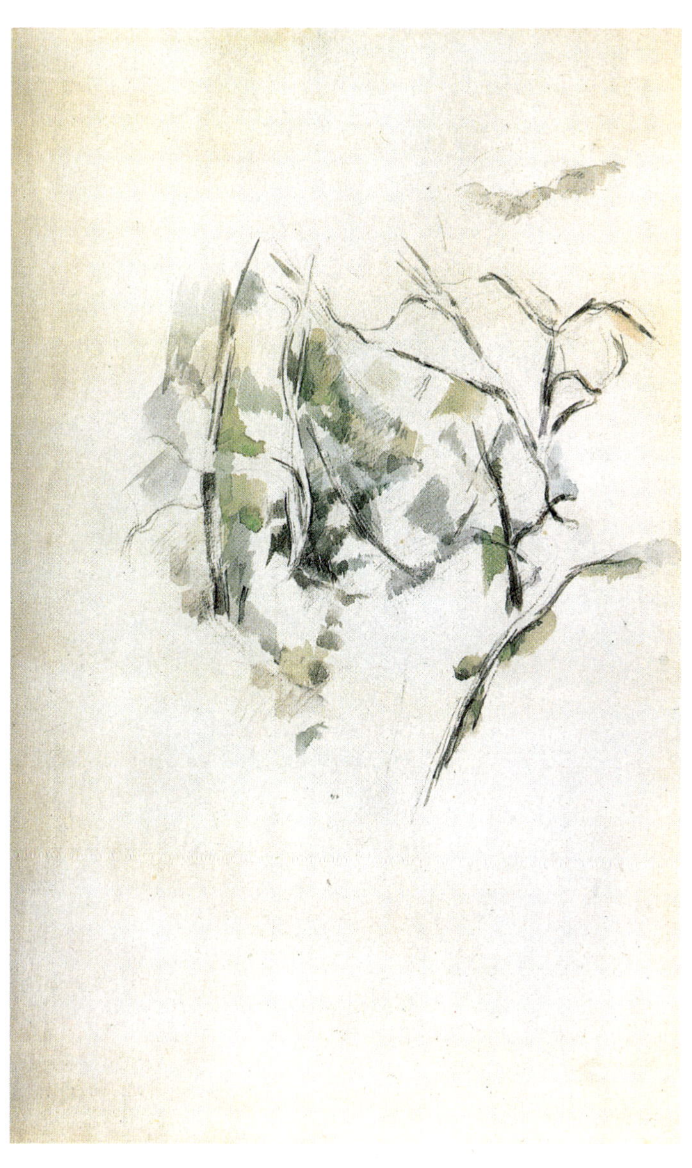

176. *Trees and Rocks, c.* 1890.
Pencil and watercolour, 31.2 × 47.8 cm (18⅞ × 12¼ in.).
Von der Heydt Museum, Wuppertal

177. *Statue under Trees*, 1898–1900.
Pencil and watercolour, 48.2 × 31.3 cm (19 × 12⅜ in.).
The Courtauld Gallery, London

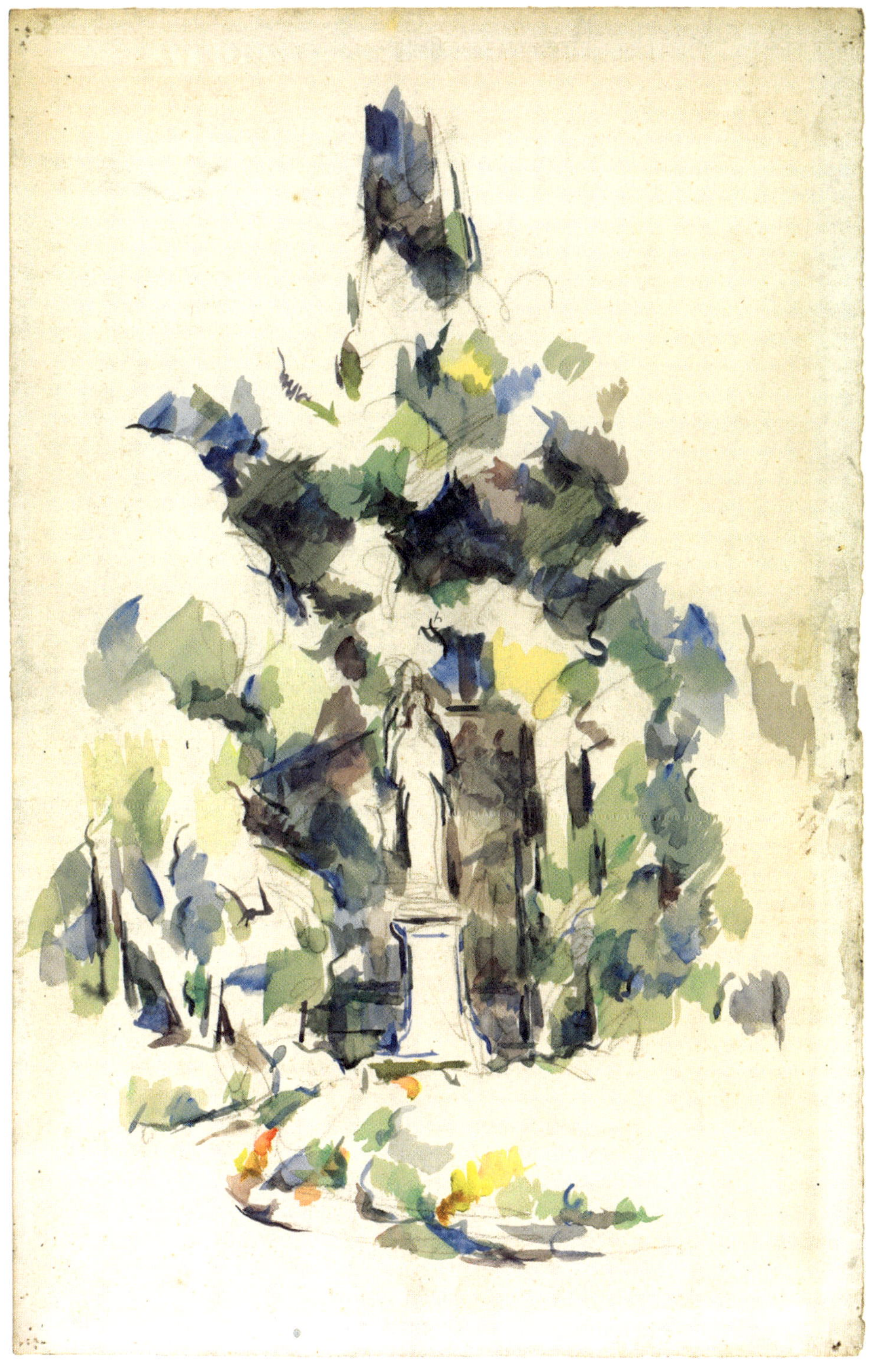

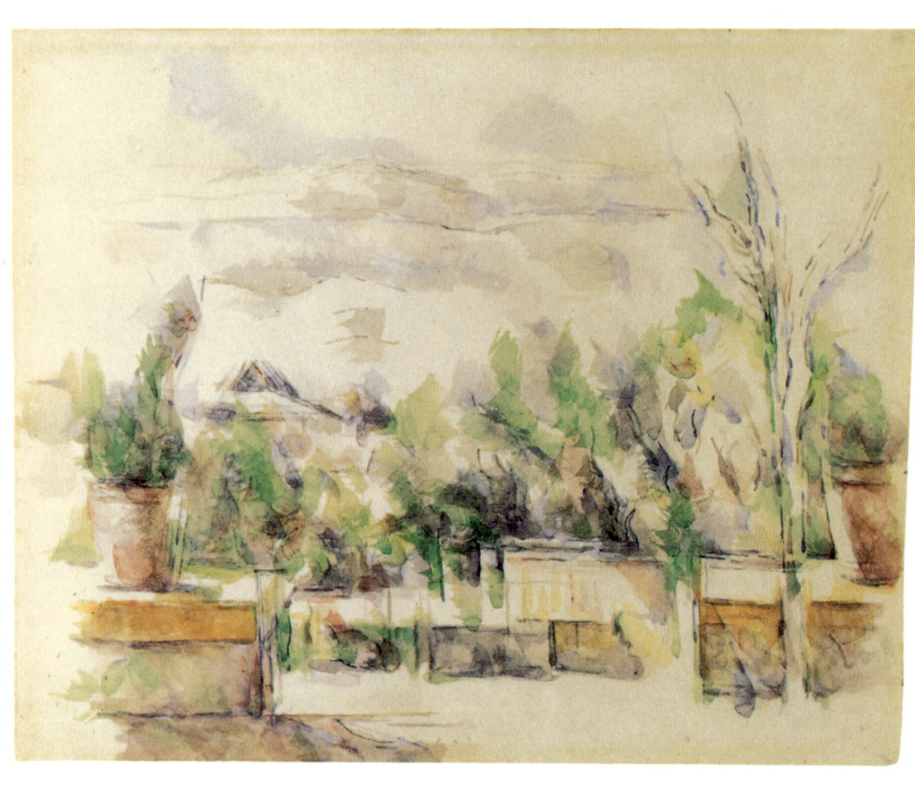

178. *The Garden Terrace at Les Lauves*, 1902–06.
Pencil and watercolour, 43.2 × 53.4 cm (17 × 21 in.).
Pierpont Morgan Library, New York

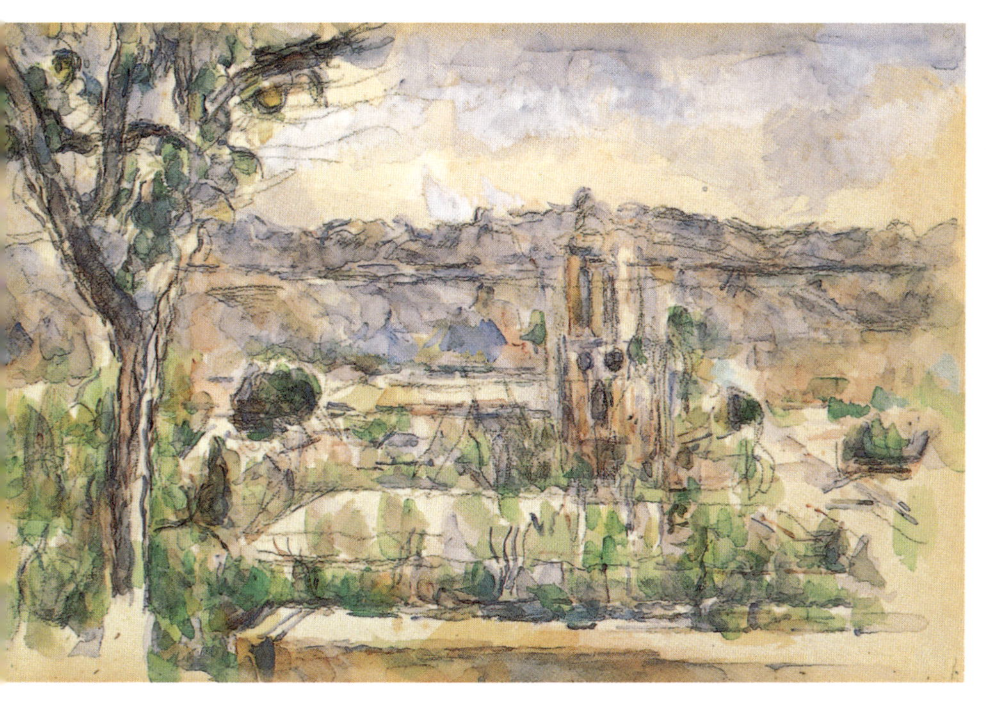

179. *The Cathedral at Aix-en-Provence from Les Lauves*, 1902–06.
Pencil and watercolour with gouache, 31.8 × 47 cm (12½ × 18½ in.).
Metropolitan Museum of Art, New York

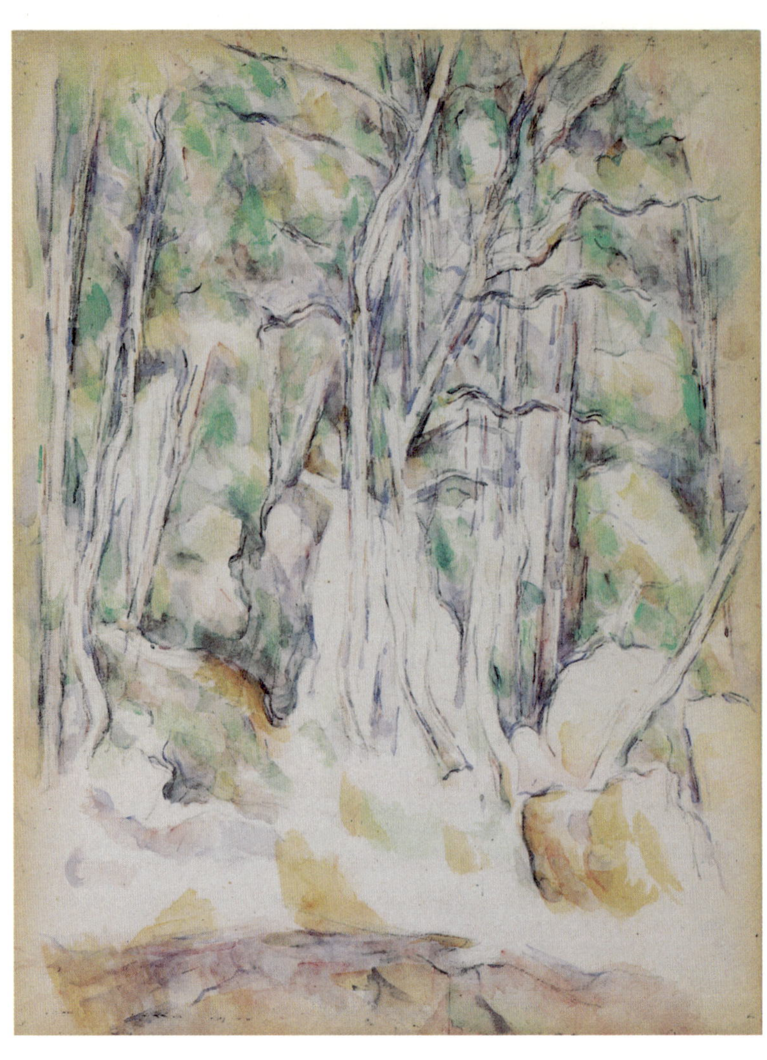

180. *The Forest*, 1900–04.
Pencil and watercolour, 56.8 × 43.5 cm (22⅛ × 17⅛ in.).
Newark Museum, New Jersey

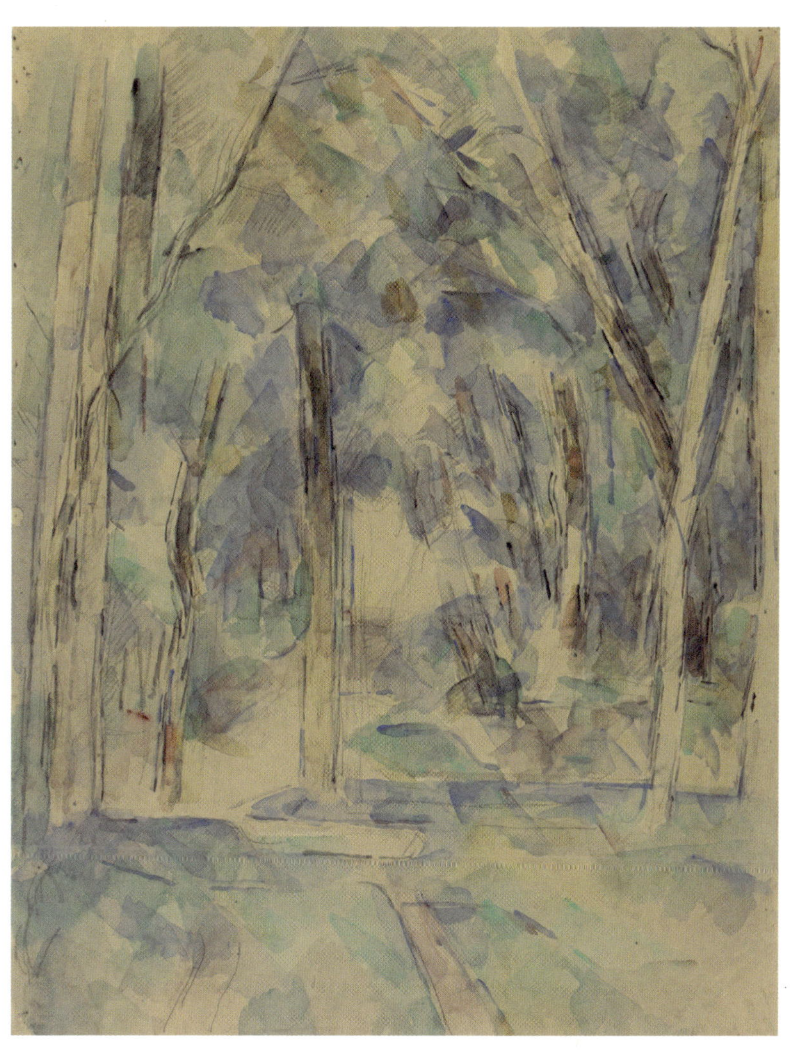

181. *Trees Forming an Arch*, 1904–05.
Pencil and watercolour on buff paper, 60.2 × 45.8 cm (23¾ × 18 in.).
The Henry and Rose Pearlman Foundation, on loan to
Princeton University Art Museum, New Jersey

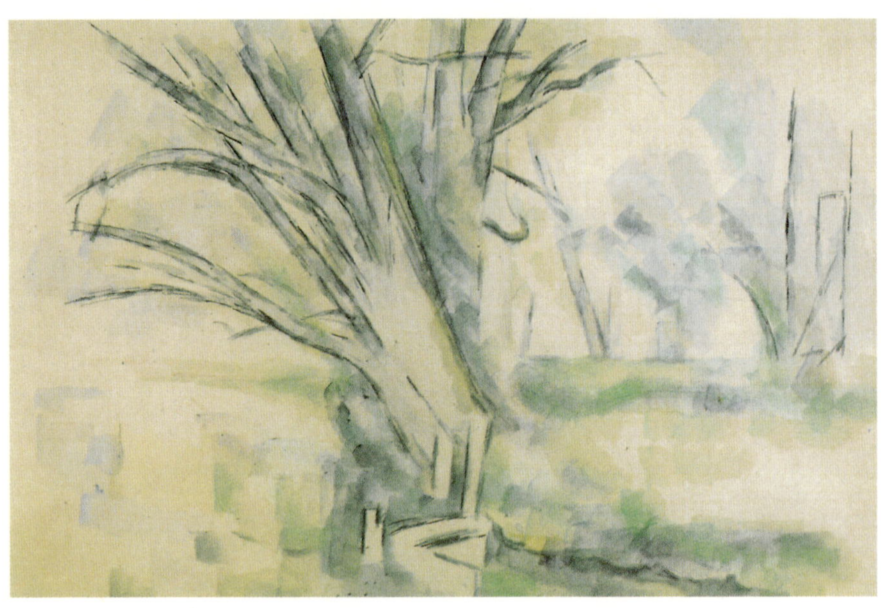

182. *Bare Trees by a River, c.* 1904.
Watercolour, 31.2 × 48.7 cm (12⅛ × 19¼ in.).
Pierpont Morgan Library, New York

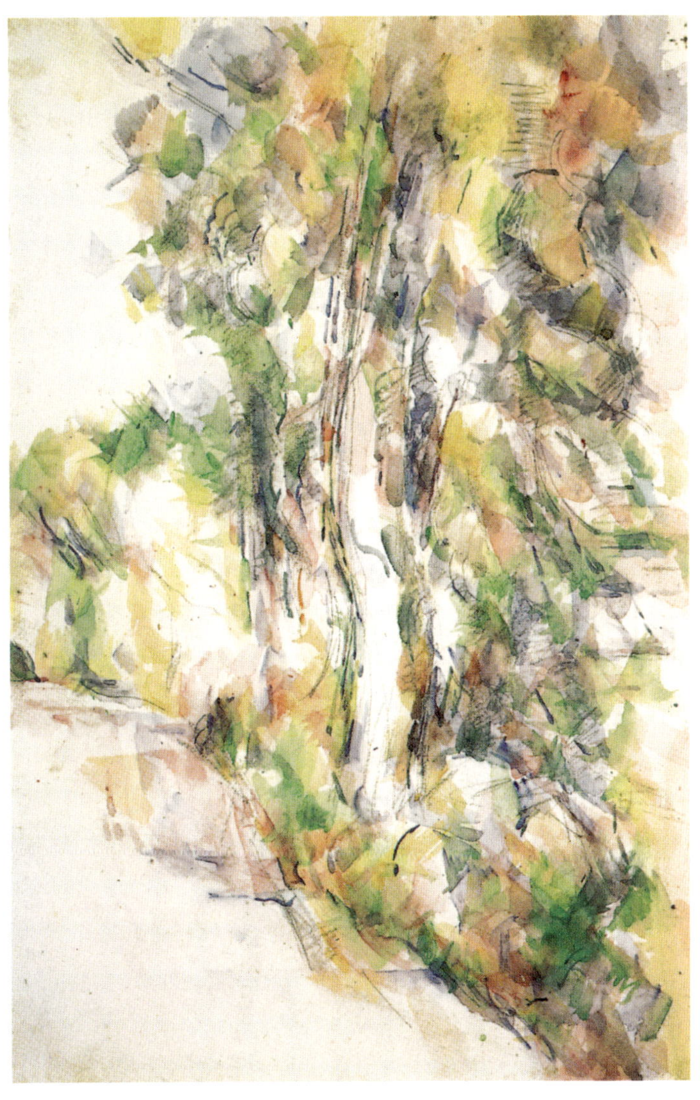

183. *Road with Trees and an Embankment*, c. 1904.
Watercolour, 46.7 × 30.5 cm (18⅛ × 12 in.).
Fondation Beyeler, Riehen, Basel

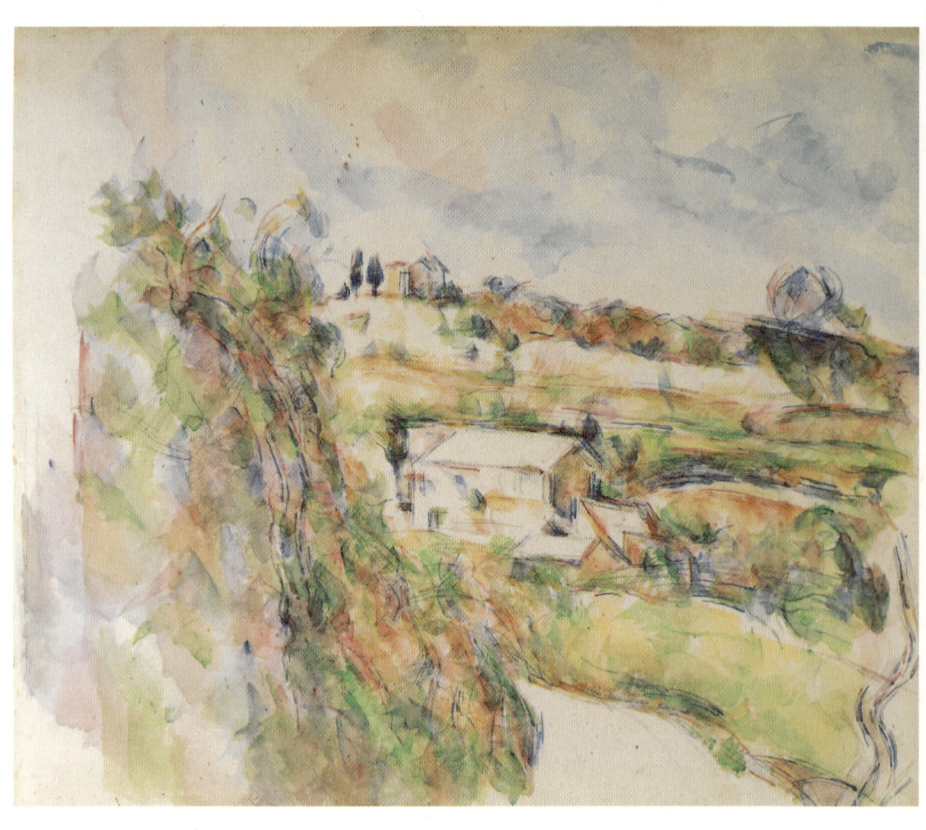

184. *Chemin des Lauves: The Turn in the Road*, 1906.
Pencil and watercolour on cream paper, 47.9 × 58.6 cm (18⅞ × 23⅛ in.).
The Henry and Rose Pearlman Foundation, on loan to
Princeton University Art Museum, New Jersey

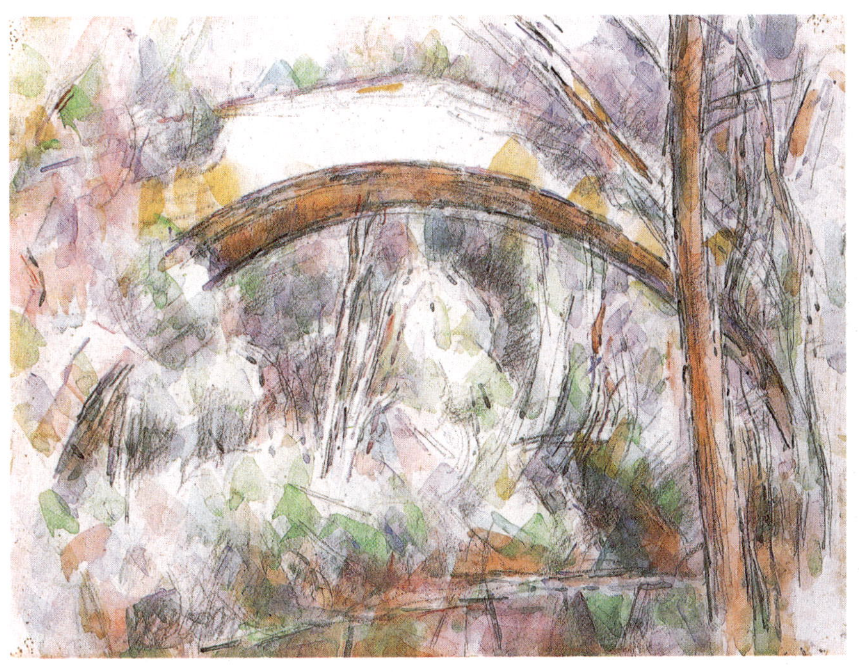

185. *The Trois Sautets Bridge*, 1906.
Pencil and watercolour, 40.8 × 54.3 cm (16⅛ × 21⅜ in.).
Cincinnati Art Museum

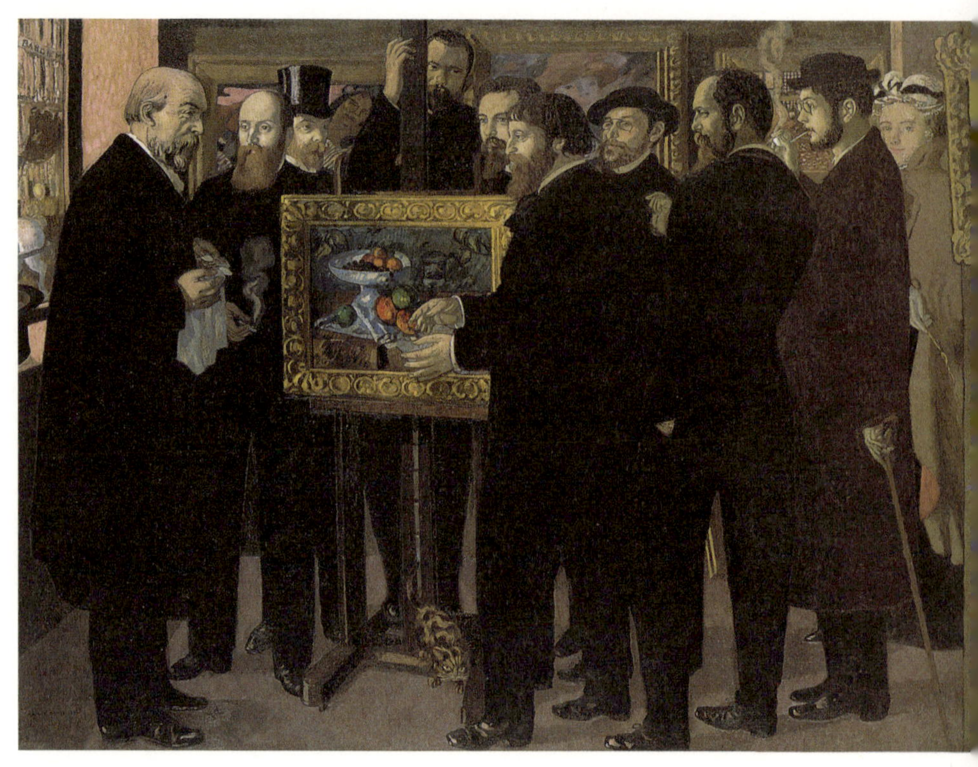

186. *Maurice Denis, Homage to Cézanne,* 1900.
Oil on canvas, 182 × 243.5 cm (71⅝ × 95⅞ in.).
Musée d'Orsay, Paris

CHAPTER SIX

The Ultimate Construct in Still Life

'He went beyond Chardin.' Joachim Gasquet

A painting by Maurice Denis dating from 1900 entitled *Homage to Cézanne* shows a group of admirers looking at a picture on an easel [186]. The painting is a still life by Cézanne – *Compotier, Glass and Apples* of 1880 – and the admirers include the artists Odilon Redon, Edouard Vuillard, Paul Sérusier, Pierre Bonnard and Denis himself, as well as the dealer Vollard, who stands protectively behind the easel. The still life itself (now in the Museum of Modern Art, New York) was owned by Gauguin, for whom Cézanne was a formative influence. Denis's painting indicates how highly regarded Cézanne's work had become by the turn of the century, but it also suggests that of all the subjects the ageing artist had undertaken during his lifetime it was the genre of still life that had come to be recognized as the most significant for the development of art. Still lifes of one type or another constitute only about a fifth (roughly one hundred and seventy pictures) of Cézanne's output, but among these are undoubtedly some of the artist's greatest and most striking compositions either in oil or watercolour.

Even within Cézanne's lifetime the apple had become a symbol of his modernity. He himself said, according to Geffroy, 'With an apple I want to astonish Paris', and it seems that he did indeed succeed in doing this even if at first it was only a conquest that his fellow artists found notable. Degas, for example, acquired in 1896 the small but perfectly composed *Apples* of *c.* 1877–78, which Huysmans may have seen in 1891, describing the fruit as 'brutal, rugged, built up with a trowel, abruptly subdued with the thumb' [187]. Neat parallel brushstrokes of pure colour – red, yellow and ochre with touches of green – define the rotundity of the forms and the lustre of the skins seen against a shadowy background. After Degas's death in 1917 this picture was bought by the economist John Maynard Keynes, through whom it became known to members of the Bloomsbury Group. On first seeing the picture Virginia Woolf recorded in her diary, 'The apples positively got redder and rounder and greener'.

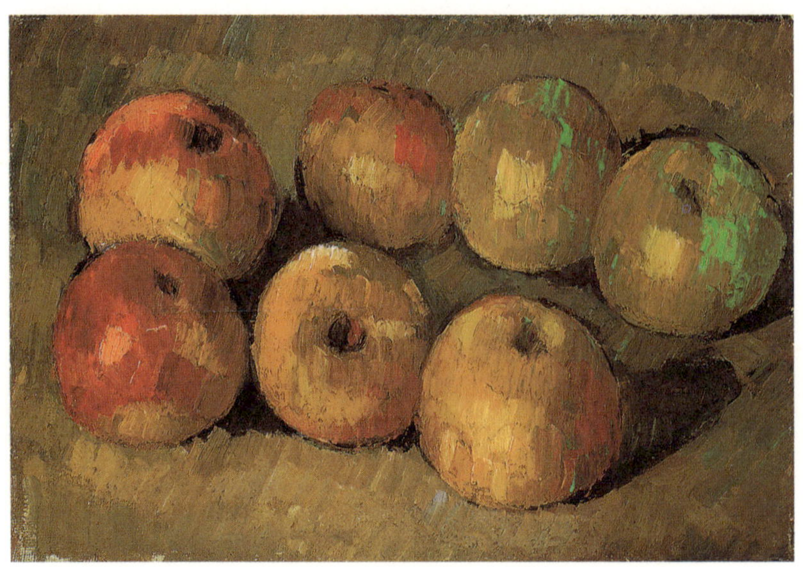

187. *Apples*, c. 1878.
Oil on canvas, 19 × 27 cm (7½ × 10⅝ in.).
King's College, Cambridge (Keynes Collection),
on loan to the Fitzwilliam Museum, Cambridge

Such a reaction was not unusual. For, as Denis reported, when Sérusier looked at Cézanne's still lifes of fruit he remarked, '"Of an ordinary painter's apple, you say, 'I could take a bite out of it'. Of Cézanne's apple, you say, 'It's beautiful'. You don't dare to peel it, you want to copy it."' Artists have continued to find Cézanne's apples challenging. Looking back on his career in 1970, the American Abstract Expressionist painter Barnett Newman described them as 'superapples' comparable with 'cannonballs'.

Cézanne's interest in still life manifested itself early in his career as he was deciding what kind of painter he wanted to become. He would have been aware of the long tradition of still-life painting in all schools of European art. The Dutch in particular specialized in different types of still life, often imbued with symbolism: flower pieces or food to suit all tastes displayed with a variety of utensils. Flowers combined scientific curiosity with economic boom, whereas the so-called 'breakfast' and 'banqueting' pieces balanced out the mundane with the exotic. Some of these paintings are linked to the theme of *vanitas*, reminding the viewer of the transitoriness of human existence and, as such, are replete with various symbols, including, for example, skulls, clocks and candles. Others are an effulgent outpouring of appreciation for the beauty of the natural world and the fecundity of nature, sometimes emphasized by means of obliquely referenced sexual symbolism. Cézanne would have seen examples of such art in the Musée du Louvre, including Jan Davidsz. de Heem's *La Desserte* of 1640, which later so impressed Matisse.

The French tradition of still life was more closely allied to sporting art, owing to the continuing influence of Rubens and his followers. Painters such as Alexandre-François Desportes and Jean-Baptiste Oudry revelled in the hunting scenes where the discarded equipage and piles of dead game destined for the larder provided wonderful opportunities for still-life painting. It was Chardin, however, who introduced a more domestic theme to the subject. Chardin could paint charming genre scenes and learned allegories, but his still lifes attracted just as much attention in his own lifetime and even more so in Paris during the nineteenth century when there was a revival of interest in his work. Its appeal lay in the very ordinariness of the objects he chose to paint and the way in which they were fitted together, often on a small scale but without sacrificing any sense of monumentality. It was the elevation of the mundane on to a higher level that made Chardin's work seem so advanced and ahead of its time. Cézanne particularly admired Chardin, remarking to Gasquet of him that in his still lifes, 'Objects enter into each other … They never stop living, you understand … Imperceptibly they extend beyond themselves through intimate reflections, as we do by looks and words … Chardin was the first to have glimpsed that and rendered the atmosphere of objects.'

In addition, when Spanish painting became popular in Paris in the mid-nineteenth century, examples of still-life painting from that school were included in the new galleries that were then being opened in the Musée du Louvre. Works by Velázquez and Goya were closely examined by artists such as Manet, who travelled to Spain in 1865 and was strongly influenced by the degree of realism in their work, further dramatized by a pronounced use of chiaroscuro.

The earliest still lifes painted by Cézanne during the 1860s allude to each of these traditions that were possibly known to him indirectly, at first through other artists. *Bread and Eggs* of 1865 (Cincinnati Art Museum) is comparable to works by realist painters such as François Bonvin and Théodule Ribot, while the brushwork of *Sugar Bowl, Pears and Blue Cup* of *c.* 1866 (Musée d'Orsay, Paris, on loan to the Musée Granet, Aix-en-Provence), which is shown hanging above the *The Artist's Father, Reading L'Evénement* [see 2], is close to that of his friend

Monticelli. The vibrant colour and fluid handling of *Still Life with Green Pot and Pewter Jug* from *c.* 1869–70 (Musée d'Orsay, Paris), as well as the greater degree of contrivance in the composition, are redolent of Manet. Two early still lifes by Cézanne, however, prefigure the artist's fascination with this genre: *Skull and Candlestick* of 1866 [188] and *The Black Clock* of *c.* 1870 (Private collection). Both have all the iconographical ingredients associated with the *vanitas* subjects of traditional still lifes, but the asymmetrical composition of the former and the strong handling in the latter prepare the viewer for what was to emerge later. During the 1870s Cézanne begins to distance himself in the first place from the still lifes painted by Delacroix, Courbet, Millet and Henri Fantin-Latour and, secondly, from those of his immediate Impressionist contemporaries. Whereas Pissarro, Monet, Renoir and Sisley relished the surface qualities of the objects they selected for their pictures and Caillebotte virtually served up a gourmet meal, Cézanne's purpose was to go beyond mere representation and engage with the materiality of the objects themselves, seeking their very essence by means of colour and mark-making.

The painting of still lifes was a very personal act for Cézanne and it is perhaps in this genre above all others that he manages to merge content and form most successfully. The more elaborate still lifes dating from the 1890s (*Still Life with Onions* of 1896–98 and *Apples and Oranges*, *c.* 1899, both in the Musée d'Orsay, Paris, and *Still Life with Flower Holder*, *c.* 1905, in the National Gallery of Art, Washington, DC) are symphonic in structure and the equal of the finest examples by any of his forerunners. By necessity, and indeed like every other artist, Cézanne was forced to paint his still lifes in his studio, which amounted to what may be described as ideal laboratory conditions. Fruit, vegetables and flowers could be readily obtained at local markets or from the gardens of friends, but wine bottles, water pitchers, jars, ginger pots, candle burners, kitchen utensils, sugar bowls, cups, baskets, milk jugs, tablecloths and draperies were the artist's constant companions either in Paris or Aix-en-Provence, ready to be set up in special displays on basic studio furniture. In the end his relationship with these objects was possibly as close as it was with people. As Cézanne described it to Gasquet,

> People don't think of a sugar bowl as having a face, a soul. But it
> changes every day too. You have to know how to catch them, how
> to win them over, those gentlemen … These glasses and plates,
> there's talk going on between them … As for flowers I've given
> them up. They wilt right away. Fruit are more faithful. They love
> having their portraits done. It's as if they're asking to be forgiven
> for fading. They exhale their message with their scent. They reach
> you with all their smells and tell you about the fields they've left,

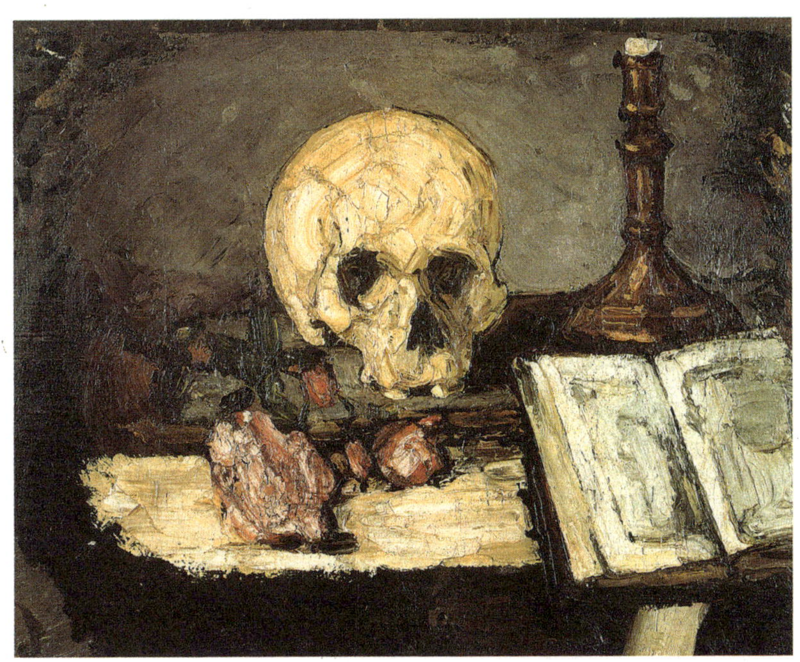

188. *Still Life: Skull and Candlestick, c.* 1866.
Oil on canvas, 47.5 × 62.5 cm (18¾ × 24⅝ in.).
Private collection

the rain that made them grow, the dawns they've watched. When
I'm outlining the skin of a lovely peach with soft touches of paint,
or a sad old apple, I catch a glimpse in the reflections they exchange
of the same mild shadow of renunciation, the same love of the sun,
the same recollection of the dew, a freshness …

Or, as Wassily Kandinsky expressed it in *On the Spiritual in Art*
(1912), 'Cézanne made a living thing out of a teacup or rather in a teacup
he realized the existence of something alive. He raised still life to such
a point that it ceased to be inanimate. He painted these things as he
painted beings, because he was endowed with the gift of divining the
inner life in everything.'

Examination of the drawings and watercolours reveals a surprising
variety in Cézanne's approach to still life. A study of drapery in the
early sketchbook in Paris (Musée d'Orsay) anticipates the attention
he paid to fabrics, which in his still lifes either served as crumpled

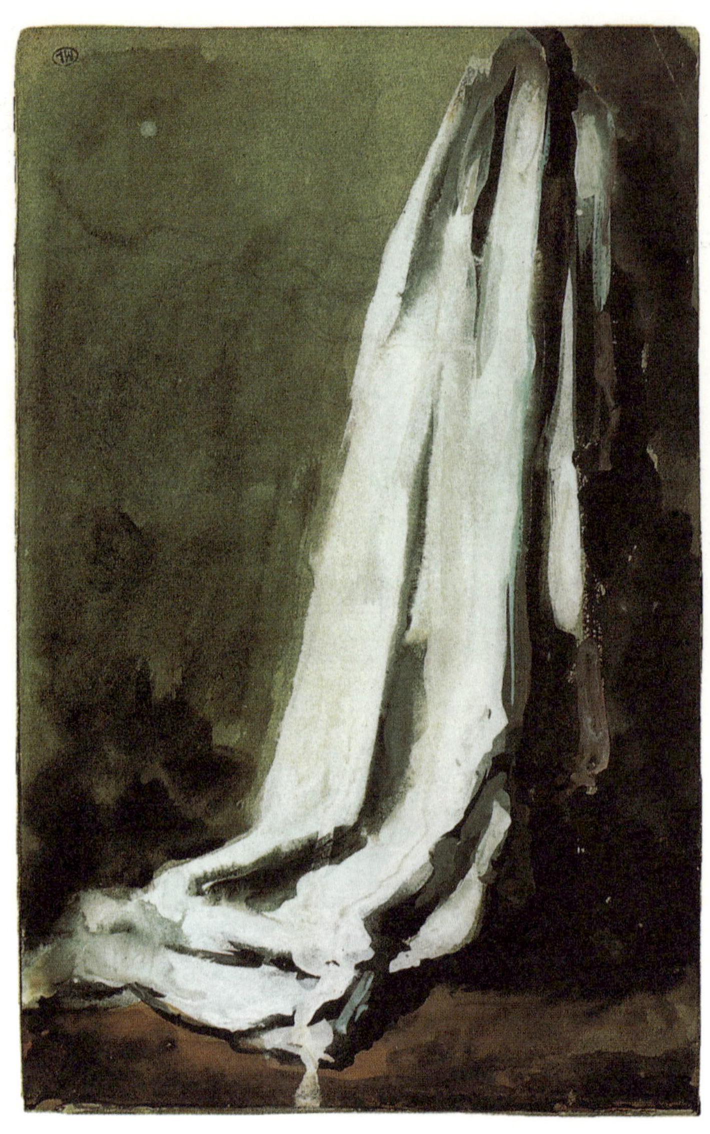

189. *Study of Drapery, c.* 1862–63.
Brown and grey ink with gouache, 15 × 23 cm (5⅞ × 9 in.).
Musée du Louvre, Paris

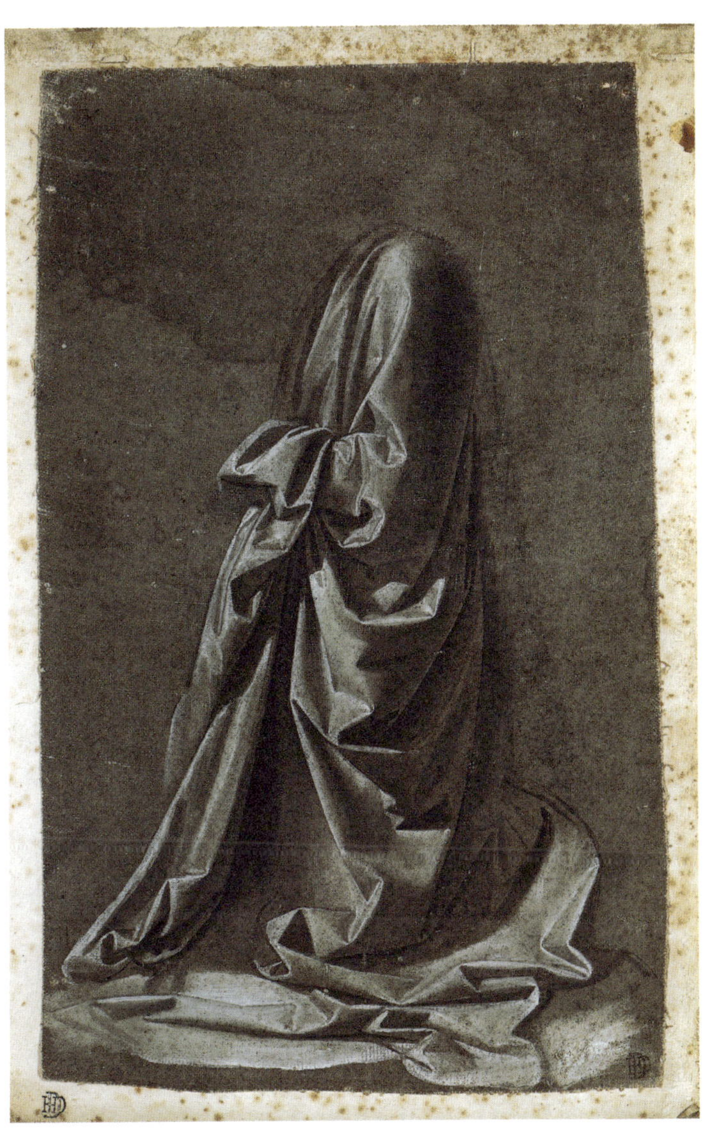

190. Follower of Leonardo da Vinci,
Drapery Study of a Kneeling Figure, c. 1490.
Brown-grey wash, heightened with white, on linen
prepared grey-green, 28.8 × 18.1 cm (11⅛ × 7⅛ in.).
Private collection

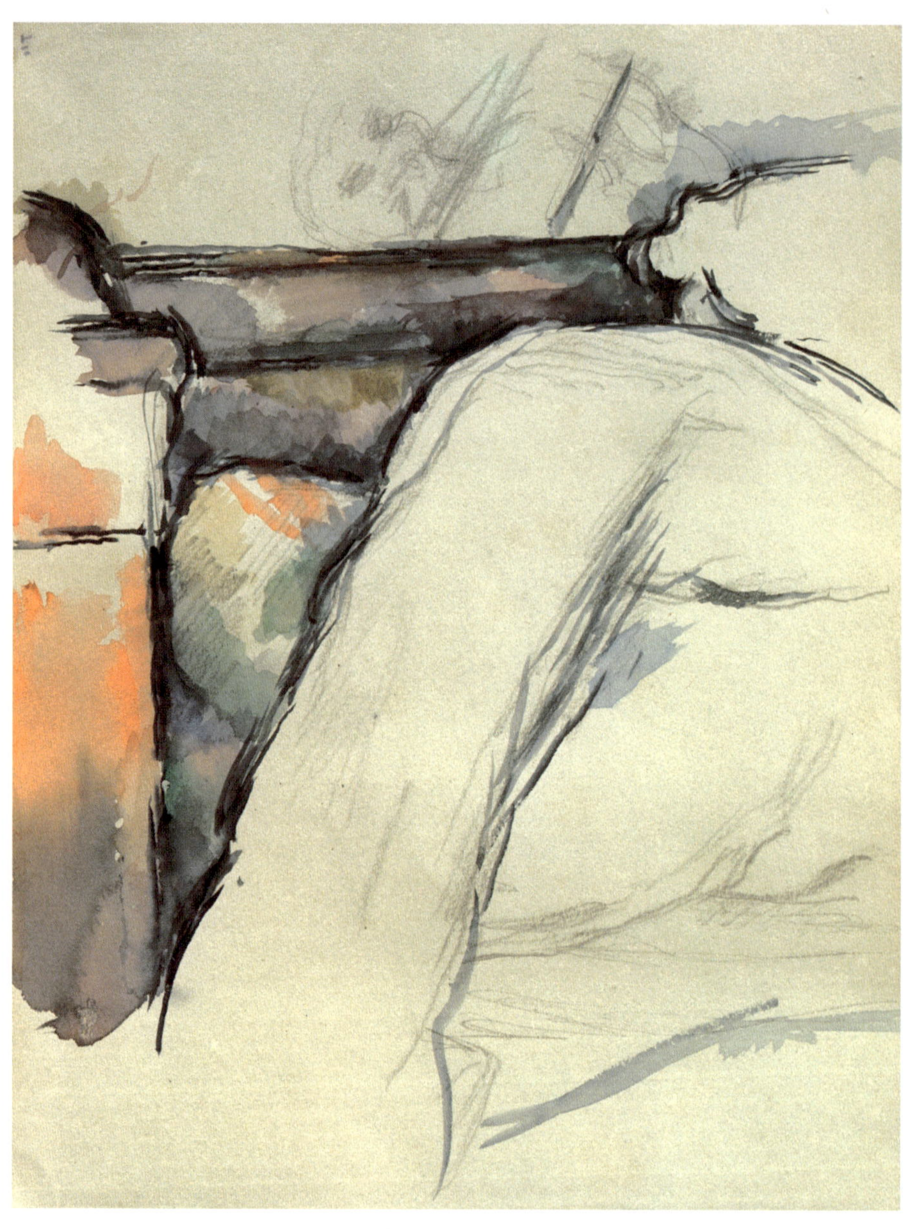

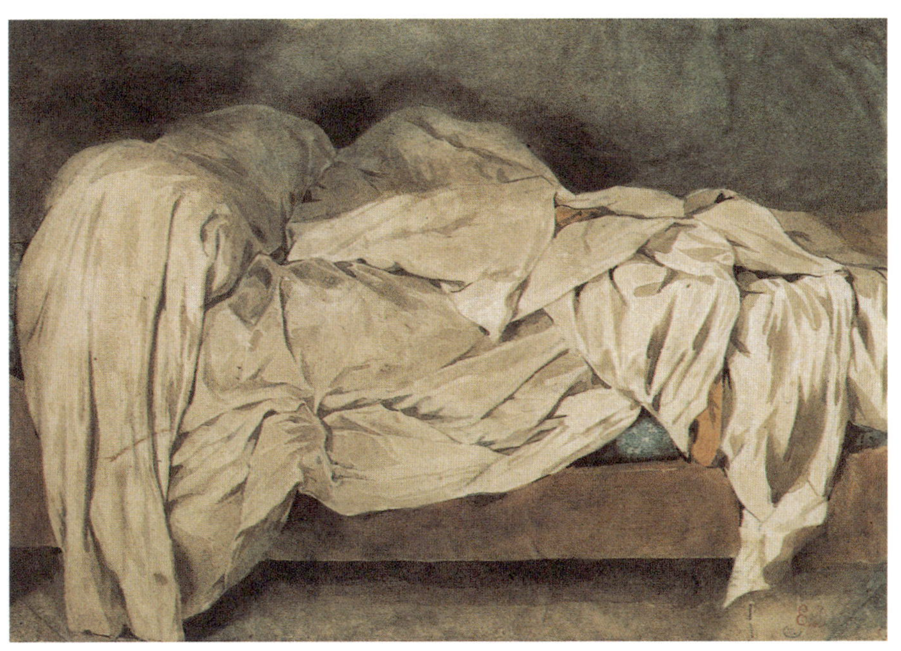

ABOVE
192. Eugène Delacroix, *Unmade Bed*, c. 1827.
Pencil and watercolour, 18.5 × 29.5 cm (7¼ × 11⅝ in.).
Musée National Eugène Delacroix/Musée du Louvre, Paris

tablecloths – 'white like a bed of new fallen snow' – or backdrops. The study in Paris [189] recalls those by Leonardo da Vinci and his studio, which, according to Giorgio Vasari, were made by soaking linen in wet plaster and allowing it to set [190]. The purpose of Cézanne's study was to learn how to imitate folds of cloth, as well as to appreciate how light defines its shape. He returned to this subject in the early 1890s using a crumpled coat left on a chair [193], which rises up like a mountain range. Other discarded garments, such as hats, also caught Cézanne's attention, as much for their form as their texture, and when seen in isolation the lure of symbolism can be felt [194]. Mundane domestic objects of a type in which Delacroix also found a certain elegance, such as *Towel on a Washstand* or *Unmade Bed* [192], also appealed and are recorded in an almost invasive way [191].

Furniture of different types, especially seat furniture, is treated with a similar deference. The eye lingers as much over the curvature of a simple chair-back as it is dazzled by the abrupt foreshortening of a more capacious armchair [195]. Patterned hangings added to the sense of drama so that the arrangement of the drawn-back curtains in the artist's apartments creates a theatrical air [196]. Such drawings recall the artist's passion for Venetian Renaissance painting and especially the work of Veronese. Later, in the grandest, more complex of Cézanne's still lifes, highly coloured carpets and colourful fabrics produced in Aix-en-Provence, where they were known as *indiennes*, flowed decorously over pieces of furniture and formed the backdrop for fruit, faience and ultimately skulls.

Pride in local products is one of the principal features of Cézanne's still lifes. The pottery and porcelain wares seen in the paintings and watercolours were undoubtedly produced in Provence, even though many of the factories were going out of business during the artist's lifetime. The watercolour known as *The Green Jug* [197] features a Provençal *dourgo*, an earthenware pitcher decorated with a thick green glaze. Cézanne captures the rounded form of the vessel by placing it at an angle slightly off-centre. Its shape is emphasized by the firm outline and dense shadow on the left; the viscous quality of the rough texture of the glaze is suggested by the green washes heightened with a patch of blue. At the foot is a puddle of light brown wash, which is not a shadow but perhaps a splashed liquid implying the contents of the *dourgo* itself. It is clear from the technique that Cézanne himself identified very readily with the artisanal practices that produced this object.

In a similar fashion, Cézanne was aware of intricate patterns in architecture such as the scrolled ironwork found in balconies [198]. Typically, unlike Pissarro, Caillebotte or Georges Seurat, it was not the view out of the window or any aspects of the interior that intrigued Cézanne so much as the foliated shape of the balcony itself.

It has been seen that the artist admitted to Gasquet that he found the depiction of cut flowers difficult, mainly on the grounds that they died too quickly. Although there are only a few works either in oil or on paper of this subject, those that he did make are not lacking in proficiency as is apparent from the magnificent watercolour of *Madame Cézanne with Hortensias* [see 94]. Cézanne's interest in flower painting was no doubt heightened by Delacroix's example. A large watercolour of a bouquet of flowers by Delacroix dating from 1848–50 owned by Chocquet was especially relished by the artist. When offered for sale with Chocquet's collection in 1899 it was acquired by Vollard who passed it on to Cézanne who then made a copy of it (Pushkin State Museum of Fine Arts, Moscow). The fact that this copy was made in oil and not in the same medium as the original indicates how unified Cézanne's style had become by the final decade of his life, in the sense that any distinction between painting and drawing had ceased to exist. Even so, the technique used by Cézanne for his watercolours of flowers or foliage perhaps reflects his impatience or even inadequacy: they are broadly handled and clearly executed at speed as though the artist is taking the subject by surprise rather than studying nature closely [201]. Cézanne chooses not to linger over the blooms or encourage the viewer to reach forward to savour the scent, as in Monet or Renoir. Just occasionally is there a sense of composure similar to that found in the supremely elegant and understated flowerpieces painted towards the end of Manet's life. And in *Vase of Flowers* [200] Cézanne emphasizes the translucency of a glass vase with the stems of the flowers visible in the water while above the blooms emerge out of the white of the paper. By contrast, *Roses in a Bottle* [199] concentrates less on translucency and more on compositional aspects.

Cézanne perhaps preferred to depict the potted plants that were to hand in the conservatory at the Jas de Bouffan or on the terrace at Les Lauves. The most majestic of these is the magnificent *Flowerpots* [202] in which ten terracotta pots are aligned on a shelf. The pale sunlight directed from the left (enhanced by the application of gouache) and the sparse foliage of the geraniums suggest that it is the end of winter. The view from below makes the linear shoots rising out of the pots in the upper half of the composition more pronounced while the green leaves contrasted with the blue shadows are stilled by the warm atmosphere. In another watercolour [203] of the same subject and of about the same date the pots are seen from above and yet Cézanne manages to give a sense of the upward thrust of the foliage as though the leaves are climbing on top of one another in a competition to reach the upper edge of the piece of paper. Such spatial disjunctions gradually increased in Cézanne's later still lifes throughout the 1890s, just as in *Foliage* [204] the plant seems to float in the air as if it has been lifted from the ground by a gust of wind.

Many of the finest still lifes on paper made by Cézanne after 1890 are 'set-pieces' as works of art in their own right. Certainly, they share the same concerns as the paintings regarding composition, form and the emphasis on materiality. But it is important to realize that at the end the artist painted more still lifes in watercolour than in oil. The challenge of depicting objects of varying textures and consistencies in the more liquescent and diaphanous medium of watercolour, rather than relying on the viscosity of oil paint, not only demonstrated his technical accomplishments but also enabled him to give an even more personal interpretation of the genre. As such, the later still lifes in watercolour are the summation of Cézanne's career as an artist in so far as they are so deeply felt and technically unsurpassed.

The most pressing requirement in any attempt at still life was to settle upon a composition. This could be limited to an arrangement of selected items on a flat surface such as a table, but it could be extended to include some indication of the architectural context, invariably an interior in which that table or any other supporting piece of furniture might be placed. One of the most intriguing aspects of many of Cézanne's still lifes is the spatial ambiguities that he introduced into them, as for example in the painting *Still Life with Plaster Cupid*, *c.* 1894 (Courtauld Gallery, London).

Cézanne deliberately chose steep and unlikely viewpoints usually from high up, or in exaggerated close-up, so that the spectator is often at first disorientated or visually confused. Added to these spatial ambiguities is the precarious arrangement of the objects themselves, which often teeter on the edge and seem as though they might at any minute fall over, roll off, or drop to the ground. In fact, the artist fixed the objects in their positions by artificial means at the angles he needed for his compositional requirements. This made the compositions even more complicated and so much more audacious. And by becoming detached from reality in this way the viewer's attention in turn becomes more fully engaged.

Hints of these complexities can be found in drawings such as *Corner of a Studio*, which could well have been intended to serve as the background for one of Cézanne's still lifes [205]. Similarly, in *Still Life: 'Pains sans Mie'*, which in its use of commercial typography anticipates works by Picasso, Braque, Léger and Marcel Duchamp, three of the objects are placed on a diagonal in front of the box of biscuits on the right, whereas those to the left on the same diagonal are seen against the patterned wallpaper set further back in the room [206]. The eye, therefore, weaves its way around the objects while receding more deeply into the composition.

At first, Cézanne's tendency to complicate matters was kept at bay. Two watercolours dating from the end of the 1880s (*Ginger Pot and Fruit on a Table* and *Ginger Pot and Fruit on a Table with a Napkin*) have a remarkable clarity stemming from their light tone and sparing application of watercolour, in addition to the daring reliance on the blank paper serving as a positive agent in the composition – a part of the artist's technique, which at this stage he developed more and more as a vital part of his working process [207, 208]. These characteristics are also the reason for the undeniable beauty of those watercolours where Cézanne does not try to overwhelm the viewer, but limits the number of objects to a minimum: *Three Pears* (*c.* 1882; Museum Boijmans Van Beuningen, Rotterdam), *Peaches and Figs* [209], or *Oranges on a Plate* (*c.* 1900; Philadelphia Museum of Art). Another *Three Pears* in Princeton [210], where the fruit is displayed on a tilted white plate set against a cloth decorated with arabesques, so impressed Degas and Renoir when they saw it on exhibition at Vollard's in 1895 that they drew lots for it: Degas won. These spellbinding works are among Cézanne's most beautiful and profound.

At the opposite extreme are those still lifes with elaborate compositions comprising a multiplicity of objects of varying sizes crowded on to tables that positively groan with the effort of supporting the weight [211–221]. These watercolours are the equal of any of the paintings in their inventiveness, complexity and clash of different forms. The wealth of the imagery is comparable with the leading Baroque still-life painters in Holland – Jan Davidsz. de Heem, Willem Kalf, Abraham van Beyeren – but surpass them in the sense that they have been achieved with a medium that is so difficult to control and one that had never before been associated with the genre to this extent. Furthermore, Cézanne has not reined in his brushwork in order to obtain the necessary precision but, on the contrary, he has adopted a broader style of execution involving a wide variety of brushmarks, some seen in isolation, others in clusters, and yet others overlapping. It is an 'all-over' technique where no distinction is made between the origin or status of the object. The overwhelming sense of unity in each of these final works on paper, however, is due to the free-flowing forms, unified colour and treatment of light – what, in effect, Cézanne referred to as the 'envelope'. As two young painters, R. P. Rivière and Jacques-Félix Schnerb, who visited

the artist towards the end of his life, observed, Cézanne 'did not seek to
represent forms by a line. The outline existed for him only as the place
where one form ended and another began … In principle there is no line,
a form exists only in relation to the neighbouring forms.'

The eye alone alerts you to the magnitude of Cézanne's achievements
in these last still lifes, which were probably never made in a single session
and are of considerable dimensions. Apart from identifying the various
items, the viewer is shown objects from above and below, from directly
in front and from the side, from near and far. The viewer is also invited
to look over and beneath objects or around and into them, as well as to
move the eye across empty surfaces, along edges of tables, and then to
slide down waterfalls of drapery. And the only assistance given by the
artist is the interplay between the horizontals and verticals, the gradual
emergence of geometric forms and the jostling of colours. As Cézanne
told Gasquet, 'There are two things in a painter: the eye and the brain,
and they need to help each other, you have to work on their mutual
development, but in a painter's way: on the eye by looking at things
through nature; on the brain, by the logic of organized sensations which
provides the means of expression.' By applying this principle in his
late watercolours Cézanne triumphantly reaches a transcendental state
beyond which few artists have ventured.

The subject of several watercolours of this late phase in the artist's
life is the human skulls that Cézanne kept in his studio. A niece records
that he had three of these. Previously, in early pictures from the 1860s,
a skull had been used as a prop in a still life [188] or an attribute in a
religious composition. However, the skull suddenly reappears at the
end of the 1880s before becoming a stalwart in the artist's repertoire
during his final years, perhaps owing to intimations of his mortality
[222–225]. Apart from any symbolic significance, it is also possible
to appreciate how the rounded shape of the cranium had a certain
macabre fascination for Cézanne as an artist. He shows the skulls either
singly or in pairs, and even as part of a triad. Set on a table, the artist
deliberately offsets the curvature against the straight edges of barely
suggested tables, balustrades and windows. Equally, he contrasts the
chalky white of the skull against the pattern of coloured drapery in the
manner of a Dutch seventeenth-century painting. According to Gasquet,
Cézanne often quoted lines about death from the poetry of Baudelaire
and Verlaine and so the symbolism of the human skull could hardly have
escaped him. Yet these watercolours have an engrossingly eerie beauty.
Skull on Drapery [225] is a particularly striking, almost choreographed,
composition where the skull is centrally placed and literally cushioned
on a carefully folded piece of drapery. It is seen directly from the front

and its centrality is emphasized by the four blank corners of the paper.
It is as though Cézanne has created an altar for a charnel house and it is
a subject that has a peculiarly chilling resonance for our modern times.
Skull on Drapery combines terror with beauty.

What must have been Cézanne thinking as he painted these images
of skulls? Did he recall Poussin's paintings of *Et in Arcadia Ego* or
Delacroix's illustrations to Shakespeare's *Hamlet*? He was evidently
aware that life was ebbing away, for, as he wrote to Bernard on
21 September 1906, a month before he died: 'But I am old, and ill, and
I have vowed to die painting rather than sink into the degrading senility
that threatens old people who let themselves be ruled by passions that
dull the senses.'

This echoes a statement made when signing off a letter to his son
a few weeks earlier, on 14 August: '*Mon cher Paul*, the only thing I have
left is painting, I embrace you with all my heart, you and maman, your
old father.'

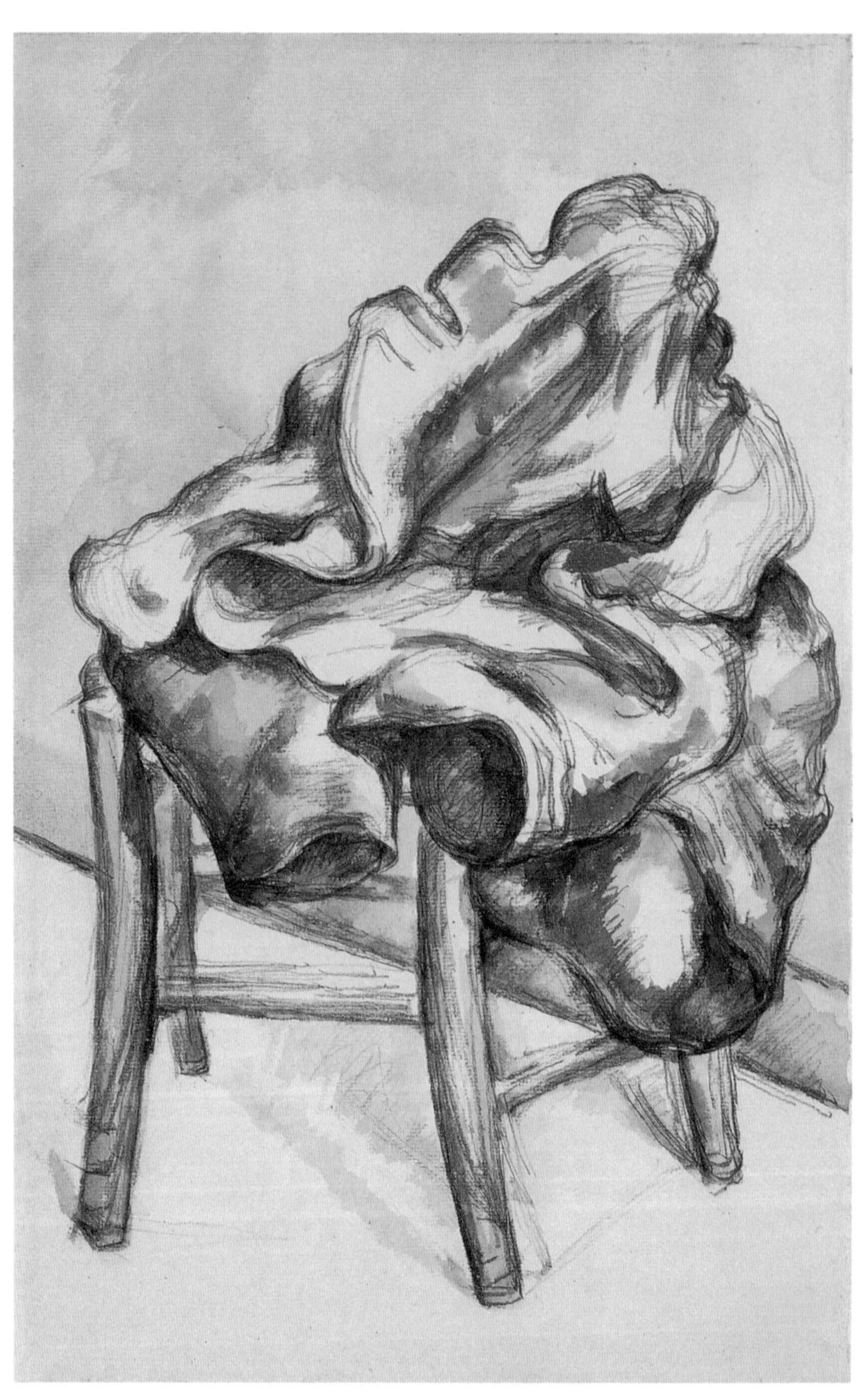

276   *The Ultimate Construct in Still Life*

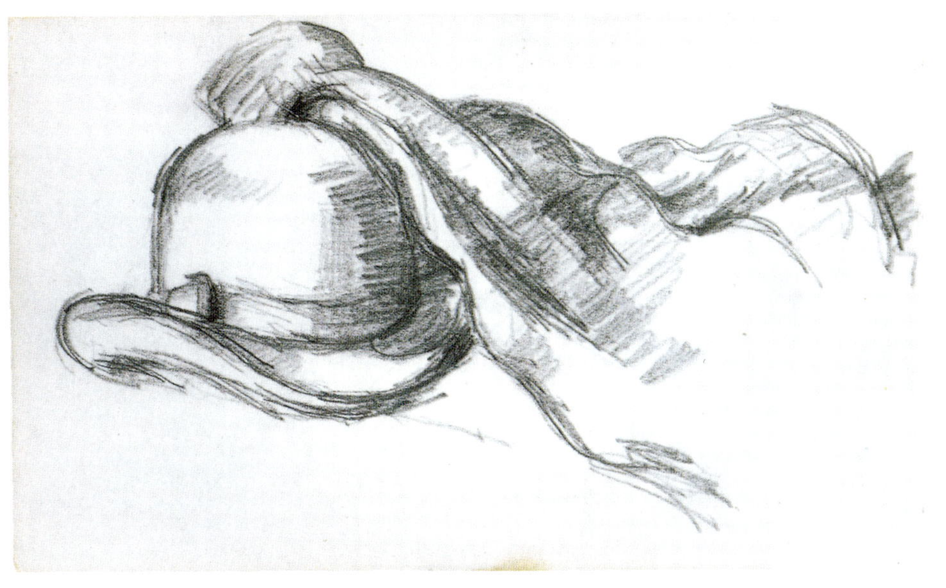

OPPOSITE
193. *Coat on a Chair*, 1890–92.
Pencil and watercolour, 47.5 × 30.5 cm (18¾ × 12 in.).
Private collection

ABOVE
194. *Derby Hat and Garment*, 1884–87.
Pencil, 12.7 × 21.6 cm (5 × 8½ in.).
Philadelphia Museum of Art

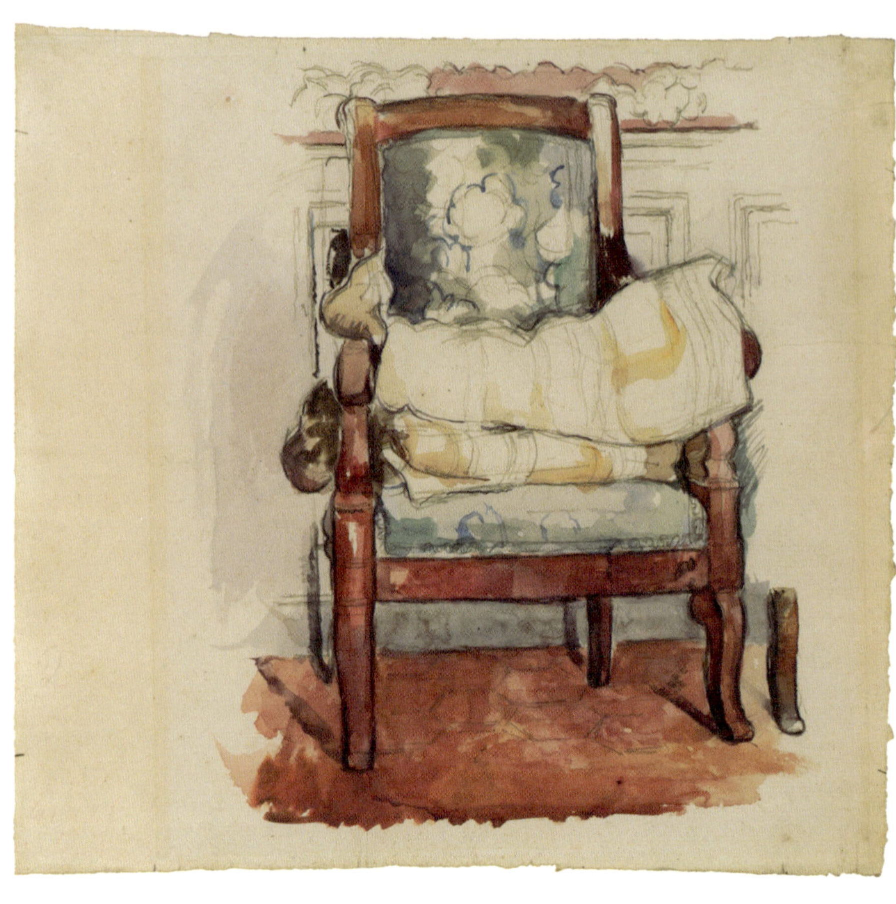

ABOVE
195. *Armchair*, c. 1885–90.
Pencil and watercolour, 32.2 × 33.8 cm (12⅝ × 13¼ in.).
The Courtauld Gallery, London

OPPOSITE
196. *Curtains*, c. 1885.
Pencil and watercolour with gouache, 49 × 30.7 cm (19 × 12 in.).
Musée d'Orsay, Paris

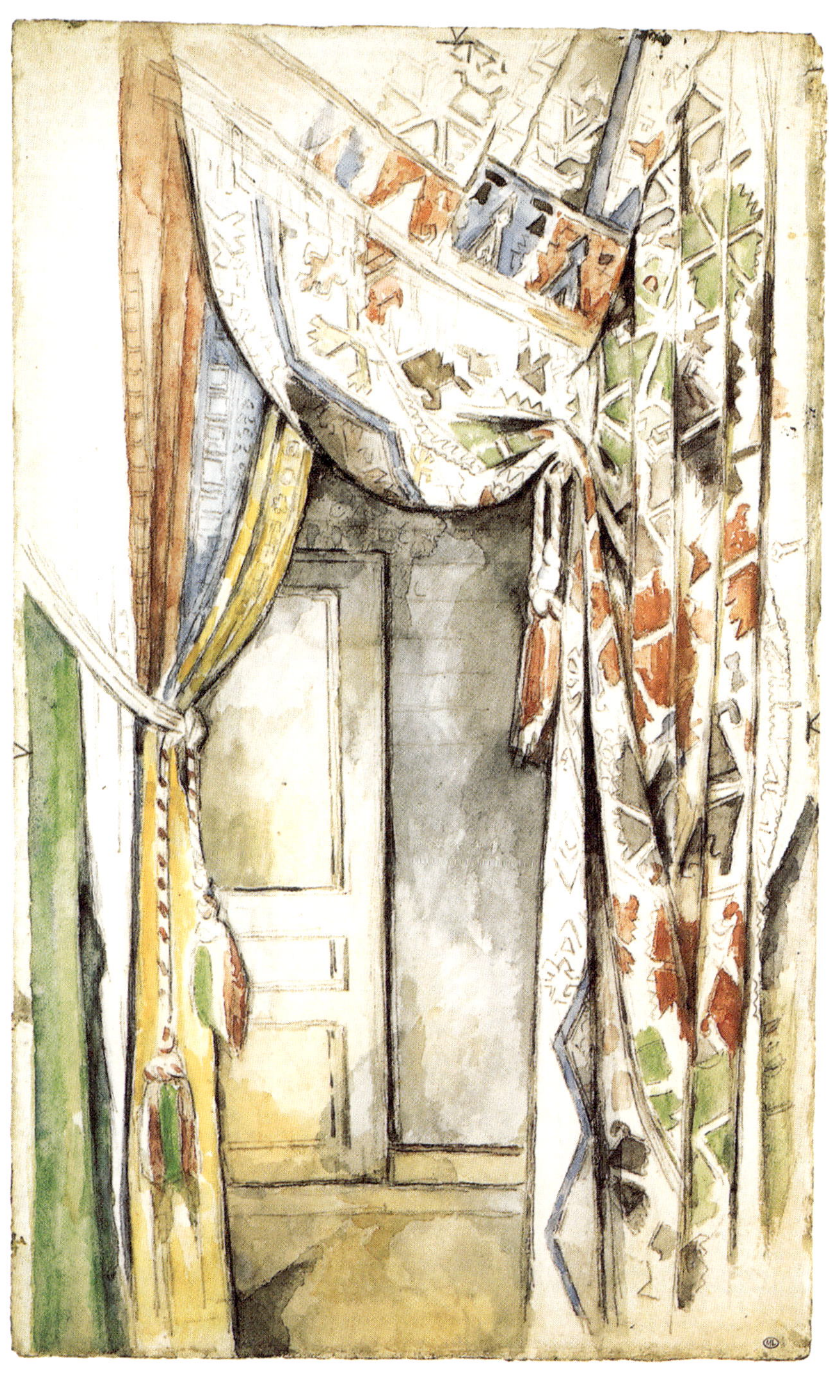

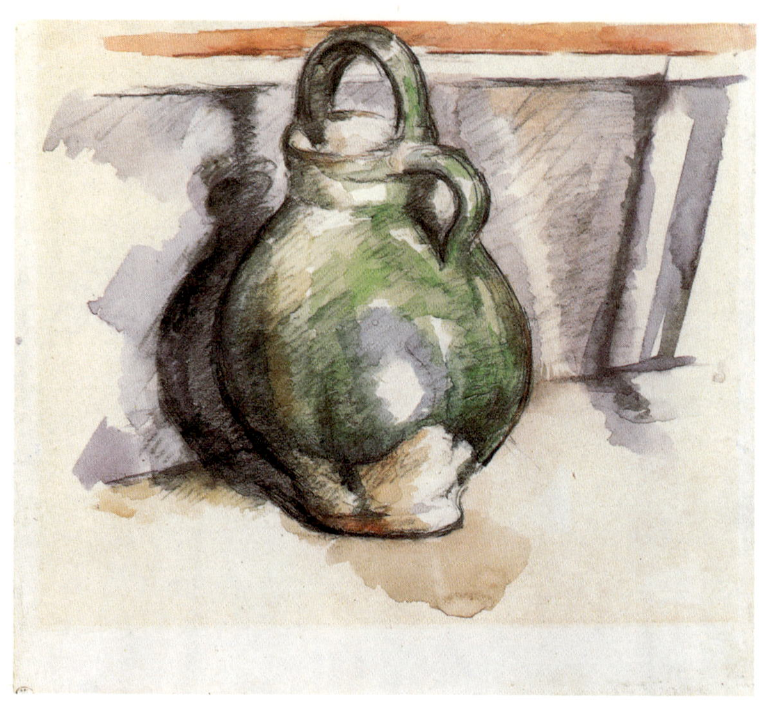

197. *The Green Jug*, 1888–90.
Pencil and watercolour, 22 × 24.7 cm (8⅝ × 9¾ in.).
Musée d'Orsay, Paris

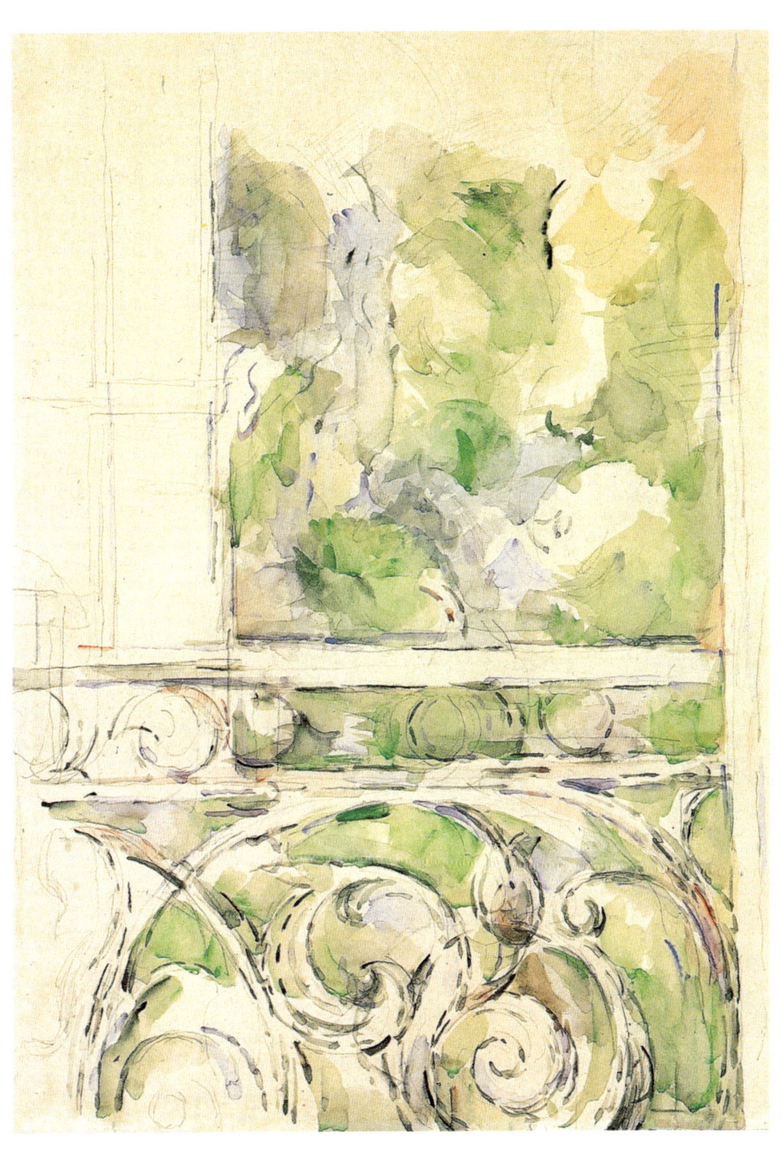

198. *The Balcony*, c. 1900.
Pencil and watercolour, 56.5 × 40.3 cm (22¼ × 15⅞ in.).
Philadelphia Museum of Art

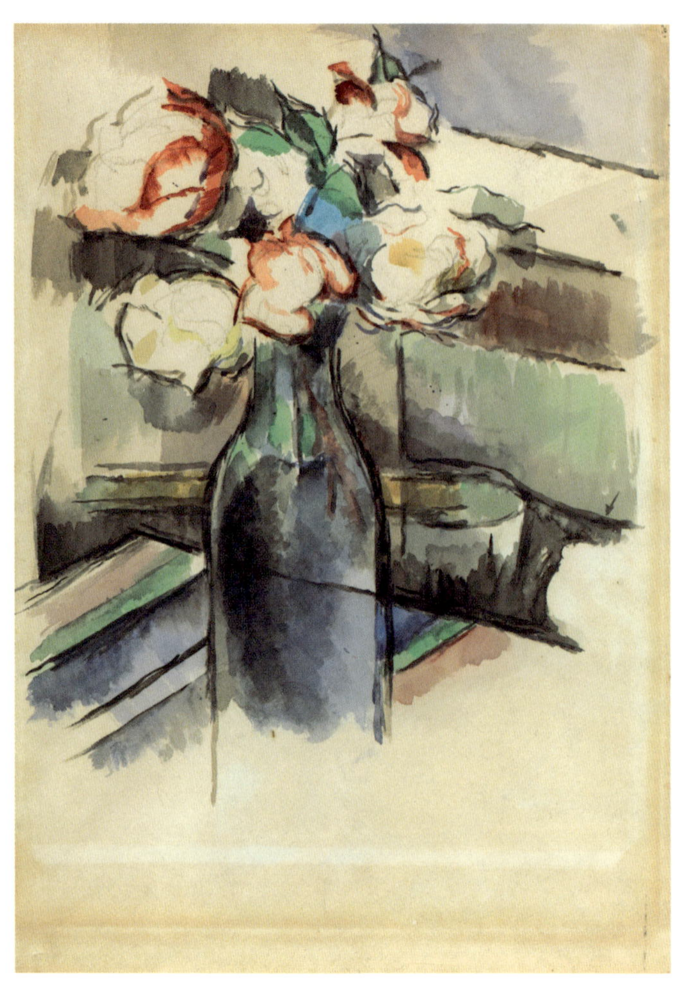

ABOVE
199. *Roses in a Bottle*, 1900–04.
Pencil and watercolour, 43.6 × 31 cm (17⅛ × 12¼ in.).
National Gallery of Art, Washington, DC

OPPOSITE
200. *Vase of Flowers*, 1885–88.
Pencil and watercolour, 46.6 × 30 cm (18⅜ × 11⅞ in.).
Fitzwilliam Museum, Cambridge

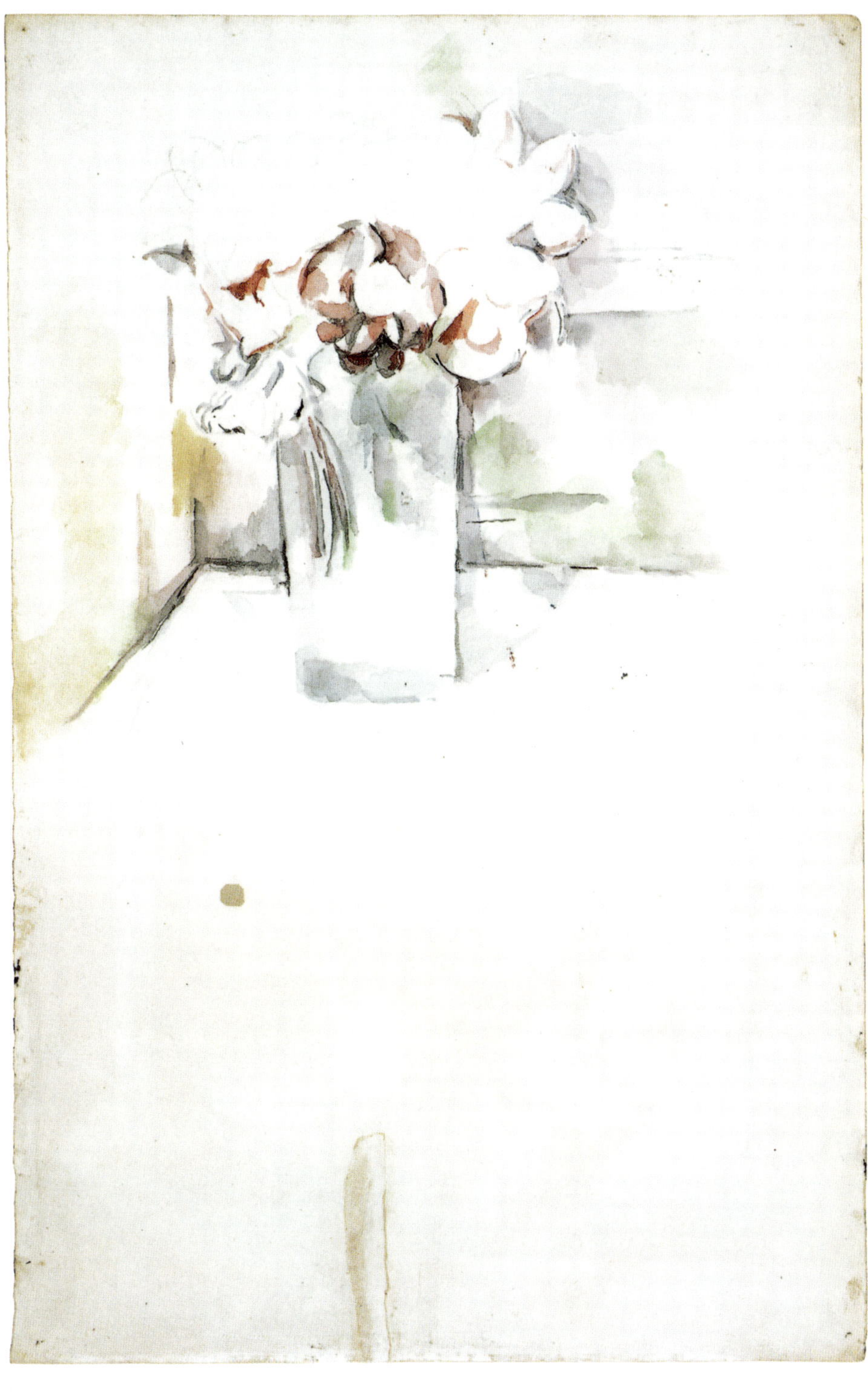

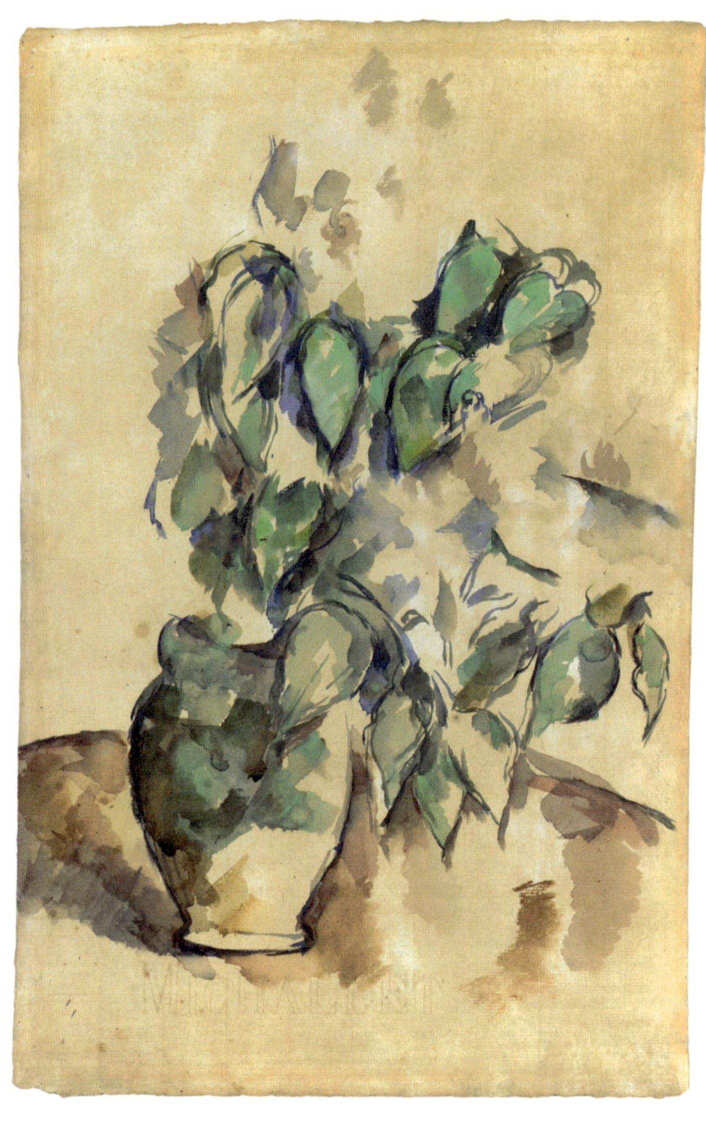

201. *Leaves in a Green Pot*, 1890–92.
Watercolour, 47.5 × 30.5 cm (18¼ × 12¼ in.).
Private collection

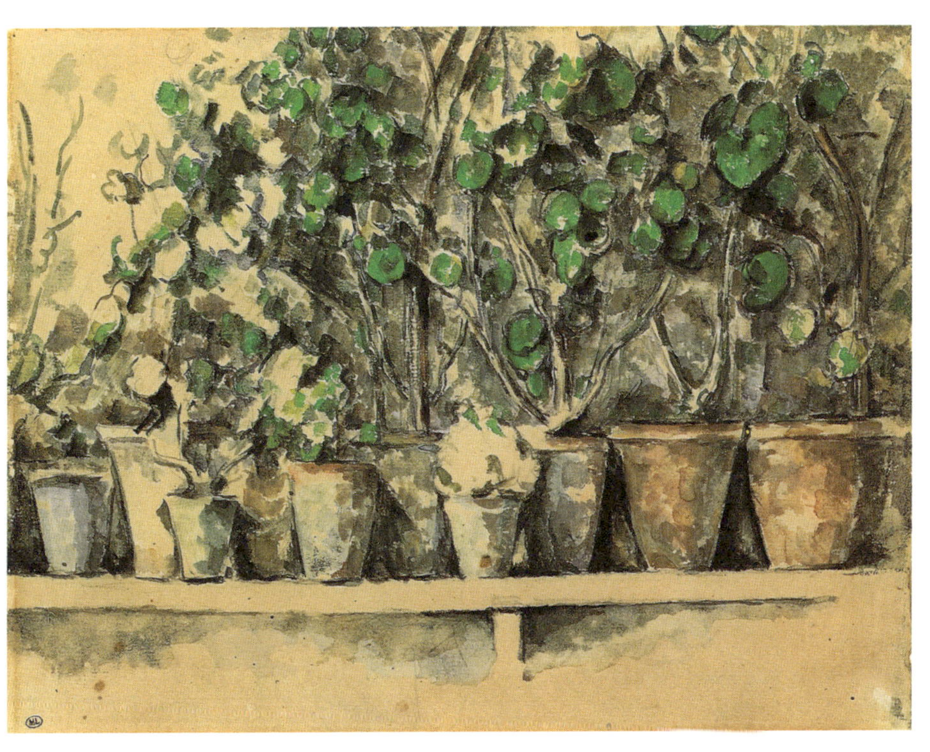

202. *Flowerpots, c.* 1885.
Pencil and watercolour with gouache on yellowed paper,
23.6 × 30.8 cm (9¼ × 12⅛ in.).
Musée d'Orsay, Paris

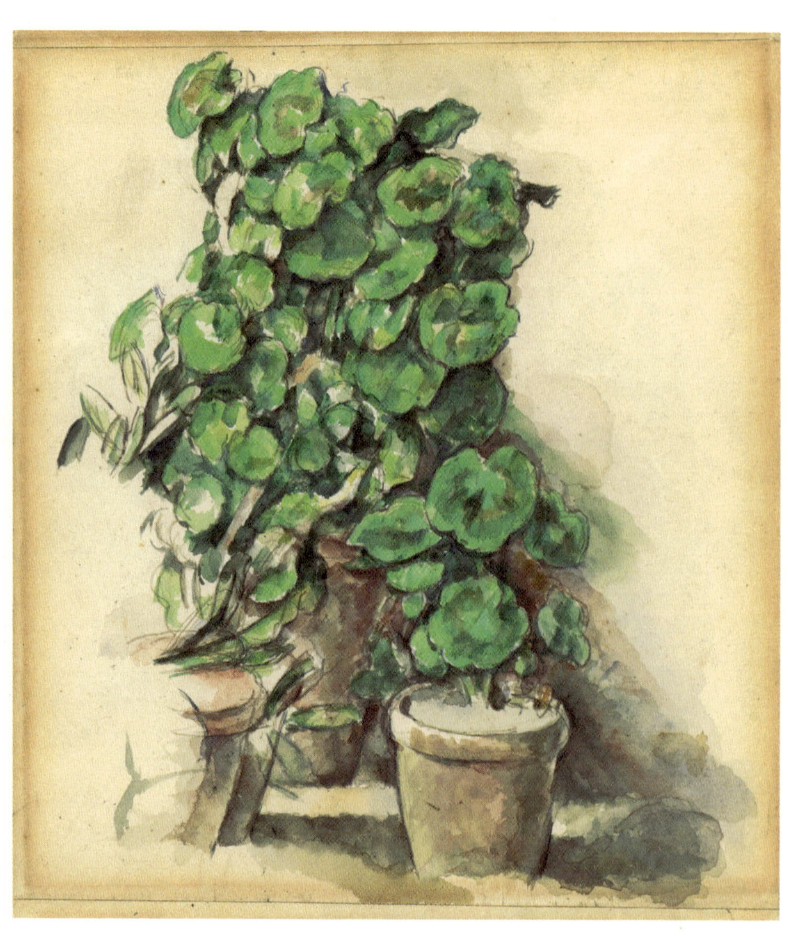

203. *Pots of Geraniums, c.* 1885.
Pencil and watercolour on buff paper, 31 × 27 cm (12¼ × 10⅝ in.).
National Gallery of Art, Washington, DC

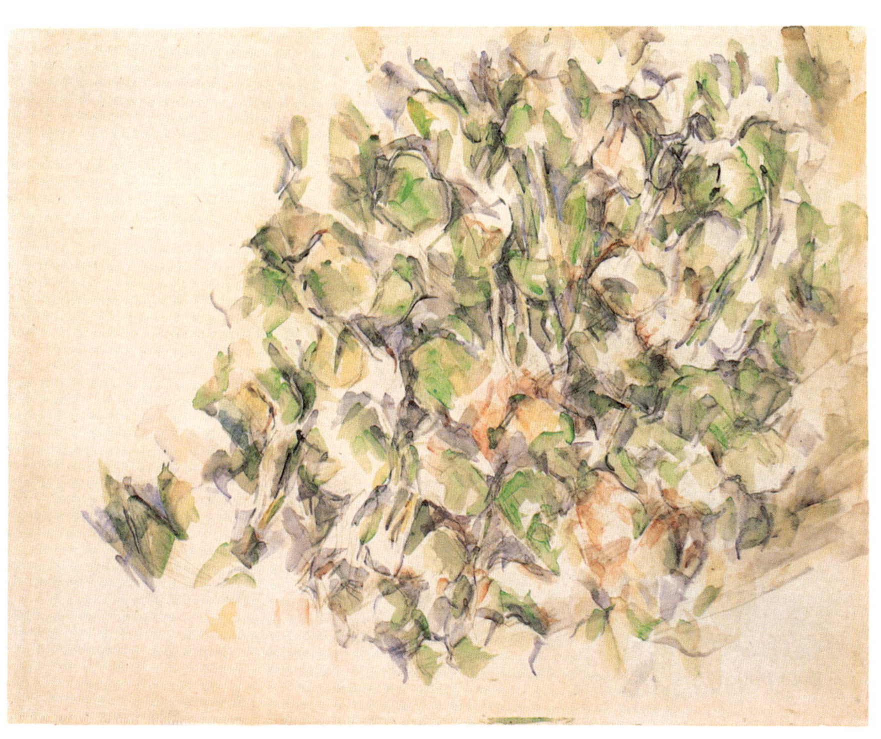

204. *Foliage*, 1895–1900.
Pencil and watercolour, 44.8 × 56.8 cm (17⅝ × 22⅜ in.).
Museum of Modern Art, New York

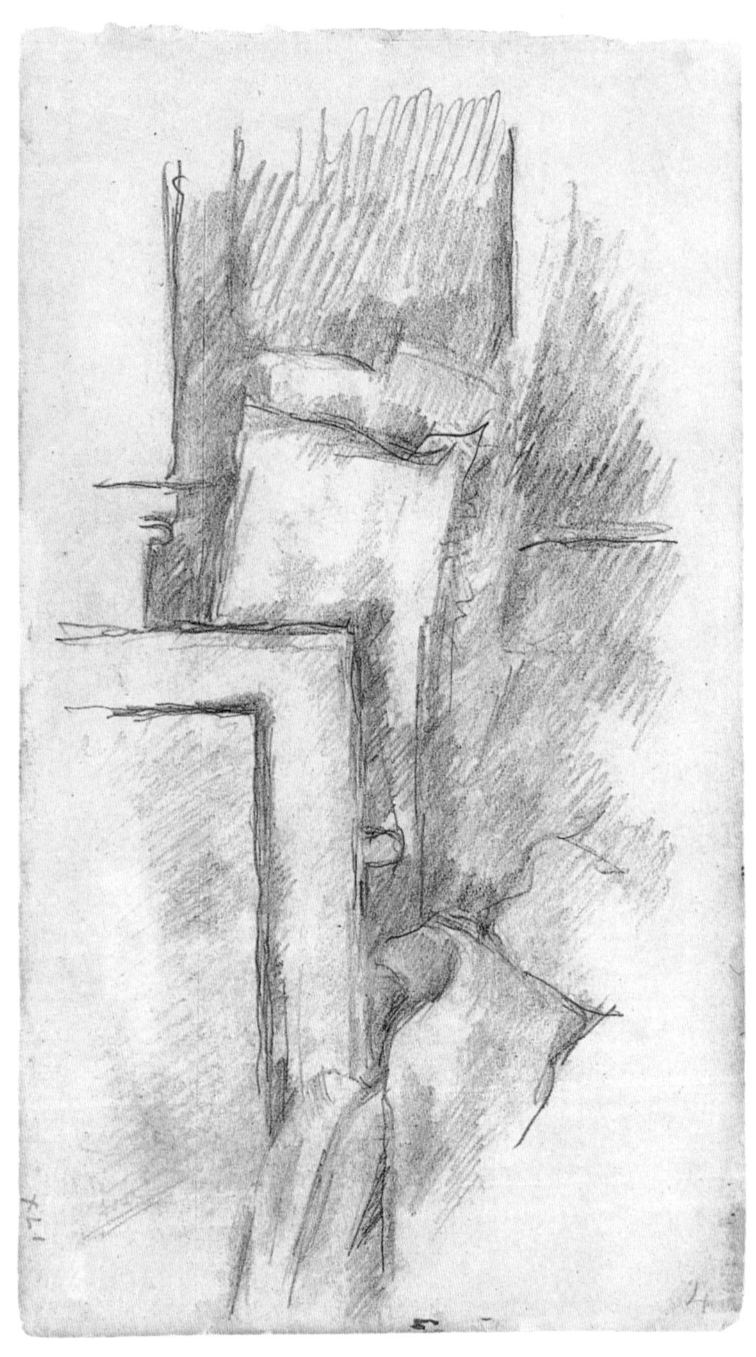

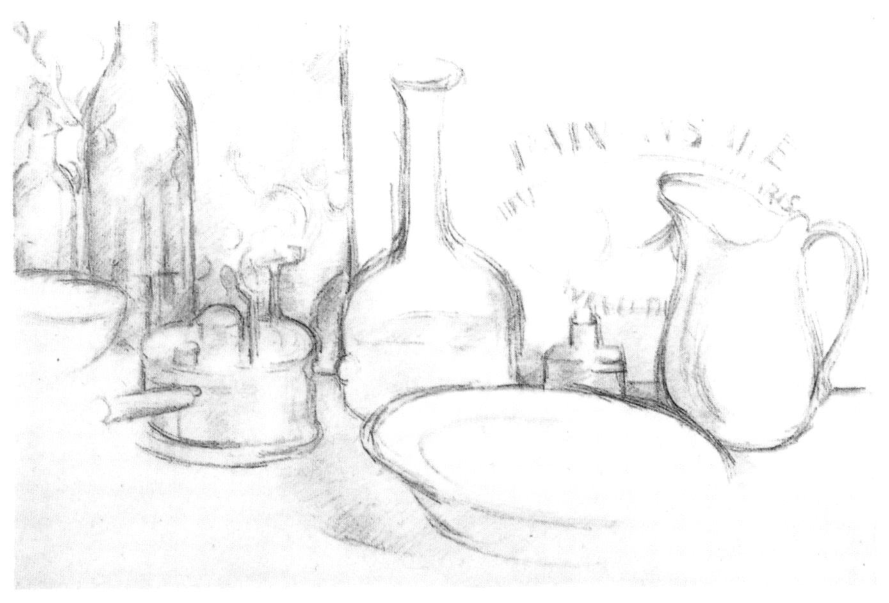

OPPOSITE

205. *Corner of a Studio*, 1877–81.
Pencil, 21.8 × 12.4 cm (8⅝ × 4⅞ in.).
Fogg Museum, Cambridge, Massachusetts

ABOVE

206. *Still Life: 'Pain sans Mie'*, 1887–90.
Pencil, 31.8 × 49.2 cm (12½ × 19⅜ in.).
Private collection

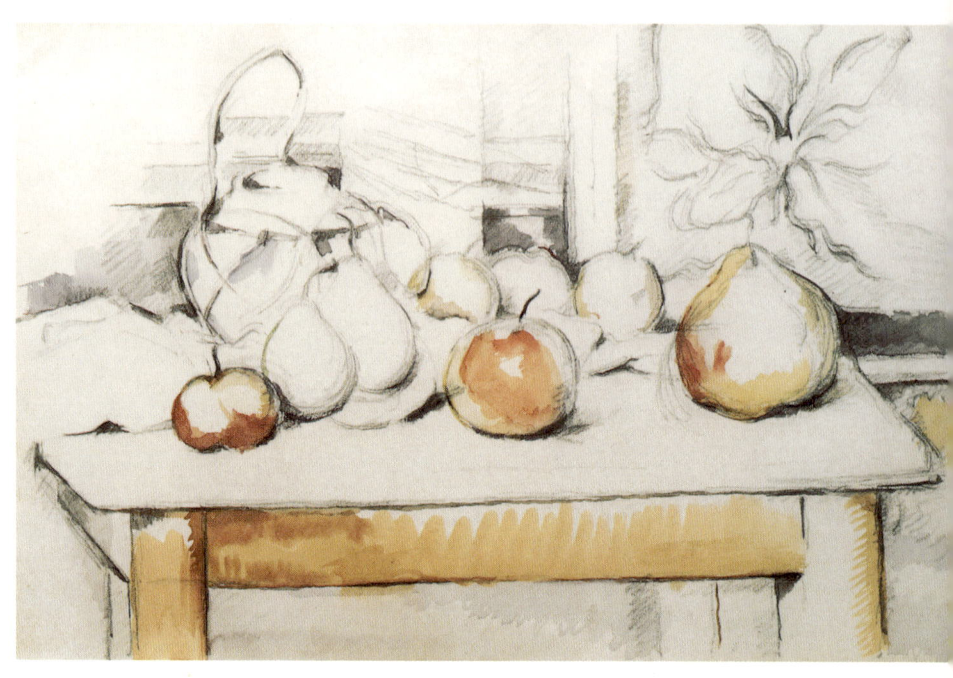

207. *Ginger Pot and Fruit on a Table*, 1888–90.
Pencil and watercolour, 24 × 36 cm (9½ × 14¼ in.).
Private collection

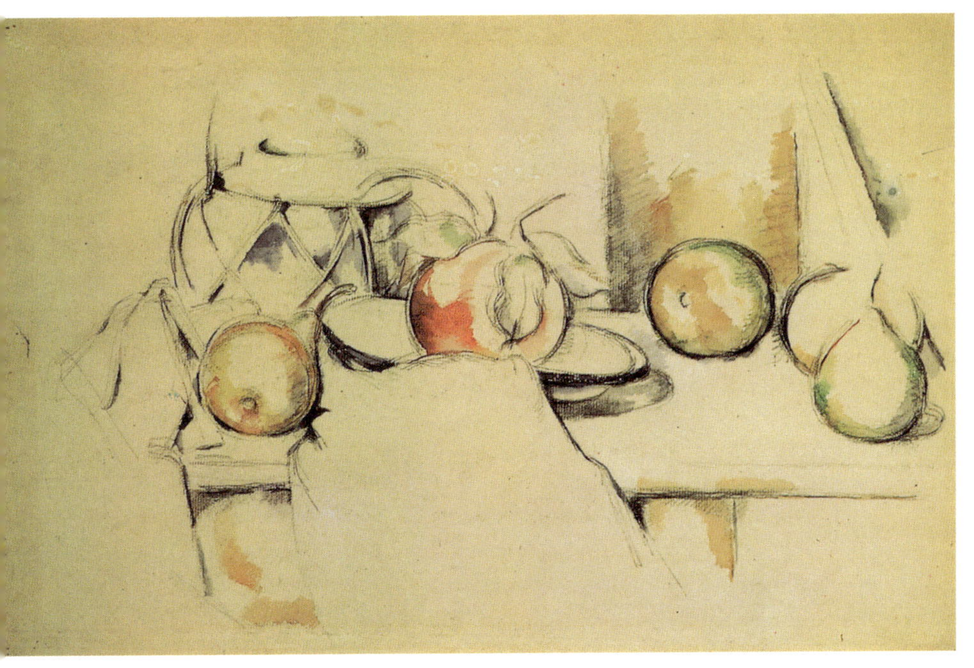

208. *Ginger Pot and Fruit on a Table with a Napkin*, 1888–90.
Pencil and watercolour on yellowish paper, 28 × 45 cm (11 × 17¾ in.).
Private collection

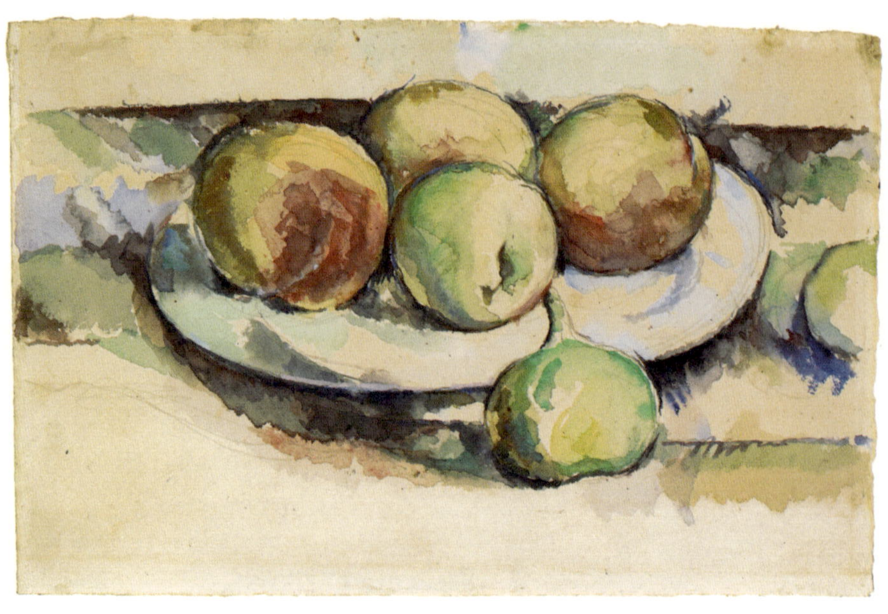

209. *Peaches and Figs*, 1885–90.
Pencil and watercolour, 19 × 30 cm (7½ × 11⅞ in.).
Ashmolean Museum, Oxford

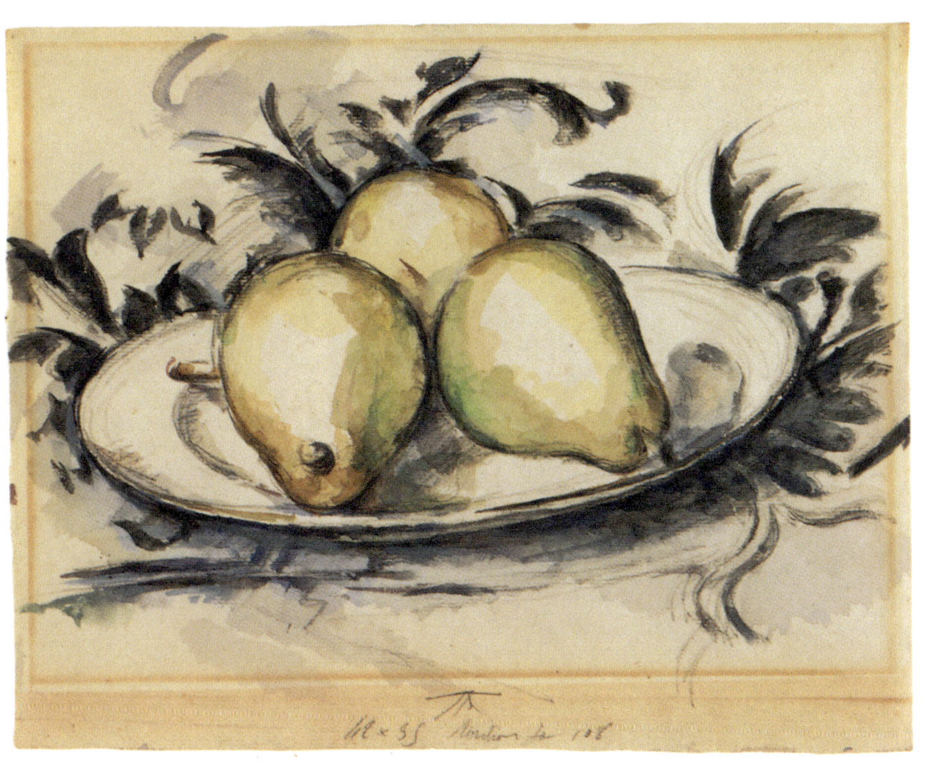

210. *Three Pears*, c. 1888–90.
Pencil and watercolour with gouache
on cream paper, 24.2 × 31 cm (9½ × 12¼ in.).
The Henry and Rose Pearlman Foundation, on loan to
Princeton University Art Museum, New Jersey

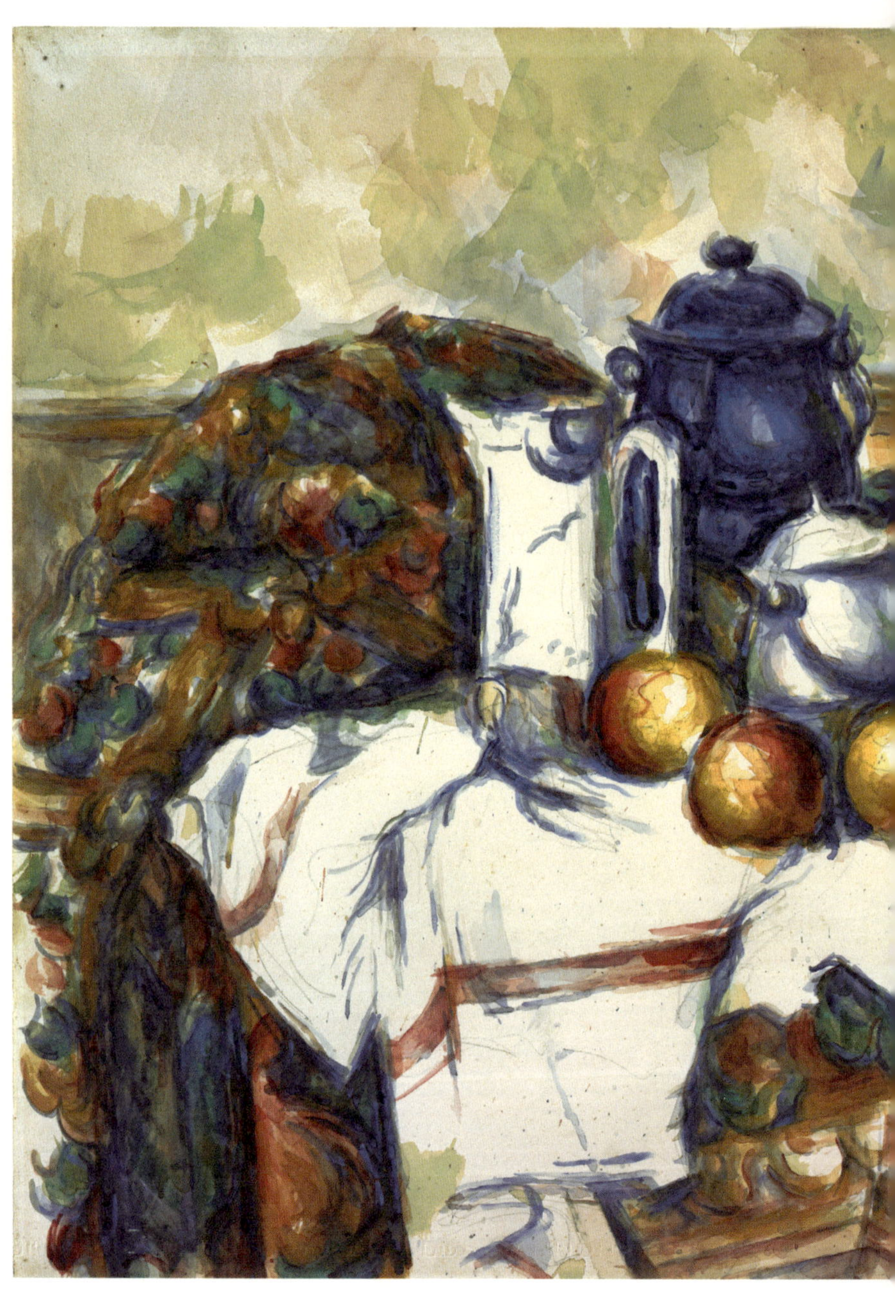

294   *The Ultimate Construct in Still Life*

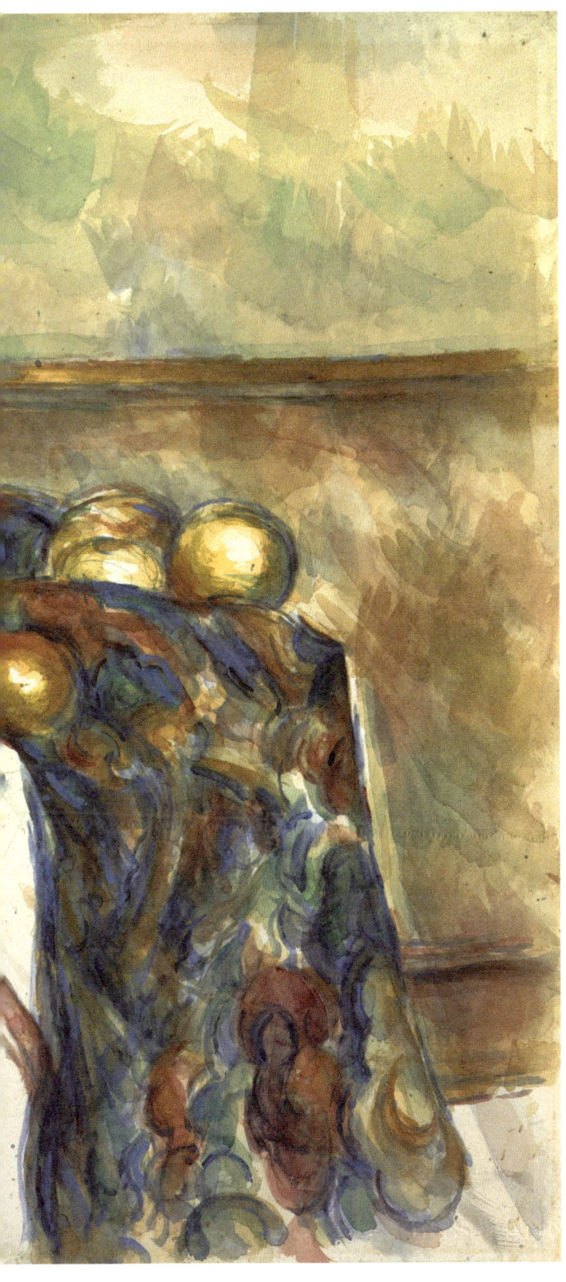

211. *Still Life with Blue Pot*, *c.* 1900. Pencil and watercolour, 48.1 × 63.2 cm (18⅞ × 24⅞ in.). J. Paul Getty Museum, Los Angeles

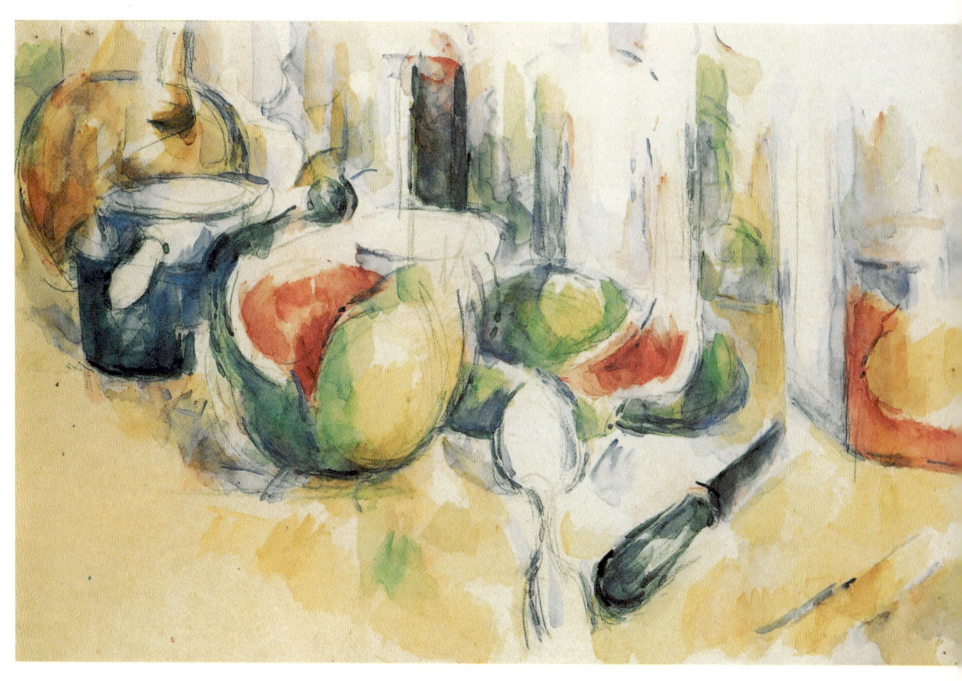

212. *Still Life with Melon, c.* 1900.
Pencil and watercolour, 31.5 × 47.6 cm (12⅝ × 18¾ in.).
Foundation Beyeler, Riehen, Basel

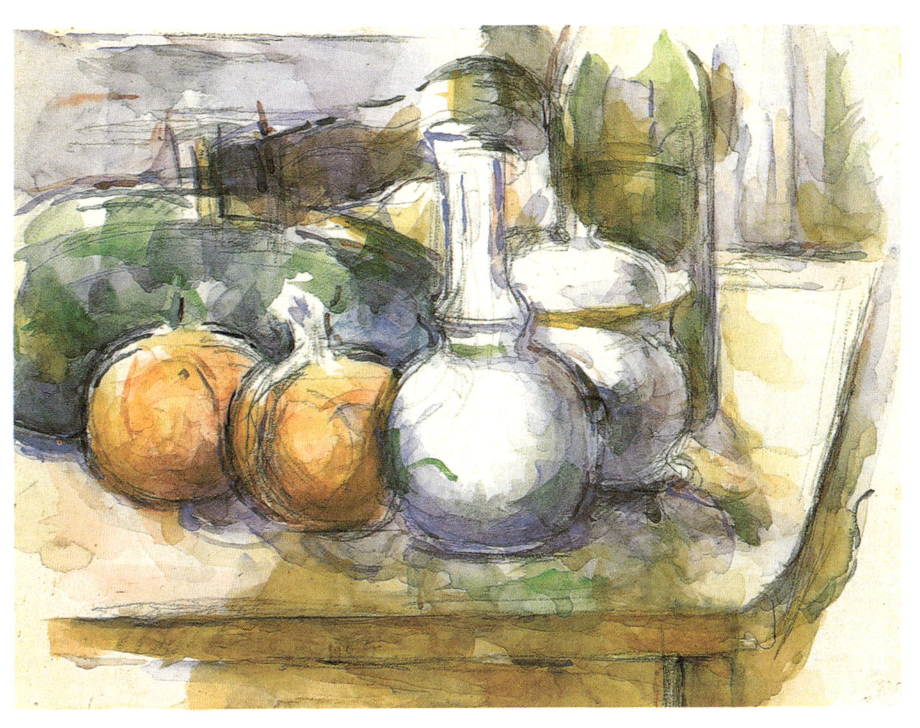

213. *Still Life with Pomegranates, Carafe, Sugar Bowl,*
Bottle and Water Melon, 1900–06. Pencil and watercolour,
31.5 × 43.1 cm (12⅜ × 17 in.).
Musée du Louvre, Paris

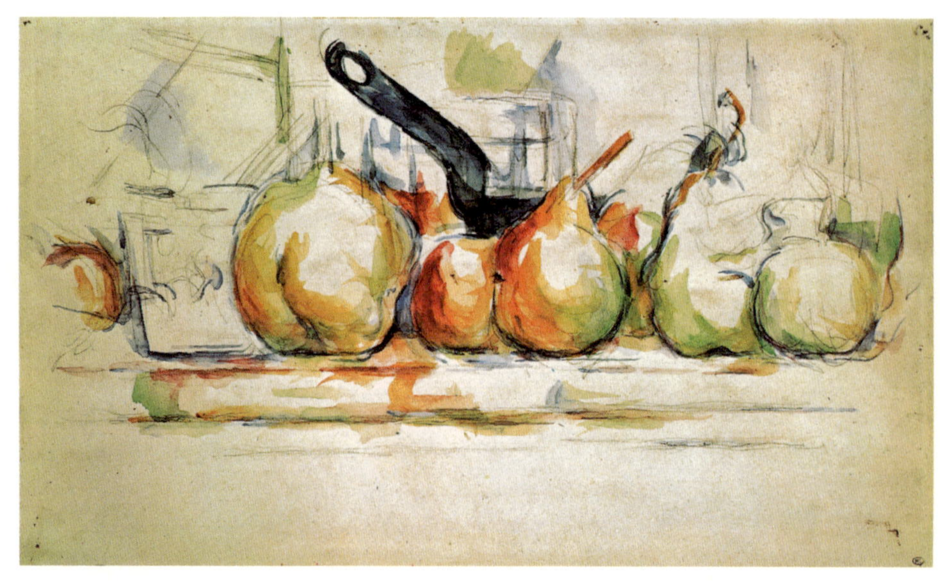

214. *Apples, Pears and Casserole (La Table de Cuisine)*, 1900–04.
Pencil and watercolour, 26 × 45 cm (10¼ × 17¾ in.).
Musée d'Orsay, Paris

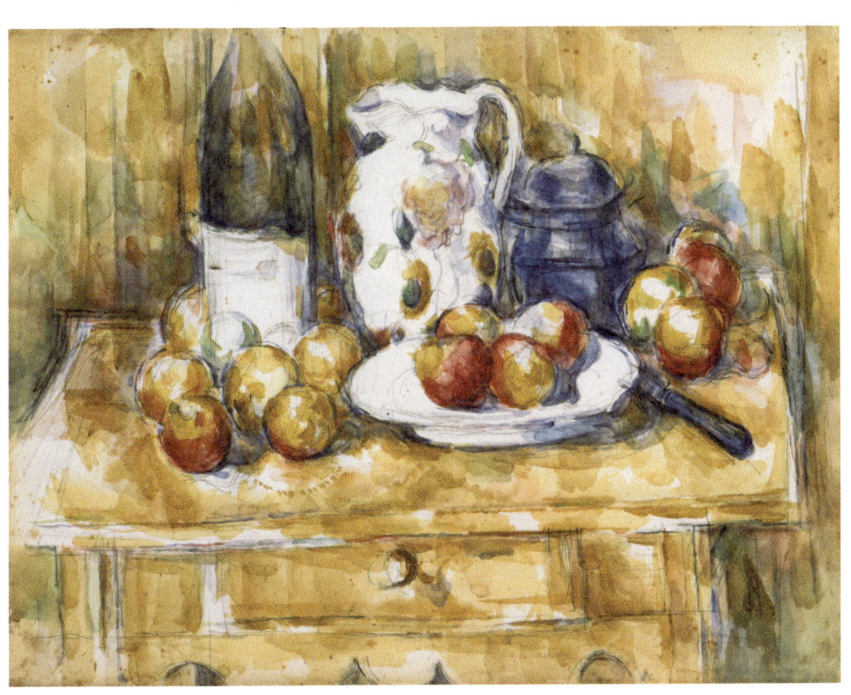

215. *Apples with Bottle, Water Jug and Blue Pot*, 1900–06.
Watercolour, 48 × 62 cm (18⅞ × 24⅜ in.).
Dallas Museum of Art, Texas

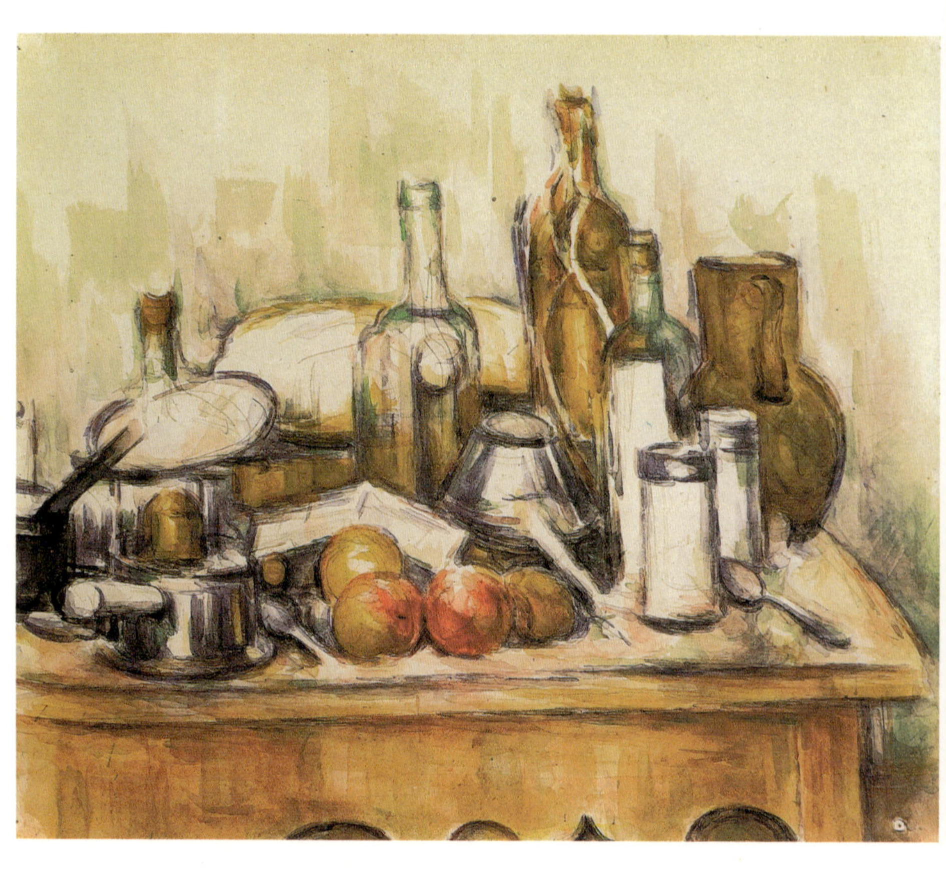

216. *Still Life with Bottles, Alcohol Stove and Apples, 1900–06.*
Pencil and watercolour, 47 × 56 cm (18½ × 22 in.).
Private collection

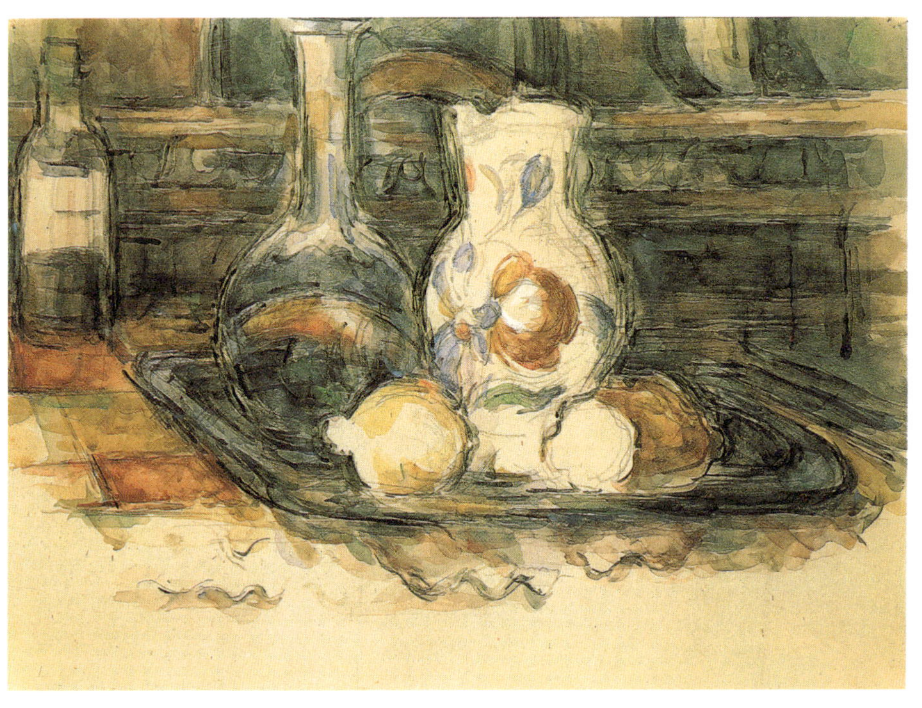

217. *Bottle, Carafe, Jug and Lemons*, 1902–06.
Pencil and watercolour, 44.5 × 60 cm (17½ × 23⅝ in.).
Museo Thyssen-Bornemisza, Madrid

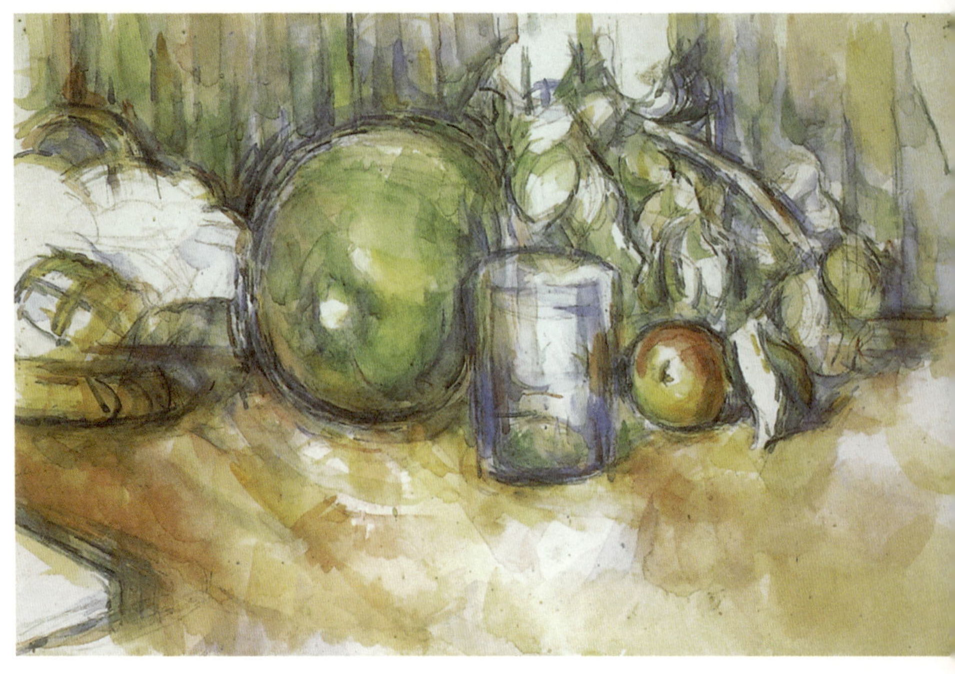

218. *Still Life with a Green Melon*, 1902–06.
Pencil and watercolour, 30.5 × 48.3 cm (12 × 19 in.).
Private collection

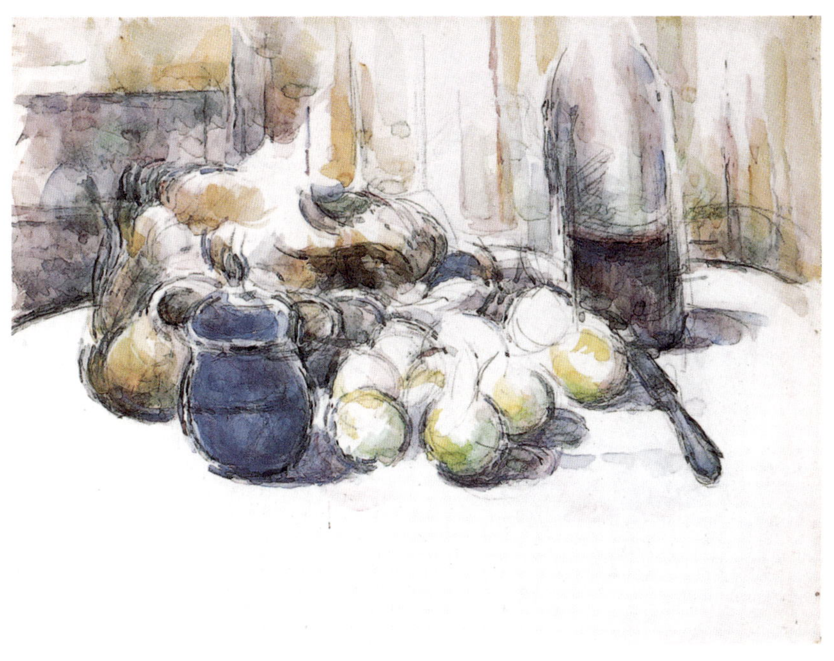

219. *Blue Pot and a Bottle of Wine*, 1902–06.
Pencil and watercolour on yellowish paper,
47.6 × 59.7 cm (18¾ × 23½ in.).
Pierpont Morgan Library, New York

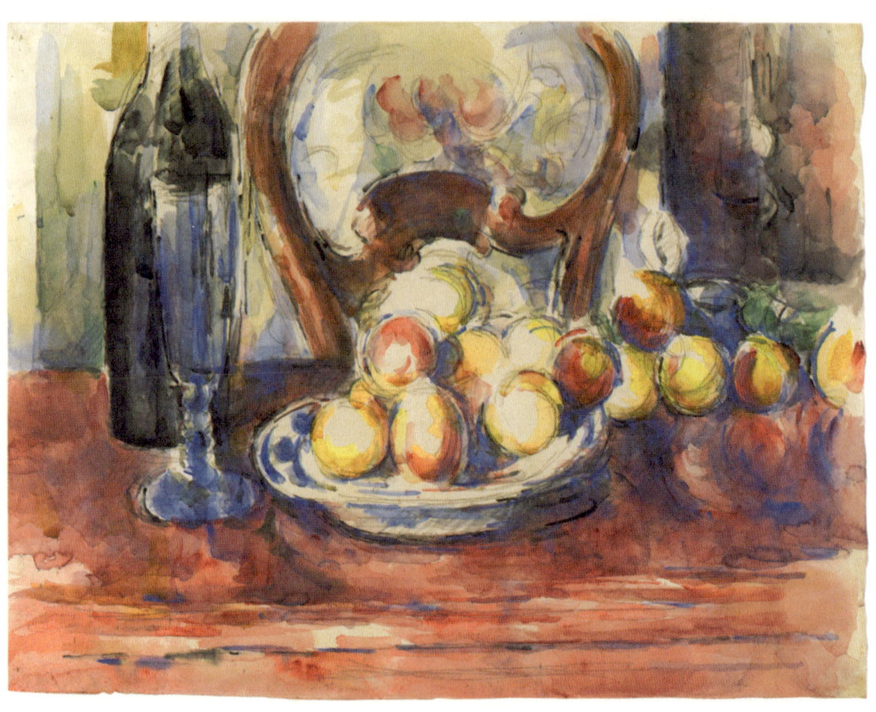

220. *Apples, Bottle and Chairback*, 1904–06.
Pencil and watercolour, 44.5 × 59 cm (17½ × 23¼ in.).
The Courtauld Gallery, London

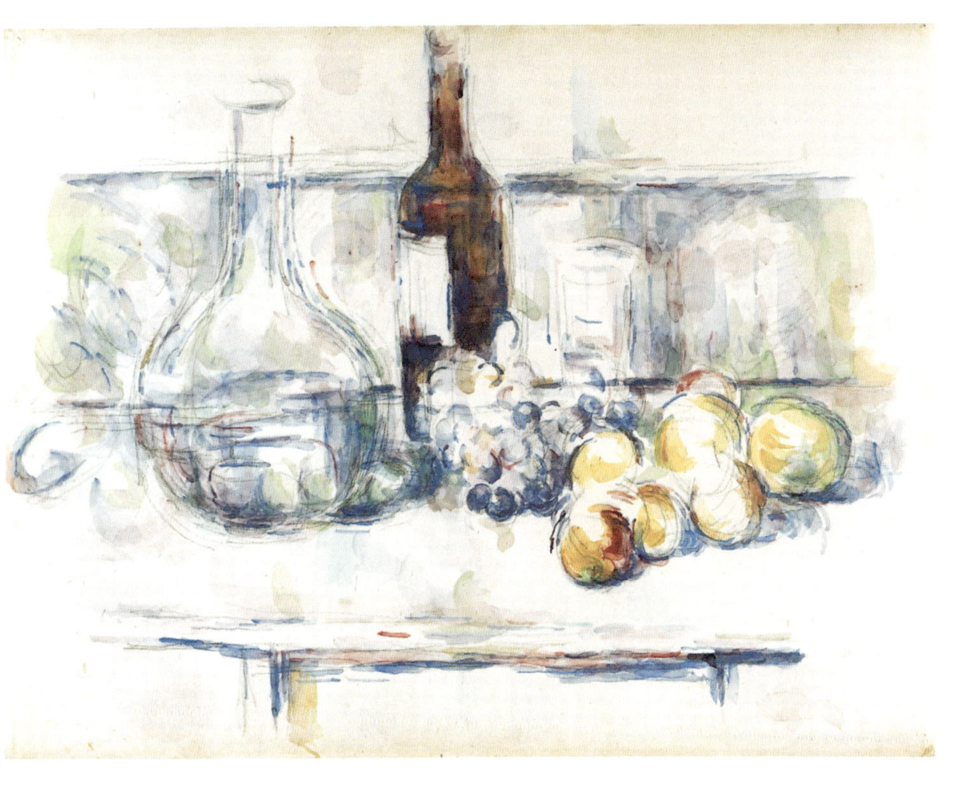

221. *Still Life with Carafe, Bottle and Fruit*, 1906.
Pencil and watercolour on pale buff paper, 48 × 62.5 cm (18⅞ × 24⅝ in.).
The Henry and Rose Pearlman Foundation, on loan to
Princeton University Art Museum, New Jersey

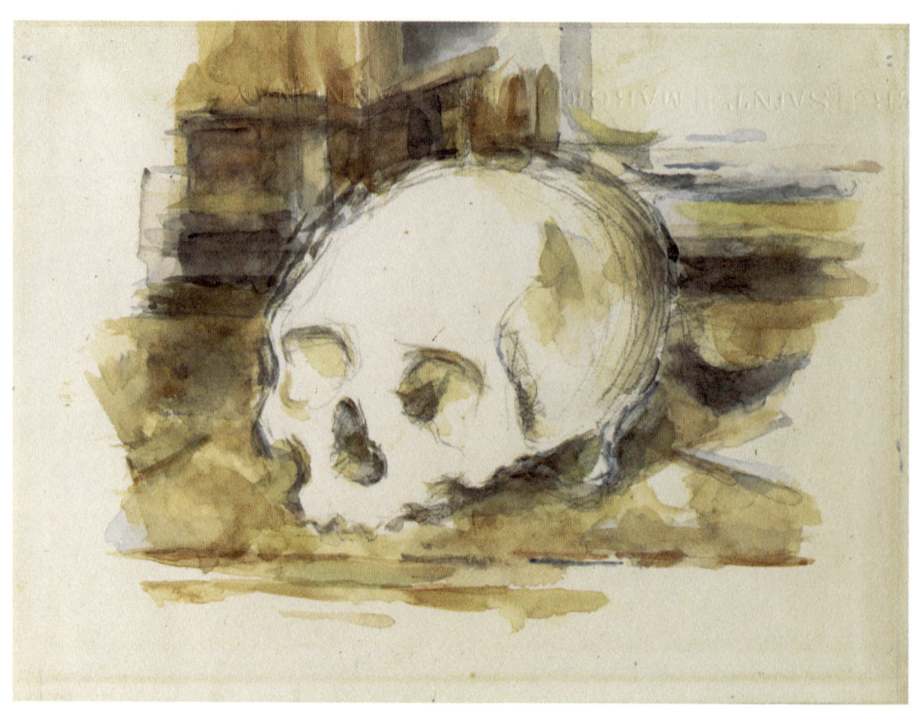

222. *Study of a Skull*, 1902–04.
Pencil and watercolour on pale buff paper, 22.9 × 31 cm (9 × 12¼ in.).
The Henry and Rose Pearlman Foundation, on loan to
Princeton University Art Museum, New Jersey

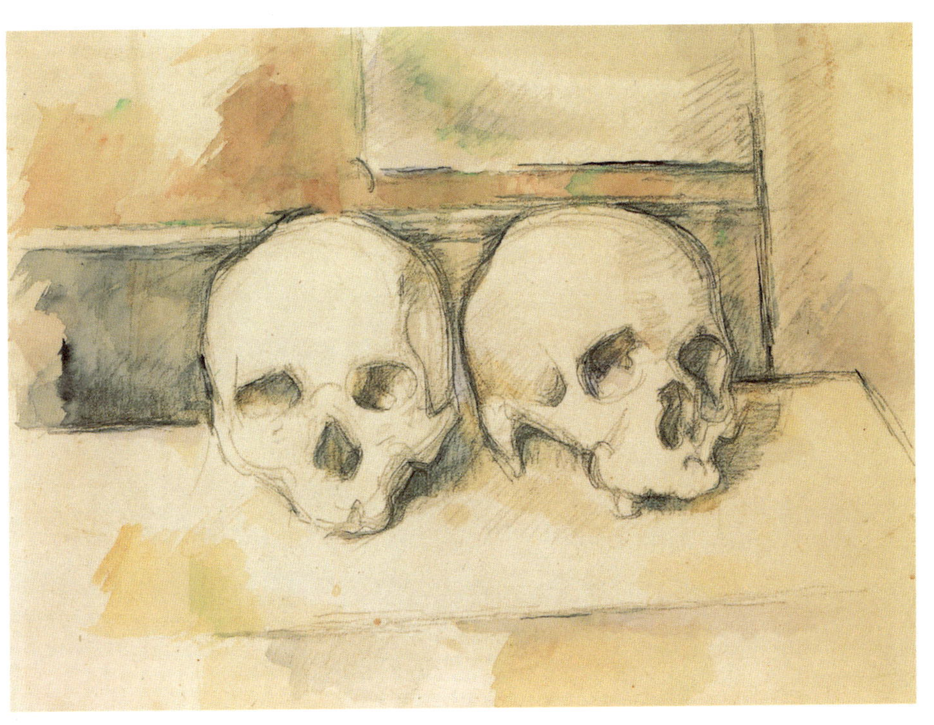

223. *Two Skulls*, 1890–1900.
Pencil and watercolour, 24.2 × 31.4 cm (9½ × 12⅜ in.).
Private collection

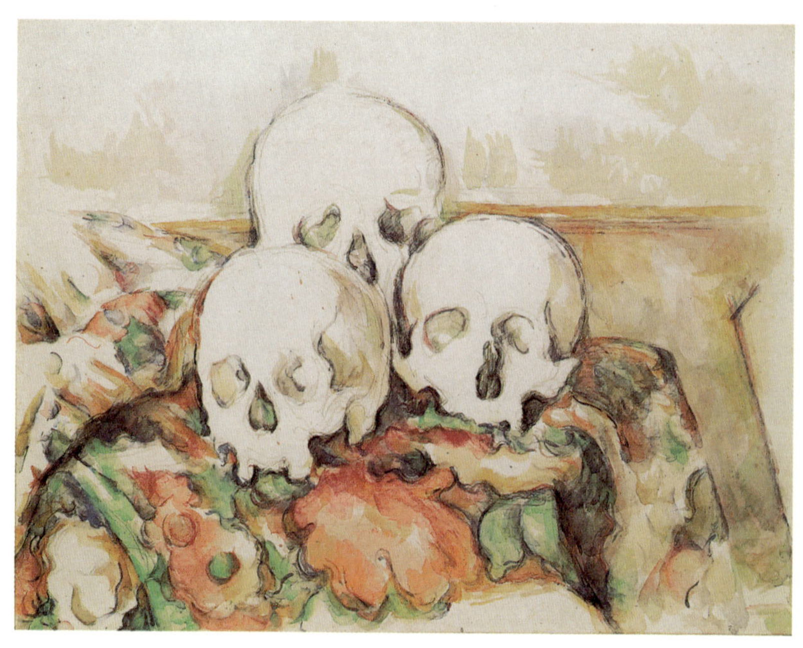

224. *Three Skulls*, 1902–06.
Pencil and watercolour with touches of gouache,
47.7 × 63.2 cm (18¾ × 24⅞ in.).
The Art Institute of Chicago

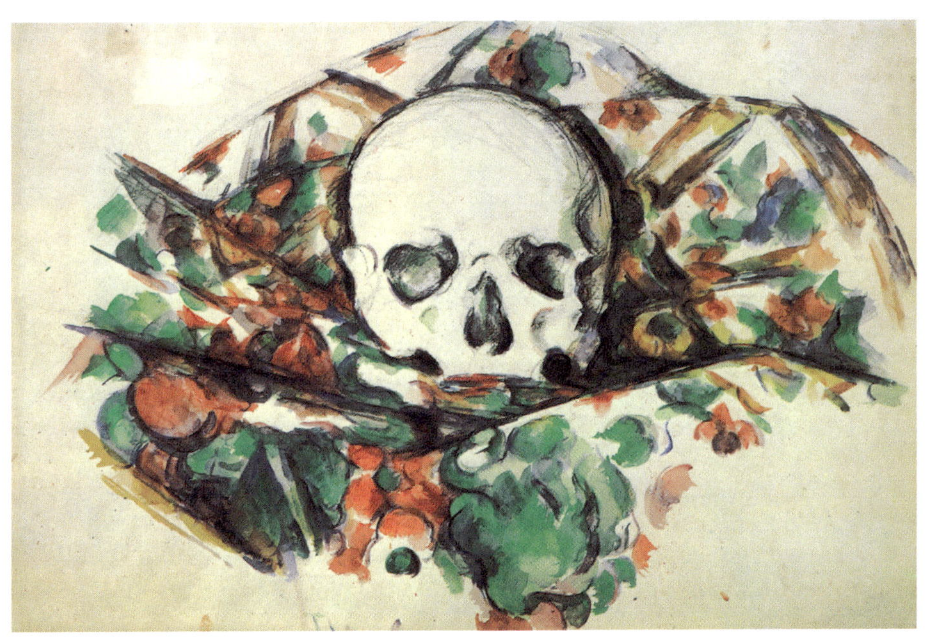

225. *Skull on Drapery*, 1902–06.
Pencil and watercolour, 31.7 × 47.6 cm (12½ × 18¾ in.).
Private collection

Epilogue

In a discussion that took place in Paris between the elderly Pissarro and
the young Matisse at the end of the 1890s the senior painter asserted that
'Cézanne is not an impressionist because all his life he has been painting
the same picture.' Asked by Matisse to define what an impressionist is
Pissarro replied, 'An impressionist is a painter who never paints the same
picture, who always paints a new picture' and nominated Alfred Sisley as
an example. In a gloss on this observation, Matisse remarked, 'A Cézanne
is a moment of the artist whereas a Sisley is a moment of nature.'

Pissarro's comment on Cézanne that 'all his life he has been painting
the same picture' does not of course refer to the subject matter since he
was immensely versatile, but, rather, to the inexorability of the artist's
attempt to portray what was in his line of vision with the greatest
possible accuracy. As Meyer Schapiro expressed it in his monograph of
1952 on the artist, 'The whole presents itself to us on the one hand as an
object-world that is colourful, varied, and harmonious, and on the other
hand as the minutely ordered creation of an observant, inventive mind
intensely concerned with its own process.' Effectively, Cézanne liberated
painting from the supremacy of the subject matter and established the
autonomy of the picture itself. His art existed in order to reconcile not
only the contradictions in his own personality, but also those found in
nature. And it is this attempted reconciliation, which was not always
successfully achieved, that invests his work with a moral grandeur. The
critic David Sylvester in 1994 described Cézanne's style as 'uncertainty
made beautiful' and it is the viewer's consciousness of the artist's
inner struggle and recurring sense of failure (what Picasso referred to
as Cézanne's 'inquiét') that heightens interest in each of his works.
It is, however, the very dichotomy created by Cézanne in his painting
between subject matter and process that has made him so influential.
Just as he was eager to explore new methods of representation, so the
results demanded new ways of looking and so provided later artists with
unforeseen opportunities. Certainly, Cézanne's art raised more problems
than he personally could solve, but the identification of those problems
and his concern to address them accounts for the respect in which he
was held by his immediate successors and why he is still so venerated by
artists today.

Drawing was central to the art of Cézanne and many of his watercolours are equal to his paintings. In the final analysis, he made no real distinction between painting and drawing, just as he chose not to define the difference between 'finished' and 'unfinished' works. Both painting and drawing were exploratory activities and part of a systematic examination of the mechanics of vision. Some drawings were made as a way of finding the answer to a particular difficulty, either by accessing the past or by fresh observation, but each individual challenge was always connected with the overall search for the most convincing method of recording the artist's sensations as he experienced them in front of nature. This, in turn, presented him with a paradox since nature comprised both fugitive and permanent elements. Or, as the poet Rainer Maria Rilke expressed it after seeing the memorial exhibition mounted at the Salon d'Automne in 1907, which came to him as a revelation and resulted in numerous return visits, Cézanne aimed to discover 'the inexhaustible nature within by seriously and conscientiously studying her manifold presence on the outside'. Drawing, therefore, was not an end in itself for Cézanne, but an analytical exercise for the purpose of comprehending the world as he saw it. He never sought realization or understanding simply by the act of drawing so much as through the overall practice of drawing, which is why Cézanne's works on paper constitute such a memorable and significant part of his *oeuvre*.

Bibliography

The literature on Cézanne is manifold and varied. The items listed here include only those titles that have been of direct use in the preparation and writing of this book. Suggestions for further reading on all aspects of the artist's work and life can be found in the books and articles cited below.

SOURCES

Danchev, Alex (ed. and trans.), *The Letters of Paul Cézanne*, London, 2013

Doran, Michael (ed.), *Conversations avec Cézanne*, Paris, 1978

—, *Conversations with Cézanne*, trans. Julie Lawrence Cochran, Berkeley, CA, and London, 2001

Gasquet, Joachim, *Joachim Gasquet's Cézanne: A Memoir with Conversations*, trans. Christopher Pemberton, London and New York, 1991

Kendall, Richard (ed.), *Cézanne by Himself: Drawings, Paintings, Writings*, London, 1988

Rilke, Rainer Maria, *Letters on Cézanne*, ed. Clara Rilke, trans. Joel Agee, New York, 1985, and London, 1988

Vollard, Ambroise, *Paul Cézanne*, Paris, 1914

CATALOGUES RAISONNÉS

Chappuis, Adrien, *The Drawings of Paul Cézanne*, 2 vols, London and Greenwich, CT, 1973 [to be consulted in conjunction with the article by Karsten Schubert, 'Cézanne, Chappuis and the limits of connoisseurship', *Burlington Magazine*, 148 (2006), pp. 612–20]

Rewald, John, *Paul Cézanne: The Watercolours. A Catalogue Raisonné*, London and Boston, 1983

Rewald, John with Walter Feilchenfeldt and Jayne Warman, *The Paintings of Paul Cézanne: A Catalogue Raisonné*, London and New York, 1996

BOOKS

Andersen, Wayne, *Cézanne's Portrait Drawings*, Cambridge, MA, 1970

Athanassoglou-Kallmyer, Nina Maria, *Cézanne and Provence: The Painter in His Culture*, Chicago and London, 2003

Barr, Alfred H., Jr., *Matisse: His Art and His Public*, New York, 1951

Berthold, Gertrude, *Cézanne und die alten Meister*, Stuttgart, 1958 [Reviewed by Theodore Reff, *Art Bulletin*, 42 (1960), pp. 145–49]

Clark, T. J., *Farewell to an Idea: Episodes from a History of Modernism*, New Haven and London, 1999 [see Chapter 3, 'Freud's Cézanne', pp. 139–67]

Danchev, Alex, *Cézanne: A Life*, London and New York, 2012

Dombrovski, André, *Cézanne, Murder, and Modern Life*, Berkeley, CA, 2013

D'Souza, Aruna, *Cézanne's Bathers, Biography and the Erotics of Paint*, University Park, PA, 2008

Feilchenfeldt, Walter, *By Appointment Only: Cézanne, Van Gogh and some Secrets of Art Dealing*, London and New York, 2006

Fry, Roger, *Cézanne: A Study of His Development*, London, 1927; new edn, Chicago and London, 1989

Kendall, Richard (ed.), *Cézanne and Poussin: A Symposium*, Sheffield, 1993

Platzman, Steven, *Cézanne: The Self-Portraits*, London and Berkeley, CA, 2001

Rewald, John, *Studies in Impressionism*, edited by Irene Gordon and Frances Weitzenhoffer, London, 1985, and New York, 1986 [includes 'Achille Emperaire and Cézanne', 'Cézanne and his father', 'Cézanne and Guillaumin' and 'Chocquet and Cézanne']

Rewald, John, *Cézanne and America: Dealers, Collectors, Artists and Critics 1891–1921*, London and Princeton, NJ, 1989

Richardson, John, *A Life of Picasso,
Volume 1: 1881–1906*, London and
New York, 1991; *Volume 2: 1907–1917*,
London and New York, 1996
Schapiro, Meyer, *Paul Cézanne*, London
and New York, 1952
Schmitt, Evmarie, *Cézanne in Provence*,
Munich and London, 1995
Shiff, Richard, *Cézanne and the End of
Impressionism*, Chicago and London,
1984
Sidlauskas, Susan, *Cézanne's Other: The
Portraits of Hortense*, Berkeley, CA,
and London, 2009
Simms, Matthew, *Cézanne's Watercolours:
Between Drawing and Painting*, New
Haven and London, 2008
Smith, Paul, *Interpreting Cézanne*, London,
1996
Stratis, Harriet K. and Britt Salvesen (eds),
*The Broad Spectrum: Studies in the
Materials, Techniques, and Conservation
of Color on Paper*, London, 2002
[see Faith Zieske, 'Paul Cézanne's
watercolors: his choice of pigments and
papers', pp. 89–100]
Sylvester, David, *About Modern Art:
Critical Essays, 1948–96*, London, 1996,
New York, 1997 [see 'Uses of still life:
Cézanne, Braque, Bonnard (1961–62)',
pp. 90–110, and 'Cézanne (1996)',
pp. 437–44]
Venturi, Lionello, *Paul Cézanne: Water
Colours*, London, 1943
Verdi, Richard, *Cézanne*, London and
New York, 1992

ARTICLES

Fry, Roger, '"Paul Cézanne" by Ambroise
Vollard: Paris, 1915', *Burlington
Magazine*, 31 (1917), pp. 52–61
Lichtenstein, Sara, 'Cézanne and
Delacroix', *Art Bulletin*, 46 (1964),
pp. 55–67
—, 'Cézanne's copies and variants after
Delacroix', *Apollo*, 101 (1975), pp. 116–27
Reff, Theodore, 'Cézanne's drawings',
Burlington Magazine, 101 (1959),
pp. 171–76

—, 'Reproductions and books in Cézanne's
studio', *Gazette des Beaux-Arts*, 56
(1960), pp. 303–9
—, 'Cézanne's drawings' *Burlington
Magazine*, 117 (1975), pp. 489–91
Schapiro, Meyer, 'The apples of Cézanne:
an essay in the meaning of still life',
Art News Annual, 34 (1968), pp. 34–53.
Reprinted in *Modern Art: 19th and
20th Centuries*, New York and London,
1978, pp. 1–38

EXHIBITION CATALOGUES

Retrospectives

Pickvance, Ronald, et al., *Cézanne*, Isetan
Museum of Art, Tokyo, Hyogo Prefectural
Museum of Modern Art, Kobe, and Aichi
Prefectural Art Gallery, Nagoya, 1986
Cachin, Françoise, et al., *Cézanne*, Galeries
Nationales du Grand Palais, Paris, 1995,
Tate Gallery, London, and Philadelphia
Museum of Art, 1996

Drawings and Watercolours

Gowing, Lawrence, *Watercolour and Pencil
Drawings by Cézanne*, Laing Art Gallery,
Newcastle-upon-Tyne, and Hayward
Gallery, London, 1973
Adriani, Götz, *Paul Cézanne: Aquarelle*,
Kunsthalle, Tübingen, and Kunsthaus,
Zürich, 1982; Cologne, 1982 (*Cézanne
Watercolors*, trans. Russell M. Stockman,
New York, 1983)
Gowing, Lawrence, *Paul Cézanne: The
Basel Sketchbooks*, Museum of Modern
Art, New York, 1988
Reff, Theodore and Innis Howe Shoemaker,
*Paul Cézanne: Two Sketchbooks. The
Gift of Mr and Mrs Walter H. Annenberg
to the Philadelphia Museum of Art*,
Philadelphia Museum of Art, 1989
Armstrong, Carol, *Cézanne in the Studio:
Still Life in Watercolors*, J. Paul Getty
Museum, Los Angeles, 2004[–05]
Lloyd, Christopher, *Impressionism: Pastels,
Watercolors, Drawings*, Milwaukee Art
Museum and the Albertina, Vienna,
2011[–12] [includes essays by Christopher

Lloyd, 'Impressions on paper', 'The
beginnings of Impressionist and
Post-Impressionist drawing: methods,
materials and modes', 'The autonomy
of drawing']
Haldemann, Anita, et al., *The Hidden
Cézanne: From Sketchbook to Canvas*,
Kunstmuseum, Basle, 2017

Specific Topics
Rubin, William (ed.), *Cézanne: The Late
Work*, Museum of Modern Art, New
York, Réunion des Musées Nationaux,
Paris, and Museum of Fine Arts,
Houston, 1977[–78]
Gowing, Lawrence, *Cézanne: The Early
Years, 1859–1872*, Royal Academy of
Arts, London, National Gallery of Art,
Washington, DC, and Musée d'Orsay,
Paris, 1988[–89]
Verdi, Richard, *Cézanne and Poussin:
The Classical Vision of Landscape*,
National Galleries of Scotland,
Edinburgh, 1990
Rathbone, Eliza E. and George T. M.
Shackelford, *Impressionist Still Life*, The
Phillips Collection, Washington, DC, and
Museum of Fine Arts, Boston, 2001[–02]
Pissarro, Joachim, *Pioneering Modern
Painting: Cézanne and Pissarro 1865–
1885*, Museum of Modern Art, New
York, Los Angeles County Museum of
Art and Musée d'Orsay, Paris, 2005[–06]
Conisbee, Philip and Denis Coutagne,
Cézanne in Provence, National Gallery
of Art, Washington, DC, and Musée
Granet, Aix-en-Provence, 2006
Robbins, Anne with Ann Dumas, *Cézanne
in Britain*, National Gallery, London,
2006[–07]
Rabinow, Rebecca A. (ed.), *Cézanne to
Picasso: Ambroise Vollard, Patron of the
Avant-Garde*, Metropolitan Museum
of Art, New York, The Art Institute of
Chicago and Musée d'Orsay, Paris,
2006[–07]
Ireson, Nancy and Barnaby Wright (eds),
Cézanne's Card Players, Courtauld
Gallery, London, and Metropolitan
Museum of Art, New York, 2010[–11]

Geskó, Judit, *Cézanne and the Past:
Tradition and Creativity*, Museum
of Fine Arts, Budapest, 2012
Amory, Dita, *Madame Cézanne*,
Metropolitan Museum of Art, New York,
2014[–15] [includes Marjorie Shelley,
'Cézanne as draftsman: sketchbooks and
graphite drawings', pp. 107–27]
Ailing, Alexander et al., *Cezanne:
Metamorphoses*, Staatliche Kunsthalle,
Karlsruhe, 2017

Collections
Rishel, Joseph J., *Cézanne in Philadelphia
Collections*, Philadelphia Museum of
Art, 1983
Buck, Stephanie, et al., *The Courtauld
Cézannes*, Courtauld Gallery, London,
2008
Friedman, Jane, et al., *Cézanne and the
Modern: Masterpieces of European
Art from the Pearlman Collection*,
Ashmolean Museum, Oxford, Musée
Granet, Aix-en-Provence, High Museum
of Art, Atlanta, Vancouver Art Gallery
and Princeton University Art Museum,
2014[–15]

SOURCES FOR THE EPIGRAPHS

Page 6 Roger Fry, '"Paul Cézanne"
by Ambroise Vollard: Paris, 1915',
Burlington Magazine, 31 (1917),
pp. 53–54
Chapter 1 Joachim Gasquet, *Joachim
Gasquet's Cézanne: A Memoir with
Conversations*, trans. Christopher
Pemberton, London and New York,
1991, p. 158
Chapter 2 Alfred H. Barr, Jr., *Matisse:
His Art and His Public*, New York,
1951, p. 38
Chapter 3 Gasquet, op. cit., p. 212
Chapter 4 Adrien Chappuis, *The Drawings
of Paul Cézanne*, London and Greenwich,
CT, 1973, vol. 1, p. 49, Question 9 of 30
Chapter 5 Chappuis, op. cit., vol. 1, p. 52,
Question 26 of 30
Chapter 6 Gasquet, op. cit., p. 102

Acknowledgments

For me Print Rooms are hallowed spaces where great works of art on paper
are carefully and lovingly preserved. My work over the years on drawings by
Impressionist and Post-Impressionist artists in general, and more recently
on Cézanne in particular, has led me to numerous Print Rooms in Europe
and America. I am grateful to the curators and staff in these various public
institutions for being so welcoming and helpful. The same applies to many
private collectors, especially Walter Feilchenfeldt in Zurich, who for so long
has been at the centre of Cézanne studies. Anyone who works on the artist
is conscious of the huge contribution made by a host of scholars and writers
who have risen to the challenge (see Bibliography) and my debt to others in
this respect is very considerable.

My wife, Frances, and our children, Alexander, Benedict, Oliver and Rupert,
together with their growing families, have given encouragement and exercised
forbearance, for which many thanks.

As on previous occasions, I have been extremely fortunate in having the
pleasure of working with the team at Thames & Hudson that has brought this
book to fruition, particularly Julia MacKenzie (editor), Allie Boalch (picture
research), Lauren Necati (design) and Louise Ramsay (production); their skills
and interest in Cézanne have made all the difference.

I would like to thank the following for quotations of copyright material:
The Letters of Paul Cézanne, edited and translated by Alex Danchev. © 2013
Alex Danchev. Reprinted by kind permission of Thames & Hudson Ltd, London;
Joachim Gasquet's Cézanne: A Memoir with Conversations, translated by
Christopher Pemberton. Copyright © 1991 Thames & Hudson Ltd, London.
Reprinted by kind permission of Thames & Hudson.

Picture Credits

Aix-en-Provence, Musée Granet 125; Avignon, Musée Calvet 77; Basel, Kunstmuseum 20, 21, 22, 26, 29, 30, 31, 51, 52, 55 (Purchased 1934, inv. 1934.207), 68, 75, 81, 84, 93, 102 (Gift of Martha and Robert von Hirsch 1977, inv. 1977.168), 103, 122 (with contributions from the Basel government, Max Geldner Foundation and private art lovers 1960, inv. G 1960.1), 127 (Purchased 1934, inv. 1934.196); Berlin, Nationalgalerie, Museum Berggruen, Staatliche Museen zu Berlin 72, 113 (Photo Scala, Florence/bpk, Bildagentur für Kunst, Kultur und Geschichte, Berlin); Boston, Museum of Fine Arts 5 (44.776); Budapest, Museum of Fine Arts 86; Cambridge, The Fitzwilliam Museum 126, 187 (Lent by the Provost and Fellows of King's College, Keynes collection), 200; Cambridge, MA, Fogg Museum, Harvard Art Museums 90 (Bequest of Marian H. Phinney), 147 (Gift of Samuel Sachs, Bridgeman Images), 153 (Gift of Henry P. McIlhenny), 155 (Gift of Mr and Mrs Joseph Pulitzer, Jr. in honor of Agnes Mongan), 164 (Bequest of Theodore Rousseau; jointly owned by The Metropolitan Museum of Art, New York and the Fogg Museum, Harvard University), 205 (Bequest of Marian H. Phinney); Cardiff, National Museum of Wales 44, 132; The Art Institute of Chicago 12, 57 (Gift of Justin K. Thannhauser, 1964.79R), 65 (Gift of Janis H. Palmer in memory of Pauline K. Palmer, 1983.1498), 73 (Anonymous loan, 475.1983), 85, 91 (Arthur Heun Fund), 92 (Arthur Heun Fund), 98 (Arthur Heun Fund), 104 (Margaret Day Blake Collection, 1944.577), 130 (Gift of Tiffany and Margaret Blake, 1947.36), 152 (Gift of Marshall Field, IV, 1964.199), 168 (Mr and Mrs Martin A. Ryerson Collection, 1937.1030), 224 (Olivia Shaler Swan Memorial Collection, 1954.183); Christie's Images/Corbis 25, 66 (Private collection), 148, 190 (Private collection), 201; Dublin, National Gallery of Ireland 158; Frankfurt am Main, Städel Museum 46, 63; Hanover, Hood Museum of Art, Dartmouth College 131 (Gift of Josephine and Ivan Albright); Hartford, Wadsworth Atheneum 123; Collection Jan Krugier and Marie-Anne Krugier-Poniatowski 191 (inv. no. JK 6160, akg-images); London, British Museum 18; London, The Trustees of the British Museum 13, 14, 71; London, The Samuel Courtauld Trust, The Courtauld Gallery 154, 165, 177, 195, 220; London, National Gallery 35 (on loan from the collection of Laurence Graff, OBE); London, Tate 160; London, Victoria & Albert Museum 175 (Purchased with the assistance of The Art Fund, P.6-1966); Los Angeles, The J. Paul Getty Museum (83.GC.221) 211; Madrid, Museo Thyssen-Bornemisza 217 (489, 1979.18); Moscow, The Pushkin State Museum of Fine Arts 39; Munich, Staatliche Graphische Sammlung 172; New Haven, Yale University Art Gallery 54 (Gift of Philip L. Goodwin, BA 1907, 1952.1.1); New Jersey, The Newark Museum 180 (Gift of Mrs C. S. Cutting 1950); New York, The Metropolitan Museum of Art 33 (Gift of C. Douglas Dillon, 1982, 1982.375), 56 (Bequest of Mary Cushing Fosburgh, 1978, acc. no. 1979.135.4), 74 (Bequest of Stephen C. Clark, 1960, 61.101.1), 88, 137 (Maria DeWitt Jesup Fund, 1951; acquired from The Museum of Modern Art, Lillie P. Bliss Collection, 55.21.2), 179 (Gift of Alex Hillman Family Foundation); New York, Museum of Modern Art 23 (The Joan and Lester Avnet Fund, 463.1980), 120 (Lillie P. Bliss Collection, 1.1934), 146 (Lillie P. Bliss Collection, 21.1934), 204 (Lillie P. Bliss Collection, 9.1934.a-b); New York, Pierpont Morgan Library 45 (Gift of Donald Oresman in honor of the 75th anniversary of the Morgan Library and the 50th anniversary of the Association of Fellows), 79, 139, 178, 182, 219 (Thaw Collection); Northampton, MA, Smith College Museum of Art 59; Ohio, Cincinnati Art Museum 185 (Gift of John J. Emery, 1951.298); Oregon, Jordan Schnitzer Museum of Art, University of Oregon 62 (Eugene, Gift of Mr and Mrs Douglas E. Walwyn); Oxford, Ashmolean Museum 70, 97, 129, 143, 145, 166, 209; Paris, Musée d'Orsay 40, 69, 78 (Département des Arts Graphiques), 124, 167 (Département des Arts Graphiques, Bequest of Comte Isaac de Camondo), 186, 196, 197 (Département des Arts Graphiques), 202, 214; Paris, Musée du Louvre 135; Paris, Cabinet des Dessins, Musée du Louvre 11, 24, 28, 32, 47, 80, 101, 189, 213; Paris, Musée National Eugène Delacroix/Musée du Louvre 192; Paris, Musée Picasso 117; Paris, Petit Palais, Musée des Beaux-Arts de la Ville de Paris 67, 116; Philadelphia Museum of Art 49 (The Louis E. Stern Collection, 1963, 1963-181-123), 162, 194 (Gift of Mr and Mrs Walter H. Annenberg, 1987, 1987-53-67b), 198 (A. E. Gallatin Collection, 1943, 1943-75-1); Photographer unknown 1, 4; Princeton University Art Museum 142 (on long term loan from The Henry and Rose Pearlman Collection), 157 (on long term loan from The Henry and Rose Pearlman Collection), 171 (Anonymous gift, x1941-166), 173 (on long term loan from The Henry and Rose Pearlman Collection), 181 (on long term loan from The Henry and Rose Pearlman Collection. Photo Bruce M. White), 184 (on long term loan from The Henry and Rose Pearlman Collection), 210 (on long term loan from The Henry and Rose Pearlman Collection), 221 (on long term loan from The Henry and Rose Pearlman Collection), 222 (on long term loan from The Henry and Rose Pearlman Collection. Photo Bruce M. White); Private collection 3, 9 (Photo Elmer de Haas), 10, 15, 16, 17, 34, 36, 37, 38 (on permanent loan to the Kunstmuseum Basel), 42, 43, 50, 53, 82, 83, 87 (Photo Elmer de Haas), 94 (Photo Elmer de Haas), 100, 105, 106 (Photo Elmer de Haas), 107, 109, 112, 114, 118, 119, 121, 133 (Photo Elmer de Haas), 136, 140, 141, 149 (Photo Elmer de Haas), 159, 170, 174, 188, 193, 206, 207, 208, 216, 218, 223, 225; Providence, Museum of Art, Rhode Island School of Design 108 (Gift of Mrs Murray S. Danforth, 42.211); Richmond, Virginia Museum of Fine Arts 163 (collection of Mr and Mrs Paul Mellon); Riehen, Basel, Fondation Beyeler 183, 212; Rotterdam, Museum Boijmans Van Beuningen 61, 76, 89, 95, 110, 134, 169; Texas, Collection Mr and Mrs Jay Pack, Dallas 41; Texas, Dallas Museum of Art 215 (The Wendy and Emery Reves Collection, Bridgeman Images); Tokyo, Bridgestone Museum of Art, Ishibashi Foundation 128, 138; Tokyo, The Eisei-Bunko Museum 48; The Granger Collection/TopFoto 7; Vienna, Albertina 27, 99, 115, 151, 156; Washington, DC, The Phillips Collection **frontispiece**; Washington, DC, National Gallery of Art 2 (collection of Mr and Mrs Paul Mellon, 1970.5.1), 6 (Chester Dale Collection, 1963.10.100), 19 (collection of Mr and Mrs Paul Mellon, in Honor of the 50th anniversary of the National Gallery of Art, 1992.51.9.hhh), 96 (collection of Mr and Mrs Paul Mellon, in honor of the 50th anniversary of the National Gallery of Art, 1992.51.9.h), 150 (Collection of Mr and Mrs Paul Mellon, 1985.64.82), 199 (Collection of Mr and Mrs Paul Mellon, 1995.47.26.a), 203 (collection of Mr and Mrs Paul Mellon, 1995.47.25); Winterthur, Oskar Reinhart Collection 'Am Römerholz' 161; Wuppertal, Von der Heydt Museum 176; Zurich, Kunsthaus 8, 58, 64, 111, 144

Index

111, 207; portraiture *58–61*,
106, 107–8, 111, 112, *158-67*;
work accepted at the Paris
Salon (1882) 17; *realisation*
9, 219; exhibiting at the
Salon d'Automne (1904–7)
20–21, 170, 311; *sensations*
9, 219; sketchbooks 7,
10–11, 113, 116, 117–20,
177; use of visual references/
sources 30–31, 34; Vollard's
exhibition (1895) 20, 66, 76,
273; watercolour technique
11, 34, 64–66, 79–81, 124,
125, 180–81, 184, 212,
218–19, 271, 273–74
Subject matter/motifs: 10–11,
63, 64; architectural detail
270–71, 281; bathers 15,
19, 20, 37, 39, *168*, *170–72*,
174, *175*, 177–80, *178*, *179*,
181–85, *182*, *183*, *193–96*,
198–203; Bibémus, quarry at
210, 217, 218, 245, 246; card
players 108, 122, 123, 124,
161; Château Noir *204*, *210*,
213, *216*, 218, 229, *241–44*;
eroticism 17, 79, *see also*
nude, the; fabrics/drapery
265–70, *266*, *268*, 274, *276*,
279, *309*; figural studies *32*,
33, 33, 36–37, *see also* nude,
the; flowers/foliage *264–65*,
271–72, *282–87*; fruit
65, 261–62, *262*, *290–93*,
296–302, *304*; Paris/Parisian
landscape 14, 69, 71, *73*, *73–
78*, 79–81, *75*, *79*, *94–97*, 207;
Provençal landscape 14, 15,
39, *88*, *98–102*, *223–25*, *239*,
252–59, *see also* Château
Noir; Mont Sainte-Victoire;
Mont Sainte-Victoire 14, 17,
78, 185, *206*, 210–11, 212,
219, 223, *226–35*; nude, the
32, *33*, *44–55*, 169, 171, 173,
176, 177, 181, *186–91*, 192,
19, *see also* bathers; pine
tree 212–13, *214*, 224, *236*,
237; portraits of friends and
family *13*, 23, 108–11, *109*,
110, 113, *114–115*, 116–21,
126–33, 142, 143, *151–55*,
see also Fiquet, Hortense;
self-portraits; rocks/boulders
210, 213–16, *216*, 217,

244–47, 249; self-portraits
2, 21, 113–16, *134–41*; skulls
265, 274–75, *306–9*; still-
life paintings 20, *65*, 117,
261–62, *263–70*, *272–73*,
280, 289, *290*, *291*, *294–305*,
see also fruit
Cézanne, Paul (son) 11,
21, 23, 25, 26, *120–21*;
Cézanne's letters to 121, 219,
275; portraits of 113, 116,
120, 121, *151–55*
Cézanne, Rose (sister) 12
Chardin, Jean-Siméon 36, 263
Château Noir *204*, 210, *213*,
216, 218, 229, *241–44*
Chantilly 208
Chatou 206
Chocquet, Victor 15–16, 20,
35, 69, 113, *132*, *133*, 271
Chocquet, Marie 26
Conil, Marthe 24
Conil, Maxime 12, 14
Conil, Paule 24
copying/copies of
artworks 29–30, 31
Corot, Jean-Baptiste-
Camille 111, 207
Coste, Numa 14
Courbet, Gustave 19, 67, 76,
111; Pavilion du Réalisme
(Universal Exhibition, 1855)
67; still-life paintings 264
Couture, Thomas 30
Crouching Venus 38, *53*
Cubism 72

Daubigny, Charles-
François 207
Daumier, Honoré 19, 30
David, Jacques-Louis 30
de Heem, Jan Davidsz 273;
La Desserte 263
Degas, Edgar 9, 20, 30, 79,
176, 185, 261, 273
Delacroix, Eugène 30,
34–36, 43, 67, 76, 120, *128*,
180; *Apollo Vanquishing
the Serpent Python* 34;
Cézanne copying work by
28, 34, 35–36, 41, 42; *The
Entombment* 34, 42; flower
painting 271; illustrations
to *Hamlet* 275; *Journal* 35;
Medea 35–36; *Self-Portrait*
35; still-life paintings 264,

270; *Unmade Bed* 269, *270*;
use of watercolour 64;
*Women of Algiers in their
Apartment* 34
Delaunay, Robert 9
Denis, Maurice 10, 83, 219,
262; *Homage to Cézanne*
260, 261
Derain, André 72, 169
Desjardins, Cézanne copying
work by *60*, *61*
Desportes, Alexandre-
François 263
Domenichino 177
Duchamp, Marcel 272
Durand-Ruel, Paul 21
Dürer, Albrecht 113, 117, 211;
Welsch Pirg 211
Dutch art 111, 262–63, 273,
274

El Greco 36, 111
Emperaire, Achille 112–13,
114, *115*, 129
Escholier, Raymond 169

Fantin-Latour, Henri 264
Fauvism 72
Félibrige Society 14
Fiquet, Hortense 11, 21, 26;
marriage 25; portraits of
22, 25, 26, 113, 116–20, *119*,
142, *143*, *144*, *145*, *146*, *147*,
148, 271
Fontainebleau 80, 208
Forain, Jean-Louis 30
Fra Bartolommeo 31; Cézanne
copying work by 173
Fragonard, Jean-Honoré 177
Fry, Roger 6, 218

Gachet, Dr Paul 69, 113, *131*
Galerie Bernheim-Jeune 21
Gardanne 208
Gasquet, Henri 107
Gasquet, Joachim 12, 14, 38,
107, 210, 261; Cézanne's
correspondence with 24,
112, 205, 211, 219, 263, 264–
65, 274; visiting Cézanne in
Provence 10
Gauguin, Paul 9, 11, 15, 82,
185, 207, 261
Geffroy, Gustave 20, 24, 107,
184, 261
Géricault, Théodore 64